MW00795754

The Confederac
Last Northern Offensive

The Confederacy's Last Northern Offensive

Jubal Early, the Army of the Valley and the Raid on Washington

STEVEN BERNSTEIN

McFarland & Company, Inc., Publishers

Jefferson, North Carolina, and London

LIBRARY OF CONGRESS CATALOGUING-IN-PUBLICATION DATA

Bernstein, Steven, 1953–
The Confederacy's last northern offensive :
Jubal Early, the Army of the Valley and the
raid on Washington / Steven Bernstein.
p.   cm.
Includes bibliographical references and index.

ISBN 978-0-7864-5861-5
softcover : 50# alkaline paper ∞

1. Maryland Campaign, 1864.   2. Early, Jubal Anderson, 1816–1894.
3. Washington (D.C.)— History— Civil War, 1861–1865.   I. Title.
E476.66.B47 2011   973.7'336 — dc22   2010041764

British Library cataloguing data are available

Front cover: Rifle (Civil War Press); Jubal Early (Library of Congress);
Shenandoah Valley © 2011 Pictures Now

Manufactured in the United States of America

*McFarland & Company, Inc., Publishers
Box 611, Jefferson, North Carolina 28640
www.mcfarlandpub.com*

To my mother and father
and
to Thomas Fleming, a friend

Acknowledgments

I would like to thank the many people whose encouragement and prompt, generous service helped produce this book. First, I would like to thank the very courteous, professional, and knowledgeable staffs at the Maryland Room archive, C. Burr Artz Library, Frederick, Maryland; the National Park Service, at Monocacy National Battlefield Visitor Center, Frederick; and the Maryland Room, and Social Sciences Department, Enoch Pratt Free Library, Baltimore. I would also like to thank the staffs of the Montgomery County Historical Society, Rockville, Maryland; the Thomas Balch History Library, Leesburg, Virginia; Handley Memorial Library and Stewart Bell Jr. Archive, Winchester, Virginia; Hardy County Public Library, Moorefield, West Virginia; Mt. Jackson Museum, Mt. Jackson, Virginia; the Franklin County Historical Society, Chambersburg, Pennsylvania; the Pennsylvania Room, Carnegie Library, Pittsburgh; and the reference desks at Cook Library, Towson University, Towson, Maryland, and Loyola College Library, Baltimore. Last, but certainly not least, I would like to thank Mrs. Betty Smith, of Frederick, Mr. Paul Gordon, former mayor of Frederick, and historians Jeffry Wert, Stevan Meserve, and Robert E. Lee Krick, for patiently answering many questions.

Table of Contents

Preface

The American Civil War was a complex affair that had more than one cause, ending 145 years ago. While the tremendous number of recent books and articles on the war has contributed to our understanding of it, the amount of misinformation on it has also increased. Partly because of this misinformation, very real questions about the war remain. One source of misunderstanding concerns the war's length. A few historians have stated to the effect that, with the loss of East Tennessee, in November-December 1863, the Southern cause was finished. Why did it take President Lincoln and the Union armies four long years to defeat a smaller, less well-equipped foe?

Part of the answer lies in the cumbersome Federal command structure, and in the inordinate amount of time it took Lincoln to find a general, a suitable commander for the Union Army. Yet even when Lincoln discovered Ulysses S. Grant, in January 1864, it still took well over a year to end the conflict. During that time, the South could have won some measure of independence. Why didn't it?

Many military historians are of the opinion that taking the war into enemy territory, for an appreciable length of time, or capturing the enemy's capital, make winning more likely. Yet, in four years, the South made only one, half-hearted, attempt to capture Washington, D.C. This is particularly intriguing, since throughout most of the war, Washington was ripe for the taking. The South's one attempt to capture Washington was Jubal Early's July 1864 expedition into Maryland.

The capture of Washington was a proud southern soldier's dream, discussed by Early and Robert E. Lee. Had that occurred, the northern war effort would have been temporarily halted, and Lincoln probably would have lost the fall presidential election. And had *that* occurred, the South would have won some measure of independence. Jubal Early, a strong Unionist before the war, was a good soldier and a competent commander with a lot of experience under fire. As a lieutenant, he had fought in the Seminole war, in the late 1830s; as a major, he fought in the Mexican war. He began the Civil War as a colonel, and by mid–1864, he had risen still higher, to the rank of lieutenant general. He had demonstrated loyalty, sound judgment, and bravery many, many times. However, during the Washington raid, and thereafter, success eluded him. The reasons, set against a backdrop of an uncooperative political situation, are the subjects of this book.

CHAPTER 1

Northern Civilian Sentiment, Spring 1864

Tranquility Sundered

Most Northerners began the year 1864 very weary of the Civil War, having developed a strong sense of uncertainty as to the conflict's direction and eventual outcome. They were tired of endless casualty lists; of relatives, friends, and neighbors returning from the battlefields dead or maimed; of conscription and its attendant evils; of unending inflation and economic sacrifice; and of President Lincoln's suspension of civil liberties.

The all-encompassing and seemingly endless conflict would soon enter its fourth year. When it began, in April 1861, very few had any idea that it would last much longer than a year, nor any idea of how many troops would be needed. In fact, on 15 April 1861, three days after Fort Sumter surrendered, President Lincoln issued a call for 75,000 90-day volunteers. At the time, most thought 75,000 volunteers fighting for 90 days would be sufficient to put down the rebellion. Three months later, the shock of Confederate victory at First Manassas (Bull Run) would cause many to understand that the conflict might be a prolonged one.

In the beginning, the great majority of the Northern public cheerfully supported the war, sending their young men off to fight, while holding meetings, rallies, and sanitary fairs on the home front. They endured the many battlefield reverses of 1861 to 1863, pressing on through the disappointing victories of Antietam and Gettysburg, where Union forces failed to pursue the Rebels, and the morale-crushing defeats of McClellan's failed Peninsula campaign; 2nd Manassas, Jackson's Valley campaign, Fredericksburg, and Chancellorsville.

However, anti-war sentiment had surfaced shortly after the war began. In August 1861, some residents of Stepney, Connecticut, assembled on the town square to protest "the unrighteous war." No sooner had they begun than a group of war supporters, including Connecticut soldiers who had recently returned from stinging defeat at 1st Manassas, along with some whose enlistments had expired, came down the road from Bridgeport and assaulted the protesters. There was an altercation, and the peace group fled the scene. The war supporters returned to Bridgeport, where they descended on the offices of a southern sympathizing newspaper, the *Bridgeport Farmer*, and promptly destroyed the presses.[1] During the opening months of the conflict, similar scenes replayed throughout the North, particularly where southern leaning newspapers and their editors were concerned. Anti-war sentiment reflected widespread division among Northern civilians, influenced by local loyalties, concerning the need for war.

Political Opposition

Opposition to the war soon transcended anti-war rallies in small towns but was fairly well confined to the Democratic Party. Republicans largely favored the war, with Radical Republicans strongly favoring immediate abolition of slavery, punishment of the South, and congressional oversight of war legislation, to the exclusion of the president. For them, the war couldn't have been prosecuted strongly enough. Their dissatisfaction was expressed as opposition to Lincoln's war and reconstruction policies. As the war dragged on, seemingly without decisive Northern battlefield victory, through 1863, and well into 1864, Radical Republican opposition to Lincoln's policies grew ever stronger, and threatened to scuttle his renomination.

The New York City draft riot of July 1863 spotlighted, in glaring relief, opposition to the draft, and by extension to the war. Lasting for four days, the riot was caused by a corrupt and inefficient draft system, exacerbated by class tensions, racial antagonism, and war-induced price inflation. Food prices had nearly tripled since 1861: beef rose from 8 to 18 cents a pound, coffee from 10 cents to 50 cents a pound, and sugar rose from 5 cents to 20 cents a pound. The costs of housing and heating fuel also rose; rents went up about 20 percent; the price of wood increased by 20 percent, that of coal rose 30 percent. Wages, however, had risen only 12 percent since 1860.[2]

Prior to 1863, calls for additional troops had been successfully filled by volunteer enlistments. However, by August 1862, enlistments had all but ceased, mostly because large numbers of dead and wounded were returning from the front. Congress responded by instituting an unprecedented draft, that failed miserably, providing only a few thousand men out of about 509,000 total recruits for 1862.[3]

New York City was ripe for a large scale riot in the summer of 1863. In the crowded slums and shantytowns of Brooklyn and Five Points, Irish immigrants lived side by side with African Americans, many of whom had come North, seeking work, in the wake of the Emancipation Proclamation. Acts of racial animosity towards them were commonplace. Wretched living conditions and competition between the two groups for employment made matters worse. Inflation was eroding purchasing power, and when workers responded by striking for higher wages, employers sometimes broke the strikes by hiring African Americans. As a result, mob violence against African Americans flared up periodically, in several Northern cities, beginning in the summer of 1862. Longshoremen became particularly outraged at African American strikebreakers. Anti-war orators, such as Democratic congressman Samuel "Sunset" Cox, fanned the flames of working class discontent and racial animosity, making incendiary statements, such as workers joining the army would find "Negroes filling their places" on the job when they returned.[4]

Exemption provisions in the draft law exacerbated class tensions as well. Substitutes could be procured for $300 on up, and shortly after the draft was announced, a cottage industry of finding substitutes for a fee appeared. Bounty jumpers appeared — those who enlisted, collected the Federal and local bounties offered volunteers, then fled to other localities, repeating the process. In addition, the Federal draft law of March 1863 provided that draftees could be excused by paying a $300 commutation fee, a loophole favoring the well-to-do. Many localities provided funds for residents who were too poor to purchase commutations. These funds became a heavy economic burden, and were often financed by increases in property taxes.

When the Federal draft began on Saturday, 11 July, most of the troop units that could have stopped a riot were at the front, in Maryland and Pennsylvania. A minimal number of troops were on hand in New York, along with the regular city police force. The names of the draftees were in the newspapers the next day as casualty lists from Gettysburg were posted around town. Around mid-morning on Monday, 13 July, city police learned that the streets were filling up with angry gangs of men and boys, armed with crowbars, searching for firearms.

The crowds converged on draft offices, vandalizing them and setting them ablaze, while individual police and soldiers cornered by the mob were beaten and killed. By Monday afternoon, the mob had taken control of the streets. African Americans were assaulted; a few were lynched; some were chased into the East River. An orphanage for African American children was burned down. The 237 children living there were escorted to safety. However, a number of Irish clergymen and police risked their lives to protect African Americans. The outnumbered and outgunned police and militia were hard pressed, defending the Union Steam Works, on 2nd Avenue, where several thousand rifles were stored. The struggle for control of New York City's streets see-sawed back and forth all day, Tuesday and Wednesday, 14–15 July. The riot finally ended on 16 July, as veteran troops of the New York 7th infantry arrived. By nightfall, there were 4,000 troops in town. The four day long orgy of destruction had left 119 dead, with 306 injured and $1.5 million in property damage. However, the draft was continued, a month later, without disturbance, as 43 regiments were stationed in the city. Draft riots also occurred in Boston, Troy, New York, and a few other Northern cities.[5]

Anti-War Sentiment in the Midwest

Anti-war sentiment got a big push from Southern-born residents of southern Illinois, Indiana, and Ohio, who had migrated northward, across the Ohio River, where they farmed and traded. Many were the sons and daughters of Jeffersonian Republicans and Jacksonian Democrats of earlier days, and many favored slavery. The majority were fiercely opposed to the Northern war effort. Abraham Lincoln knew some of these transplanted Southerners well, having been born in Kentucky, and having married Kentuckian Mary Todd, whose family had strong southern connections. Most of these erstwhile southerners were Democrats, and many became Peace Democrats.

The war divided the Northern Democratic Party into two opposing factions. The War Democrats were against secession, favoring the war and reunification of the country, albeit with slavery intact. Among their leaders was party chairman August Belmont. In August 1864 they would nominate General George B. McClellan as their presidential candidate. In response to outspoken anti-war rhetoric from Peace Democrats, some elite Democratic war supporters migrated to Lincoln's new National Union Party, into an uncomfortable alliance with the Republicans. They later became disillusioned with the Unionists over their adherence to abolition.

The Peace Democrats tolerated secession, as far as allowing the southern states to establish the Confederacy. However, secession had strong support in the Antebellum North. In 1814, New England nearly seceded from the Union when a group of anti-war Federalists met at Hartford, Connecticut, to consider the issue. Many in the North favored peaceful southern secession in lieu of holding the Union together at gunpoint. There was widespread sentiment favoring secession in New York, New Jersey, Pennsylvania, Delaware, and Maryland; New York City, Philadelphia, and Baltimore were strongholds of secessionist sentiment.[6] Fernando Wood, mayor of New York, suggested that the city secede, partly because of $300 million worth of southern contracts that local businessmen had to forfeit because of the war. Rodman Price, an 1850s governor of New Jersey, was a southern sympathizer, as was Baltimore mayor George W. Brown.

However, Peace Democrats wanted peace at any price; thus they were so portrayed by newspapers and Republicans, and became known, derisively, as Copperheads, the name alluding to a poisonous snake. James Gordon Bennett, editor of the *New York Herald*, said of them, "Of all the small, insignificant, contemptible cliques that have ever disgraced the politics of this country the peace clique is the worst. It is equally despised by honest Union men and honest rebels." Copperheads were also described as having "all the instincts of a traitor without the pluck to be a rebel."[7] They numbered among their leaders Democratic congressmen Clement L. Vallandigham, of Dayton, Ohio; Daniel Vorhees, of Indiana; Alexander Long, of Ohio; and Benjamin Harris, of Maryland. War Democrats wanted North and South to reunite, with slavery intact, and a Constitution that allowed it; Peace Democrats were willing to allow Southern independence. Vallandigham was later arrested, dragged from his home, and jailed for his views. When he was released, Union troops escorted him to Confederate lines, in Kentucky, where they left him, per Lincoln's orders. After a short time as an uninvited guest of General Braxton Bragg, Vallandigham left the country, traveling to Canada. Upon returning, he spoke out provocatively against the war, hoping to be arrested again. His re-arrest was supposed to signal a general uprising, but Lincoln ignored him. However, the Peace Democrats weren't particularly peaceful.

In the spring of 1863, hundreds of Copperheads attended a mass meeting in Indianapolis. From the evening trains returning from the meeting, hundreds of pistol shots were fired at buildings near the tracks. Police and militia later confiscated nearly a thousand pistols from train passengers who had attended. On 23 March 1864, a full-fledged riot occurred in Charleston, Illinois, about 25 miles west of Terre Haute, Indiana, in which more than 100 Copperheads fired on Federal troops.[8]

The Charleston riot proved the Copperheads belligerent. However, during the spring and summer of 1864, their anger provided Indiana Republicans with an opportunity to make Lincoln's 1861 suspension of habeas corpus look benign. Indianans had become very disenchanted with the war and wouldn't support politicians whose policies had failed to produce victory. The resumption of the draft, in response to Lincoln's July call for 500,000 additional troops, ominously portended defeat for Indiana's Republican administration.

In addition, the state legislature had recently adjourned without voting on funds to run the government. In response, Republican governor Oliver P. Morton had adopted questionable financial measures, subjecting him to possible prosecution should the Democrats win the upcoming elections.[9] Morton and the Republicans thus had to win, whatever the cost. The Copperheads soon gave him an opportunity.

In the waning days of 1863, Democratic operatives formed a secret society — the Sons of Liberty — to aid the Democratic Party in the fall elections. However, rank and file members weren't informed of anti-administration covert actions planned by their leaders. Through spies employed by Morton and General Henry B. Carrington, Union Army commander in Indiana, the Republicans learned of Sons of Liberty plans. In June 1864, one of the spies procured the Sons of Liberty constitution and copies of their secrets and rituals, and turned them in to Carrington. He edited the material, and turned it into a report, which was given to Morton. Republican newspapers obtained the report and published it on 30 July. Representing the Sons of Liberty as a vital part of the Democratic Party, they called the rebellious group the "most criminal and atrocious conspiracy that has existed since the Jacobin societies crimsoned France with their blood."[10] That evening, the Republicans held a mass meeting at Indianapolis, where orators spoke against the Sons of Liberty, demanding that they be arrested and hanged. Morton promised to shut down the Sons of Liberty; the Democrats were alarmed, while the flagging Republican campaign was revived.

One particularly disgruntled member of the Sons of Liberty, Harrison H. Dodd, wanted immediate action taken against the Republicans. His desires were intensified by the Democrats' nomination of a moderate gubernatorial candidate, Joseph E. McDonald, at the state convention in July. Dodd had also been rebuffed by the leadership of the Sons of Liberty. Acting on their own, Dodd and a few others, funded by a Confederate agent in Canada, devised a scheme to free prisoners at Camp Morton in Indianapolis and capture the arsenal. This was to be in conjunction with Confederate agents freeing prisoners at Chicago's Camp Douglas, supposed to touch off a general Midwestern rebellion against the Union, later called the Northwest Conspiracy.

However, Dodd unwittingly revealed the plan to Carrington's detective on 2 August. That evening, Morton and Carrington were informed. Curiously, Morton did nothing for a few weeks. The state Democratic Party leadership refused to cooperate with Dodd (who had informed the state Democratic chairman of the plan), forcing him to promise that he wouldn't carry it out. Dodd complied, and the Northwest Conspiracy never occurred. Nevertheless, on 20 August, on orders from Morton, Federal troops broke into Dodd's business, seizing large quantities of ammunition and 400 revolvers. They also seized a list of several Sons of Liberty who were candidates for state office. Word of the raid was given to the Republican press, which promptly published sensational tales of alleged treason by Indiana Democrats.

Citizens of Indianapolis became angry at the stories, and at a Republican rally on 22 August, Morton shouted that the entire state Democratic Party was behind the plot. As August ended, he decided to arrest Sons of Liberty leaders and try them by military tribunal. Carrington pleaded lack of authority to arrest them, seriously doubting the legality of military trials, especially since regular courts were available. Morton brushed aside Carrington's objections, opining that an immediate trial was "essential to the success of the national cause in the autumn elections." However, there were no openings on the U.S. District Court docket until after the elections.[11] He then removed Carrington from command, replacing him with the more pliant General Alvin P. Hovey.

Upon returning from the Democratic National Convention at Chicago, Dodd was arrested and confined in the Indianapolis Federal Court building. Hovey created a military commission of local officers, and Dodd's trial began on 22 September. Dodd denied the military commission's authority to try him, and demanded trial by jury in Federal District Court. His demand was overruled, and charges of conspiracy against the government, giving aid and comfort to the enemy, inciting insurrection, and disloyal practices were filed against him. Dodd pleaded not guilty to each one. Morton's detective testified against him but couldn't offer evidence of an overt act, or proof that the Sons of Liberty were a *de facto* conspiracy.

The trial quickly became a sham, turning into an effort to indict the entire Democratic Party. Reporting daily, the Republican press distorted the evidence, making the treason charges more convincing, successfully publicizing charges of Democratic treason throughout Indiana. Then, on 7 October, Dodd escaped from prison, and fled to Canada. As a result, the trial ended, but the Republican press concluded that his escape was conclusive proof of guilt. Some days later, Morton won re-election by more than 20,000 votes; the Union party gained control of the state legislature and 8 of 11 congressional seats.[12]

Dodd's comrades were then arrested, tried, and found guilty. Three were sentenced to be hanged, and one was sentenced to hard labor for the remainder of the war. With the specter of military executions before him, Morton suddenly reversed course, acknowledging the illegality of military tribunals. Not wanting Indiana to witness military executions, he tried to have their sentences reduced. On 30 May 1865, President Andrew Johnson commuted the defendants' sentences to life in prison. A year later, Johnson pardoned the prisoners, just as the U.S. Supreme Court was hearing their case, on a writ of habeas corpus. The court ruled that military tribunals had no jurisdiction over the defendants, and they were released. Lamdin Milligan, one of the defendants, sued the military tribunal, for damages resulting from his illegal imprisonment. He was awarded the token sum of five dollars.

Lincoln had played a role in reducing their death sentences. However, there were no overt acts of treason committed, yet the defendants were convicted and sentenced to death or hard labor. There is perhaps no better example of Republican abuse of civil liberties and due process in the entire war. That Morton found it necessary to indict the entire Democratic Party, in a sham trial, exploiting the defendants on overblown charges of treason, exposes Republican desperation to win re-election, and the strength of antiwar sentiment in the Midwest.

Republican Opposition to Lincoln

In the first months of 1864, there was little support in the Republican Party for Lincoln's renomination. Various Lincoln Clubs had appeared in New York City, but Republican Party operatives discounted their influence, as they had perceived the president's declining popularity in his own party.[13] Much of the opposition to Lincoln centered around the widely held perception that on important issues he moved too slowly. In February, Senator Lyman Trumbull wrote a letter to H.G. McPike, of Alton, Illinois:

> The feeling for Mr. Lincoln's reelection seems to be very general, but much of it ... is only on the surface. You would be surprised, in talking with public men ... to find how few, when you ... get at their real sentiment, are for Mr. Lincoln's reelection. There is a distrust and fear that he is too undecided and inefficient to put down the rebellion. You need not be surprised if a reaction sets in before the nomination, in favor of some man supposed to possess more energy and less inclination to trust our brave boys ... under the leadership of generals who have no heart in the war. The opposition to Mr. L. may not show itself at all, but if it ever breaks out there will be more of it than now appears.[14]

The perception that Lincoln moved too slowly on important issues was particularly strong among Radical Republicans. In early 1864, Thaddeus Stevens introduced someone to Representative Isaac N. Arnold, Illinois Republican: "Here is a man who wants to find a Lincoln member of Congress. You are the only one I know, and I have come over to introduce my friend to you." Arnold thanked Stevens, stating, "I know a good many such ... and I wish you, Mr. Stevens, were with us."[15] However, neither Stevens nor the rest of the powerful Radical contingent were with Lincoln. They were harshly critical of the president; he wasn't sufficiently committed to emancipation, and his position on Reconstruction — that a state could be reconstituted when 10 percent of eligible voters signed loyalty oaths to the Union — was nowhere near punitive enough. They were also alarmed that Lincoln had overly expanded executive power — suspending habeas corpus, declaring martial law, and greatly increasing the size and powers of the Army and Navy — at the expense of Congress.

The Radicals pressured Lincoln almost daily, throughout the war, for enactment of stronger measures against the South. Senator Zachariah Chandler, of Michigan, exemplified Radical thinking on the Confederacy: "A Rebel has sacrificed all his rights. He has no right to life, liberty, property, or the pursuit of happiness. Everything you give him, even life itself, is a boon which he has forfeited."[16] Radical policies after the war reflected Chandler's thinking, and a dozen years passed before the seceded states were fully re-admitted to the Union.

Eager to replace Lincoln, Radical Republicans called a separate convention that met on 31 May, in Cleveland. John C. Fremont was nominated by acclamation, despite the presence of a large contingent of Grant supporters. Among the planks on the convention agenda were the confiscation of all southern lands and their distribution among Union soldiers. Fremont accepted the nomination on 4 June, rejecting confiscation of lands as too malicious and thereby lowering himself in Radical estimation.

Lincoln was renominated on 8 June by the Republican National Convention, meeting at the Front Street Theater in Baltimore. To appease the Radicals, a plank was inserted into the agenda allowing for the removal of any cabinet member that didn't support Radical ideas, the first time in American history that one faction of a political party had direct control over a president's sitting cabinet. Nevertheless, the Radicals would go further, impeaching President Andrew Johnson and nearly removing him from office.[17] However, given the strength of opposition to the war, and the uncertain military situation, in the spring of 1864, Lincoln's chance for victory in the fall election was very slim. As spring turned into summer, that chance would diminish still further.

Military Stalemate Continues

By January 1864, some of the military goals necessary for Northern victory had been achieved. The day after the battle of Gettysburg, 4 July 1863, Vicksburg fell to a Union army, led by Major General Ulysses Grant, splitting the Confederacy in two. More important, despite the Confederate victory at Chickamauga, the Army of the Cumberland, led by Grant and Major General George Thomas, had captured eastern Tennessee with victories at Lookout Mountain and Missionary Ridge. Solidifying their victory, Union forces at Knoxville repulsed several Confederate attempts to recapture that city in December 1863. Knoxville was a crucial manufacturing center that the Confederacy could ill-afford to lose. Nevertheless, these victories, though important, still hadn't provided any indication of ultimate Union victory.

However, they were won at tremendous cost in high battlefield casualties and in rapidly declining Northern civilian morale. And despite these victories, the impression of Northern battlefield incompetence continued to haunt the Federal high command and the northern public. On 20 February, Union military hopes in Florida were dashed when Federal arms suffered a humiliating defeat at the Battle of Olustee (Ocean Pond) near Jacksonville. Union casualties numbered about 1,800 out of a force of approximately 5,000 troops. The Confederates, with a similar sized force, suffered about 950 casualties.[18] The Rebel victory at Olustee kept Federal troops from invading Georgia from the south. On 22 February, Confederate cavalry, led by Major General Nathan Bedford Forrest, defeated Federal cavalry at Okolonna, Mississippi. Some days later, on 1 March, a large Federal cavalry force, led by Major General Hugh Judson Kilpatrick and Colonel Ulric Dahlgren, was defeated in their attempt to burn Richmond and free Federal prisoners held at Libby Prison and Belle Isle. Kilpatrick and Dahlgren led nearly 3,600 troops, while opposing Confederate cavalry numbered no more than 366.[19] As spring approached, the Southern cause was still very much alive, and Northern victory seemed no closer than it did a year earlier.

On 26 February, the Senate passed a bill that revived the moribund rank of lieutenant general, after the House passed it, the previous December. The bill was passed with the understanding that the high rank was intended specifically for Ulysses S. Grant, who was to be made overall commander of all Federal armies. He accepted the promotion, with Lincoln presenting the commission, at a White House ceremony, on 10 March.[20] Public reaction to Grant's promotion was enthusiastic, and was manifested at New York City's Sanitary Fair that began the first week in April. There were various popular exhibits, and at the Knickerbocker Kitchen Restaurant, with a seating capacity of a thousand, waitresses dressed in colonial garb served waffles and coffee.

However, an exhibit in the Department of Arms and Trophies, consisting of two exquisite swords, indicated the strength of public support for Grant. They were to be awarded to the most popular Army and Navy officer, to be determined by ballot, each vote costing $1. Democratic Party operatives donated $1,000, purchasing 1,000 votes, making General McClellan the leading contender for the Army sword. However, at the last moment, Grant supporters made a large donation, causing Grant to win the Army sword, by a 15,000 vote margin, over McClellan. Little interest was shown in the Navy sword. Nevertheless, the fair was very successful, raising over $1,000,000 for the Sanitary Commission.[21]

The Army of the Potomac's spring campaign began on 4 May as Major General George G. Meade's columns pushed across the Rapidan River into a forested, low-lying area overgrown with scrub pines and tinder-dry brush called The Wilderness. The following day they encountered the Army of Northern Virginia, beginning a two-day bloodbath. The Battle of the Wilderness produced 17,000 Federal killed, wounded, and missing; the South lost 7,500. Lieutenant General James Longstreet, arriving with 10,000 troops just in time to prevent a Federal assault from overwhelming Confederate lines, was severely wounded. He was replaced by Major General Richard H. Anderson. Grant, however, didn't retreat, as previous Federal commanders had. Instead, on 7 May, he gave marching orders to Meade, and the Army of the Potomac marched southeast, attempting to get between the Army of Northern Virginia and Richmond.

The Army of the Potomac narrowly lost the race when Anderson's Confederates marched throughout the night, 7-8 May, arriving first at the vital crossroads at Spotsylvania Courthouse. The battle there climaxed on 12 May when a Federal assault nearly broke the center of the Confederate line; 4,000 gray-clad troops were captured, including Generals Edward "Allegheny" Johnson and George H. "Maryland" Steuart. However, the fight resulted in another draw, deciding nothing.[22] Grant and the Army of the Potomac again maneuvered closer to Richmond; towards the end of May, the Cold Harbor campaign began.

On the evening of 2 June, many a Union infantryman, anticipating an assault the next day, inscribed his name on a tag, and placed it conspicuously on his body, for identification. Early the next morning, Grant ordered a suicidal assault against the horseshoe-shaped Confederate breastworks, bristling with guns. The attack failed, and within 20 minutes, 7,000 Federal troops were killed or wounded, earning Grant the sobriquet "Butcher." The failed assault allegedly haunted Grant the rest of his life.

The indecisive spring slaughter in Virginia brought Northern civilian morale back down once again. One writer stated,

> General Grant might not have received such a strong popular vote if the Metropolitan (Sanitary) Fair had been held in May or June. He was then fighting in the Wilderness and at Cold Harbor, Virginia, where his casualties were counted in the tens of thousands. Appeals went out in the city for more linen and rags, "thoroughly clean and sweet," for the Medical Bureau and Sanitary Commission. Grant appeared to be brutal and reckless, and Lincoln's strategy seemed endless and aimless. Plans to replace him in the White House made more sense than ever. Northern civilians, tired of war, listened more intently to politicians calling for an end to the butchery.[23]

Northern civilian morale was at its lowest in mid–June 1864. The stage was set for a decisive Confederate victory.

CHAPTER 2

Two Generals Gamble

Soldiers of the 2nd Corps, Army of Northern Virginia, relaxing in a tree-lined rest area close to the Cold Harbor battlefield, knew the Confederate high command had important plans for them, when they found out that their commander, newly minted Lt. General Jubal Anderson Early, had called a special conference with the heads of his commissary, quartermaster, medical, and ordnance units, on 12 June 1864.

Earlier that day, Early had conferred with the Army commander, General Robert E. Lee, probably in Lee's headquarters tent, just west of the battlefield, on a slope above Powhite Creek.[1] In their conference, Lee gave Early orders to take the 2nd Corps and defend Lynchburg, then in danger of capture by Union Major General David Hunter's 18,500-man Army of the Shenandoah. Hunter had assumed command of Union forces in the Shenandoah Valley on 19 May, four days after their defeat at New Market. Beginning their march southwards on 22 May, Hunter's army defeated a scratch force of 5,000 Confederates under Brigadier General William E. "Grumble" Jones, at Piedmont, on June 5, then captured Staunton, where they destroyed large quantities of supplies. Hunter's 8,500 troops were joined on 8 June by 6,000 troops under Major General George Crook, and by 4,000 cavalry under Brigadier General William W. Averell. Future president Rutherford B. Hayes, serving under Crook, wrote in his diary on June 8, "We reached the beautiful Valley of Virginia yesterday over North Mountain and entered this town (Staunton) this morning."[2]

One writer said that Hunter "was one of the most unpleasant generals to serve on either side during the Civil War."[3] Hunter neither drank, smoked nor cursed, but he was subject to fits of intense anger, which seriously impaired his ability to objectively assess any number of military situations. Shortly after assuming command of Union forces in the Valley, Hunter began to display a vindictive streak—a penchant for burning the homes of innocent civilians, including that of his first cousin, Alexander Hunter. Entering Lexington on 11 June, he burned the homes of ex-governor John Letcher, General "Stonewall" Jackson, and a number of buildings on the campus of the Virginia Military Institute. Jackson's sister-in-law, Mrs. Margaret Preston Junkin, hid the general's sword under her skirts, and later on, as Jackson's house burned, in the privy out back.[4] Hunter's army unnecessarily spent three days in Lexington, then began its advance on Lynchburg, a vital manufacturing, transportation, and hospital center. The excess time spent in Lexington would cost Hunter dearly several days later, as his force approached Lynchburg.

Hunter's sojourn up the valley was marked by his emphasis on civilian targets, a heretofore seldom used type of warfare. Although civilians had been targeted since 1861, the first two and a half years of the war saw a certain level of restraint, by both sides, in making war on civilians. A notable exception was the burning of Lawrence, Kansas, by a Confederate guerrilla force, led by William C. Quantrill, in August 1863. In 1864, however, the demarcation line between military and civilian targets vanished, due in no small way to Hunter's burning of hundreds of private homes, barns, and outbuildings in the Valley of Virginia. The Union Army's path between New Market and Lynchburg was marked by burned crops, dead animals, the burned-out shells of homes and outbuildings, and the resulting homelessness and starvation of their former inhabitants. Lee wanted to intercept and severely punish Hunter. However, if Hunter captured Lynchburg, punishing him would be very difficult, as re-taking that city would involve time-consuming, high-casualty house to house fighting. Also, Hunter's force occupying Lynchburg would be a grave threat to Lee's force at Petersburg and to Richmond itself.

Lee also realized that with General Ulysses Grant's huge army daily increasing the pressure on the Army of Northern Virginia, and with General William T. Sherman's Army of the Cumberland moving ever closer to Atlanta, only daring maneuvers could save the Confederacy from final defeat. Thus Jubal Early was ordered to stop Hunter short of Lynchburg, destroy the Army of the Shenandoah, then either re-join Lee's forces at Petersburg, or march northwards, down the Valley, cross the Potomac River, and threaten Washington, D.C. Thus Grant would be forced to detach substantial numbers of troops from the Army of the Potomac for the defense of Washington, lessening the pressure on Lee's troops. Lee's written instructions, sent in confirmation of his verbal orders, stated, "Move with the whole of the Second Corps toward the Shenandoah and prepare to meet Hunter."[5]

At 3 A.M. on Monday, 13 June, Early's force of 8,000 infantry and 2 battalions of artillery, with 24 guns, began to file out of their camps near Gaines Mill, marching steadily into the pre-dawn darkness.[6] Major General Robert Rodes' division was leading, followed by those of Major Generals John B. Gordon and the 27-year-old Stephen D. Ramseur. Brigadier General Armistead Long, formerly General Lee's military secretary, commanded Early's artillery, with Lt. Colonels William Nelson and Carter Braxton commanding one battery each. As yet they had no cavalry. Many troops who had served under Stonewall Jackson, in the old Army of the Valley, were still in their units, as were the officers who handled the commissary, ordnance, quartermaster, and medical departments.

The new Army of the Valley marched westward through Mechanicsville, crossing the Chickahominy River at Meadow Bridge, then turned straight north, away from Richmond. Sometime thereafter, they turned northwest, and late that afternoon, Early at last gave the order to halt. They camped by the South Anna River, near Auburn Mills. There he finally decided that Charlottesville would be the army's immediate objective, since that city stood at the junction of the Orange & Alexandria and Virginia Central railroads, giving it strategic value. However, Early had no information concerning the whereabouts or condition of Major General John C. Breckinridge, whose troops were supposed to join the Army of the Valley, nor did he know the whereabouts of Hunter's force. Breckinridge was bedridden, having fallen from his horse at Cold Harbor, aggravating an old wound.

Many of the troops began to guess that the Shenandoah Valley was their ultimate objective as the army marched northwest at first light on 14 June. Marching roughly parallel with the South Anna River, they camped that night at Gardiner's Crossroads, in Louisa County. At dawn on 15 June, the Army of the Valley was on the march again, with Early riding at the column's head. At Louisa Courthouse, he dispatched a telegram to Breckinridge, who was thought to be in the vicinity of Charlottesville. He advised Breckinridge that he would be "near Charlottesville" the following evening, and inquired about conditions in the Valley. A few miles west of Louisa Courthouse, Early's force passed near the battlefield at Trevilian Station, where Confederate cavalry under Wade Hampton had recently defeated a Federal cavalry force under "Little Phil" Sheridan. However, when the Army camped that evening, they were still a few hours' march from the city.

The next morning, impatient to be in Charlottesville, Early galloped several miles ahead of his troops, and into the city. There he found a telegram from Breckinridge, then in Lynchburg. Breckinridge's message told Early that Hunter's Army of the Shenandoah was in Bedford County, 20 miles west of Lynchburg, and approaching rapidly. If Lynchburg was to be saved from capture, Early's army had to get there fast.

Charlottesville is 60 miles north of Lynchburg; Hunter's force was much closer. How could Early get the 2nd Corps to Lynchburg ahead of Hunter? The Orange & Alexandria railroad ran between the two cities, however the O & A suffered from severe problems common to many southern railroads, especially late in the war. The rails were badly worn, with the gaps between the rails (normally a tiny fraction of an inch) widening, with no replacement rails available. Worn rails necessitated trains moving less than 20 miles per hour; higher speeds greatly increased the chance of derailment. Rolling stock — engines, passenger and freight cars — suffered from want of replacement parts. Also, some southern railroad companies were more devoted to profits than to military transportation; they often ignored Confederate government demands to share their resources with one another.[7]

Prior experience caused Early to mistrust O & A management, and his telegrams of 16 June to Breckinridge were worded accordingly: "Send off at once all engines and cars of the Orange and Alexandria Railroad to this place, including everything at its disposal. I will send troops as soon as I get cars.... See that there is no lack of energy in railroad management," and again, "Let me know what the railroad agents can and will do. Everything depends upon promptness, energy, and dispatch. Take the most summary measures and impress everything that is necessary in the way of men or means to insure the object. I have authority to direct your movements, and I will take the responsibility of what you may find it necessary to do. I will hold all railroad agents and employees responsible with their lives for hearty cooperation."[8]

However, the troops were tired from their long day's march, and by mid-afternoon some had not yet arrived in Charlottesville, so Early decided to wait until the next morning, 17 June, to embark the 2nd Corps for Lynchburg. Since Hunter's force was much closer to Lynchburg than the 2nd Corps, Early must have anxiously wondered whether he could get there first. However, Federal incompetence intervened. On 15 June, the day the 2nd Corps passed through Louisa Courthouse, advance units of Hunter's Army of the Shenandoah passed the Peaks of Otter, eastwards through the Blue Ridge, towards Lynchburg. They spent that evening in Liberty, 24 miles directly west of the city. Despite the rough terrain between Liberty and Lynchburg, had Hunter's force advanced steadily the next day, they could have arrived in the city by late afternoon and captured Lynchburg that evening or the following morning.

However, a strange inertia had taken hold of Hunter. His columns had been harassed by fatigued units of Confederate cavalry under Generals John McCausland and John Imboden since they left the Shenandoah Valley. McCausland's cavalry burned the bridge over the James River at Buchanan, in the Blue Ridge, in front of Hunter's advancing host, with McCausland himself supervising the destruction from a small boat in the river. Hunter called in his outlying units, and his troops spent June 16 destroying the Virginia & Tennessee railroad, as they moved slowly eastward, towards Lynchburg. By nightfall, however, they had covered a paltry seven miles.

Hunter was paralyzed by indecision and rumor; while he didn't know the size of the Confederate force awaiting him at Lynchburg, the grapevine had it that 20,000 Confederates under John C. Breckinridge garrisoned the town. Regardless, he knew that his victory at Piedmont and his acts of destruction in the Valley would elicit retaliation from the Confederate high command. However, deciding that caution was the better part of valor, he directed that his 200-wagon supply train retreat towards the safety of the Blue Ridge. Had Hunter arrived at Lynchburg on the morning of 17 June, he would have found a city weakly defended by a few thousand invalids, local militia, and the remnants of the Confederate force from Piedmont, unofficially commanded by General Daniel Harvey Hill (Breckinridge was still bedridden). Lynchburg would have been Hunter's for the taking, but he never got there. Hunter's Federals continued their trek towards Lynchburg, marching northeast on the Salem Turnpike on the morning of 17 June with Averell's cavalry in the lead.

While Early had good reason to mistrust O & A management, his own actions made their relationship worse. In the wee hours of the morning of 17 June, in Charlottesville, Early awakened the Army of the Valley. They assembled and marched to the railroad depot, 8,000 strong, and waited. They waited and waited, grumbling in the pre-dawn darkness, while railroad officials struggled with scheduling problems. As the first hint of dawn brightened the eastern sky, Ramseur's division, and one brigade of Gordon's division, boarded the Orange & Alexandria's rickety passenger and freight cars, with Early in the lead train, for the ride to Lynchburg. However, Early refused to leave Charlottesville until every locomotive and car had arrived from Lynchburg, that didn't occur until a few minutes before 8 A.M.[9] The wagons and artillery were ordered to start for Lynchburg on the main roads.[10] The entirety of Early's force would not arrive in Lynchburg until the following evening.

The ride to Lynchburg was anything but comfortable and occasioned an accident which underscored the dilapidated condition of the Orange & Alexandria. Even with rickety cars and worn out rails, the journey should have taken no more than three and a half hours. The hours disappeared as various points on the line — Rockfish Depot, Amherst Courthouse, McIvor's Depot — faded behind the slow moving cars. Then, as one of Early's troops stated: "Just as we got on the high bridge over the James River at Lynchburg, the rear car jumped the track; but as we were going very slowly and the soldiers commenced hallooing to the engineer, he stopped. Some of the men jumped off for fear the whole train would be pulled off the bridge. One or two were killed and some fell on the bridge, and some caught in the timbers and were badly hurt. But they soon tumbled the rear car off the track and rushed on to the depot."[11] Finally, at 1 P.M., after a journey of five hours, the train rumbled across the James River, and into Lynchburg.

The Battle of Lynchburg

When Confederates greeted Early's train, "Old Jube" breathed a sigh of relief, realizing that the Army of the Valley had arrived in Lynchburg ahead of the Federals. He ordered the trains back towards Charlottesville to pick up the remainder of the 2nd Corps. Early then located Breckinridge, still bedridden and unable to command. Fortunately, General Daniel Harvey Hill, a friend of Breckinridge's, had undertaken to organize the city's defense.

Although Early and Hill didn't get along, and Hill's authority hadn't been officially approved, he offered to take Early on a tour of the city's defenses. Early first wired Richmond for authority to put Hill in command of Breckinridge's troops, then rode with him to inspect the city's defenses.

Hill's defensive works were located right at the city limits, in intermittent lines facing the southwestern, western, and northern approaches to Lynchburg. Early seriously doubted their effectiveness. The lines were over a mile long, manned by invalids, militia units, and VMI cadets, with a few cannon on College Hill facing the Salem Turnpike. The Forest Road, approaching from the west, was only sparsely defended. Early noticed immediately that Hill's defensive configuration would expose the city to Union artillery fire, and the probability of house-to-house fighting in the streets of Lynchburg should Hunter's Federals attack in force. He decided the defenses should be farther away from town, and to weigh the risks involved in attacking Hunter.

Early and Hill then rode southwest, along the Salem Turnpike, towards Imboden's cavalry, which was still harassing Hunter, trying to slow down the Federal advance. About four miles southwest of Lynchburg, near a Quaker meetinghouse, they located Imboden's force and heard rifle and cannon fire. The stone meetinghouse was on top of a ridge, overlooking part of the turnpike, and Imboden's troops had taken cover behind it and an adjacent stone fence. They forced Averell's cavalry to halt and called for infantry support. Around 4:30 P.M., General Crook's infantry and Averell's cavalry began to outflank Imboden's troops atop the ridge. A few of Imboden's tired troopers began to withdraw towards the city.

Realizing that Imboden's force could not hold their ridgetop position for long, Early sent a messenger back to Lynchburg with orders for Ramseur to bring up his lead brigades. Early's orders to Ramseur were to move two miles beyond the city, take position at a "certain commanding redoubt," and hold the front.[12] Impatient for Ramseur's force to appear, Early rode back towards Lynchburg, looking for them. At last they

Lieutenant General Jubal A. Early (courtesy Monocacy National Battlefield)

appeared, and he waved them forward, shouting "Deploy!" as they spread out on both sides of the road.

Despite heavy Confederate artillery fire, Crook's force, consisting of hard-bitten West Virginia mountain men and Ohio national guardsmen, advanced towards the redoubt. From somewhere behind the defenders came a faint bugle call sounding the charge. "Old Jube" was leading Ramseur's advance, the Stonewall Brigade, to reinforce the redoubt's beleaguered defenders. As he reached the redoubt, Early shook his fist and yelled, "No buttermilk rangers after you now ... damn you!" as Ramseur's counterattack drove Crook's Federals backwards.

The "buttermilk rangers" epithet referred to a popular tune about a soldier weary of fighting, sometimes sung by Early's troops during infrequent rest hours. Was Early yelling at the enemy, or at Imboden's exhausted cavalry as they retreated towards Lynchburg?[13] One account has Early yelling at a group of Confederate cavalry as they retired before Crook's advance.[14] Since Early had a well-known mistrust of cavalry, this is entirely credible. Early's biographer, Charles C. Osborne, states: "The epithet ... was a slap at the hapless troopers of Imboden's command ... it was an unfair aspersion: Imboden's men, like McCausland's, had helped delay Hunter ... until frayed nerves and exhausted bodies could hold on no more."[15] However inappropriate Early's upbraiding his own cavalry was, it was entirely consistent with his character. His low opinion of cavalry, and subsequent misuse of his mounted forces, would cost him dearly a few months later.

One writer described him as standing out "blatantly in an officer corps composed largely of genteel, well-dressed 'aristocrats.' For one thing, his dress was atrocious. He wore a great gray coat and an ancient-looking white slouch hat, decorated with a black plume. He also appeared habitually with a pair of huge field glasses slung around his neck. Junior officers took note of 'the inevitable canteen' at his side which 'was generally supposed to contain brandy or whisky,' and rightly so. Early preferred Kentucky 'Old Crow' if he could get it. His whole appearance gave an impression of carelessness and disarray, to which his thin, somewhat curly hair, short gray beard, and florid complexion (perhaps the result of too many pulls at 'the inevitable canteen') added their measure."

As nightfall approached, the fighting ended. Hunter established headquarters at Sandusky, a handsome Federalist-style brick mansion, four miles southwest of Lynchburg, near the Salem Turnpike (present-day Fort Avenue). The house was built by Richmond merchant Charles Johnston, around 1808, who named it in remembrance of a narrow escape he once had from Shawnee Indians near Sandusky, Ohio.

Hunter and his staff had dinner at Sandusky that evening, guests of the owner, Major George Christian Hutter, who had served in the pre-war Union army — the Old Army — for about 40 years, retiring in 1861. Hutter and Hunter had served together in the Mexican War; both were paymasters in the Old Army, which may have accounted for Hunter's failure to burn the house. He instead used the mansion as headquarters. *The Lynchburg Virginian* commented on the dinner the following week: "The general officers were in very high spirits at the supper table on Friday night, and boasted they would be in Lynchburg the next day." Hunter boasted to Hutter that "he had fifty thousand men and could take Lynchburg easily." Hutter warned Hunter that capturing the city "might not be an easy task."[16]

Meanwhile, Early counted just 7,000 troops as darkness ended the fighting on 17

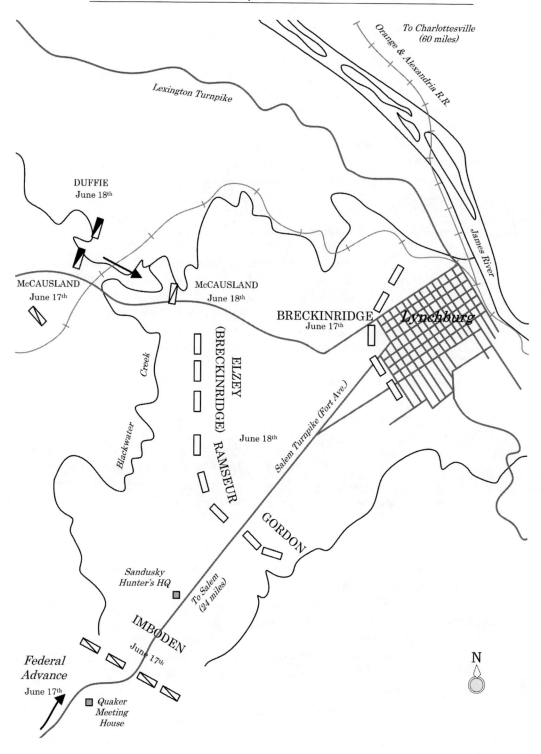

Battle of Lynchburg, June 17–18

June. The Orange & Alexandria had so far failed to deliver the remainder of Gordon's division and the entirety of Rodes' command. The artillery and wagons were still in transit. Early wanted to attack Hunter's force the next morning but had too few troops. He needed to be reasonably sure that an offensive against Hunter's 18,000 troops would be successful. Reluctantly, he decided to wait for the rest of the 2nd Corps. He spent the evening strengthening Lynchburg's defenses.

Hunter, however, was duped into not making a full-scale attack on Lynchburg. During the night, the Confederates ran a single locomotive, with a few freight cars, back and forth through the city, deliberately creating the impression that reinforcements were arriving (none were). All night long, Hunter and his staff were treated to noise from the train, martial music, bugle calls, and loud cheering. Many Lynchburg residents remained at the train station throughout the night, to cheer repeated arrivals of a single locomotive, pulling a few empty cars, that ran out of town, then turned around and came back to the depot.[17] The Confederates had on several previous occasions used trains to give the impression of being reinforced, to great effect, but Hunter apparently didn't know it.[18]

Accordingly, Hunter's plans for 18 June didn't call for a full-scale attack on Lynchburg, which could have succeeded in capturing the city. Instead, he decided to send large scouting parties forward, on the three main approach routes, to determine the strength of Early's army. On his left, Brigadier General Alfred Napoleon Alexander Duffie, an expert swordsman and French army veteran, was already leading the 1st Cavalry Division along the Forest Road towards the city. On his extreme right, a road entered Lynchburg from the south, and immediately in front the Salem Turnpike entered the city from the southwest.

However, Duffie also fell victim to Confederate ruse tactics. Early Saturday morning, 18 June, he opened an artillery barrage on McCausland's force, steadily pushing the Confederates back towards Lynchburg. Around 9 A.M., the 1st Cavalry Division came to a strategic bridge across the Virginia & Tennessee railroad. Duffie had heard nothing from Hunter; nevertheless he decided to push forward. As he surmised, McCausland's troops vigorously contested the approach to the bridge. Although McCausland had infantry support, Duffie inspired his men forward. They captured the bridge, but had to stop to repair it.

At 10:30 A.M. Duffie finally received a message from Averell, urging him to advance on the city. He deployed his dismounted cavalry in three columns, marching east along the Forest Road. However, he was soon forced to stop as Confederate fortifications, bristling with cannon, loomed on both sides of the road across a narrow creek. As reinforcements had not yet arrived, Duffie deployed his force, carefully reconnoitering the Confederate line. Federal cannon fire briefly silenced the southern batteries, but two cavalry charges failed to dislodge the Confederates. Duffie realized he couldn't advance any farther and informed Hunter. However, he couldn't have known that his force outnumbered the Confederates opposing him.

Late that afternoon, the Confederates opened a tremendous barrage of cannon and small arms fire against Duffie, creating the impression of superior numbers. Still awaiting reinforcements and further orders from Hunter, Duffie stayed put. However, by that time, Rodes' division had finally arrived in Lynchburg and had begun marching out on the Forest Road to reinforce Wharton's small brigade and McCausland's meager number of cavalry. At 5 P.M., from a hill two miles away, Duffie observed long columns of Confederates marching west on the Forest Road and heard locomotive whistles, bugle calls, and martial music emanating from the city. The sight of Rodes' columns, along with the martial music, further discouraged Duffie's advance.

Finally, at 7 P.M., orders arrived from Hunter to pull back as the Army was retreating. Duffie had been duped, and the Federals had been hoodwinked into retreating. Except for a brief probe of Lynchburg's southern defenses, on the Campbell Courthouse Road, Duffie's foray against McCausland and Wharton was Hunter's only serious attempt to capture the city.

Previously, around 11 A.M., Early had counterattacked along the Salem Turnpike. Ramseur's and Gordon's troops charged towards Brigadier General Jeremiah Sullivan's infantry, who broke and fled. But Sullivan's troops were reinforced, and the Federal line stiffened and held. Then the Federals counterattacked and drove Early's men back to their lines. Late in the afternoon, Early longed to mount a full-scale attack but didn't know precisely what Hunter's intentions were. Was Hunter in full retreat? Where exactly were his units? Although his subordinates — Generals Gordon, Ramseur, Breckinridge, Ransom, Rodes, and Elzey — urged an attack, the troops were tired from hard marching, and fighting. Early decided to wait until dawn before attacking. Major Generals Arnold Elzey and Robert Ransom had come from Richmond in response to Breckinridge's convalescence. Ransom was put in charge of Early's cavalry.

However, Early's holding back turned out to be a mistake. Hunter and his staff again had dinner at Sandusky; however, this time the mood at the table was subdued. *The Virginian* reported that the officers "took their meal at the same board in perfect silence."[19] After dinner, Hunter requested of Major Hutter the use of two rooms for a council of war. Hutter granted the request, and Hunter locked the doors as he and his staff planned their next move. Believing that large numbers of enemy reinforcements were arriving, Hunter decided to retreat. As Hunter and his staff left Sandusky, Union troops quickly forgot Hutter's hospitality, plundering Mrs. Hutter's chamber, and most of the house, stealing a large amount of clothing, and various other valuable items. The Federals also left about ninety wounded troops in Major Hutter's barn, a few of whom died the next day, 19 June.[20]

In fact, a few thousand Confederate reinforcements did arrive in Lynchburg late in the afternoon of 18 June, but even with them Early counted no more than 12,000 troops versus Hunter's 18,000.[21] Hunter didn't know that his army still outnumbered Early's, and he claimed that his troops were beginning to run low on ammunition. That may have been true; however, General Crook, whose troops comprised about one-third of Hunter's force, claimed to have plenty.[22]

A short time after 9 P.M. Saturday, the Army of the Shenandoah was in full retreat, marching west towards Salem. A skeleton force of skirmishers kept their camp fires going, but the noise of the retreat could be heard by the Confederates. Early pondered a night attack but claimed that it was after midnight when he learned of the retreat. Early stated, "it was not known whether he was retreating, or moving so as to attack Lynchburg on the south where it was vulnerable, or to attempt to join Grant on the south side of the James River. Pursuit could not, therefore, be made at once, as a mistake, if either of the last two objects had been contemplated, would have been fatal."[23] Thus by Sunday morn-

Sandusky, circa 1900 (courtesy Historic Sandusky Foundation)

ing, 19 June, Hunter had "stolen a night's march" on Early, and Early had missed a chance to catch and destroy the Army of the Shenandoah.

As events turned out, Early's postponing pursuit until the following morning didn't have immediate negative consequences. Ramseur's advance units caught Hunter's rear guard in the mountains west of Salem, destroying eight Federal cannon. Some skirmishing occurred between Ramseur's men and Averell's cavalry, but the Federals were moving fast in the bewildering mountain country. Ransom's cavalry was supposed to have circled ahead of Hunter's force, and cut off their retreat, but they took the wrong road and failed to make contact.

Perhaps the most significant confrontation during Hunter's retreat was the Battle of Hanging Rock, at Salem, on 21 June. Hunter's troops clashed with McCausland's cavalry; the Federals lost about 30 men, killed, wounded and captured, with the loss of 10 pieces of artillery. Southern losses were much less.[24] After a chase of sixty miles, Early called off the pursuit. Hunter's force escaped through the Shenandoah Valley and into the inhospitable Allegheny mountains of West Virginia.

The Army of the Shenandoah retreated through West Virginia in what became known among the troops as "The Great Skedaddle,"[25] one of the most "difficult and dangerous retreats of the war," according to Chaplain William Walker of the 18th Connecticut Infantry.[26] Hunter's men sweated and starved in the rugged West Virginia countryside.

Harassed by Confederate guerrillas, many of them were completely broken down and demoralized, unable to march or fight, by the time they reached Charleston on 30 June.

Hunter wasn't aware that Early's itinerary called for marching northwards, down the Valley towards Maryland. However, he feared, somewhat illogically, that Early might send his force rapidly northwards, on the Orange & Alexandria Railroad, to Charlottesville, then march westward to cut off a Federal retreat down the Valley. Thus, rather than conduct a fighting retreat down the Valley, he took the Army of the Shenandoah out of Virginia altogether.[27] This allowed Early free rein to march down the Valley, unmolested, cross the Potomac, threaten Washington, D.C., and menace the North for two months thereafter. Hunter claimed that there were sufficient supplies for his troops on the route through West Virginia, at Meadow Bluff and Gauley River.[28] Nevertheless, his election to retreat through West Virginia was not a good choice, since it was disastrous for the welfare of his troops and for the Union war effort.

Hunter did bring his army back alive and largely intact. They would return to the Maryland-Virginia theater of the war, by steamboat, up the Ohio River from Parkersburg, then by the B & O railroad into Maryland. But his strange month-long hiatus from the war resulted in his being re-assigned to an at large command by General Grant on 5 August. Hunter then asked to be relieved of command entirely, and his request was granted.

The March of the Barefoot

The pristine setting of a mineral springs, seven miles north of Salem, rang with the shouts and laughter of Ramseur's division, as the dirty, ill-clothed and footsore troops bathed in the waters of a well-known resort on the morning of 22 June 1864. Charles Johnston, builder and first owner of Sandusky, built a summer resort at the mineral springs in 1820, which soon became famous as Botetourt Springs, catering to Virginia's elite. In 1839, the hotel and cottages were acquired by Edward William Johnston, brother of Confederate general Joseph E. Johnston. At Botetourt Springs, Johnston later opened the Roanoke Female Seminary, today's Hollins University.[29]

Early had begun the march towards Maryland on 21 June as the Army of the Valley changed direction after breaking off its pursuit of Hunter. They swung northwards onto the Valley Turnpike, and nightfall saw most of Ramseur's division bivouac at Botetourt. Early wired Lee on 22 June, probably from Botetourt, informing him that since Hunter had exited Virginia, he would now proceed "in accordance with original instructions." Lee wired Early three days later, stating that he should press forward with "execution of the first plan."[30] The "original instructions" and "the first plan" referred to Early's force marching down the Valley, then through Loudoun County, crossing the Potomac, and threatening Washington, D.C.

Early decided to move north by the time his troops reached the mineral springs[31] because Lee had dangerously thinned the ranks of the Army of Northern Virginia so that he could march into Maryland. Early considered that Lee's confidence in him justified the risk of detachment from the Army of Northern Virginia.

Emphasizing to his assembled generals that they were duty bound to do their best to relieve Federal pressure on Lee, Early informed them that the army would march to Staunton, then head north down the Valley, starting at dawn. Leaving the mineral springs relaxed and restored, the Army of the Valley resumed their march northwards, towards Lexington, at first light on 23 June.

They toiled up the Valley Turnpike all day, with Ramseur's troops leading. Although the troops were cheerful, many were shoeless, and the uniforms of still more were threadbare and torn. Hard marching took the army through Buchanan that afternoon, with many leaving the ranks to gather cherries from roadside farms. By day's end, most of Ramseur's troops had crossed the James River, with the other divisions close behind. As the army marched northwards, Early himself rode several miles to the west, observing from a distance Hunter's retreat. Leaving Ransom's cavalry to watch the Federal retreat, he rejoined the troops at nightfall.

On 24 June, on the way to Lexington, Major Henry Kyd Douglas persuaded Early to allow some of the troops to visit wondrous Natural Bridge, close to the Valley Turnpike. The side trip delayed the army only a few hours; however, when added to other distractions and obstacles, the lost time cost Early the chance to capture Washington. Late that afternoon, the army entered Lexington, camping close to the ruins of VMI and the remains of former governor Letcher's home. They left the next day, marching past Stonewall Jackson's grave, with rifles reversed out of respect.[32]

Early faced several critical issues as the army entered Staunton on 26 June. Nearly half of the troops were barefoot, and still more lacked adequate footgear. The Valley Turnpike was stained with blood from the bare feet of many a soldier. The crippling effect of marching shoeless was illustrated by one of Early's troops: "The night we arrived there (Charlottesville) it was my turn to cook rations. The wagons were late coming up, and by the time I drew rations and cooked them the long roll beat to fall in. My feet were so sore that I had to crawl around the fire and cook on my hands and knees. I got no sleep the whole night. So when we were ordered to fall in I went to Dr. Baldwin, our surgeon, and showed him my feet and told him that it was impossible for me to march any farther. He said we would not march that day, as we were going to take the cars from there to Lynchburg. I told him I could stand that very well."[33] At Salem, Early had ordered a shipment of shoes, but they had not yet arrived. Although Richmond assured him of their imminent arrival, the shoes wouldn't catch up with the troops until 7 July, when they were in Maryland.

Fortunately, the army could feed itself. Major John Harmon, Early's quartermaster, and Major Wells J. Hawks, chief commissary officer, reported that the Valley was enjoying the biggest harvest in many years. However, the troops had marched over 200 miles since leaving Cold Harbor, and their broken down condition, along with that of their horses, necessitated a reformation of the Army.[34]

The re-organization started when Major General Arnold Elzey, who had suffered a disfiguring facial wound at Cold Harbor, asked to be relieved of command. Elzey had been in command of Breckinridge's infantry since Lynchburg, but it had become apparent that he could no longer endure hard marching. Early regretfully obliged him. However, the 48-year-old Elzey remained with the Army of the Valley and would go on to serve in Tennessee as General John B. Hood's chief of artillery in September 1864.[35]

However, Elzey's incapacity was perhaps the easiest personnel problem to solve.

Major General John B. Gordon's division was considered the most ill-disciplined and disruptive of Early's troops. These included the remnants of Brigadier General Harry Hays' Louisiana Tigers, those of Brigadier General Leroy Stafford, the Stonewall brigade, and the old 2nd and 3rd brigades. These brigades had been decimated by attrition. With Elzey's incapacity, Breckinridge's troops had no commander with Breckinridge himself with the army as an at large commander. Early thus decided to create a new corps, to give the former vice president a command that was appropriate to his level of experience, knowledge, and station in life.

In addition, he put the former Louisiana Tigers and those from Stafford's old brigade under Brigadier General Zebulon York, a former northerner who had become wealthy growing cotton in Louisiana. He put the Stonewall Brigade and the 2nd and 3rd brigades under Brigadier General William Terry. Early hoped that this consolidation would provide firm and steady leadership where it was most needed. However, consolidation is rarely easy on rank-and-file troops, and this occasion was no exception.

A Confederate officer, making an inspection of certain commands later in the war, commented on consolidation: "Both officers and men object to their consolidation into one brigade. Strange officers command strange troops, and the difficulties of fusing this incongruous mass are enhanced by constant marching and frequent engagements."[36]

To make matters worse, Gordon held an intense dislike for Early that had started when Early refused to permit Gordon to attack Grant's exposed right flank at the Battle of the Wilderness on 6 May. Such an attack would have rolled up Grant's flank, won the day for the Confederates, and might have stymied Grant's spring offensive. Gordon never forgave Early, and the daily friction between them reflected that.[37]

Breckinridge was thus challenged to shape these discordant elements into efficient fighting units; also, he doubtless acted to calm tension between Gordon and Early. In addition, the former vice president had to contend with the thorny problem of local loyalty, displayed by many troops from mountain regions of Virginia. Many of these men vigorously defended their homes and localities from the Yankee invader, gladly laying down their lives. However, when the army marched any appreciable distance from their locales, in the words of one writer, they "became high privates," disobeying orders and disappearing from the army. If they did return, it was at a time and place of their own choosing.[38] This desertion became a terrible problem for Early after the army crossed the Potomac, underscoring the fact that many of these troops felt no particular loyalty towards the Confederate government in Richmond.[39]

Colonel Bradley T. Johnson, with his Maryland Line cavalry, reported to the army on 27 June. Early also gave him command of the troops of William E. "Grumble" Jones' old brigade, most of whom had seen action at Piedmont. Johnson would become a brigadier general the next day and would have ample opportunity to justify his promotion during the expedition. Major General Robert Ransom was placed in charge of Early's cavalry, because it was thought that he could handle the ill-disciplined horse soldiers. However, many in Early's army, Johnson in particular, would have cause to regret Ransom's presence.[40]

After greatly reducing the number of wagons allowed to the army, Early issued an order forbidding excess underclothing. However, the reduction to so few wagons may have been a mistake as the troops now couldn't depend on drawing rations from army reserves. Since they were needed for the harvest, Early disbanded the army's Valley reserve force. The army then left Staunton on 28 June. However, they advanced only ten miles that day, camping near Mt. Sidney. Around noon the next day, they marched through Harrisonburg, camping that evening near Sparta.

By 1 July, the army approached the Valley's northern end, and the Potomac crossing, with the accompanying engagements with the Yankees not far beyond. That evening, they camped on and around Fisher's Hill, near Strasburg. Early had thus made certain that the Upper Shenandoah Valley contained no enemy forces. Now, however, one of Early's shortcomings came into glaring relief.

Early had some idea that he could count on Confederate partisan forces for their scouting and intelligence value. He also knew that Lt. Colonel John S. Mosby's 43rd Virginia Cavalry, well-known for their uncanny ability to harass Federal troops unmolested, operated in the Upper Valley and east of the Blue Ridge. However, he made no attempt to contact Mosby, because he mistrusted partisan units, as he mistrusted and misused cavalry, and held them in contempt.

Since his March 1863 kidnapping of Union brigadier general Edward Stoughton at Fairfax Courthouse, Mosby had proven his value to the Confederacy time and again. In May 1864, Mosby's squads raided Union wagon trains east of Fredericksburg and near Berryville. Later that month, and into June, he harassed Federal cavalry, capturing horses and prisoners, and struck Federal wagon trains moving south along the Valley Turnpike. His continued raids against Union supply bases and Federal communications elicited a strongly-worded letter of thanks from Robert E. Lee in September.

Mosby was very loyal to the Confederacy; however, he would soon develop a strong dislike for Jubal Early, which continued long after the war. In a chance encounter on 2 July, Mosby and some of his rangers met Hugh Swartz, one of Early's quartermasters, in Rectortown (Fauquier County), returning to the Army of the Valley from his home in Middleburg. Swartz gave Mosby the welcome news that Hunter had been defeated at Lynchburg and chased into West Virginia. After learning about the advance on Washington, Mosby told Swartz that there wasn't enough food or forage in Loudoun County to sustain the Army of the Valley.[41] Mosby knew that an advance through Loudoun comprised the shortest route to Washington. Swartz had some idea that Early was considering that option; in fact, the route through Loudoun was the original route that Lee and Early discussed in their 12 June meeting at Cold Harbor.

Swartz located the Army of the Valley at Winchester that afternoon. He informed Early that there wasn't enough food or forage to sustain the army in Loudoun. Mosby may well have told Swartz, with Swartz telling Early, that not enough grain had been harvested in Loudoun yet, since Early's comment on the situation reflects that

> My provisions were nearly exhausted and if I had moved through Loudoun, it would have been necessary for me to halt and thresh wheat and have it ground, as neither bread nor flour could otherwise be obtained; which would have caused much greater delay than was required on the other route, where we could take provisions from the enemy.[42]

However, neither the communication to the effect that there wasn't enough food or forage in Loudoun to sustain Early's army, nor the idea that not enough grain had been harvested, agrees with the facts on the state of Loudoun's food supply, in July 1864. By

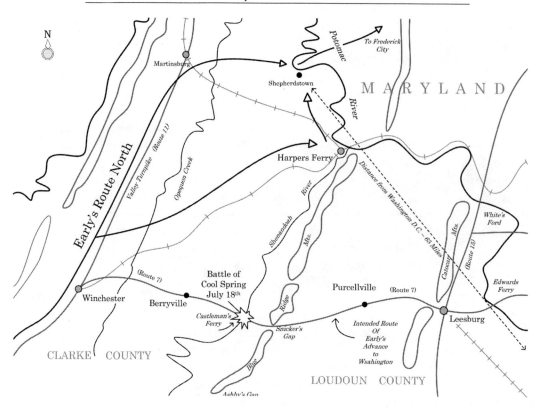

Early's Route North

1860, Loudoun County had developed the basis for what would eventually become a thriving dairy industry. As of 1 June 1860, Loudoun had 5,809 milch (milk) cows, producing thousands of gallons of milk. For the fiscal year ending on that date, approximately 417,000 pounds of butter were produced, and about 396,000 bushels of wheat. On that date, Loudoun contained 14,472 beef cattle, and "Orchard Products" valued at $3,785.[43]

Loudoun agriculture remained strong throughout most of the war, and wasn't substantially destroyed until "The Great Burning Raid," when Union General Phillip Sheridan sent three brigades of cavalry into the area, to rid the county of Mosby's men. The raid began on 28 November 1864, carried out by troops under Brigadier General Wesley Merritt. When it was over, five days later, Loudoun agriculture lay ruined.

Loudoun historian Charles P. Poland, in his book *From Frontier to Suburbia* comments on the raid: "The Union officer who supervised the operation estimated that 5,000 to 6,000 cattle, 4,000 sheep, and 6,000 hogs were driven off or destroyed. The same officer stated that, although he did not know the number of mills, barns, or quantity of forage destroyed, he estimated the damage was in the millions of dollars."[44] However, one of Merritt's brigades reported the destruction of 230 barns, 8 mills, 1 still, 10,000 tons of hay, and 25,000 bushels of grain.[45]

He also quotes an account of a Union participant in the raid:

It is one of the richest counties in cattle and pasturage, with splendid stock in horses and sheep. It fell to the lot of our brigade to go through the beautiful Valley between

Loudoun Heights and the Short Hills, and flankers were sent out so as to sweep the whole Valley. Some idea of the general destruction may be formed when I relate that in one day two regiments of our brigade burned more than one hundred and fifty barns, a thousand stacks of hay, and six flour mills, besides driving off fifty horses and three hundred head of cattle. This was the most unpleasant task we were ever compelled to undertake.[46]

Poland further states, "During Early's retreat through the county after his raid on Washington, Confederates so extensively consumed Loudoun's produce that Union pursuers could not subsist to any extent off of the county." In the supporting footnote, he explains, "Mosby and his men attempted to restrict Unionist troops in pursuit of Early from taking forage and grain from the county."[47]

However, even the Great Burning Raid didn't destroy Loudoun agriculture entirely, and just two months after the end of the war, a local newspaper proclaimed, "We are glad to hear from all parts of the county — growing crops are looking remarkably well and promise a good yield. The wheat crop is not as large as in former years, but there is a fair proportion of corn. Loudoun is a great county — her agricultural resources are immense."[48]

Loudoun agriculture was indeed very strong, and the facts show that there was enough food to have sustained the Army of the Valley. However, Early's behavior in this episode is curious. He made no attempt to verify Swartz's information even though it came from a source he mistrusted, a partisan ranger, a free-booter to use Early's term. Instead, he accepted Swartz's information at face value, demonstrating his indifference to the route his army took in their advance on Washington, despite the fact that the route through Loudoun County was part of the raid's original plan. Impartial readers might also conclude that the capture of Washington wasn't Early's most pressing concern.

However, Early's indifference didn't stop Mosby from supporting the Army of the Valley. Two days after he spoke with Swartz, thinking that Early was going to lay siege to Maryland Heights, Mosby led his Rangers on a raid on Point of Rocks, Maryland, on the Potomac. Striking at Union communications, they cut telegraph wires and burned canal boats, isolating Sigel's force atop the Heights.

Nevertheless, the undeniable fact remains that the route to Washington through Loudoun was considerably shorter than the route Early's force took — through western Maryland. And had the Army of the Valley marched through Loudoun County, arriving at the gates of Washington three, perhaps four days earlier, they would have captured and occupied the city, however briefly.

Into Maryland

Early's Confederates arrived in Winchester late on Saturday morning, 2 July, to an enthusiastic welcome. Winchester was home to many a Confederate sympathizer, and most of the city's residents turned out and cheered the army's arrival, offering food to Early's ravenous troops. Among Confederate sympathizers in Winchester was Mary Greenhow Lee, a local boarding house owner. About two weeks later, Lee would count Fanny Gordon, wife of John B. Gordon, as a guest. Winchester was also home to Early's chief medical officer, Dr. Hunter Holmes McGuire.[49]

Federal troops were at last found in the vicinity of Winchester by Bradley Johnson's aide, Captain George W. Booth.[50] About the same time, Early began to receive information concerning a large Federal garrison at Martinsburg, West Virginia, about 21 miles straight north on the Valley Turnpike, led by Major General Franz Sigel.

Sigel commanded about 5000 troops at Martinsburg, consisting of four regiments of infantry and accompanied by cavalry led by Colonel James Mulligan, also commanding the 23rd Illinois infantry. In addition, several hundred Federal troops garrisoned Harpers Ferry, led by Brigadier General Max Weber. At Winchester, Early's immediate goal was to trap Sigel's force between the Army of the Valley and the Potomac, and destroy Sigel's command before he could cross into Maryland. In addition, Lee wanted Early to destroy as much of the B & O railroad as possible and likewise wreck Maryland's C & O canal, isolating Washington from Federal troops in the west.

Putting his plan into motion, Early ordered McCausland to ride with his cavalry northwards to the mouth of Black Creek, burn the B & O railroad bridge over that stream, then ride eastward, following the tracks, to North Mountain Depot. There, he was to leave the tracks and locate and hold the highway that led from Martinsburg to the Potomac. Early then ordered Bradley Johnson to ride with his brigade northwards towards Leetown. He was then to cross the B & O tracks at Kearneysville, and join McCausland at Hainsville. Johnson and McCausland would thereby cut off Sigel's route of retreat to the Potomac. Meanwhile, Early would lead the brigades of Ramseur and Rodes towards Leetown, cutting off the escape route towards Harpers Ferry, while Breckinridge's force marched straight northwards, towards Martinsburg.

However, the operation didn't go quite as planned. On the evening of 2 July, McCausland's force, consisting of the 14th, 16th, 17th, and 22nd Virginia cavalry, along with a company of Virginia artillery, left Winchester. They went around North Mountain, passing up the Black Creek Valley, towards Hedgesville, West Virginia. At first light on 3 July, McCausland passed through Hedgesville. Their goal, as described by an officer of the 14th Virginia, was to "arrive at Hedgesville, meet the enemy and drive them in their blockhouse and order up the artillery."[51]

Opposing McCausland at the blockhouse were two companies of the 135th Ohio infantry, led by Captain Ulysses Westbrook. The order to abandon North Mountain Depot failed to reach the 135th Ohio as the telegraph wires west of Harpers Ferry had been cut. After receiving word that their pickets had been driven in, the 135th Ohio quickly formed a skirmish line. Ignoring a Confederate flag of truce, they fired a volley at McCausland's advancing cavalry, then retreated into the log blockhouse.

They kept McCausland's 1,500 men at bay for two hours. Then the Confederates brought up artillery. Two shots from a 6-pounder cannon destroyed the 25-foot-square blockhouse, and Westbrook surrendered to McCausland. Most of the 200-odd troops of the 135th Ohio were taken to Andersonville prison. Only 65 survived the war.[52]

While McCausland's part in the operation to trap Sigel was successful, Bradley Johnson's was not. Major John L. Yellott, provost marshal in Frederick, Maryland, had learned on 1 July that a lady in that city had been notified that a large Confederate army would attack Martinsburg on 3 July. Sigel learned of Early's advance on 2 July and immediately began to empty Federal warehouses, loading supplies onto wagons, and waiting B & O railroad cars.[53] Sigel was depending on Colonel Mulligan's force, numbering nearly 3000 cavalry, infantry, and artillery, to provide rear guard cover for the Federal retreat towards Shepherdstown. He ordered Mulligan to delay the approaching Confederates and slowly fall back towards Shepherdstown by way of Kearneysville.

Johnson's brigade of 1300 troops, consisting of the 1st Maryland Cavalry, several battalions of Virginia cavalry, and two cannon of the Baltimore Light Artillery, left Winchester around midnight, 3 July. Seven miles north of Winchester, they turned right, heading northeast, towards Leetown. Approaching Leetown, Johnson's advance learned that Federal cavalry were somewhere ahead.

The 10th West Virginia infantry, anticipating a defensive fight, had been digging trenches. Mulligan told them to stop digging as a retreat was planned. Around 6 A.M. on 3 July, Johnson's brigade collided with Mulligan's. A Confederate cavalry charge was initially successful but dissipated. Mulligan counter-attacked, leading the 10th West Virginia out of their trenches, forcing Johnson's brigade into a hasty retreat towards Martinsburg. In addition, Major Harry Gilmor's 2nd Maryland Cavalry, screening Breckinridge's advance, had engaged the cavalry of Brigadier General Julius Stahel.

Meanwhile, Breckinridge's division had entered Martinsburg. Gordon's troops arrived around 3:30 P.M. When Mulligan realized that a large force of Confederate infantry occupied the town, he stopped pursuing Johnson's brigade and backtracked towards Shepherdstown. However, he had prevented the Confederates from attacking Sigel's wagon train. Sigel burned some supplies, retreated to Shepherdstown, crossed the Potomac, and entrenched his force on Maryland Heights. From there, his big siege cannon controlled the approaches to Harpers Ferry and the river crossings in the vicinity. Early had failed to catch Sigel and lost precious time in pursuing him as well as in pursuing Weber's troops on their retreat from Harpers Ferry. He also began to lose control of his men. Although he had decided against an attack on Harpers Ferry, some of his troops were there on 4 July, feasting on Federal rations.

Ramseur's and Rodes' divisions arrived after nightfall, exhausted from their 24-mile march from Winchester. For the troops, the consolation for having failed to catch Sigel was the sack of Martinsburg, beginning that evening and lasting all night, well into 4 July. Sigel had removed most of the supplies, but a very large quantity remained, and Early's ravenous scavengers helped themselves to several kinds of meat, fruit, oysters, cakes, sardines, and wine.[54] Neither Gordon, Rodes, or Ramseur attempted to stop the looting. Only Breckinridge was able to stop most of his troops from plunder, and it appears that Early himself made no effort to do so. Early did offer a mild rebuke to Breckinridge for the pillaging, then issued a General Order, stating that any further depredations would be "summarily punished."[55]

Supply wagons would have been very useful in Martinsburg, as they could have stored captured food supplies and followed the army into Maryland. While the feasting at "The Dutch General's Barbecue" gratified the troops, it had a price. The army was now spread out and disorganized, greatly increasing the time needed to cross the Potomac. However, for Early, it was fortunate that General Grant, at City Point, Virginia, as of 3 July, thought that the 2nd Corps was still with Lee at Petersburg.[56] Grant wouldn't realize Early's absence from Lee's army until 5 July, when the Army of the Valley was crossing the Potomac.

The Army of the Valley crossed the Potomac into Maryland, at Boteler's Ford, about a mile downstream from Shepherdstown, over a two day period, 5–6 July. Only a few had found shoes in Martinsburg's warehouses, and far too many remained barefoot. The experience of crossing the Potomac shoeless was related by a Virginia infantryman:

> I walked into the water and commenced to ford. About one-third of the way the bottom of the river was covered with large round stones, then a smooth and level bed of granite which extended nearly to the opposite bank. I got along very well until I reached the level granite bottom, which was covered with minute shells, adhering to the granite, so very sharp that they stuck into my feet at every step. I walked on them until I thought I could not take another step, stopped, but could not keep my feet still, — thought of sitting down, but the water was just deep enough to cover my mouth and nose if I had sat down. I thought I would turn back, but I saw it was just as far back to the other side. Tears actually came into my eyes. I was never in as much torture for the same length of time in my life. Finally I got over, with the resolve never to ford there again without shoes.[57]

The army remained scattered after crossing the Potomac. On the evening of 5 July, Gordon's division camped at Antietam Furnace, where Antietam Creek runs into the river. One of Breckinridge's divisions, led by General John C. Vaughn, bivouacked near Sharpsburg. Early himself crossed the Potomac on the morning of 6 July. Major Henry Kyd Douglas invited Early, Breckinridge, Gordon and Ramseur to visit his father's house, near Sharpsburg. After leaving the Douglas house, they took a brief tour of the Antietam battlefield.

However, Early seems to have temporarily forgotten about capturing Washington. Throughout 6 July, and part of 7 July, he was pre-occupied with making a reconnaissance of Maryland Heights, thinking about ways to push Sigel's force off of the mountain. Had Early decided to attack Sigel's troops, the Army of the Valley would have been at a pronounced disadvantage. Major Frank Rolfe, of the 1st Massachusetts Heavy Artillery, described Maryland Heights: "The batteries were situated from 250 to 1,065 feet above the river and the roads (were) very rocky, steep and crooked and barely wide enough for a wagon. Over these roads, the guns, ammunition, and supplies of all kinds were hauled."[58] (The 1st Massachusetts had occupied Maryland Heights in the spring of 1863.) From the sides and crest of Maryland Heights, more than 1,400 feet above the town, Federal siege guns dominated Harpers Ferry and the surrounding countryside. An attack on the mountain would have been extremely risky and time-consuming, yet Early seriously considered it.[59]

On the morning of 6 July, Early participated with Gordon's troops in the destruction of the C & O Canal, smashing canal locks and burning a few boats. However, that afternoon, Captain Robert E. Lee, Jr., galloped into camp with a message for Early from his father. The message contained orders from General Lee authorizing Early to dispatch a cavalry force to liberate 18,000 Confederate prisoners at Point Lookout, Maryland, after first creating a diversion — a raid on Baltimore. The liberation of the Point Lookout compound was to be a cooperative effort with the Confederate navy. Early scribbled a reply to Lee, who knew only a bare outline of the plan. Forgetting about Sigel on Maryland Heights, Early decided to march east, through the passes of South Mountain and Catoctin Mountain. The morning of Thursday, 7 July, found the Army of the Valley still scattered far and wide. Gordon's troops were still pressuring Sigel on Maryland Heights, while Ramseur's men, near Sharpsburg, were still feeling the effects of alcoholic lemon punch.[60]

Skirmishing at Frederick

Meanwhile, Bradley Johnson had decided to take the initiative by attempting to capture Frederick, his hometown. Johnson had left Frederick in May 1861, with his wife and 5-year-old son, to join Confederate forces at Harpers Ferry. He had made a few brief visits during the war, and the desire to capture his hometown and redeem himself after failing at Martinsburg was irresistible.[61]

For Johnson's cavalry, the first scene of action that Thursday morning was the beautiful Middletown Valley, bisected by Catoctin Creek, with the hamlet of Middletown about halfway between South Mountain, and Catoctin (Braddock) Mountain, on the Valley's eastern edge. Around 10 A.M., Johnson's regiments, cantering eastward, had just left Middletown when they spotted a wave of Union cavalry, blue uniforms in sharp relief, bearing down upon them. These were the approximately 250 troops of the 8th Illinois Cavalry, led by Lt. Col. David Clendenin. They had been sent from Monocacy Junction, by General Lew Wallace, to scout the area west of town to determine the strength of Early's approaching army.[62] Johnson's men, surprised, fell back several hundred yards where reinforcements met them. They advanced again, ultimately pushing Clendenin's men back into Catoctin Pass. Clendenin didn't have enough troops to hold the pass, and fell back towards Frederick.

A few minutes later, around 11 A.M., some of Johnson's troops stood in the pass, near the thousand foot high summit of Braddock Mountain, and gazed down on Frederick. The town fairly glistened in the sunshine, with blocks of handsome brick rowhouses and church spires conspicuously visible. To the east was the Monocacy River, and to the southeast lay Sugarloaf Mountain, which had been used by Confederates as an observation post in earlier forays into Maryland. The surrounding countryside was checkered with farm fields with corn and wheat crops waiting for harvesting. However, this "smilingly arcadian" vista was marred by a line of Union infantry, with accompanying artillery, advancing towards them.[63] These were troops that Wallace had sent from Monocacy Junction, led by Colonel Charles Gilpin, to reinforce Clendenin.

Johnson realized that he had to determine the strength of Union forces in Frederick; his plan was a frontal attack advancing down from Braddock Heights while simultaneously sending flanking units to attack the Federals from the south, along the Georgetown Pike, and from the north, along Market Street, rolling up the Union line in his front. The Baltimore Light Artillery positioned their guns on Hogan's Hills and Red Hills just below Braddock Heights, and opened fire around 4 P.M. They sent a few shells into Frederick, one reportedly striking Johnson's former residence. Federal artillery, at the head of Patrick Street, returned fire, and managed to quiet Johnson's big guns. The Federals in Johnson's front stymied his dismounted cavalry, however his flanking units were threatening the town from the south. By 6 P.M., Union fire had tailed off considerably, and Johnson's force began to advance.

Then seemingly from out of nowhere, Major General Robert Ransom appeared. Johnson assured Ransom that his plan would work; his flanking columns were encountering little or no resistance, and he was receiving information concerning Federal troop alignments from old friends and neighbors. Ransom, however, wasn't convinced and thought the advance on Frederick was solely for Johnson's personal gratification. He was satisfied that his attack hadn't encountered any Union veteran units. He ordered Johnson to call off the attack, and withdraw to Catoctin Mountain. Johnson, furious, obeyed the order. As his troops retreated from the outskirts of Frederick, he became further annoyed at Federal pursuit since they were beginning to retreat when he cancelled the attack. Remaining angry, he went sullenly into his tent, staying there until well after dark.

Wallace was convinced that he had won a victory, which casualty figures appeared to confirm. The Confederates had lost about 140 killed, wounded and missing, while Union casualties were 2 killed and 18 wounded.[64] This not entirely accurate perception no doubt gave Wallace confidence that his force, assembling at Monocacy Junction, could successfully delay Early's main army. As General Erastus B. Tyler, commanding Clendenin and Gilpin, had requested reinforcements, Wallace sent three companies of the 144th Ohio National Guard and seven companies of the 149th the following morning. They joined Gilpin's skirmish line west of town.

Meanwhile, Early's infantry was rapidly approaching from the west by way of the Hagerstown turnpike and from the south by the Harpers Ferry road. Gordon's and Breck-inridge's forces passed through Middletown while Ramseur's troops marched through Boonsboro. The troops lived off of the countryside, eating cherries and apple butter, while stealing horses and cattle from roadside farms.[65] While they needed the food, impressments of farm animals only served to antagonize already indifferent Maryland residents. While Early was concerned about troops plundering local farms, he did little to stop it. In fact, he had already begun his own economic warfare campaign against the North by ransoming Maryland towns on the army's route.

By late Friday afternoon, 8 July, Frederick residents and Federal troops had begun to notice Early's advance. Roads leading out of town became crowded with residents leaving Frederick in anticipation of the coming fight. Early had deliberately encouraged rumors about the size of his army by sending his cavalry to attack Federal troops far and wide and by ordering them to attack as many Federal bridge guards as possible just before the army crossed the Potomac. One observer noted Early had "spread his little army, like a fan."[66] These tactics worked, and by that afternoon Wallace had heard that the Confederates might have as many as 30,000 troops. That morning, Confederate cavalry were observed advancing south of the city, towards the Buckeystown Road, indicating to Wallace that the Confederate goal was Washington, not Baltimore.[67]

Early received Ransom's report of Johnson's attack on Frederick at his headquarters tent near Sharpsburg. The report indicated weak Federal resistance; Early realized, however, that the Federal high command now knew of his army's presence in Maryland. He also realized that the army needed to advance on Frederick — quickly. However, he didn't know of a message that Wallace had sent the previous day to the troops fighting Johnson: "I have a telegram announcing veterans from Grant landing at Baltimore, and they will be up some time tonight.... The fellows fighting you are only dismounted cavalry, and you can whip them. Try a charge."[68]

That Friday, the Army of the Valley rose early, and marched from the vicinity of Sharpsburg and Rohrersville, laboring up the 2½-mile-long western slope of South Mountain and into and through Middletown Valley. That evening, Early established headquarters on the long western slope of Catoctin Mountain.[69] Breckinridge's and Ramseur's troops camped near Middletown while Rodes' units spent the night near Jefferson, Maryland.

Wallace had realized that he couldn't defend Frederick with his small command, and resolved to make a stand at Monocacy Junction, along the Monocacy River, three miles southeast of town. Accordingly, he ordered Federal forces to withdraw from Frederick that evening, 8 July. He also ordered some Federal supplies removed from Frederick but had only a vague idea of their extent.

Many of the town's Federal sympathizers had come out the previous day to watch the action against Johnson's Confederates and cheer Union troops, exposing themselves to Confederate fire. Wallace deeply regretted having to abandon them. As the Federals withdrew from the town, Frederick's Unionist residents placed barrels of fresh water on street corners for the troops to drink from. Wallace telegraphed Washington at 8 P.M., "Breckinridge, with a strong column moving down the Washington pike towards Urbana, is within six miles of that place. I shall withdraw immediately from Frederick City and put myself in position on the road to cover Washington, if necessary."[70] Wallace knew his duty. He would have an excellent chance to carry it out the following day.

CHAPTER 3

Economic Warfare — Southern Style

Forward — to the Future

On Wednesday, 2 August 1972, a subcommittee of the Committee on the Judiciary, United States Senate, met to consider S. 1842, a bill "To reimburse the City of Frederick, MD., for Money Paid Saving Harmless Valuable Military and Hospital Supplies Owned by the United States Government" during the Confederate occupation of Frederick, 9 July 1864. Senator Charles McC. Mathias, Jr., of Maryland presided. Senator J. Glenn Beall, also of Maryland, testified, as did Maryland congressman Goodloe E. Byron, Frederick mayor E. Paul Magaha, treasurer Louis E. Eichelberger, special counsel Samuel D. Schell, and Maryland state senator Edward J. Mason. S. 1842 had been introduced in May 1971 as authorizing the secretary of the Treasury to reimburse Frederick "a sum of money ... for moneys paid to General Early during the Civil War resulting in savings to the government of the United States due to the preservation of certain government supplies."[1]

The August 1972 subcommittee meeting wasn't the first congressional hearing on the subject of reimbursing Frederick for their losses incurred in satisfying Early's ransom demand. Senator Mathias introduced legislation for compensating Frederick in each of the 13 Congresses in which he served. Appeals on Frederick's behalf were first introduced in Congress in 1889 by Representative Louis J. McComas, Rep. Byron's great-grandfather. Further appeals were made in 1891, 1898, 1902, 1912, 1955, and 1961. A few of the measures passed in the House but failed in the Senate. Mathias first became interested in the case in the early 1950s when he was Frederick city attorney. During his tenure as city attorney, Frederick made the last interest payment on the debt incurred to pay Early's ransom, on 1 October 1951.[2]

In 1986, Mathias tried for the 13th time. On 3 October 1986, the Senate approved a Mathias sponsored amendment to a $550 billion fiscal appropriations bill, that would have compensated Frederick in the amount of the ransom demand, $200,000. "I am pleased to see that my patience and persistence has been rewarded," said Mathias. "The thirteenth time has indeed been lucky."[3] However, he was to be cruelly disappointed.

Advance units of the Army of the Valley entered Frederick around 6 A.M., Saturday 9 July, with Early focused on continuing his economic warfare campaign against the residents of Maryland. Three days earlier, McCausland, leading 1500 cavalrymen, had ransomed Hagerstown for $20,000. Early originally directed that Hagerstown's ransom be set at $200,000; however, an aide misunderstood the amount and wrote $20,000 on the ransom note. McCausland and his troops also received a large amount of clothing for their efforts.[4]

Soon after their arrival in Frederick, a squad of soldiers raised the Confederate flag above the courthouse. Some of the Confederate officers strolled over to the nearby City Hotel for breakfast while others walked several blocks south, across Carroll Creek, to the United States Hotel, a name that aptly illustrated Frederick's patriotism and predominately Unionist sympathies. The City Hotel was owned by John Need, a southern sympathizer. During the 1862 Antietam campaign, Need had welcomed Rebels to the City Hotel but barred them when they offered only Confederate scrip in payment. A short time later, Early's commissary officer issued a demand: "Hon. Mayor: I am directed by Lieut. General Early, commanding, to require of you for the use of his troops, (500) five hundred barrels of flour, (6,000) six thousand pounds of sugar, (3000) three thousand pounds of coffee, (20,000) twenty thousand pounds of bacon. I am respectfully your obedient servant, W.J. Hawks, Chief Com. C.S. Army of Va." However, the Confederates were told that the requested food could not be procured.

A short time after their arrival, Early and a few staff officers approached the three-story brick home of Dr. Richard Thomas Hammond, a practicing physician in Frederick. Early had been informed that the Hammonds were slave owners and southern sympathizers. Since their home was on nearby 2nd Street, it seemed a logical place to take care of a pressing matter. With Hammond in the house were his wife, Mary Agnes, and their young son, Robert Lee. Dr. Hammond answered the door bell, and was greeted in the urbane manner common to southern officers. They inquired whether General Early might do some writing in the house, and Hammond readily consented.

Early was escorted into the sitting room, where he dictated the ransom demand to one of his officers. It stated: "By order of the Lt. Gen'l comd'g, we require of the Mayor & town authorities $200,000 in current money for the use of this army. This contribution may be supplied by furnishing the medical department with $50,000 in stores at current prices; the commissary department with stores to the same amount: the ordnance department with the same; and the quartermaster's department with a like amount."[5] The ransom demand was signed by Lt. Col. William Allan, chief quartermaster, W.J. Hawks, Dr. Hunter McGuire, and John A. Harmon. Early read and approved it in that part of the house that served as Dr. Hammond's office.[6]

Upon the signing of the ransom demand, Early turned to Mary Agnes, and remarked: "Madam, we are going to make a demand upon the banks of Frederick for $200,000, and if the demand is granted, very good, if not, Frederick will be reduced to ashes. We do this in retaliation for similar acts done by the Federal forces within our borders. You need not fear as timely warning will be given you to leave with your family."[7]

In later years, Mary Agnes frequently recalled the ransom note incident, and as Robert Lee explained, she often "pointed to the table whereon the historical demand was written and said that table should be preserved," because of the role it played in the war. The whereabouts of the drop-leaf maplewood table are presently unknown. The ransom demand was accompanied by a threat to destroy the city if it wasn't obeyed. Upon receipt of the order, Mayor William G. Cole immediately called a meeting of available aldermen and Common Council members. Ransom negotiations commenced in Cole's office, on North Market Street, about a block away from the Hammond home.[8]

Cole and the officers of The Corporation, as Frederick's administration was called, haggled over the ransom demand, with Allan, Hawks, Harmon, and Dr. McGuire. They were guarded by a contingent of Confederate troops, ready to burn the city, if the ransom wasn't met. Cole, the aldermen, the City Council members spoke strongly against the harsh demand. Frederick counted barely 8000 residents, with annual tax revenues of just over $8,000, and a tax base of just $2,200,000, they protested. The ransom note was demanding one-tenth of the city's taxable base, they contended. Citing the fact that Early had demanded only $20,000 of nearby Hagerstown, Cole and Frederick's leading citizens asked that Early reconsider the amount demanded. They put their request in writing, stating:

> To Lieutenant General Early, Commanding the Confederate forces in Maryland.
>
> The undersigned citizens of Frederick City respectfully represent, that the assessment of Two hundred thousand dollars imposed upon the City of Frederick will bear most ominously upon the people of this place. We beg leave to represent that the populations of our city does not exceed 8000—that the entire basis of the city, does not exceed two million, two hundred thousand dollars, that the tax now levied at the rate of 37½ cents on the 100 $ produces 8000 $, as the annual corporate tax of the city.
>
> The assessment imposed by your order will take from the Citizens of this place nearly one-tenth of the taxable property of the city. The Corporation by assuming this large debt, has met your requisition, and paid the amount. In view therefore of the great and onerous burthen thrown upon our citizens, many of whom are indigent and unable to bear the loss, and as the assessment made in other places in Maryland is relatively much less than that imposed upon our city, We respectfully request you to reconsider and abate the said assessment.
>
> Very respectfully submitted,
> Wm. G. Cole, Mayor of the City of Frederick,
>
> L.J. Brengle
> R.H. MacGill
> R.H. Marshall
> Jos. Baugher
> July 9, 1864

Allan and the other officers, speaking for Early, refused. Cole and his corporate officers, fearful of the Confederates burning Frederick, gave in to the ransom demand late in the afternoon. There probably was enough food in the city to satisfy the food requisition; however, most of it was owned by the Federal government and stored in private warehouses. The city thus had no authority to take it. Since Frederick didn't have the money to satisfy Early's ransom demand, the mayor, Common Council, and Board of Aldermen had no choice but to turn to Frederick's banks. Their appeal read:

> Whereas, the Lieut. General Commanding the Confederate Army now occupying this Town had made a demand on the corporate authorities for the sum of Two hundred thousand dollars ($200,000). And, whereas, at a meeting of the Corporate authorities of said town held this day, the following proceedings were had, with the concurrence and approval of the Citizens present.

Resolved by the Mayor, Aldermen & Common Council of Frederick, That the several
Banking and Savings Institutions of the town is requested to furnish so much of said
sum of Two hundred thousand dollars pro rata according to their several & respective
abilities and that the corporate authorities will proceed at the earliest possible moment
to reimburse said Banks & Savings institutions by levying upon the Citizens of said
Corporation in proportion to their ability to pay a sufficient tax to cover the same.

Resolved by the authority aforesaid, That the Mayor, Messrs. Sifford, Bruner, of
the Board of Aldermen, Jno. A. Simmons & J.M. Holbruner of the Board of Common
Council & Joseph Baugher, R. H. Marshall, Lewis N. Nixdorff, Calvin Page & E.
Albaugh, Esq. be authorized to demand said funds & pay over the same to the proper
officials of said Army.

By the order of the Board 1864 July 9th passed Wm. Maloney, Thomas M. Holbrunner,
Edward Sinn, John A. Simmons, Jno. Sifford, James Brunner, Wm. G. Cole, Mayor.[9]
Charles E. Trail, a prominent Frederick resident and a great-grandfather of Senator
Mathias, helped persuade the local banks to lend the city the money to pay the ransom
demand.

The money was obtained, as a loan to the city, from five banks. It was delivered to
Major Braithwaite late in the afternoon, in baskets, about 5 P.M., when city administrators
realized that Early's troops had won the Battle of Monocacy, about a half hour after it
ended.[10] Braithwaite gave the city a receipt:

Received of the Mayor, Aldermen, and Common Councils of Frederick, the sum of Two
hundred thousand dollars in full payment of said sum, which was this day levied and
demanded to be paid to the Confederate States Army, by said corporation of Frederick.

J.R. Braithwaite Maj

	Capital	Ratio
Farms. & Mech.	$125,000	$ 28,000
Franklin Sav. B.	$136,000	$ 31,000
Fred. Co. Bank	$150,000	$ 33,000
Central Bank	$200,000	$ 44,000
Fred. Twn. Sav. Inst.	$282,000	$ 64,000
	$893,000	$200,000

After receiving the money, Early kept his agreement not to take or destroy private
property. The U.S. government rented several warehouses filled with medical, commissary,
and quartermaster supplies, valued at a minimum of $262,500.[11] There were two ware-
houses for quartermasters stores, one commissary store, bakeries with capacity for baking
10,000 loaves of bread per day, a forage house with a capacity of 8000 barrels of corn,
stables for 504 horses, various repair shops, and everything needed for the use of the U.S.
General Hospital, located on the southern edge of town. The facilities on the grounds of
Frederick's several hospitals were valued at between $1,000,000 and $1,500,000.[12]

Despite Early's agreement not to take private property, many Confederates, especially
cavalry, looted private stores. However, while a few Rebel troops undoubtedly looted
from one or two of the warehouses, taking items such as blankets, clothing, and camp
supplies, Early himself didn't know of their existence until late that afternoon. As he
entered Frederick, Early's informants told him that government warehouses in the city
had been emptied, by quick-acting Federal authorities before midnight on the 8th.[13] In
fact, this wasn't so. The Federal commanders then in Frederick, Generals Lew Wallace

and Erastus B. Tyler, were occupied with directing Federal troop movements west of the city and evacuating the wounded. Wallace ordered some supplies removed but had only a vague idea of their extent. By midnight on the 8th, for want of railroad cars and time, nearly all of the supplies remained in the city. They remained in Frederick throughout the 9th, and were there when Union troops re-occupied the city, the next day.[14]

However, in trying to make the city's case before the Senate subcommittee, Mayor E. Paul Magaha claimed that because of his friendship with generals William N. Pendleton and Bradley T. Johnson, Early was very familiar with Federal activities in Frederick. Pendleton had been the pastor at Frederick's All Saints Episcopal Church before the war, and Johnson was a well-known attorney who edited *The Maryland Union*, one of the city's newspapers. However, Pendleton had left Frederick in 1853, when he resigned as pastor over a dispute with parishioners about the dilapidated condition of the church building. He then took a position with a congregation in Lexington, Virginia. Pendleton returned to Frederick on only one occasion, 8 September 1862, with the Army of Northern Virginia, during the Antietam campaign. He left the following day, making it unlikely that he knew about the Federal supplies in the city in July 1864.

Johnson left Frederick in May 1861 to enlist in the Confederate army and organize a Maryland detachment. He too returned in September 1862, with Lee's army, for the Antietam campaign. He was made provost marshal in Frederick for a few days. Wounded at Antietam, Johnson was sent to Winchester, Virginia, to recover, while serving on court-martial tribunals. Although he made a few very brief visits to Frederick in 1863, it's unlikely that Johnson knew of the existence of the supplies the following summer.[15] Thus Early didn't know, for example, that there existed at least seven warehouses containing government supplies. These were partially or completely filled, having a collective storage capacity of 380,872 cubic feet.[16]

Thus Frederick did "save harmless valuable military and hospital supplies owned by the United States government." Early undoubtedly would have fired the city, destroying the supplies, but for the ransom payment, as he destroyed Chambersburg, Pennsylvania, three weeks later. His desire for revenge, and for making Maryland residents experience war first-hand, in retaliation for Hunter's incendiary deeds in Virginia, was too strong to resist. Nevertheless, the issue played a role in the U.S. Army preventing Frederick's reimbursement, during the 1961 appeal to Congress.

Congress's rejection of Frederick's 1961 appeal was based on a Defense Department–Army report, dated 26 April 1955. The report's main points:

1. The goal of Early's expedition was to threaten, and possibly capture Washington, thereby relieving Federal pressure on Lee's forces at Petersburg. Since Early kept his agreement not to destroy private property, the Army concluded, "it can hardly be believed" that the existence of the supplies induced an attack on Frederick.

2. Union troop withdrawal did not result from carelessness or failure of duty, but by military necessity — the superiority of the Confederate army.

The Army also contended that had Early known of Federal supplies in Frederick, it was his right to confiscate or destroy them, and that he could remain within his rights by demanding a contribution without regard to the supplies; the threat to burn the town would be only a means of enforcing the contribution.

The Army doubted that large amounts of Federal supplies remained in Frederick during the day-long Confederate occupation, basing this conclusion on their assertion to the effect that it was doubtful whether the witnesses could accurately remember or estimate the value of the supplies "as the affidavits were executed between 38 and 48 years after the witnesses had seen the property." They were referring to the various eye-witnesses who testified to notaries concerning the extent of the supplies.

The Army further concluded that "there could not have been very large quantities of Union stores in Frederick that were likely to be taken or destroyed by Confederate forces, and ... the $200,000 was merely a contribution demanded ... enforced by a threat to destroy the town, if the demand was not complied with. It further appears that the money was paid only to prevent the destruction of the town, and primarily to protect private property therein. Therefore, there are no peculiar facts to distinguish this case from other cases in which contributions were demanded of towns by enemy forces, or from cases where private property was destroyed, or taken by an enemy force for its own use." The Army then recommended that Congress reject the bill.

While the report's main points were true, the Army's conclusions were incorrect. The fact that Mayor Cole and the aldermen and Common Council members knew they didn't have the authority to take the food supplies to satisfy Early's requisition, and didn't take them, is clear evidence that the ransom payment was made, at least partly, to save the supplies. The $200,000 was therefore more than a contribution given on demand. The money was a ransom paid that saved at least $262,500 in Federal property, and many times that amount in private property.

Was it Early's right to take or destroy the supplies, as the Army contended? General Franz Sigel, who had been in charge of Federal warehouses in Martinsburg, W. Va., was relieved of command on the recommendation of General Grant, for burning Federal supplies when Union forces evacuated Martinsburg, on 3 July.[17] Since Sigel didn't have the right to destroy Federal property, it's self-evident that Early didn't. In fact, Early did find out about the existence of the supplies around 5 P.M. on 9 July, after the battle of Monocacy had ended. However, according to the terms of the agreement he made with Frederick's mayor and aldermen, "Old Jube" and his officers left them alone.

Was it doubtful that "any large amounts" of Federal supplies remained in Frederick when the Army of the Valley occupied the town? There were nearly 20 eye-witnesses to the events of 9 July 1864 in Frederick who executed affidavits affirming that a large quantity of Federal supplies were then in the city. While the affidavits were executed 38 to 48 years after the fact, the witnesses would never forget the events of 9 July; they remembered the supplies, and it's doubtful they would forget their extent or their value.

However, for the city of Frederick, saved from the Confederate torch, the financial ordeal of repayment to the banks was just beginning. Between 1864 and 1868, the mayor, Board of Aldermen, and Board of Common Council had various meetings with bank representatives. After proving their claim in court against the city (necessary because the sessions in which the aldermen and council members demanded the loans were unofficial—rump sessions), the parties reached a tentative agreement in April 1868. Included in the agreement was a provision by which the Frederick County Commissioners would contribute to repaying the loans. However, they never did. The banks agreed to withdraw the court actions establishing the validity of their claim, and a final compromise was reached.

By an ordinance dated 15 April 1868, the city delivered certificates and bonds to the five banks worth more than $125,000, dated 1 July 1868.[18] They were to earn interest at 6 percent, payable for 30 years, and were redeemable before maturity by the mayor until the debt was paid. By another ordinance of the same date, an annual property tax of 20 cents per hundred dollars was levied until the city's debt to the banks was satisfied. The ordinance exempted the bank's capital stock from the tax, costing the city nearly $36,000 in lost tax revenue.

In May 1888 the city redeemed the first issue of certificates and bonds. On 30 June, Frederick refinanced the debt owed to the banks, by issuing coupon bonds valued at over $500,000, each payable for 30 years, bearing interest at 4 percent. From 1868 to 1888, the city paid more than $150,000 interest on the first bond issue. Thus the total cost to Frederick, through 30 June 1888, was over $311,000, for $200,000 borrowed to satisfy Early's ransom demand.

Through the bond issue of July 1888, $123,000 of the debt was carried forward; that month another city ordinance imposed a tax of 12½ cents per hundred dollars, to pay the interest. A March 1916 Act of the Maryland General Assembly authorized yet another city ordinance, dated April 1917, for a $380,000 bond issue to redeem and pay off the July 1888 city bond issue. With the 1917 bond issue, the last payment to satisfy Early's ransom demand was made on 1 October 1951. The total cost to the city to pay the direct loan debt to the five banks was $539,602. Interest at 4 percent, for the various amortizations and tax exemptions involved, added another $1,769,893, for an aggregate total cost of over $2,300,000.[19] Thus Frederick was ransomed, and paid for, 87 years later.

However, Congress decided to reject Senator Mathias' $550 billion funding bill. After the Senate passed it on 3 October 1986, the bill was referred to House-Senate conferees for adjustment. When they finished their modifications, Mathias' amendment for compensating Frederick had been removed. The reason, as given by a report from the House conferees, was that the Department of Defense objected on the grounds that reimbursing Frederick would "open a Pandora's box" for similar claims.[20] Commenting on the rejection by the House conferees, Senator Mathias stated, "They [the House] took the wrong view that if they paid the Frederick ransom, they'd have to pay ransoms all over the country where there had been Civil War incidents. The fallacy of that argument is that they weren't repaying the Frederick ransom; they were repaying the ransom on United States government supplies that were stored here. That would have made a distinction that would have saved them from having to pay all over the country."[21]

"It is apparent that the government of the United States received the benefit of the ransom in the savings of its stores," wrote Rep. David J. Lewis, as part of the 1912 reimbursement appeal.[22] However, while other towns paid ransoms, only one — Frederick, Maryland — saved harmless several hundred thousand dollars worth of government supplies by doing so and sacrificed for 87 years to pay the debt. These are the "peculiar facts" that distinguish Frederick's case. Nevertheless, as of this writing, no reimbursement has been made.

CHAPTER 4

A Pyrrhic Victory

The Battle of Monocacy was perhaps the most important engagement of the Civil War, but throughout most of the past 146 years, one of the least appreciated. It was a hard, brutal struggle, sanguinary as some called it, between the Army of the Valley, numbering about 15,000, and a hastily assembled Federal force of 6,000, led by General Wallace, blocking the road to Washington. Altogether, the contest lasted a little over nine hours. When it was over, around 4:30 P.M. on Saturday, 9 July, Wallace's army was driven from the field. However, the significance of the "hard, sharp fight" in the "smilingly arcadian" setting along the Monocacy River wasn't in who won or lost. Technically, the Army of the Valley won, occupying the field at day's end. But as General Grant stated, "General Wallace contributed on this occasion, by the defeat of the troops under him, a greater benefit to the cause than often falls to the lot of a commander of an equal force to render by means of a victory."[1] And in fact, Wallace himself stated, proposing a monument to his fallen troops, "These men died to save the National Capitol, and they did save it."[2] Had the battle of Monocacy not occurred, the Army of the Valley would have arrived at Fort Stevens a day earlier, without the casualties resulting from the battle, and in better condition to fight.

Wallace commanded the Middle Department of Maryland, with the Monocacy River at the extreme western boundary. (The eastern boundary was the western shore of Chesapeake Bay.) He had first realized that his military acumen might be needed when B & O railroad president John W. Garrett visited him at his headquarters, the former Reverdy Johnson home, in Baltimore on 2 July. Garrett told Wallace that he had received communications warning of an increase in the number and duration of cavalry raids in the Upper Valley, probably screening a large force of Confederates approaching Maryland. Garrett further expressed his unease about the unsatisfactory state of Washington's defenses and inquired whether Wallace would cooperate with Major General Christopher C. Augur (District of Columbia commander) to defend the area between Harpers Ferry and Monocacy Junction. Wallace was convinced that Garrett was looking for a way to defend the B & O's especially prized iron bridge over the Monocacy. He thought he could successfully defend the structure "from my end of it to the other" and promised that the valued bridge would be strongly defended.[3]

Garrett was encouraged by Wallace's promise; the Indianan dispatched the well-regarded 3rd Maryland Potomac Home Brigade to defend the bridge. The following day, Wallace was alarmed by newspaper reports that Hunter's army had retreated through West

Virginia, leaving the Valley open to any Rebel force marching northward. Hunter's force was now in the Kanawha River Valley. Wallace spent the remainder of 3 July gathering troops from the Middle Department. These comprised the 3rd Regiment, Potomac Home Brigade; the 11th Maryland Volunteer Infantry; seven companies of the 149th Ohio National Guard; three companies of the 144th Ohio National Guard; four companies of the 1st Regiment, Potomac Home Brigade; and a light artillery unit, totaling about 2300 troops.[4] That afternoon, Wallace ordered advance units, led by Brigadier General Erastus B. Tyler, west to Monrovia, several miles east of Monocacy Junction (hereafter "the Junction"). Some had battle experience, some had none.

By the evening of 4 July, Wallace had learned that generals Sigel and Weber had retreated from Martinsburg and Harpers Ferry and that their commands now occupied Maryland Heights. He had spent the day studying maps of western Maryland, deciding to move his headquarters to the Junction. Just after midnight, 5 July, he quietly left Baltimore, on a special B & O train, accompanied by a lone aide, without the War Department's knowledge. He acted on his own because at the Battle of Shiloh, in 1862, he had failed to come to the support of Grant's brigades, under attack at Pittsburg Landing.[5] He was thereby blamed for the terrible casualties Union forces suffered and was assigned to administrative duties in Cincinnati and Baltimore. Wallace badly wanted to prove that Shiloh had been a fluke. However, he was a Democrat serving under a Republican administration and a non–West Pointer in an army dominated by West Point graduates. Thus, had either Stanton or Halleck known of his westward trip, he feared they would relieve him of command.

Arriving at the Junction some hours later, Wallace and his aide ate "a soldier's breakfast" and at first light inspected their immediate surroundings. He was impressed with the landscape's physical beauty and potential as a defensive battleground. He realized the need to locate the Army of the Valley and concentrate troops to stop it. Wallace spent part of 5 July hiring civilians to trek west of Frederick, over rugged Catoctin Mountain, and report any sightings of, or contact with, Confederates; he then settled down, awaiting their return. On 6 July, the civilian scouts confirmed that large concentrations of Rebels were beyond South Mountain, not allowing them to pass through, gathering for an advance on Frederick. A scouting party led by Provost Marshal John Yellott also reported a "large portion of Ewell's corps are in the neighborhood of Boonsboro."[6] The Federals still believed that Ewell commanded the advancing Confederates. Later that day, Wallace received a message from Sigel that a large Confederate force, consisting of three divisions, with 3000 cavalry, was advancing on Frederick.

Wallace responded by moving the remainder of his troops westward from Baltimore. The 11th Maryland Volunteer Infantry, led by Colonel William Landstreet, 100-day men, and Captain Frederick W. Alexander's Baltimore Light Artillery, boarded a troop train for the Junction at 9 P.M. on 5 July. Arriving at the Junction several hours later, they disembarked at dawn. After an uncomfortable night on the train, neither Landstreet nor his troops made a good impression on Wallace, who later described them as "a good looking, clean body of city men, but like their commander, green to a lamentable degree."[7] They encamped along Bush Creek, a wide, fast-flowing stream, south of the Junction, a short distance north of Gambrill's Mill. On 7 July, Wallace's Federals, led by Colonel Charles Gilpin, repulsed Bradley Johnson's cavalry, west of Frederick.

On Thursday evening, 8 July, Wallace directed the evacuation of Federal troops from Frederick. He returned to the Junction around midnight on a lame horse commandeered from a civilian. He forthwith went to his headquarters, the home of Captain John Leith (of the Confederate 1st Maryland Regiment), near the railroad, on the east bank of the Monocacy. He immediately drew up a battle plan, anticipating the 1 A.M. arrival of Grant's veteran 6th Corps, led by Brigadier General James B. Ricketts. The plan was based on the correct assumption that Early's target was Washington, not Baltimore. Wallace based his plan on the defense of the Junction where Garrett's prized iron bridge spanned the river and where a sturdy wooden covered bridge carried the road to Washington across a few hundred yards to the south.

The river crossings north of the Junction included the Old Stone Bridge, or Jug Bridge, carrying the Baltimore Turnpike (the National Road) over the Monocacy; Crum's Ford, about halfway between the Jug Bridge and the Junction; and Hughes Ford, a mile or so north of the Jug Bridge. The Jug Bridge, so named for a large ceramic urn mounted on the east end, had been built in 1807–1808, and witnessed the arrival and enthusiastic welcome of the Marquis de Lafayette to Frederick in 1824.[8] A mile or so south of the Junction, the Worthington-McKinney farm ford allowed an easy river crossing. It would play a pivotal role in the coming battle.

Wallace's plan called for placing his less experienced troops — including Landstreet's 11th Maryland, the 1st and 3rd Potomac Home Brigade, and various Ohio National Guard units — north of the Junction. Ricketts' 6th Corps veterans, including Colonel William Henry's 10th Vermont Infantry, the 14th New Jersey Infantry, Lt. Colonel William H. Seward's (the son of the secretary of state) 9th New York Heavy Artillery, and the 87th Pennsylvania Infantry, would be deployed south of the Junction, on both sides of the river. Their deployment area included Gambrill's Mill, the Georgetown Turnpike, and the 240-acre Thomas farm, known as Araby, immediately south of the road. Wallace's line thus extended for at least three miles: north of Hughes Ford, southward past the Junction, to the Worthington-McKinney Ford, southwest of the Worthington farm.

After halting civilian refugee traffic in the area, Wallace lay down to rest on the hard wooden floor, using his long, dark blue uniform coat as a pillow. Rest, however, proved unattainable; no sooner had he reclined than he was plagued by doubts. How could a three-mile front be adequately manned by so few troops? Winning the coming fight was unlikely; he thought of "the desperation of the work — how hopeless it was of victory." He questioned his own authority: "To what extent did my right as a commander go in the exposure of the men under me?" His worries drowned out the train whistle, at 1 A.M., heralding the arrival of 6th Corps reinforcements. His aide, Major James Ross, appeared in the doorway, a stranger behind him, disturbing his ruminations. Wallace arose from the floor and was introduced to Brigadier General James B. Ricketts, leading the 3rd Division of the 6th Corps, Army of the Potomac. They shook hands and settled down to business. Ricketts began by asking, "Is it true, then, that Jubal Early is here?" "Yes, at Frederick City. His camp fires are in sight," Wallace replied. "How many men has he?" asked Ricketts. Wallace replied, "Twenty to thirty thousand. I know nothing personally beyond the fact yesterday ... my people whipped his advance guard under Bradley Johnson." Ricketts then inquired, "What are you going to do?" The Indianan replied, "I came here to fight."

Wallace then told Ricketts that he had twenty five hundred troops. Ricketts was incredulous: "Twenty five hundred against thirty thousand!" The Indianan asked Ricketts how many troops he had. "About five thousand," was the reply. "Seven thousand five hundred," Wallace exclaimed, then expressed approval. Ricketts asked what he was fighting for. Wallace replied that he had "three objects." The first was to make Early reveal his destination: Baltimore or Washington? The Indianan further explained, "There are two turnpikes within two miles of here. The one he makes his main fight for will expose his object. I am already convinced he means Washington."

Ricketts expressed doubt, "How far is it from here to Washington?" Wallace replied, mistakenly, "About sixty miles." He commented, "He [Early] had the reputation of being a good soldier. That he will now lose." Wallace further explained how Early's crossing the Potomac at Shepherdstown had been a mistake. "He should be in Washington now," he said. Ricketts retorted, "Impossible!" "Not at all," the Hoosier rejoined, "He had only to cross the Potomac at Edwards Ferry below Harpers Ferry. No power on earth could have saved the city from him. As it is, he has fooled away his time and chances, and an opportunity which, if now lost by him, the Confederacy can never hope to regain." Ricketts laughed, inquiring of Wallace his remaining objectives. The second, replied the Hoosier, was "to push the curtain aside," referring to Early's cavalry screen, "and make him show us what all he has." Wallace further explained that he also wanted to "get thirty six or forty hours on Early, that ... will give General Grant ample time to get a Corps or two into Washington and make it safe."

Wallace then complained about Halleck's reinforcing Harpers Ferry and ignoring him, explaining that he had been urged to join the troops on Maryland Heights. Ricketts allegedly replied, "What! And give Early a clear road to Washington! Never — never! We'll stay here. Give me your orders." Ricketts read them, inquiring, "You expect the fight in the morning?" Wallace answered affirmatively, and Ricketts assured him that he would be fully deployed "before daybreak." The Hoosier in turn assured Ricketts that his post would be "across the pike behind the wooden bridge," because "it is the post of honor. There the enemy will do his best fighting." He then instructed Major Ross to show Ricketts where to deploy.

Major General Lew Wallace (courtesy Monocacy National Battlefield)

Ricketts departed, and Wallace "lay down and slept never more soundly."[9] Wallace was taking a calculated risk, one that saved Washington, D.C., and the Lincoln administration and redeemed his reputation.

The Fighting Begins

As Wallace finished breakfast and began troop inspections, around 6 A.M., the battle of Monocacy began, two miles to the north. Advance units of Brigadier General Robert D. Lilley's Virginia Infantry, part of Ramseur's division, had marched eastward from Frederick, along the National Road. Their objective was to defeat Union forces at the river crossing, and capture and hold the Jug Bridge. They marched into the slowly breaking dawn, for the better part of an hour, before the high green ridge comprising the Monocacy's east (south) bank became visible. As they approached the indestructible stone bridge with the strange urn, advancing down a slight grade they were fired upon by pickets of Colonel Allison Brown's 149th and 144th Ohio National Guard. Lilley's Rebels deployed, fanning out on both sides of the road.

At daybreak, Brown had deployed a skirmish line on the west (north) bank, quickly becoming engaged with Lilley's men. Brown had seven companies of Ohio National Guardsmen; nevertheless, they were outnumbered by the Confederates. Heavy skirmishing continued for several hours. Around 10 A.M., from a rise overlooking the field, Brown spotted Confederate cavalry, probably from Johnson's 1st Maryland, attempting to turn his right flank at Hughes Ford, about a mile north of the bridge.[10] In response, Brown sent Company E and a company of mounted infantry, led by Captain Edward Leib, to reinforce troops guarding Hughes Ford. Arriving at the ford, Leib "drove the rebels off," then returned to support Brown. As Leib drove the mounted Confederates away from the ford, gray-clad infantry attacked Brown's left flank in force.

Meanwhile, Robert Rodes' Georgia Infantry had replaced Lilley's men. Using the terrain to his advantage, Rodes positioned his troops to overlap Brown's left flank. They attacked around 11:30 A.M., and their numerical superiority pushed Brown's line backwards, subjecting them to a fierce enfilading fire. In response, Brown ordered Company B, of the 149th, to charge Rodes' line; they were repulsed. Reinforced by three companies of the 144th, they made a bayonet charge against the Georgia infantry, driving Rodes' men backwards, restoring the Federal battle line. Brown's Ohio Guardsmen then held their position the remainder of the afternoon.

Farther south, fighting had begun in earnest, near the Washington Turnpike, near the "gray-stained, roofed" wooden bridge. According to Wallace, the Federals got off the first shot. Around 7 A.M., right after inspecting Ricketts' deployments, the Hoosier observed Rebel cavalry advancing down the Buckeystown Road, then spied another gray-clad column moving east on the turnpike towards the covered bridge. Corroborating Wallace's sightings, Ricketts ordered Captain Alexander's three-gun battery, overlooking the Junction, to open fire. Wallace and Ricketts, close to the covered bridge, soon heard the discharge of one of Alexander's 3-inch Parrott rifles, and Ricketts, familiar with artillery, expressed his disappointment. "A Parrott!" he exclaimed. "Have you nothing better?"[11] In response, Wallace ordered their 24-pound howitzer forward. Captain William H. Weigel, qualified to properly serve the gun, promptly reported to Wallace, and the big gun was soon firing at the Rebels.

However, the Confederates responded with a soldierly acumen. After Weigel's first shot, they rapidly cleared the Washington Turnpike, finding cover behind houses and outbuildings, haystacks and trees. Rebel artillery was soon in operation, thundering against Federals on the south bank, a mile and a half distant. Wallace counted sixteen 12-pounder brass cannon (Napoleons); the four guns of Captain L.J. Kirkpatrick's Amhurst Artillery, firing from the Cronise farm, were particularly effective. A little after 7:30 A.M. Federal troops breakfasting near Gambrill's Mill suddenly found themselves the targets of Kirkpatrick's guns. The scene around the mill became chaotic as the first shells exploded, killing two from the 151st New York Infantry. Shouted orders added to the pandemonium as men retrieved weapons and formed ranks as shells continued to burst among them and whistle overhead.[12]

Nevertheless, the deadly southern barrage had a more telling effect. Wallace had arranged with the engineer of a B & O train, behind a ridge several hundred yards northeast, to evacuate the wounded. But as the Confederate cannonade intensified, the engineer panicked and steamed away to the east, leaving Wallace with no way to evacuate his wounded. Gambrill's Mill, used as a make-shift hospital, was soon filled. With no ambulance service, ambulatory Federal troops who were badly wounded had nowhere to go. Those who couldn't walk were forced to lie where they fell. Wallace's telegrapher was also aboard the train, and he was now cut off from contact with Washington and headquarters in Baltimore.

The Hoosier learned of the train's withdrawal around 12:30 P.M. He later wrote, "It took me some time to recover from this blow. Indeed, could hands have been laid upon him, I think yet I could have stood quietly by and seen the cowardly wretch hanged. But there was no remedy. The hurt and the maimed must lie where they fell — in that respect like the dead."[13]

The defense of the Monocacy bridges was crucial to Wallace's strategy. The Confederate objective was to capture the crossings, but without undue loss; they wanted to avoid a repeat of Burnside's chaotic crossing of Antietam Creek two years before. However, as the morning wore on, Ramseur's troops steadily increased pressure on the Federals defending the bridges. The defense of the bridges near the Junction was portrayed by Lieutenant (later Captain) George E. Davis, commanding Company D, 10th Vermont Infantry:

> Early in the morning of July 9th, with Second Lieutenant ... and seventy-five men
> of our regiment, I was ordered to report as skirmishers, to Capt. Charles J. Brown,
> commanding companies C and K, First Maryland Regiment, Potomac Home Brigade,
> near the block house, on the west bank of the Monocacy River. He and his two hundred
> men had just entered the service for one hundred days, to repel this invasion, and knew
> nothing of actual service. I was sent to General Wallace's headquarters on the hill east,
> for orders, which were to hold the two bridges across the river, the wooden bridge and
> the railroad bridge, at all hazards, and to prevent the enemy from crossing. No intima-
> tion was made that the wooden bridge might be burned. General Ricketts' division
> was in two lines of battle in our rear on the east bank of the Monocacy. Some of the
> Ninth New York Heavy Artillery pickets were at our left, near the northwest end of
> the wooden bridge, making something over three hundred men in all, on the west

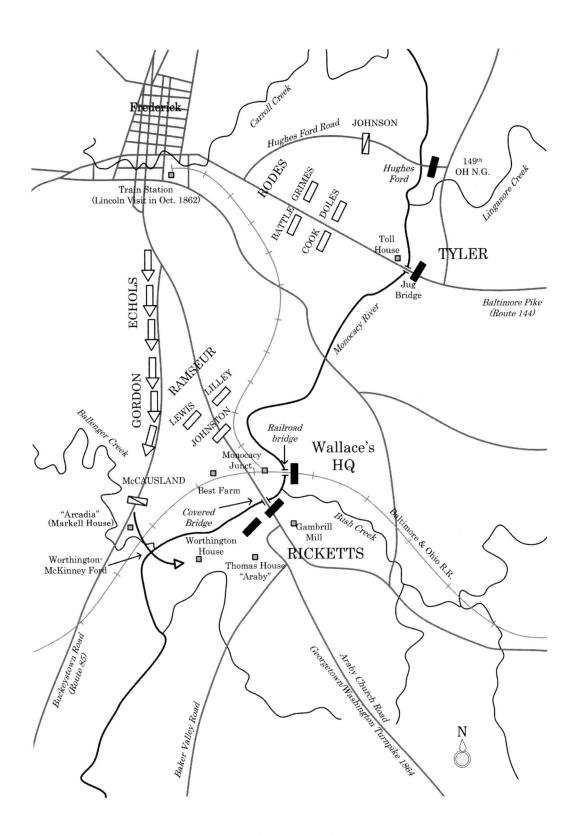

Battle of Monocacy, July 9

Gambrill Mill, 1934 (courtesy Monocacy National Battlefield)

bank, and we were the only Union troops on that side of the stream, confronted with Ramseur's division of Confederate troops. We faced north and west to cover a triangle, the north line of which was three hundred fifty yards from the railroad bridge to the turnpike over the railroad....

When the enemy advanced, about 8:30 A.M. along the pike from Frederick ... Captain Brown turned to me in disgust and insisted upon my taking command. I assumed command instantly, brought up my Tenth Vermonters to this point, and after a severe fight of about one hour, the enemy retired.... About 11 A.M. a second and much severer attack was made on our right and rear, by which they intended to cut us out, take us prisoners, cross the railroad bridge and turn Ricketts position.... I had, on assuming command, sent pickets up and down the river, who warned me of this flank movement, that was entirely hidden from my view, so that I drew back my men to the west end of the railroad bridge, faced north, repelled the attack, then assumed my former position on the pike, which we held until the retreat about 5 o'clock. In the early part of the noon attack, the wooden bridge over the Monocacy was burned, without notice to me. At the same time, the Ninth New York pickets were all withdrawn, also without notice.

The third and last attack began about 3:30 P.M. The situation was critical; the enemy came upon us with such overwhelming numbers and desperation, it seemed that we must be swept into the river. The place of the Ninth New York pickets at my left had not been filled for want of men. The hundred day men at my right were melting away and went over the iron bridge to the rifle pits on the east bank of the river. Nevertheless, we fought for over an hour and kept back a much larger force than ours. Apprehending an advance on my left, I sent Corp. John G. Wright, Company E, Tenth Vermont, through the cornfield to examine and report. He was killed at once....

Immediately the enemy was seen passing around my right to cut off my retreat by the iron bridge.... We must leave now or never. Our noble band of Vermonters stood by me till I gave the order to retreat, when we kept together and crossed the railroad bridge, stepping upon ties, there being no floor.[14]

The Vermonters were watched closely, by Confederate artillerists, as they retreated across the bridge, with the swift and treacherous current 45 feet below. Nevertheless, southern gunners held their fire. One writer commented on this restraint, "Thus even in the heat of battle the chivalrous spirit of American manhood asserted itself, and Southern artillerists refused to commit needless slaughter even of their enemies. To their praise be it said."[15]

Brown was given command when Major Charles Chandler, of the 10th Vermont, had inexplicably re-crossed the river. The inexperienced Brown gave his command to Davis because he couldn't identify advancing Confederates clad in Federal uniforms. Davis was surprised by the sudden burden of grave responsibility; nevertheless he immediately aligned his units with Ricketts' division, across the river, using their firepower to keep open his line of retreat. The 10th Vermont, and a few troops of the 9th New York Heavy Artillery, though greatly outnumbered, managed to keep Ramseur's troops at bay well after 4 P.M. when Wallace ordered a retreat.

Meanwhile, in Frederick, as the sun climbed towards noon, Jubal Early realized time was passing. Taking a break from ransom negotiations, he rode out to assess his army's progress. Observing fierce Federal resistance, he realized that a direct advance down the Washington Turnpike could be achieved only with heavy casualties. The Rebels had to find a way to flank the bridge crossings. Somewhere, there must be another ford. He thought of McCausland's cavalry, those "buttermilk rangers," usually long on bravado, but short on results. Hadn't he ordered them, the previous evening, to find another ford? He had. And lo and behold, he soon caught sight of them, splashing across the river, dismounting, marching up the steep east bank. Reluctantly, "Old Jube" realized that his "buttermilk rangers" had solved his problem, providing his army with a way to outflank Wallace.[16]

McCausland Attacks

From a second story window in his house, farmer John T. Worthington watched, with growing consternation, as the line of gray-clad, dismounted cavalry, led by General McCausland, advanced through his front yard. They had crossed the Monocacy, at the Worthington-McKinney Ford, several hundred yards southwest, at a little past 10 A.M. They quickly overcame stiff resistance from Lt. George W. Corbit's Company B, 8th Illinois Cavalry, and pressed on towards Worthington's house, an imposing red brick, two story structure with a large front porch. Assembling in his front yard, they advanced through a field of waist-high corn, towards the boundary fence with the Thomas farm, three hundred yards north. However, unknown to the Rebels, Wallace had alerted Ricketts to their approach. Ricketts responded by quickly extending his line towards the Worthington farm.

McCausland led the 14th, 16th, and 17th Virginia Cavalry, somewhat more than 900 troops. They had become the spearhead of Early's flank attack and expected some resistance but were unaware that veteran Union troops, led by Ricketts, were strongly posted behind the fence. They crossed the Worthington property, in the words of one writer, "as if on parade," standing straight with their rifles at their sides, flags and guidons waving in the bright July sunlight. As they approached the Thomas property, a line of blue-clad troops, heretofore concealed by the cornstalks, appeared behind the fence, a hundred yards away, rifles aimed and ready. Worthington watched helplessly, as Ricketts' Federals loosed a withering volley into the stunned Confederates. The survivors hid in the tall corn; crawling out of range, then running back the way they had come. They ran past the Worthington house, all the way to the river, where they regrouped.[17] Brigadier General John Echols had discovered earlier that the Army of the Valley faced Union veterans. McCausland's repulse caused Early himself to believe that they faced veterans, not 100-day militia.[18]

As morning became afternoon, near the turnpike's covered bridge, the fighting abated somewhat, skirmishing north of the Junction notwithstanding. At the Worthington farm, all was quiet. Wallace and his staff enjoyed a lunch of sardines and crackers, and he rejected an offer to open a bottle of wine.[19] In his memoirs, Wallace celebrated the hours gained in keeping the Army of the Valley from accessing the Washington Turnpike: "Five hours from my very able antagonist, General Early! I counted them, beginning at seven o'clock, not once but many times, much as I fancy a miser counts his gold pieces."[20] Commendably, he had determined to hold on until "five or six o'clock," as it "would not be in General Early's power to move his main body before the next day."[21] However, circumstances began to change for Wallace's Federals, in early afternoon, prompted by events beyond his control.

The first was the aforementioned departure of the hospital train, after Wallace told Ricketts it would stay. Next, an inexperienced artilleryman servicing the 24-pound howitzer loaded the shell before the powder, jamming the gun. Neither Weigel nor any of his troops could get the gun to work; Wallace had lost his best cannon, significantly reducing his army's firepower. Perhaps in response, he ordered the turnpike's covered bridge burned, as Captain Davis stated, "in the early part of the noon attack," around 12:30 P.M., confirmed by Private Alfred S. Roe, 9th New York Heavy Artillery.[22] Years later, Wallace wrote that he ordered the bridge fired around 2 P.M., the hour generally accepted by present-day historians. Whenever it was fired, the bridge's destruction made it more difficult for Ramseur's Confederates to cross the river; it also stranded Davis' 10th Vermont on the north (west) bank. The Hoosier sent Major Ross to advise Davis of the bridge's imminent destruction. Observing that the 10th Vermont was several hundred yards away after crossing the bridge, Ross retreated, back across the bridge, failing to deliver the warning.

Around 2 P.M., the pace of the fighting increased, causing Wallace to realize that promised reinforcements hadn't arrived. These were 1050 troops of the 122nd Ohio, 6th Maryland, and 67th Pennsylvania Infantry, comprising the 2nd Division of the 6th Corps. They had been on three troop ships that hadn't docked when Ricketts' 3rd Division left Baltimore. Led by Colonel John F. Staunton, they left Locust Point (near Ft. McHenry) aboard two B & O trains. They were badly needed, and were expected to arrive at the Junction by 1 P.M., but never did. The two trains stopped at Monrovia, eight miles east of the Junction, well within hearing range of the battle, remaining there all afternoon. On 23 August, Staunton was cashiered from the Army, for failing to reinforce Wallace.[23]

McCausland Tries Again

Humiliated by their thrashing on the Worthington farm that morning, McCausland's cavalry prepared to attack Wallace's left flank again. Urged on by surviving officers, they crossed the shallow Monocacy again, numbering about 900, around 2 P.M. As they surged up the steep south bank, they were cheered by Breckinridge's reserves, lounging on the grass at Arcadia, a large Victorian era mansion on the Buckeystown Pike, overlooking the area.

Having learned not to attack the veteran 6th Corps head on, McCausland opted for a flanking attack. This time, the dismounted cavalry marched southeast of the Worthington house, passing between it and 800-foot high Brooks Hill. Using the uneven terrain and forested areas on the lower reaches as cover, they attacked an undefended section of the boundary fence, catching Ricketts off guard. Ricketts frantically tried to shift his troops to meet the threat without result. McCausland's stalwarts thereby achieved an irresistible momentum straight towards Araby, the Thomas farmhouse, supported by enfilading artillery fire, from across the river.

Ricketts' line swung southeast, facing this new threat. McCausland's troops disappeared from sight, into the shallow valley between Brooks Hill and the Thomas farm, the shrill "yip-yip" of the Rebel yell on their lips. A minute or so later, they came out of the valley, covering the remaining quarter mile to Araby in a few minutes. They pushed Ricketts' defenders backwards, to the Washington Turnpike (today's Araby Church Road). At the turnpike, they formed behind an embankment where the road passed the entrance to the Thomas farm. McCausland's advance overran Araby — so named by the original owner for an estate in Scotland — as the C. Keefer Thomas family, and their servants and neighbors, huddled in the basement. However, McCausland's advance was unsupported, save for friendly fire from across the river. As they occupied the grounds of Araby, that friendly fire ceased (for fear of hitting them) and the 16th and 17th Virginia Cavalry now found themselves outnumbered and outgunned, taking increasing casualties.

Peering through his field glasses, from his vantage point on the bluff, on the east bank, Wallace saw McCausland's troops begin to falter. He sent Major Ross to tell Ricketts to counter-charge. Instead of Ricketts, Ross met Captain W.H. Lanius, on the staff of Colonel William Truex, commanding Ricketts' 1st Brigade. Under fire, and without informing Ricketts, Lanius directed the 87th Pennsylvania and 14th New Jersey infantries to charge the farmhouse and evict the gray-clad cavalry.

The two regiments charged up Araby's front lane, through the front yard, slowly driving the Rebel cavalry away from the main house and off the farm. Shortly thereafter, a Confederate shell crashed through Araby's dining room wall, landing on a table and scattering silverware throughout the room. The Virginia cavalry launched their attack around 2 P.M., captured Araby about 2:25 P.M., and held it for about twenty minutes. Faced with superior numbers and firepower, they were forced to retreat again, angrily falling back to the Worthington farm. McCausland's brigade suffered about 100 casualties in their two assaults.[24] Araby was badly damaged by rifle and cannon fire, as hundreds of bullets from both sides found resting places in the exterior woodwork and interior walls, while gaping holes were created by shells crashing through the outer brick walls.

With the retreat of the Virginia cavalry, fighting momentarily ended; however, the

Federals paid a price for stopping McCausland again. Captain Alexander's six Parrott rifles were now nearly out of ammunition, and as Federal ordnance officers failed to send any, there was no way to obtain more. Alexander's nearly useless artillery, along with the jammed howitzer, were major factors in Wallace's decision to retreat.

Gordon Attacks

With the second repulse of McCausland, Early realized that an assault in strength was needed to drive Wallace's Federals from the field, to gain access to the Washington Turnpike. Early thereupon told Breckinridge to order Gordon to attack, with his entire division, Wallace's Federals arrayed on the Thomas farm and along the turnpike. The Georgian's attenuated division, numbering about 2,500, likewise crossed the river at the Worthington-McKinney Ford. Gordon later stated, "My hope and effort were to conceal the movement from Wallace's watchful eye until my troops were over, and then apprise him of my presence ... by a sudden rush on his left flank, but ... he discovered the maneuver of my division before it could drag itself through the water and up the Monocacy's muddy and slippery banks."[25]

After riding part-way up Brooks Hill, Gordon took a long look at Wallace's lines. Using the uneven terrain and forested areas on the lower part of the hill, Gordon's force advanced through the shallow valley in front of it. Around 3:30 P.M., they emerged from the woods on the Worthington property: three lines of infantry, preceded by a line of skirmishers, advancing towards the Thomas farm.

Gordon advanced by brigade, en echelon — piecemeal. Ricketts had turned his lines southeast, facing his advance. As Gordon stated, his forward movement "presented new difficulties" that included finding himself "separated from all other Confederate infantry, with the bristling front of Wallace's army before me. In addition ... I found difficulties which strongly militated against the probable success of my movement. Across the intervening fields ... there were strong farm fences, which my men must climb while under fire. Worse still, those fields were thickly studded with huge grain stacks which the harvesters had recently piled. They were so broad and high and close together that no line of battle could possibly be maintained while advancing through them. Every intelligent private in my command, as he looked over the field, must have known before we started that my battle-line would become tangled and confused.... I knew, however, that if any troops in the world could win victory against such adverse conditions, those high-mettled Southern boys would achieve it here."[26]

Clement A. Evans' brigade, comprising several regiments of Georgia infantry, advanced first, straight towards Araby. Killing and wounding a number of officers, Federal defenders slowed their momentum. Evans himself was severely wounded, the bullet penetrating a box of sewing pins in his coat pocket, driving needles into his side and hip. He took a bad fall, and doctors were unable to remove the pins until a decade later. Evans advance revealed that many in Gordon's division, perhaps Gordon himself, were unaware that they were facing Union veterans. As they approached Araby, encountering the tail end of McCausland's retreating cavalry, they taunted them, in a friendly way: "We will show these cavalrymen how to fight, these are only one-hundred days men and can't stand up against our troops."[27] Gordon's lack of knowledge about the quality of opposing troops was the result of poor communication in the Valley Army. General Echols knew that morning that Wallace's troops were veterans; apparently that knowledge wasn't communicated to other units. Their lack of communication also points to Early's feud with Gordon, war weariness, and the beginning of a decline in morale.

Under a nasty enfilading fire from Colonel Henry's 10th Vermont, on the Baker Valley Road, Evans' brigade nevertheless advanced, moving around the huge grain stacks. Bulls-eye shooting by the 87th Pennsylvania and 14th New Jersey slowed, then stopped Evans' surging infantry. Evans' best officers went down, including Gordon's brother, Major Eugene C. Gordon, and at least six flag bearers.[28] Evans' brigade lost over five hundred killed and wounded.

With Evans' brigade stopped, the momentum of Gordon's attack shifted to the center, where Brigadier General Zebulon York's Louisiana Infantry was beginning their charge against the troops of colonels Matthew McClennan and William Truex of the 87th Pennsylvania and 14th New Jersey. Rolling, uneven ground a few hundred yards west of Araby obscured part of York's command. Unnoticed by Federal defenders, they discovered an opening between the regiments of Truex and McClennan and charged forward to exploit the gap. York's Louisianans pushed the Federals backwards, towards the Washington Turnpike. At the turnpike, Truex's and McClennan's men took cover behind breastworks, stopping York's Louisianans, and a second charge by Evans' Georgians. They held the Confederates at bay until well after 4 P.M. York's brigade lost 163 killed, wounded, and missing in the attack.[29]

With Evans' and York's brigades temporarily halted, Gordon realized that reinforcements might be needed. Accordingly, he dispatched messengers to Breckinridge, at the Worthington house, requesting additional troops. Gordon, however, decided that he would first use all of his resources to break fierce Federal resistance. He sent for Brigadier General William Terry, leading a Virginia infantry brigade. Meanwhile, a 12-pounder Napoleon from Lt. Colonel John Floyd King's battery was placed in Worthington's front yard. The gun crew began to fire at Federal sharpshooters on the second floor of Araby. They quickly found the range, badly damaging the house and driving the Federal marksmen out. One of those so evicted, Private Spangler Welsh, of the 87th Pennsylvania, was captured by Gordon's troops. King would visit the battlefield fifty years later, on 9 July 1914.[30]

Terry's troops surged across the Thomas farm and encountered an isolated line of Federal skirmishers, Company F of the 151st New York Infantry, protecting artillery. Terry's men ran past Gordon, on his horse, calmly giving commands. They ran through the Federal skirmish line, capturing the fence immediately behind them. With Gordon leading, Terry's Virginians gained the pasture near the river bank, several hundred yards northwest of Araby. Ahead lay still another fence, near an abandoned road cut, defended by the 9th New York Heavy Artillery and the 110th Ohio Infantry. These far-flung Federal units were protecting the Thomas Hill field, looming above the Washington Turnpike near the remains of the covered bridge.

The New York and Ohio troops fiercely resisted Terry's advance. He thereupon dispatched survivors of the 2nd, 4th, 5th, 26th, and 33rd Virginia Infantry up the river bank on a flanking maneuver led by Colonel J.H.S. Funk. Out of sight, Funk's infantry

Araby, Monocacy Battlefield, 20th century (courtesy Monocacy National Battlefield)

marched past the line of Federal guns. Turning right from the riverbank, they loosed a withering volley into the Federals, driving them down the hill towards the turnpike and Gambrill's Mill. As the 9th New York and 110th Ohio fled, Gordon's men pressed their attack along the length of Wallace's front on the turnpike. Lacking artillery support, the Federals began to retreat towards Gambrill's Mill. Wallace thereupon lost control of his troops. Per his 3 P.M. agreement with Ricketts, he ordered a retreat, around 4:20 P.M.

Wallace Retreats

Funk's breaking Federal resistance above the Thomas Hill field, along with Gordon's increasing pressure on Wallace's lines, effectively ended the battle near the turnpike. The Federals began a long, slow and disorganized retreat, dictated partly by the geography of the Monocacy River Valley.

According to Wallace's autobiography, he conferred with Ricketts around 3:30 P.M., just before Gordon's attack. After Ricketts expressed his desire to stay "a while longer" and fight Gordon, they discussed the whereabouts of the reinforcements, Colonel Staunton's troops, then "some hours overdue." Wallace remarked, "The arrival of the brigade would be good when we have to retreat. As a rear-guard it would be infinitely serviceable. I will wait for it." Wallace then explained the retreat; it would occur by the "country roads north to the Baltimore Pike, thence towards Baltimore." He agreed to send Ricketts the retreat order, and then explained, "As everything will depend on the bridge on the Baltimore Pike, it shall be held, if possible, until your command gets stretched out behind it."[31]

Uppermost in Federal plans, immediately after the fighting ended, was how to best get away from the hard-charging Confederates. Coordinating with Gordon's 3:30 P.M.

attack, Ramseur's troops had finally forced Davis and the 10th Vermont to retreat across the river. As Wallace's lines began to crumble, Davis gave the order, "Follow me, and every man for himself!" as they left their triangular position on the north (west) bank. Crossing the B & O's iron railroad bridge, stepping on the railroad ties, about two-thirds of Davis's 275 troop command made it safely to the east bank. Even though Confederate artillerymen held their fire, several of Davis' men were hit by rifle fire, and fell into the fast-flowing Monocacy, 45 feet below. A few were captured and wound up in Georgia's Andersonville prison. Ramseur's Confederates followed them over the bridge, with the 20th North Carolina Infantry fairly close on their heels. However, Davis would win the Congressional Medal of Honor, issued 27 May 1892, for the day-long defense of the two bridges "against repeated assaults of superior numbers, thereby materially delaying Early's advance on Washington."[32] Once across, Ramseur's men merged with Gordon's troops as they overran the Federal field hospital at Gambrill's Mill.

Wallace's beaten Federals began their retreat, walking briskly (some ran) up a wagon road northwards from Gambrill's Mill. Some were mounted, most were on foot. They crossed fast-flowing Bush Creek, climbing up the bluff on the far bank, marching along narrow dirt trails, towards the hamlet of Bartonsville, the Baltimore Turnpike, and the railroad. The unfamiliar landscape was heavily forested, filled with narrow streams, ravines, and deadfalls. Not surprisingly, a few hundred of Wallace's men were captured. The experience of Colonel Henry and the 10th Vermont was typical. They were nearly cut off and captured as Gordon's men overwhelmed Ricketts' far left, near the Baker Valley Road. Leaving his wounded behind, Henry ordered his troops to run past Gambrill's Mill and over the ridges north of Bush Creek. Both of his flag bearers, exhausted from the fast pace, fell in the confusing countryside. Corporal Alexander Scott retrieved the flags and carried them to safety. He was thereby awarded the Congressional Medal of Honor in 1897. Henry's command — 69 troops and 2 officers, made it to Monrovia, where the Baltimore Pike crossed the railroad. There they found a locomotive and several empty passenger cars, sitting idly on the track, waiting.[33]

Meanwhile, at the Jug Bridge, Robert Rodes' Georgia infantry pressed the attack against Colonel Brown's stalwart National Guardsmen. By 6 P.M., after having stood their ground for twelve hours, the Ohio troops were again under heavy pressure. Around 5 P.M., the retreating Wallace met Brown, ordering him to hold the bridge "to the last extremity" and when "pressed so hard that nothing more could be done, to command my men to disperse and to take care of themselves," Brown later stated.[34] Shortly after Wallace departed, General Tyler, commanding the northern sector, arrived and began directing the defense of the bridge. He ordered his reserves, Landstreet's 11th Maryland, to assist Brown's Guardsmen. However, Rodes' Georgians and Brigadier General Cullen Battle's Alabama Infantry had somehow found a way across the Monocacy. Tyler learned that the Rebels were in the woods, on the east bank, fast approaching the bridge's east end. In response, Brown's Buckeyes double-timed it across the bridge. From a ridge overlooking the stone span, they fired several volleys at the gray-clad infantry, trying to cut off Wallace's retreat.

Seized with a momentary panic, as it seemed that they would be surrounded, Brown's Ohio Guardsmen suddenly bolted, discarding their weapons as they ran. With great difficulty, Brown persuaded about 300 to return. They made a brief stand, covering Wallace's withdrawal, then began their own. Captain Edward Leib covered Brown's retreat. Nearly cut off and captured, he escaped by riding his horse straight down a steep bluff into the river, then northwards towards Hughes Ford.[35] Several hours later, Leib found himself in New Market, with some troopers of the 8th Illinois Cavalry, led by Lt. Colonel Clendenin. Near New Market, Leib and a few of the 8th Illinois repulsed scattered units of Confederate cavalry. That evening, Wallace's army was scattered between Bartonsville and New Market, some finding succor from sympathetic Unionist residents near the Baltimore Turnpike. Most made it back to Ellicott City by late Sunday afternoon where grateful citizens fed them and serenaded them with patriotic songs, including "Battle Cry of Freedom." Brown's Buckeyes had successfully kept Battle's Rebels from cutting off the Federal retreat, and few Confederates were seen on the road to Baltimore that Saturday evening.[36]

The Last Casualty

Six-year-old Glenn Howard Worthington bent low over the smoldering fire, in the back yard of his father's house an hour after the fighting ended. The Worthington farm, known as Clifton, had seen a lot of the fighting, and many a Confederate had been

Worthington House with 12-pounder Napoleon on front lawn (courtesy Monocacy National Battlefield)

mortally wounded near the house. The imposing L-shaped, two-story brick structure, with a large front porch, served as a hospital during and after the fighting.

That afternoon, as Gordon's brigades assembled on his front lawn, John T. Worthington held a pleasant conversation with General Breckinridge. Worthington was a southern sympathizer and slave owner. However, Federal fire caused Breckinridge to remind Worthington that as a civilian, he wasn't obliged to expose himself; Breckinridge further suggested that he go back inside. Despite having spent most of the day in the basement, listening with his family to the continuous tramping of feet, and rifle and cannon fire, Worthington took the advice. Nevertheless, as the afternoon wore on, they emerged from below and began tending to the wounded.

In the aftermath of the battle, rifles discarded by retreating Federal troops were gathered into a pile in the Worthington back yard, for disposal. With the muzzles all pointing towards Brooks Hill, they were set ablaze. Amid the chaos, as surgeons worked on the wounded, young Worthington watched the fire consume the wooden stocks. As the fire died down, leaving little but the barrels, the six year old decided that one of the bayonets would make a fine souvenir. He approached the fire's perimeter, eager to acquire a bayonet. Using part of a barrel stave as a stick, he began moving the sharp metal object closer. However, as the bayonet approached, a glowing coal from the fire stuck to it. Unnoticed by Worthington, the coal sideswiped a paper cartridge left behind in the wake of the fighting.

As he bent over to retrieve the bayonet, the heat from the coal penetrated the cartridge, and it exploded, badly burning his face. Blinded, with eyebrows burnt away, and face seared, he yelled in agony. A nearby soldier picked him up, and carried him up the front steps, into the house, where he was put to bed. Unable to open his eyes that evening, he regained his sight the following morning. Thus Glenn Worthington became the last casualty of the battle of Monocacy. He would go on to become a circuit court judge in Frederick. Largely through his efforts, the battlefield was declared a national park in June 1934. Worthington died in August of that year.[37]

CHAPTER 5

The Road to Silver Spring

The Army of the Valley awakened very early Sunday morning, well before dawn, after having slept on the battlefield. The pitiful cries of the wounded had died down, but as the army rose and began to make breakfast, their plaintive supplications increased. Many of the dead still lay where they had fallen the previous day, but Early's veterans didn't have time to put them to rest that morning. After a breakfast of bacon and hardtack, washed down with black coffee, the long roll beat to fall in, and about 14000 battle-hardened but sleepy men prepared to begin their advance on Washington, D.C. After buckling on their knapsacks, Early's veterans joined their units. With McCausland's cavalry out in front, followed by Breckinridge's infantry, they began the long climb up the ridge east of the battlefield, trudging southeast along the Washington Turnpike (present day Araby Church Road) in the cool darkness of early morning. Rodes' infantry followed Breckinridge, and Ramseur's division brought up the rear. They would stay in the vicinity of Monocacy Junction for a few more hours, unsuccessfully attempting to destroy the iron B & O railroad bridge over the river.

As the eastern sky began to brighten, they tramped through the tiny crossroads hamlet of Urbana, in the shadow of Sugarloaf Mountain, with a few early risers observing their advance. The temperature rose with the sun, and the day became oppressively hot and humid as the mercury climbed well above 90 degrees. The long butternut columns passed through Hyattstown and Clarksburg, their sore feet pressing down on the unpaved road, raising tremendous dust clouds. Mile after endless mile they marched as the number of stragglers grew in proportion to their discomfort and the distance marched. And as they advanced, Early rode up and down the lines, exhorting them forward, promising that he would shortly have them in Washington, where they could avail themselves of the capital's various comforts. However, even more than Early's encouragement, a hard core of veterans, whom nothing fazed, kept the army going.

However, their march towards Washington didn't lack contact with the enemy. Ramseur's division was followed by Cole's Maryland cavalry, with elements of the 8th Illinois, who shot at them and captured stragglers, forcing them to deploy several times. This harassment further delayed Ramseur's troops, and some of them weren't able to join the rest of the army, at Gaithersburg, until nearly 1 A.M. Monday, 11 July.[1] Late Sunday afternoon, Breckinridge finally called a halt, and the Army of the Valley bivouacked on and around the Summit Hall farm, in Gaithersburg, over 20 miles from Monocacy battlefield, about five miles northwest of Rockville.

Built in 1813, Summit Hall was a two-story Federalist style frame house, situated on a rise about 500 feet above sea level. It offered a commanding view of the surrounding countryside, and the farm's owner, John T. DeSellum, "daily beheld the smoke, and hazy atmosphere — caused by battle, campfires and conflagration" at the Battle of Cedar Mountain and "heard the firing on Saturday" from the Battle of Monocacy, and "Sunday morning ascertained that Early was advancing."[2] DeSellum had been a Federal recruiting officer in Montgomery County in 1862 and 1863 and had suffered the abuse and occasional threat that came with that job.

At the Summit Hall farm, Early ruminated on the day's activity. McCausland's cavalry, the frontal screen of the Army of the Valley, had fought a sharp engagement with about 500 troops of the 16th Pennsylvania Cavalry, a motley assortment of Federals led by Major William Fry, about a mile above Rockville. Fry had sent a warning message to the commander of Washington's defenses, Major General Christopher C. Augur, around 4 P.M.: "General: I have taken position and formed. My rear guard is fighting the enemy near Rockville. I have been joined by a Squadron Eighth Illinois cavalry and expect to be engaged in a few moments. I would respectfully suggest that the forts in the vicinity of Tennallytown be strongly guarded as the enemy's column is a mile long." Augur received the message about an hour later. McCausland's veterans, accompanied by two cannon, slowly pushed Fry's troops back through Rockville, with dead troops and horses left in the streets. Fry's inexperienced Federals fought McCausland's troops by slowly retreating from one skirmish line to the next, forcing McCausland's men to deploy each time, then retreating before combat could begin. However, as they approached Rockville, Confederate sympathizers informed McCausland that Fry's force was a hurriedly assembled battalion of only 500 troops. In response, rather than deploy again, McCausland's force charged the Federals in a column, driving them back through Rockville. The Federals retreated, but made a strong stand on a hill about a mile and a half south of town, retiring only when McCausland opened fire with his artillery.[3]

As commonly occurs in warfare, misperception magnified the size of Early's approaching host, resulting in exaggerated panic among residents of Montgomery County. Major Coe Durland, commanding a detachment of the 17th Pennsylvania Cavalry, near Leesborough (Wheaton), sent the following message to Augur on Sunday evening: "I have the honor to report that I arrived at this place at 9 P.M. this evening. Would respectfully state that it has been reported to me by a citizen who has just left Rockville that 5,000 of the enemy's cavalry came in and took possession of the town between the hours of 5 and 6 this afternoon."[4] McCausland commanded about 1,500 troops. However, most Federals believed that the Army of the Valley numbered at least 20,000 troops.

Despite Fry's defeat, Federal commanders in Washington now knew where the Army of the Valley was located. Fry's exhausted command was relieved the next day by the 2nd Massachusetts Cavalry, known as the California Brigade, led by Colonel Charles Russell Lowell and composed largely of Californians. McCausland's cavalry continued down the Georgetown Pike and River Road, approaching forts Reno, Kearney, and Bayard at Tennallytown, drawing fire from their heavy artillery. Over breakfast at Rockville's Montgomery House hotel the next morning, McCausland would report to Early that Washington's defenses at Tennallytown and farther south were impregnable.

Meanwhile, on Sunday evening, the rearward troops slowly trickled in to Gaithersburg, with the larger portion camping on Summit Hall farm while the nearby farm of Ignatius Fulks hosted about 1800 of Early's cavalry.[5] While hungry Confederates in the ranks butchered cattle and chickens, stole grain and demolished fences for firewood, Early and his officers sat down to dinner with DeSellum and his sister. They soon engaged in verbal combat with DeSellum, a Unionist slave owner. As he related their differences, "a conversation commenced about the war and the cause. They saw I was a slave holder, and my remarks about John Brown's raid suddenly caused a Col Lee to abruptly demand of me, 'whether I was for coercing the south.' As I did not intend to lie, or act the coward, my reply was, 'I wanted the south whipped back under the Constitution, Union, and government of the United States — with the rights and privileges she had before the war.'"[6] Lee, by now very angry, replied, "'You are an abolitionist; it is no use to blame the devil and do the devil's work.' and was very insulting." While the conversation most likely occurred about the way DeSellum remembered it, who was Colonel Lee? Fitzhugh Lee didn't often display a quick temper and at that time wasn't with the Army of the Valley. Most historians agree that neither were any of Robert E. Lee's sons.

In any case, "Gen. Arnold Elsey [*sic*: Elzey] arose from the table and with the dignity and politeness of a gentleman stated his reasons for joining the Southern Confederacy, his polished manner was an indirect reproof for Lee's violation of common politeness in the presence of my Sister." Elzey, from Maryland, may have been at the dinner table; he had remained with the Army of the Valley after Early had reorganized them on 26 June. Nevertheless, he had suffered a terrible facial wound at Cold Harbor, involving his jaw and tongue, bringing DeSellum's description of his role in the debate into question. However, he credits Elzey's "gentlemanly manner" with preventing "a serious termination of the conversation." He next describes how his farm was ransacked, "fences torn to pieces and general wreck and ruin followed, it was a night and day of horror as our lives were in imminent danger." Early the next morning, DeSellum approached Early, and asked if "he intended to give me up to be indiscriminately plundered." "Old Jube" replied, "You don't simpathise with the south and you can't expect favour, or protection." Early wrote an order leaving him two barrels of corn, but after leaving Summit Hall, sent two men to ransack the house. In her bedroom, DeSellum's sister hid $3,000 in government bonds under her dress just before they burst through the door, pistols in hand.[7]

The plundering and destruction at Summit Hall was fairly typical of how Early's Confederates treated property owners in Maryland. Their wanton looting created animosity among Maryland residents and contributed to Early's inability to sufficiently control his men, but he did little or nothing to stop it. As they were advancing on Frederick, some of Early's outriders attempted to ransack the farm of Unionist George Blessing. Using their guns to deadly effect, Blessing and his two sons drove them off, and kept them at bay until Federal cavalry arrived. However, Early was concerned that only a few Maryland "secesh" had come out to greet them, and particularly concerned that very few had come out from Washington, probably indicating the arrival of Federal reinforcements in the city.[8]

Early the next morning, the Army of the Valley left Gaithersburg, the heat and humidity largely responsible for their sleepless night. The summer of 1864 was also one of the driest on record — no rain had fallen in the Washington area for 47 days, causing tremendous dust clouds with every movement of a body of men or horses. As Early's troops stumbled down the road towards Washington, the humid morning promised another relentlessly hot day. They passed the scene of McCausland's engagement with Fry's Federals, straggling into the tiny crossroads community of Rockville, population 600. With streets muddy barriers during wet weather, the town nevertheless boasted a courthouse, at least two hotels, a Chinese laundry, a female seminary, a few stores and taverns, and a newspaper, the *Montgomery County Sentinel.* County Unionists considered Rockville a "vile secesh hole," and they prudently stayed out of sight during Early's visit. Jeb Stuart's cavalry had stopped there the previous year, during the Gettysburg campaign, and Stuart had captured and detained a number of the town's prominent residents, including Richard Johns Bowie, chief judge of the Maryland Court of Appeals.[9] Early had no time for chasing distinguished Unionists; he stopped at the Montgomery House Hotel for breakfast. There he met with a courier sent by McCausland who told him that the Federal fortifications at Tennallytown were too strong to be breached. Early then decided to change the army's route, and enter Washington at Fort Stevens, astride the Seventh Street road, a few miles farther away than Tennallytown. The change of direction added an hour or two to the army's schedule, but Early believed he had little choice. As they left Rockville, the troops swung northeast, marching down Viers Mill Road, past Samuel Viers' grist mill, then along the New Cut Road (Forest Glen Road), arriving at Leesborough (Wheaton) about three hours later. There they turned south onto the macadamized Seventh Street Road (Georgia Avenue), towards the tiny crossroads hamlet of Sligo (Silver Spring), bringing Early ever closer to realizing a proud southern soldier's dream, capturing Washington, D.C.

Washington Prepares

Because of Washington's unique location, nearly surrounded by southern territory, the city had been vulnerable to Confederate attack since the war began. Like an arrowhead driven into the body of secession, the city was thrust into southern sensibilities and presented an inviting target, particularly before southern military strategy had been completely worked out. The day after First Manassas, General Thomas J. "Stonewall" Jackson reportedly asked Jefferson Davis for 10,000 troops so he could capture Washington the next day. Davis turned him down. However, on 2 October 1861, there was a meeting at Fairfax Courthouse between Davis and Generals Joseph Johnston, Pierre Beauregard, and Gustavus W. Smith, commanders of 40,000 Confederate troops then at Manassas Junction. Beauregard had conceived a plan for attacking Washington "by the back door"—Fort Massachusetts (Fort Stevens), then persuaded Johnston and Smith that it would work. The trio hoped to get reinforcements from Davis. The plan was that a Confederate force would cross the Potomac after leaving a diversionary force at Manassas and capture Washington before the Union commander, General George B. McClellan, could send enough troops into the city from their camps south of the Potomac to defend it. However, the plan was shelved when the southern generals told Davis that they would need at least 50,000 troops; Davis replied that he could spare only 2,500 reinforcements (which would have brought Confederate strength to 42,500).[10] The idea of a Confederate force capturing Washington (or Baltimore) ran counter to Davis' defensive strategy, and Robert E. Lee steadfastly ignored a number of proposals from Beauregard for doing so. However, the idea never completely disappeared from southern military strategy.

From the Federal perspective, some of the anxiety concerning Washington's vulnerability, partly created by Baltimore's Pratt Street riot of April 1861, had subsided when Maryland was gradually brought under strong Federal control over the next few months. At Antietam and Gettysburg, Confederate armies only indirectly threatened the city, and Washington's civilian residents temporarily forgot about the threat of capture by a Confederate force. However, the threat of Washington's capture was never far removed from the consciousness of the city's military leaders. After Lee and Jackson defeated a Federal army led by Major General John Pope at Second Manassas, and fought Union forces to a standstill at the battle of Chantilly, Washington succumbed to widespread panic, and a steamship stood offshore in the Potomac, waiting to evacuate the president and his cabinet. However, Navy secretary Gideon Welles remained calm, correctly assuming that Lee's Confederates wouldn't risk an assault against the city's fortifications.[11] The panic in the city subsided after Lee's withdrawal from Maryland after Antietam. However, consternation among Washingtonians flared up again after the Union defeat at Chancellorsville. The Army of the Potomac in the spring of 1863 was led by Major General Joseph Hooker, who retained neither the confidence of Lincoln and the cabinet, nor that of his troops. Federal thinking on Washington's safety in June 1863 was exemplified by Brigadier General Alpheus S. Williams, referring to the imminent battle at Gettysburg: "If we are badly defeated there is but little hope, I think, of saving Washington. The troops held so sacredly about that 'corruption sink' would make a poor show before the victorious Rebels."[12] However, Hooker was replaced as commander of the Army of the Potomac on 28 June by Major General George G. Meade, a more effective commander. Nevertheless, the city was isolated from the fighting throughout most of the war.

Thus Washington's residents sweltered uncomfortably through the first week in July, but their discomfort was because of the heat and humidity and the paucity of information on troop movements north and west of the city. On 4 July, the telegraph to Harpers Ferry went dead, destroyed by Mosby's Rangers in their raid on Point of Rocks, Maryland. Suddenly, enemy troop movements west of Washington were hidden by the silence of the telegraph. The War Office, where Lincoln spent many hours communicating with Federal commanders, was informed of the evacuation of Harpers Ferry by B & O railroad personnel. The commander of Washington's defenses, General Augur, responded by sending 250 troops of the 8th Illinois Cavalry, led by Lt. Colonel Clendenin, on a reconnaissance mission towards Harpers Ferry, and Halleck sent General Albion P. Howe and the 170th Ohio National Guard to relieve General Sigel's command on Maryland Heights. Halleck, however, made the situation worse by incorrectly informing Grant, on 5 July, that General Hunter's army had arrived back in the threatened area on the upper Potomac. He further muddled the situation by rather pompously telling Grant a short time later, "I think your operations should not be interfered with by sending troops here. If Washington and Baltimore should be so seriously threatened as to require your aid, I will inform you in time."[13] However, Washingtonians' attitude of uncaring indifference to the war abruptly changed when word of Wallace's defeat on the Monocacy reached the city.

Crowds of frightened refugees, their belongings hastily piled in wagons, began arriving from upcountry, telling Washingtonians in emphatic tones that this was no mere cavalry raid — that the countryside north and west of the city was occupied by Confederates. City residents began hoarding food and supplies, causing shortages and high prices for both, and increasing the general sense of panic. Herds of horses began to appear in the streets, adding to the chaos and uncertainty.[14] Government officials and workers also succumbed to panic. Secretary of War Edwin Stanton handed over $5,000 from a personal account along with $400 in gold, belonging to Mrs. Stanton, to his clerk, A.E.H. Johnson, and gave him instructions to hide the money in his (Johnson's) house. That Sunday, Treasury register Lucius Chittenden found the staff in the Treasury Building hastily filling sacks with government bonds and securities to be loaded aboard a steamship and taken out of the city.* Chittenden also put his family on the evening train for New England, the last train out of Washington before the Confederates destroyed the railroad north of Baltimore.[15] However, the calling out of local militia units did little to calm the tension gripping the city.

Indeed, Washington was home to thousands of Union Army troops. While they gave the impression of a strong military presence, the city was in fact woefully unprepared to meet Early's advancing army. Washington was ringed by 53 forts and 22 batteries, north and south of the Potomac, for a distance of 37 miles. They housed powerful siege cannon which could destroy or stop an attacking force at long range, but at short range they were ineffective. Most of the forts were connected by trenches or rifle pits, and some had abatis between them. However, fortifications are considered only as good as the troops that garrison them. In the fall of 1862, a commission of army engineers and department heads, led by Major General John G. Barnard, designer of Washington's forts, spent two months inspecting them. They recommended that the fortifications needed 34,000 experienced troops — 25,000 infantry and 9,000 artillerists, with 3,000 additional cavalry. However, in July 1864, the city had, on paper, 31,231 troops available for defense, but these were largely convalescents, militia, bridge guards, and government clerks, most of whom had never fired a gun. In fact, Washington had only about 9,600 troops on the ground, of varying quality, available to meet an attack.[16]

Just as important was the alarming lack of trained artillerists in the city, and the lack of a mobile force which could meet and deter an attacking army, some distance removed from the fortifications. Most of the heavy artillerists had been sent to the Army of the Potomac, at Petersburg, and two battalions of the 9th New York Heavy Artillery had gone with General Ricketts to Monocacy Junction without Halleck's knowledge. On 6 July, Halleck wired Grant, asking for the return of heavy artillerists from the Army of the Potomac. However, the deplorable state of Washington's defenses in July 1864 was partly the result of the high casualty rate in the Army of the Potomac at the battles of the Wilderness, Spotsylvania Court House, and Cold Harbor. The city garrison, designated the XXII Corps in 1863, had sent 48,265 troops to reinforce Grant, leaving them poorly prepared to repulse an invading force.[17]

However, the city's porous defenses were also the result of low morale, poor discipline, and insufficient procedures, particularly in regard to the three bridges spanning the Potomac. Lt. Colonel B.S. Alexander, a former aide to General Barnard, and recently appointed chief engineer of Washington's defenses, inspected the bridges the first week

---

There was probably no gold in the Treasury Building in Washington in July 1864. Most of the Federal government's gold supply was kept in the Treasury Building on Wall Street, New York City.

in July and found them practically inviting attack. He toured the Chain Bridge and Aqueduct Bridge, and sent an assistant to examine the Long bridge. At the Washington end of the Chain Bridge, Alexander found that none of the guards knew how to load the guns protecting the approaches to the bridge; the east end battery was in charge of an Ohio National Guard private who knew nothing about ordnance. He merely cleaned the guns, swept the platform, and opened the munitions boxes. Alexander found no procedure in case the bridge was fired, and the guards had no means of escape in case of an attack. He found a similar state of unpreparedness at the Aqueduct Bridge and at the Long Bridge, Alexander's assistant found the bridge defense "imperfect, owing to the dilapidation and decay of Fort Jackson" at the Virginia end. In addition, garrison duty at Washington's forts afforded little opportunity for the troops to do anything but eat, sleep, drill and patrol designated areas in and around the forts, and guard duty was more arduous and unpleasant in cold weather. Because of unsanitary living conditions, disease was an ever-present danger, and more than a few garrison troops suffered from typhoid, smallpox, and various other ailments. The city offered a variety of diversions, and the troops were occasionally able to indulge in them. However, the cost was often prohibitive, with a hack ride from Virginia into the city costing $6.50.[18]

In addition, the lack of clear lines of authority weakened Washington's defenses and hampered the Federal response to Early. The issue of which commander had the authority to approve an offensive against Early's invaders wasn't decided until after reinforcements from the Army of the Potomac's 6th Corps arrived at the front. General McCook, commander of the northern defense line, wasn't sure whether he had the authority to allow an offensive against Early. When the commander of the 6th Corps divisions in Washington, Major General Horatio G. Wright, requested permission for such an assault from General Augur, the defense oriented Augur refused. Halleck then stepped in, and directed that the 6th Corps be held in reserve, and when elements of the Federal 19th Corps arrived, they were sent to Fort Saratoga, which was never threatened.[19]

Grant Responds

Upon their arrival at Baltimore, from the Monocacy battlefield, many of Wallace's Federals were put to work strengthening that city's defenses, making them unavailable for the defense of Washington. Hunter's Army of the Shenandoah was returning to the Maryland-Virginia theater of war but at a negligently slow pace. On 8 July, Hunter's force was at Cumberland, Maryland. He was ordered to make Martinsburg, West Virginia, his base of operations. However, Hunter's lead brigade, led by Brigadier General Jeremiah C. Sullivan, didn't reach that locale until 10 July, and the main body of his troops didn't arrive until 14 July as Early's army re-crossed the Potomac on their retreat into Virginia. Hunter was difficult to reach by telegraph; thus the Army of the Shenandoah was also unavailable for defending Washington. Halleck thus realized that reinforcements for the city's defense were going to have to come from either the Army of the Potomac or from Federal garrison troops in a northern state.

Grant first became aware that the Second Corps of the Army of Northern Virginia was missing from his front on 28 June when he received a report from Captain John

McEntee, a Union intelligence officer accompanying Hunter's retreating army. McEntee's report stated that Hunter "engaged part of Ewell's Corps commanded by Early" and estimated that Early had about 20,000 troops with him. McEntee also stated that Early's force was "probably in Richmond again by this [June 28]." Since McEntee was with the Army of the Shenandoah when they retreated into West Virginia, he had no way of knowing that the Army of the Valley had marched northwards towards Maryland. Grant reasoned that Lee needed every man available from Early's force to defend Petersburg (and Richmond). McEntee's assessment — that Early had returned to Lee, therefore made sense, and it was soon corroborated by information gleaned from rebel deserters. Unaware that Early's force was marching northwards down the Valley, Grant sent a telegram to Halleck on 1 July, stating in part, "Ewell's [Early's] corps has returned here."[20] John W. Garrett's warning telegram to Stanton on 29 June, implying that a strong force of Confederates was marching down the Valley, was thereby ignored. As late as 3 July, Grant informed Halleck that "Early's corps is now here" (Petersburg).

Grant first realized that Early's force might not have returned to the Army of Northern Virginia when his chief intelligence officer, Colonel George H. Sharpe, interrogated a Confederate deserter who had wandered into camp on the morning of 4 July. In an afternoon telegram to Halleck, Grant described the rebel's admission: "Ewell's corps has not returned here, but is off in the Valley with the intention of going into Maryland and Washington City. They now have the report that he already has Arlington Heights and expects to take the city soon." He advised Halleck "to hold all of the forces you can about Washington, Baltimore, Cumberland, and Harpers Ferry, ready to concentrate against any advance of the enemy." Grant still had confidence that Hunter could handle the Army of the Valley: "If General Hunter is in striking distance there ought to be veteran force enough to meet anything the enemy have, and if once put to flight, he ought to be followed as long as possible."[21]

On 4 July, Grant began to search in earnest for definitive information on Early's whereabouts. Although he was positive that Early was no longer with the Army of Northern Virginia, on 5 July he still wasn't certain that he had marched down the Valley. However, that same day, as a precautionary measure, he sent one division of the Sixth Corps to Washington. The two remaining divisions would follow shortly. On 6 July, Grant finally became convinced that Early was in the vicinity of the Potomac. On 4 July, Mosby's raid on Point of Rocks convinced Wallace that a large Confederate force was in Maryland, and he began forwarding troops to Monocacy Junction the next day. However, when Ricketts, leading the first division to leave City Point, reported to Wallace, at 1 A.M. on 9 July, he was stunned to learn that Early was massing his troops in Maryland, just west of Catoctin Mountain. Grant sent the two remaining divisions of the Sixth Corps to Washington that same day. However, but for Wallace's delaying Early at Monocacy Junction, Grant's sanguinary thinking on Early's whereabouts, and his dilatory response, would have resulted in the Confederate capture of Washington.

The Moment of Truth—Early Hesitates

Twenty-seven-year-old Brigadier General Martin Davis Hardin galloped across the long wooden bridge over the Eastern Branch, in the waning minutes of Sunday afternoon, after receiving word of Major Fry's engagement with McCausland's cavalry above Rockville. He had been inspecting the forts on the District's eastern boundary, noting that they weren't adequately manned and had no connecting trenches between them. The grandson of a senator from Illinois of the same name, Hardin had lost his left arm, the result of an ambush by Mosby's men, while inspecting his picket lines near the Rapidan River in December 1863. He had been wounded on three other occasions and spent the winter and spring convalescing. Now, however, his main concern was keeping the Army of the Valley from penetrating Washington's defenses. He spurred his mount onwards, first reporting to General Augur, at army headquarters on 14½ Street, not far from the White House. Sometime thereafter, Hardin reported to Major General Alexander McDowell McCook, soon-to-be commander of the District's northern defense perimeter, at McCook's headquarters at Crystal Spring (Piney Branch Road and 14th Street). McCook assigned Hardin to command the forts defending Washington's western boundary, south of Fort Stevens, and the sector extending southeast of Fort Sumner, down the Potomac past Fort Foote. A difficult task as Hardin had only about 1,800 infantry, 1,800 artillerists, and 60 cavalry to defend the entire sector.[22] Hardin's sector, which didn't include Fort Stevens, was expected to bear the brunt of Early's attack on Monday.

Very early Monday morning, McCausland and his 1,500 cavalrymen cantered down the Georgetown Turnpike, to reconnoiter Federal defenses at Tennallytown. They first encountered Federal outriders not far from the Montrose post office, somewhere in the vicinity of the Bethesda Presbyterian Church. Pushing the smaller Federal force back towards Tennallytown, McCausland's horsemen approached Washington by way of the Georgetown Turnpike and River Road. As they advanced, they were fired upon by gun crews at Forts Bayard, Simmons, Mansfield and Sumner. However, try as they might, McCausland's men could find no weak points in the Tennallytown defense sector.[23]

Late Monday morning, the main body of Early's bedraggled army, led by General Breckinridge, turned south, down the Union Turnpike, heading for Sligo Post Office, known locally as Sligo. As the Union Turnpike became the Seventh Street Road, the troops passed a few isolated dwellings, the half-finished Grace Episcopal Church, and a white-frame country store which occupied the southwest corner of the intersection of Colesville Road and the Seventh Street Road. Stealing liquor from the cellar, perhaps a few hundred became drunk. Another quarter mile of marching took them past a spring, from which the clearest cold water flowed, with bits of mica gleaming on the bottom of the pool. A little further on, they came to Silver Spring, the French chateau style mansion of Francis Preston Blair and named for the spring. Originally designed as a summer retreat, the mansion had adjacent gardens and an artificial lake with a small island in the center.[24] Newspaper editor and founder of a distinguished family, Blair had come to Washington in 1830, at the request of President Andrew Jackson. Living for several years near the White House, Blair served as an advisor to Jackson, making his home just across Pennsylvania Avenue. However, the humid malaria-breeding locale of downtown Washington, where residents often had trouble keeping their basements dry, proved very uncomfortable. One day in 1842, Blair and his daughter, Elizabeth, took a horseback ride several miles northwest, where the elevation was higher and the climate healthier. Blair was thrown off his mount, and in searching for the horse, he discovered the spring. Captivated by the serene beauty of the surroundings, Blair moved there, building his estate and completing

Silver Spring, 1864 (Library of Congress)

Silver Spring in 1845. He gave his Washington townhouse to his son, Montgomery, who had come east from St. Louis. Montgomery Blair would later build a mansion of his own, Falkland, several hundred yards west of Silver Spring and about the same distance south of Sligo. In July 1864, however, the Blairs weren't home, having gone to the New Jersey shore to vacation, while Montgomery Blair had gone to Pennsylvania on a hunting trip.[25]

Thus Silver Spring sat empty as Early's advance troops spread out on the grounds, a few discovering a barrel of whiskey in the basement. They promptly became more inebriated, carousing around the spring and the mansion. For a few hours that afternoon, the mansion lay at the mercy of some of the ill-disciplined troops who wandered around inside, looting the wine cellar, destroying furniture, and tramping on the flowers and bushes outside. Confederate units led by generals Echols and Wharton camped on the grounds of Falkland.

From Fort Stevens, the landscape northwards towards Silver Spring sloped gently downwards for several hundred yards, a small stream at the bottom. Sloping gradually upwards on the far side, towards the Blair properties, the countryside offered farm fields brimming with tall corn, green meadows, and vast stretches of empty fields. The Seventh Street Road was a 15-foot-wide thoroughfare with a toll booth at the intersection of Piney Branch Road, several hundred yards north of the fort. A few scattered residences stood between Silver Spring and Fort Stevens, including the Carberry, Lay, and Rives houses. Fast flowing Rock Creek was about a mile west of Fort Stevens, down a long hill. Across the half mile wide Rock Creek Valley, occupying a prominence near Milk House Road (today's Military Road), stood Fort DeRussy. Heavy artillery from both forts commanded the valley, and any force advancing south into the city along Rock Creek would be subject to their fire.[26]

In addition, General McCook had his men block the passageways along the stream with fallen trees, brush, and various abatis, sealing off that path into the city. West of Fort DeRussy, in Tennallytown, forts Kearney, Reno, and Bayard stood on and around the highest ground in the District (highest point: 518 feet). Farther south and west stood forts Simmons, Mansfield, and Sumner.

Measuring 375 yards around the perimeter, Fort Stevens' artillery included four 24-pound coastal defense cannon mounted on barbettes, six 24-pound siege guns, two 8-inch siege howitzers, and five 30-pound Parrott rifles, all firing through embrasures. Early described the forts defending Washington as "exceedingly strong, and consisted of ... enclosed forts for heavy artillery, with a tier of lower works in front of each, pierced for an immense number of guns, the whole being connected by curtains, with ditches in front, and strengthened by palisades and abatis. The timber had been felled within cannon range all around and left on the ground, making a formidable obstacle, and every possible approach was raked by artillery fire. On the right was Rock Creek, running through a deep ravine which had been rendered impassible by the felling of the timber on each side, and beyond were the works on the Georgetown Pike which had been reported to be the strongest of all. On the left, as far as the eye could reach, the works appeared to be of the same impregnable character."

Pickets from Fort Stevens stationed along the Seventh Street Road had kept watch for Early's advance throughout Sunday night and Monday morning, observing carefully the steady stream of refugees coming into the District. Signal stations at Forts Reno and Stevens had observed Early's advance down the Seventh Street Road, relaying the information to McCook at his reserve camp on Piney Branch Road at the Crystal Spring. McCook ordered his meager command into the fort on the double.

As local residents were sitting down to their noon meal, advance units of Rodes' infantry arrived in the vicinity of the fort. Skirmishing began almost immediately, as McCook ordered his troops into a line in front of the works. Taking cover behind anything they could find, they were greeted by Confederate sniper fire emanating from the Carberry House, a wooden structure with a distinctive cupola, west of the Seventh Street Road, about a thousand yards from the fort. The Rives and Lay houses, east of the Seventh Street Road, and a few other structures were also used by southern snipers.

Edward A. Paul, a *New York Times* correspondent stationed in Washington, had rented a house along the Seventh Street Road, about a mile north of Fort Stevens. He had left Washington on Sunday to return to the front at Petersburg. Around noon the next day, Mrs. Paul was unpleasantly surprised to see long lines of gray-clad troops, "creeping along the fence rows on either side of the pike." She had received no warning of their approach. Inquiring of them, she asked if they were rebels. An officer straightened up, and replied, "Yes, madam, we are rebels." She then inquired of their intentions. The officer replied, "We shall not injure you, but your friends may," referring to the fact that the house was within range of the fort's cannon. Passing the house, the Confederates formed a skirmish line at right angles to the road, and a short time later commenced firing at McCook's men. For the next hour or so, a number of Confederate generals and their staffs, including Early and Breckinridge, occupied the grounds around Paul's house, suggesting to Mrs. Paul that she and her family evacuate and go to the rear. She refused to go, however, until one of her daughters was injured by a shell fired from the fort. She finally left when the Confederates promised to post a guard around the house. However, the promise was not kept, and when Paul returned from Petersburg a few days later, he found his home completely ruined by Early's scavengers, providentially saved from the torch by a passing squad of Union troops. Paul was certain that the Confederates knew of his activities as a northern reporter.[27]

The brisk exchange of rifle fire occupied both sides all afternoon, punctuated by cannon fire from the works. Many Confederate officers spent an inordinate amount of time rounding up stragglers, looking for soldiers who had wandered off in search of water or had succumbed to heat prostration. As Early stated, "When we reached the sight of the enemy's fortifications the men were almost completely exhausted and not in condition to make an attack." Nevertheless, atop his horse about a half mile from the fort, Early peered through his field glasses and also observed that the works were "but feebly manned." At that time there were but 209 troops in and around the fort, consisting of Company F, 150th Ohio National Guard, part of the 13th Michigan Artillery, and 52 convalescents, the entire group led by Lt. Colonel John Frazee, commander at Fort Stevens.[28] In addition, the rifle pits and trenches on each side — east and south of the works — were unmanned.

Concentrated Confederate sniper fire pushed back the Federal picket line, and at one o'clock, Lieutenant A.T. Abbott, at the fort's signal station, sent an emphatic message to General Augur, "The enemy is within twenty rods (120 yards) of Fort Stevens." At that point, General Gordon responded to "annoying" Federal cannon fire, by ordering a battery of 20-pound Parrott rifles, the rebel's heaviest guns, to unlimber and open fire from a quarter mile away. The southern artillery rounds found resting places in the red clay earthworks of the fort, showering the garrison with dirt, but failed to silence the big siege guns. However, many in the Army of the Valley dismissed Federal artillery as ineffective: "Long before we came in sight we knew that the city was protected by militia, or home guards, from the way they handled the big guns. The shells from these passed over our heads at a great altitude and burst far to our rear, doing no damage to any one. Some one jokingly remarked that the enemy was shelling our wagon train, which was at that time many miles in the rear, and their wild shooting produced in our minds a great contempt for the 'melish.'"[29] Federal artillery fire, though annoying, and dangerous to targets a mile or more distant, would have been largely ineffective against a strong Confederate infantry charge on the fort, as the muzzles of many of the big siege guns couldn't have been lowered enough to meet it.

The Army of the Valley numbered about 14,000 when they began their advance on

Washington early Sunday morning; roughly 10,000 answered muster in front of Fort Stevens. The remainder had either deserted or succumbed to heat related illness. Three-fourths of those present in front of the Federal defenses were "not in condition to make an attack," perhaps more. However, a few hundred troops, healthy enough to charge the works, were in the vicinity. Curiously though, Early didn't order an attack, which perplexed and frustrated the troops. Colonel Thomas F. Toon, leader of the 20th North Carolina Infantry, responded accordingly: "I know one thing, I could have easily taken everything in my front if I had been allowed to continue my advance. Major DeVane, a gallant spirit, urged me to disregard the order to fall back, and rush forward, whatever the consequences might be. I hated to withdraw, but always tried to obey orders."[30] Virginia cavalryman John Newton Opie voiced similar sentiments, and undoubtedly many in the ranks agreed with them, and one writer has stated that "they [Early's troops] could never figure out why Early had denied them a chance to capture the works and the city."[31]

Early, however, looking through his field glasses again, had spotted large dust clouds over the city, indicating the arrival of Federal reinforcements. He realized that, at that point, capturing Washington was probably out of the question. The jaded condition of most of his troops militated against any advance into the city, and Federal reinforcements were, in fact, close at hand. At 1:30 P.M. the first steamer carrying 6th Corps veterans from the Army of the Potomac docked at the Sixth Street wharf in downtown Washington, and the troops disembarked. Lincoln was there to greet them, munching on a piece of hardtack and good naturedly rallying them that they had better hurry if they wanted to catch Jubal Early. Through a misunderstanding, Halleck had ordered their commander, General Wright, to march to Tennallytown. They had marched a mile or so towards that locale when the error was discovered. Wright then turned his two attenuated divisions around, and they marched out the Seventh Street Road, the head of the column arriving at Fort Stevens about two hours later, at 4:10 P.M.[32] Also around 1:30 P.M., the fort was reinforced by 500–600 dismounted troops of the 25th New York Cavalry, who pushed the Confederate skirmish line backwards until they were well over a thousand yards from the works, causing General McCook to observe that the Army of the Valley was not "developing any force other than their skirmish line." Had Early ordered his troops into the city, the Army of the Valley might have been destroyed in high casualty, time consuming fighting in the streets of Washington.

However, a strong rush by a few hundred Confederate infantry between 2 o'clock and 4 o'clock most likely would have captured the fort. Once inside, they might have turned the big guns around and bombarded the city. The resulting embarrassment to the Lincoln administration could have resulted in McClellan winning the November election. Yet despite all that the Army of the Valley had experienced in the preceding month — defeating Hunter at Lynchburg, chasing him into West Virginia, marching down the Shenandoah Valley, defeating Generals Sigel and Weber at Martinsburg, defeating Wallace at Monocacy Junction, and despite the thought that a Confederate force might never be that close to Washington again (doubtless occurring to Early and many of his troops) — Early didn't order an attack on Fort Stevens, on 11 July or 12 July. Such an attack, even if it had failed, would have done much to quiet his critics after the war.

Lincoln Faces Enemy Fire

Towards five o'clock that Monday afternoon, as skirmishing continued in the vicinity of the fort, Generals Early and Breckinridge rode together onto the grounds of Silver Spring. While vice president in the Buchanan administration, in the late 1850s, Breckinridge often visited the Blairs, spending many a pleasant afternoon and evening at the mansion. Now, however, as the two generals rode up to the house, Breckinridge spotted a number of troops looting. A few soldiers were inebriated, after having looted the wine cellar. Cursing emphatically, Breckinridge caught one soldier coming out of the house with a piano cover which the trooper intended to use as a horse blanket. He ordered the man to return it, had him arrested and detained, then assigned a regiment to guard the mansion.

As Early and Breckinridge entered the house, they found no sign of the Blairs, but noticed that valuable silverware, china and clothing had been left unlocked, as had the basement wine cellar. Ruminating on the reason, Breckinridge was greeted by a former servant of the Blairs, who had been taken prisoner by the troops. He inquired as to the Blair's whereabouts, and was told that the women of the house had abruptly gone vacationing, to Cape May, New Jersey, and the men on a fishing trip to Pennsylvania. Puzzled by the Blairs' strange behavior, the generals made the mansion their headquarters, after clearing the premises of looters.[33]

Major General John C. Breckinridge (Library of Congress)

Sometime after dark, Breckinridge and Early were joined at the mansion by Rodes, Ramseur, and Gordon. Conviviality was the mood as the generals sat down to a council of war. With the Blairs' best French wine, they drank a few toasts to their success, good naturedly rallying Breckinridge about letting him be first to enter Washington, and returning him to his old seat as head of the Senate. Breckinridge spoke fondly of the Blairs, distant cousins, and of the many social events he had attended as their guest. A few more minutes of banter, and Early got down to reality.

He discussed the army's options, noting their position in front of Washington. He pointed out that as Hunter's army returned to the Washington area war zone, their avenues of retreat — the upper Potomac River crossings and the passes through South Mountain — would be sealed off. Gordon later wrote of their conference,

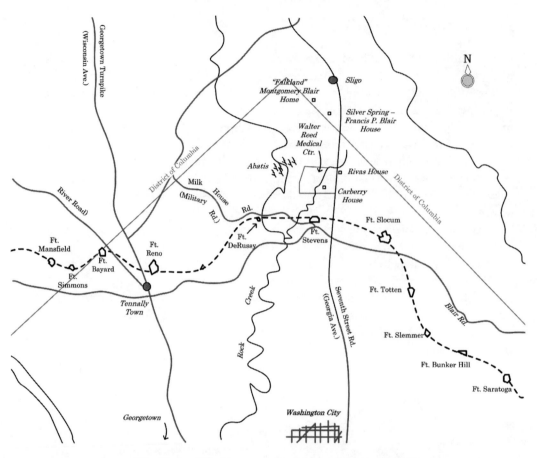

The Gates of Washington at Ft. Stevens, July 11–12, 1864

"There was not a dissenting opinion as to the impolicy of entering the city." He also commented on the opinions of the men in the ranks, the "sore-footed men in gray ... lazily lounging about the cool waters of Silver Spring, picking blackberries in the orchards of Postmaster General Blair, and merrily estimating the amount of gold and greenbacks that would come into our possession when we should seize the vaults of the United States Treasury." He further commented that the foot soldiers didn't believe "in the wisdom of any serious effort to capture Washington at that time."[34]

After entertaining each of their opinions, Early determined to make an assault on Fort Stevens at daylight, barring any information indicating the inadvisability of such a course. In fact, exactly that message reached Early during the night, from Bradley Johnson, indicating that two Federal corps had disembarked at Baltimore the previous day (10 July), and were on their way to Washington, which effectively shelved the planned assault. As Early later explained, "As soon as it was light enough to see, I rode to the front and found the parapets lined with troops."[35] He also found the trenches and rifle pits on either side of the fort were filled with blue uniforms. Reluctantly, he gave up the idea of advancing into Washington. Nevertheless, as a face-saving gesture, he determined to make a demonstration in front of the fort.

Action in front of Fort Stevens began on a "bright and glorious" Tuesday morning (in the words of one Federal observer), as it had ended the previous evening. Federal gun crews in the fort opened fire on various targets within a mile of the fort, including the Carberry and Rives houses. All together, gun crews from Forts Stevens, Slocum — about a mile east of Stevens — and DeRussy, would fire well over 200 shots that day.[36] Sometime during the first part of Tuesday afternoon, President Lincoln and his entourage arrived at the fort, to view the progress of the fighting, as they had the previous day.

Lincoln had held a cabinet meeting at the White House at noon. Navy secretary Gideon Welles asked "where the Rebels were in force." The president replied that he wasn't certain, "but he thought the main body at Silver Spring." Welles doubted "whether there was any large force at any one point, but that they were in squads ... scattered ... from the Gunpowder to the falls of the Potomac." Lincoln again stated that "there must be a pretty large force in the neighborhood of Silver Spring." Welles expressed regret on the lack of accurate information on their location and activities. Shortly thereafter, the meeting broke up, and the president and Mrs. Lincoln, with Secretary Stanton, rode out to the fort, accompanied by a cavalry escort. Welles would follow a few hours later.[37]

After leaving their cavalry escort far behind, the president's party visited the hospital, behind the fort. Lincoln conversed with the surgeons, praising the Sixth Corps, and telling those present that the "people of the country appreciated the achievements of the wearers of the Greek cross."[38] Then Lincoln and his entourage, escorted by General and Mrs. Wright, entered the fort. With sharpshooters' bullets whistling around them, punctuated by the boom of cannon fire, the Lincolns made their way towards the forward parapet.

In Wright's words, "The President evinced a remarkable coolness and disregard of danger. Meeting him as I came out of my quarters, I thoughtlessly invited him to see the fight ... without for a moment supposing he would accept. A moment after I would have given much to have recalled my words, as his life was too important ... to be put in jeopardy by ... the bullet of a sharpshooter. He took his position at my side on the parapet, and all my entreaties failed to move him, although ... the spot was a favorite mark for sharpshooters. When the surgeon was shot and after I had cleared the parapet of everyone else, he still maintained his ground till I told him I should have to remove him forcibly. The absurdity of the idea of sending off the President under guard seemed to amuse him, but in consideration of my earnestness..., he agreed to compromise by sitting behind the parapet instead of standing upon it. He could not be made to understand why, if I continued exposed, he should not, and my representations that an accident to me was of little importance, while to him it could not be measured ... failed to make any impression on him." Wright further stated to the effect that when Lincoln finally descended from the parapet, he did so out of consideration for Wright's sincerity, not from any thought of personal danger. Surgeon C.V.A. Crawford of the 102nd Pennsylvania Volunteers was shot through the thigh, standing a scant three feet from Lincoln. Another officer was reportedly killed only five feet from the president, an inviting target, dressed in a long faded yellow coat and stovepipe hat. A short time later, Welles found Lincoln "sitting in the shade, his back against the parapet towards the enemy."[39]

In addition to General Wright, at least one other person inside the fort on 12 July emphatically urged Lincoln to get out of harm's way. A number of people took credit for warning the president, "Get down you fool!" Exactly who warned him and when has never been conclusively proved. Captain Oliver Wendell Holmes (brevet lieutenant colonel) was inside the fort that day, and saw Lincoln. However, he never mentioned saying anything to the president until many years later, when in 1931, as chief justice of the U.S. Supreme Court, he visited Arlington Cemetery. There he told a friend that he shouted at Lincoln, "Get down you fool!" Holmes may well have warned the president; however, it's more likely that the apocryphal nature of the Holmes-Lincoln interaction accounts for that story's longevity. Private John Amos Bedient of the 150th Ohio National Guard, and Elizabeth "Aunt Betty" Thomas, a free African American whose home had been razed for the 1862 expansion of Fort Stevens, also may have warned Lincoln.

Thus Lincoln's well-known inquisitiveness got the better of his fear of enemy fire. However, mere curiosity doesn't explain his entire motivation for exposing himself to Confederate bullets, especially since he did so on two separate occasions. One writer has stated, "Neither he (General Lee) nor Davis nor Early ever mentioned any potential impact the raid might have had on the [presidential] election."[40] This is believable, as it was in keeping with Davis' policy of relying purely on military victory to achieve political results. However, while Early's expedition against Washington wasn't executed with the idea of defeating Lincoln at the polls, many Southerners were aware of the raid's potential for damaging Lincoln's presidency. The *Richmond Examiner* concluded that Early's raid would greatly increase the Northern desire for peace when the editor declared, "General Early, it is said, has gone over to stump the states of Maryland and Pennsylvania for the Peace party."[41] It's also difficult to believe that Early's officers and troops weren't aware of the raid's potential for damaging the Lincoln administration.

Was Lincoln exposing himself to Confederate fire, on two successive occasions, recklessness or bravado? Not likely. These were the acts of a rather desperate man, who realized his presidency was failing as a result of the war's length and incredibly destructive effects, and thus far, the lack of any definite indication of Northern victory. Lincoln's standing on the parapet indicated that he was well aware of the potential of Early's raid for destroying his presidency. There is little doubt that if Early had captured Washington, Lincoln would have been defeated in the November election. There is also little doubt that the Northern war effort would have been at least temporarily halted, with the president, his cabinet, and Congress having to meet in Philadelphia or New York City. In that case, foreign powers might have intervened to mediate the conflict, giving de facto recognition to the Confederacy, as Lee had hoped. However, even though Early failed to capture Washington, his expedition still caused the Lincoln administration, and the Federal high command, considerable embarrassment.

The Valley of Death

Lincoln's close brush with death or wounding while on the parapet, and the intensity of sharpshooter fire, resulted in Generals Wright and McCook mounting an offensive to drive the sharpshooters out of the area in front of Fort Stevens. The battle ground was about a mile and a half in length, extending northwest of the works, down the slope immediately in front and up the other side. There was a dense forest at the top of the far ridge with a wheat field in front of it and a large area of oak brushwood, up to 15 feet high, in front of the wheat field (closer to the fort). A line of large shade trees stood adjacent to the brushwood. Hiding in the brushwood and behind the trees, Rodes' Confederates had inundated the fort with a deadly barrage of minie balls all day Monday and thus far on Tuesday. Confederate sharpshooters also used, with deadly effect, two knolls overlooking the Federal rifle pits, the Carberry (Lay) house and the Rives house, on each side of the Seventh Street Road, and the orchard and large shade trees on the Rives property. A field of high brush stood on the east side of the Seventh Street Road, bisected by Piney Branch Road. A trail led to another impressive home north of Piney Branch Road, surrounded by a meadow, with a large forest of shade trees above that, bordering on the Blair property on the other side. These features on the east side of the road were also used by southern sharpshooters.

McCook asked Wright to furnish a full brigade for the assault. Wright met with his division and brigade commanders, giving the assignment of driving the Confederates out to Brigadier General Frank Wheaton, in temporary command of Brigadier General George Getty's Second Division. Colonel Daniel D. Bidwell's Third Brigade was selected to make the assault, with Wheaton's first brigade immediately behind. Wheaton told Bidwell to keep his men under cover as far forward as possible, at "trail arms," to keep the early evening sunlight from glinting off of their rifle barrels. Colonel Bidwell, of the 49th New York Infantry, would signal to begin the assault by waving the flag of the 77th New York Infantry. Artillery from forts Stevens and Slocum would open up on the houses sheltering the rebel snipers with three salvos, then Bidwell's brigade would begin their charge. A gala Washington crowd had come out to witness the assault, including Lucius Chittenden and other luminaries. They took their places in the vicinity of the fort, around their conveyances, cheering and clapping as the assault began.

With his troops lying on the ground, "on their arms," to avoid deadly Confederate fire, Bidwell gave the signal around 6 P.M. The big Federal siege guns spat fire and defiance at the hidden Confederates waiting in the houses and the brush. Clouds of smoke eddied upwards from the muzzles of the Federal cannon, covering the parapet. The main body of Early's troops could be seen, waiting in the wheat field and silhouetted against the forest, as Bidwell's men began their charge. The Carberry house caught fire and burned as Federal shells found their mark, and a few Confederate snipers jumped from the upper floor. Another house nearby also burned to the ground. Flashes of Confederate rifle fire could be seen, blinking on and off in the fading light, as Bidwell's troops gained the first ridge on the far slope. They continued their bayonet charge, but Confederate resistance hardened beyond the Carberry house, and gaps began to appear in the Federal line. Wheaton's men came up to replace Bidwell's killed and wounded, and the Federal assault fairly well succeeded in driving the Confederates out of the battle area, although undoubtedly assisted by oncoming darkness. The Confederates claimed to have stopped Bidwell's advance three times. The Battle of Fort Stevens ended around 10 P.M., but it had a high price. The Federals retained possession of the battlefield, but all of Bidwell's regimental commanders were killed or wounded, and as many as 375 in his brigade were likewise killed and wounded out of about 1,000 that had begun the assault. Federal casualties were "unusually high" as a percentage of those engaged, compared to Union losses at Antietam and Gettysburg, yet Bidwell's assault has ever since been called a skirmish. Confederate losses for the two days spent at Washington were less than 100 men killed and wounded.

However, as a result of the fight, residents of Leesborough later changed the name of their town to Wheaton.

Meanwhile, Early was planning the Army of the Valley's retreat. Later that night, he summoned Major Henry Kyd Douglas. After some good-natured banter, between Early, Douglas, and Breckinridge, Early explained that he was leaving behind a rear guard picket line of two hundred men, to be commanded by Douglas. They were to remain behind, as pickets on the Seventh Street Road, between Silver Spring and Fort Stevens, until midnight. They were then to follow the main body, which would be retreating up the Seventh Street Road, towards Rockville, then west towards Poolesville and White's Ford.[42]

Thus Early's raid on Washington ended. However, the threat to Washington posed by the Army of the Valley did not. That would continue for another three months. The raid did accomplish General Lee's goal of forcing Grant to detach a considerable number of troops from the Army of the Potomac to defend Washington. The raid also prolonged the war, by the defeat of Hunter's force before Lynchburg, and by Early's continued threat to Maryland and Pennsylvania. However, the Army of the Potomac wasn't sufficiently weakened by the detachment of a few thousand troops from the 6th Corps for Lee to attack and defeat them.

The failure to capture Washington greatly disappointed and frustrated many of Early's men. Trooper Caleb Linker stated to the effect that while they had come within sight of Washington, spending two days at the gates, they had not "accomplished anything." A few, however, naively expected that as a result of the raid, peace initiatives from the North would be forthcoming. Sergeant Major Joseph McMurran stated, "We are now victorious over our enemies.... Now the prospect of peace encourages all.... Even the people of Maryland say that Lincoln will now have to make a proposition of an 'armistics.'" However, the thinking of many in the Army of the Valley on the raid was found scrawled on the flyleaf of a copy of Lord Byron's works at Silver Spring by Union troops. A feisty Confederate trooper of the 58th Virginia Infantry had written:

> "Now, Uncle Abe, you had better be quiet the balance of your administration. We only came near your town this time to show you what we could do, but if you go on in your mad career we will come again soon, and then you had better stand from under.
> Yours respectfully,
> "The Worst Rebel you efer Saw"

Early himself put it more succinctly, telling Henry Kyd Douglas, "Major, we haven't taken Washington, but we've scared Abe Lincoln like hell!"[43]

CHAPTER 6

A Raid to Nowhere

Late Friday evening, 8 July, in a steady rain, Brigadier General Bradley Johnson reported to General Early's headquarters tent, "on the roadside just south of Middletown."[1] After having been denied the opportunity to capture Frederick the previous day, Johnson had spent some of that Friday repulsing an unexpected Federal cavalry attack on his headquarters, secessionist John Hagan's tavern, about halfway up Braddock Mountain.[2] Major Harry Gilmor and his 2nd Maryland Cavalry chased the Federals back down the mountain, losing a few killed and wounded; the Federals lost 35 killed and wounded. Now Johnson entered Early's headquarters tent with some expectation of another opportunity to capture his hometown. However, the conversation did little to lift his spirits.

Early began by mentioning the delivery by Captain Robert E. Lee Jr., on 6 July, of a special order from his father and Jefferson Davis. Johnson stated that he could have captured Frederick. With an upraised hand Early signaled for quiet then explained what Lee's order contained, describing a mission of Herculean proportions that Johnson was to accomplish in less than four days. Early directed Johnson to leave at dawn the next morning, position his brigade at a point north of Frederick, and "keep an eye" on Early's extreme left flank, making sure that all was well in the battle that was to begin south and east of Frederick soon after daybreak. Johnson would then "strike off across the country" through Westminster, towards Baltimore, destroy the railroads and telegraph lines north of that city, then turn around, "sweep rapidly around" Baltimore, and cut the B & O railroad between Baltimore and Washington. He was then to move rapidly southward and execute one prong of a joint attack on Point Lookout Prison Camp, containing thousands of Confederate prisoners of war. Johnson's brigade would attack the prison compound in tandem with a Confederate naval force sailing from Wilmington, North Carolina, led by Commander John Taylor Wood. Wood's steamers would arrive at the prison camp at 3 A.M. Tuesday. Johnson was to take command of the freed prisoners, march them up through southern Maryland, and link up with Early at Bladensburg.

Bewildered, Johnson strenuously objected. Early told him that Lee selected him because he was "a Marylander" and could thus make it down to Point Lookout and back better than anyone else. He replied to the effect that he had great respect for Early's "intellect" and "manly character," but that the planned raid was "utterly impossible for man or horse to accomplish," since it involved "near three hundred miles" of riding, "not counting for time lost" in destroying bridges and railroads, in only four days. Early told

77

him to give it his best effort, and Johnson said that he "would do what was possible for men to do."[3]

A quick salute and the two generals parted company. Johnson left Early's tent, doubtless wondering how the Point Lookout raid could be accomplished in the scant time allotted. Johnson's mission was to isolate Baltimore and Washington from the rest of the north, then ride about 150 miles to the prison camp and assist in freeing and arming an estimated ten to twelve thousand Confederate prisoners, nearly the equivalent of an entire corps of troops.[4]

General Lee first proposed a raid on Point Lookout Prison in a letter to Davis on 26 June 1864. Lee had been thinking about an expedition to free the prisoners at Point Lookout for some time. Prisoner exchanges between North and South had ceased, and the Army of Northern Virginia desperately needed the manpower the prisoners would provide. Lee first connected a raid on Point Lookout with Early's invasion of Maryland in another letter to Davis on 29 June. In this second letter, Lee mentioned the positive effect on morale in the Army of Northern Virginia of a successful release of the prisoners. By 1 July, Commander Wood had begun to assemble his force, which was to consist of marines and seamen from a Confederate naval squadron in the James River, scheduled to reach Wilmington, N.C., by 6 July. Meanwhile, 20,000 stands of small arms were to be shipped to Wilmington for distribution to the freed prisoners. Wood's marines and seamen were to have boarded two fast, blockade-running steamships on the night of 10 July, and were to have arrived at Point Lookout in the wee hours of Tuesday morning, 12 July. They were to subdue the garrison and link up with the prisoners. Wood made no mention of coordination with a land-based cavalry force in his initial plan. However, he visited Lee at Petersburg on the evening of 2 July. There the two leaders decided to send a courier to Early, requesting a brigade of cavalry to coordinate with Wood's seaborne force. Johnson's brigade was to have marched the freed and armed prisoners up through southern Maryland and meet the Army of the Valley at Washington.

Point Lookout Prison was located on a low-lying, sandy peninsula where the Potomac River flows into Chesapeake Bay, about 80 miles southeast of Washington. The prison was established in August 1863, by order of Secretary of War Edwin Stanton, who refused to allow the construction of barracks to house the prisoners. Instead, the initial prisoner contingent, approximately 10,000 Confederates, and those thereafter, were housed in tents.[5]

Living conditions at the prison were brutal at best. The prisoner camp, roughly in the middle of the prison, was a rectangular enclosure of some ten acres, surrounded on three sides by a 14 foot high wooden fence with an attached raised walkway which allowed Federal guards to keep a sharp eye on everyone inside. A well guarded gate was in one corner of the camp, which controlled access to the outside. On the fourth side, the prisoner compound faced the Bay, with three small gates jutting about 25 feet out from land, above the water. The gates were used as privies during the day, but were locked at night. The guards were housed just north of the prisoner camp, and farther north a wide channel, running between the Bay and the Potomac River, presented another barrier to any force approaching from land. Just north of the channel, isolated from the main part of the camp, was a smallpox hospital. Southward from the prisoner camp, a few hundred yards distant, were the commandant's home, the quartermaster's office, and the camp dispensary.

Continuing south, towards the tip of the peninsula, was Hammond Hospital, built in 1862 to serve Federal wounded from McClellan's failed Peninsula campaign. Hammond Hospital had wards arranged like the spokes of a wheel, around a central kitchen, chapel and library. A covered walkway led to another kitchen and dining room, and at the very tip of the peninsula sat a lighthouse.

The soil was largely white sand, and the buildings and fences were painted white, adding to the dreary monotony of the surroundings and causing blindness among the prisoners. The water was poisoned — impregnated with copperas, a brackish tasting sulfate of copper, iron and zinc[6]; the food was of poor quality and insufficient to ward off hunger. Smallpox, typhoid fever, and tuberculosis ran rampant through the camp. Sidney Lanier, an accomplished musician who later became a famous poet, died of tuberculosis contracted at Point Lookout.[7]

Sergeant Bartlett Yancey Malone, of Company H, 6th North Carolina Infantry, in his diary described daily life at Point Lookout as an unending battle against cold, hunger, and disease. The bill of fare at Point Lookout was very thin: "5 crackers and a cup of coffee for Breakfast," "a small ration of meat 2 crackers three Potatoes and a cup of soup" for dinner, and for supper, "we have non[e]." The accommodations were crude; living in tents, the men were given a scant allowance of wood for fuel, "one shoulder tirn of pine brush every other day," for a tent housing 16 men. In addition, the cruelty of their captors was a constant refrain, and Malone described how a guard shot one of the prisoners in the head for "peepen threw the cracks of the planken." Hunger, cold, and the arbitrary and violent behavior of the guards were continuing themes in his diary, and the evening of 1 January 1864 was so cold that "five of our men froze to death befour morning." In July 1864, Point Lookout Prison was ripe for a liberating raid.

Johnson and his 1500 cavalry troops left Braddock Mountain well before daylight on 9 July, heading northeast. They paused briefly at Worman's Mill, two miles north of Frederick, satisfying themselves that Early's far left flank was "getting along all right." Johnson may have detached a few horse soldiers to harass elements of the 149th Ohio National Guard, protecting Hughes Ford. Thus satisfied, Johnson's brigade moved off towards Libertytown, New Windsor, and Westminster at a trot. Only Captain

Brigadier General Bradley T. Johnson (courtesy Monocacy National Battlefield)

George W. Booth, Johnson's adjutant, Captain Wilson C. Nicholas, and the brigade's ranking colonel, William E. Peters of the 21st Virginia Cavalry, were informed of their mission and eventual goal.[8]

News of the raiders' advance spread rapidly through north central Maryland, and as the Confederates entered Libertytown and New Windsor, empty streets and locked doors greeted them. In New Windsor, they demanded that residents reopen their stores, and some looting occurred. Shortly thereafter, Johnson sent Major Harry Gilmor and twenty troops of the 2nd Maryland ahead with orders to capture Westminster, eight miles northeast. Having learned that 150 Federal troops occupied Westminster, Gilmor's men charged into town, sabers drawn. As Gilmor stated, "A few bluecoats were to be seen, and the boys gave an awful yell when they saw them, which brought everyone to the doors and windows."[9] The Federals fled towards Baltimore as the southerners cut the telegraph wires. However, Gilmor's reception at Westminster was friendly, as residents opened their doors, a few offering food and drink to the tired southern horsemen. Three hours later, as Gilmor's men swapped stories with the townsfolk, a message arrived from Johnson, asking Gilmor to demand 1500 sets of clothing, shoes and boots from the mayor. However, two hours after that, as Johnson arrived, friendly residents brought bread and crackers to the troops, and Mayor Jacob Grove was unable to assemble the town council. Gilmor personally persuaded Johnson not to burn the town.[10]

Gilmor and the 2nd Maryland left Westminster early Sunday morning, 10 July, ahead of Johnson's brigade. They would ride through Reisterstown and the Worthington Valley to Cockeysville, where they would destroy the tracks and bridges of the Northern Central Railroad and cut telegraph wires linking Maryland with Harrisburg, Pennsylvania. They would then wait at Cockeysville for Johnson and the brigade and further orders.

Gilmor and the 2nd Maryland burned their first bridge over the Gunpowder that morning, about three miles northeast of Cockeysville. Meanwhile, Johnson and the main force arrived in Reisterstown around 6 A.M.; Johnson breakfasted at the home of Mrs. Mary Worthington, in the Worthington Valley. Two hours later they were in Cockeysville, where, with Gilmor's force, they engaged in further destruction of the Northern Central Railroad.

Since it was Sunday morning, the arrival of the troops caused great excitement among the church faithful. Johnson later commented, "I fear we rather broke up the meeting. We were greater attractions than the preachers."[11] He directed the destruction of several Northern Central railroad bridges nearby. They would destroy or vandalize eleven Northern Central bridges before the raid ended. Johnson then sent Gilmor on a unique mission — to destroy the tracks and the Gunpowder River bridge of the Philadelphia, Wilmington, and Baltimore railroad at Magnolia Station, 25 miles northeast of Baltimore. The bridge was rumored to be heavily guarded by Federal troops, causing Gilmor to protest the small size of his contingent, 135 troops versus the 500 promised. Johnson rightly feared that given Gilmor's reckless nature, he would have tried to capture Baltimore with 500 troops. Johnson and the brigade then turned around and headed southwest across Baltimore County. Gilmor was not informed of the intended raid on Point Lookout.

The Raid on Magnolia Station

Harry Gilmor glanced at his watch as he sighted Magnolia Station on the Philadelphia, Wilmington and Baltimore railroad just north (east) of the Gunpowder River, several hundred yards distant. It was 8:30 A.M., Monday, 11 July. Gilmor and his command had traveled northeast, from the vicinity of Cockeysville, Baltimore County, with little rest, for the preceding 24 hours. Gilmor and 85 troops of the 2nd Maryland Cavalry, augmented by 50 troops of the 1st Maryland, led by Lt. Harry Dorsey, left Cockeysville at noon on Sunday. Riding south towards Towsontown (Towson), they turned east at Timonium then rode northeast on Old York Road, then to Meredith's Bridge over the Gunpowder. As they rode, Gilmor assigned squads of outriders to gather fresh horses from various farms along their route as replacements for tired and broken-down mounts; this was standard procedure on cavalry expeditions.

Five of Gilmor's men rode into Towsontown, and a large and eager crowd of men, women and children soon gathered around them, as contact with a real "live rebel" was a new and fascinating experience in that part of Maryland. However, these five troopers "behaved themselves remarkably well. They destroyed nothing and took nothing but what they were willing and able to pay for."[12] Meanwhile, Gilmor, who had been born and raised in that part of Baltimore County, couldn't resist the urge to visit his family. With a few officers, he left his command at Meredith's bridge, retracing his route down Old York Road. He then detoured over to the Gilmor family home, Glen Ellen, a large and imposing castle-like, early Gothic revival mansion, nearly an exact replica of Abbotsford, Sir Walter Scott's residence in Scotland. Gilmor's father, Robert, was a close friend of Scott's. "I captured the whole party on the front steps," Gilmor later wrote. After catching up on family affairs for a few hours, he "paroled and released them, and moved on with my command."[13]

Before leaving Glen Ellen, Gilmor told a relative about his destination. Knowing the small size of Gilmor's force, the relative told him that he "would not return alive."[14] Gilmor then departed Glen Ellen, returning to Meredith's Bridge where he gathered his command together, then headed northeast, towards Magnolia Station. Late Sunday night, after several monotonous hours in the saddle, fatigue began to sap the stamina of Gilmor's men. They began to doze in the saddle, and a few fell off their mounts. Gilmor, half asleep, missed the turn onto the road that he intended to take to the mouth of the Gunpowder.

Discovering his error, he decided to wait at a nearby farm until daylight, to let his men sleep. As he stated, his men "were actually so suffering for it [sleep] they were falling from their horses on the road and I was beginning to lose some of them." Thus they spent the remainder of that night on the farm of Joshua Price, at an old stagecoach stop, 14 miles northeast of Baltimore.

Gilmor's force continued eastward at dawn on Monday, 11 July. As they approached Kingsville, Gilmor heard the report of a gun up ahead. As he galloped forward, one of his men, returning to the column, told him that a local farmer, Ishmael Day, had shot Ordnance Sergeant Eugene Fields. Gilmor considered Fields one of his best troops. He hurried forward, to find Fields lying in the road, in front of Day's house, his face and chest covered with reddish-purple welts, of the kind produced by buckshot.

Day had heard the previous day that a large cavalry force was in the vicinity. He mistakenly assumed that they were Federals out to impress horses. In response, he raised a large American flag over his home, demonstrating his loyalty to the Union, so they wouldn't take his horses; and take them instead from Southern sympathizers. With labored breath, Fields told Gilmor that he had ordered Day to "take down that damned old rag!" Day allegedly responded, "Gentlemen, you may burn my house to the ground, but I will shoot any man that touches that flag."[15] When Day refused to remove the flag, Fields dismounted. While Fields was attempting to take down the flag, Day shot him, with a shotgun, from a second story window. As Gilmor's men arrived at his house, many cursing loudly, the 65-year-old Day fled. Gilmor placed Fields into one of Day's carriages, sending him to Wright's Hotel, near Kingsville, where he received medical attention. Nevertheless, he died a short time later. Gilmor's men looted then burned Day's home, and outbuildings.

From Day's farm, Gilmor's force rode northeast from Kingsville. About two and a half miles later, they crossed Little Gunpowder Falls, coming to Jerusalem Mill, with an adjacent Quaker village, hard by the Falls. Ninety-five years old in 1864, Jerusalem Mill stands five stories high with two enormous overshot waterwheels, powering four sets of grindstones, producing flour that was shipped around the world. At the store of miller David Lee, about a hundred yards away across the road, Gilmor's men requisitioned clothing, boots and shoes, causing Lee considerable loss.[16]

Gilmor then led his men towards Magnolia Station, arriving shortly after 8:30 A.M., and promptly captured the telegraph operator. A few minutes later, they heard the 8:40 train from Baltimore approaching. Gilmor ordered Captain Bailey ahead to capture the train, which he did immediately. Guards were posted around the train, and Gilmor gave strict orders against looting, on pain of death. He quickly learned that Major General William B. Franklin was aboard, along with a few other Federal officers. Franklin had fought in a number of major engagements and was convalescing from a wound he had received that spring in the Red River campaign in Louisiana. He was traveling home to York, Pa., when the train was captured. Gilmor entered one of the passenger cars, and questioned a few likely looking passengers. Dressed in civilian clothing, Franklin approached Gilmor and identified himself. Gilmor later wrote that he was "immediately impressed" by Franklin's "blunt, direct manner and gentlemanly bearing." He next ordered the train unloaded, making sure that each passenger received their personal belongings. Franklin was placed under guard, and directed into a carriage, with four other Federal officers. Gilmor wanted to drive the train to Havre de Grace, destroying the other bridges along the way. However, the train's engineer had damaged the operating controls, so it couldn't be moved. Gilmor burned the train at the station. He then learned from the conductor that another train was rapidly approaching.

Meanwhile, Federal authorities had taken steps to defend the Philadelphia, Wilmington & Baltimore railroad. Major Henry B. Judd, Federal commander at Wilmington, Delaware, sent 50 men, led by Captain Thomas Hugh Stirling, to protect the Gunpowder River bridge. When they arrived at the crossing, they met with 32 troops from Company F, 159th Ohio National Guard, sent up from Baltimore. Their commander, Lieutenant Robert Price, agreed with Stirling that Price's Ohio guardsmen would patrol the western side of the bridge while Stirling's Delaware infantry would guard the eastern end, closest to Magnolia Station.[17] Navy secretary Gideon Welles sent three gunboats to protect the Bush, Gunpowder, and Susquehanna River railroad crossings. However, the Federal gunboats were hampered by shallow water near the bridges. The U.S.S. *Teaser* was assigned to protect the bridge at Magnolia Station; however, her captain claimed that a malfunctioning exhaust pipe prevented the ship from reaching the mouth of the Gunpowder. Instead, the U.S.S. *Juanita* arrived to defend the bridge crossing.

Gilmor's capture of the second train from Baltimore was described by Helen Marie "Nellie" Noye, an Army nurse from Buffalo, New York, who had been caring for Federal wounded in Annapolis when she was ordered to accompany them northward. She had become a nurse after the Battle of Antietam, and during the summer of 1863 she began nursing duties, without pay, at the Naval Academy Hospital. She wrote: "The proximity of the Confederate Army in July 1864 caused the

Colonel Harry Gilmor (Library of Congress)

nurses to be ordered from the hospital. My train was captured at Magnolia Sta. north of Baltimore by Gilmore's guerillas [sic]. At the sound of the firing I looked out and saw the soldiers by the side of the track. A rebel soldier helped me off the train, which was subsequently backed onto the burning bridge over the river. Our luggage being placed on a handcar, we made our way to the river, where we stayed until morning, and were then taken by steamer to Havre de Grace. The appearance of the tilted stack of the engine above the wreck of the bridge is still strong in my memory."[18]

Shortly after the second train arrived, Gilmor ordered the passengers off and the baggage unloaded. He then ordered his men to attack Stirling's bridge guards. "The enemy's cavalry attacked us yesterday while the men were pitching tents, wounding one man, and afterward sent in a flag of truce demanding our surrender, which was refused. We formed a line to defend the bridge."[19] Gilmor had sent Captain Brewer to the bridge to demand the Federal surrender. While waiting for Brewer to return, the second train was fired, and backed onto the bridge. At the same time, Gilmor sent thirty men towards the bridge to occupy the Federals. The Federals promptly began to retreat across the bridge. Lt. Price then led a few of his Ohio guardsmen onto the bridge, separating two cars from the burning train, and moved them to the far side of the bridge. From front to rear, the entire train was now on fire, as it slowly backed over the bridge. As it approached the drawbridge, the bridge caught fire, and the train stopped. To escape the inferno, more than a few Federals were forced to jump into the river.

Shortly thereafter, the train and part of the bridge tumbled into the water. Lifeboats from the *Juanita* retrieved those Federals that had jumped from the bridge. Burning embers from the bridge threatened the gunboat, and she was forced to move. Stirling and his command retreated to Perryville, on board the *Juanita*, which had not assisted in the defense of the bridge. Price later noted that the *Juanita* had been "anchored 300 yards below the bridge. She had no colors hoisted, neither did she communicate with shore, which caused us to look on her with suspicion. At about 8 o'clock she hoisted the Stars and Stripes, and at the time the bridge was being fired she steamed up a little nearer, but did not use her gun."[20] Price's statement is strange, since Ensign William J. Herring, commander of the *Juanita,* didn't have any steam in the ship's boilers. Gilmor destroyed the trains and the bridge without having to fight the Federals.[21]

After destroying the bridge, Gilmor released the passengers, except General Franklin and the four Federal officers. He then signaled to Herring that he could come ashore and pick up the passengers and transport them to Havre de Grace. Gilmor and his troops then departed for Baltimore, with Franklin and the officers riding in carriages. In a hurry to rejoin Johnson's brigade, he wanted to take the Franklin Turnpike (today's Franklin Street) westward through Baltimore City. However, an old friend warned him that the streets were barricaded and Federal troops waited at various locations in the city specifically for him. Gilmor heeded the warning and changing course headed for Towsontown. Arriving with a few officers ahead of the column, they made a beeline for the bar in Ady's Hotel, where they enjoyed a glass of ale. However, a short time later, a few of Gilmor's friends warned him of the approach of a large Federal cavalry force coming up from Baltimore. Choosing to stay and fight, Gilmor ordered Captain Nicholas Owings, with ten men, to escort the prisoners west, and wait for him at Hunt's Meeting House on Reisterstown Road, near Pikesville. He then ordered Lt. William Kemp, with fifteen men from Company C, south on York Road to charge the Federal advance and then fall back on the main column.

However, the "large force of Federal cavalry" turned out to be about 75 volunteers investigating reports of Confederate raiders up county. They fell into Gilmor's trap. With sabers drawn and hats pulled down tightly, the Southerners "charged down on them, though it was so dark we could not see a man of them." The volunteers fled from Gilmor's charge, with some Confederates chasing them as far as Govanstown, near present-day Baltimore's northern boundary.[22]

Neither Johnson nor Gilmor were overly concerned about Federal pursuit. The raid had prompted Generals Wallace and Ricketts to properly garrison and strengthen the city's forts, but lacking cavalry in sufficient numbers they didn't pursue the raiders. However, had the Confederates attacked Baltimore, they would have been soundly rebuffed. The city then contained less than 2,200 experienced troops. However, armed residents, including African American units, allowed Wallace to claim that he had 13,413 soldiers present and ready for action. In addition, Baltimore's streets had been barricaded against cavalry attack. Nevertheless, there was much confusion concerning command responsibilities, between Wallace and General E.O.C. Ord, who had replaced him as Federal commander in Baltimore, immediately after the battle of Monocacy. Chief of Staff Halleck in Washington defined the situation, retaining Wallace as administrative head of the Middle Department, while Ord, by "special order of the President," was Wallace's superior.[23]

Gilmor did have some concern about serious Federal pursuit. Therefore, though the hour was late, he determined to push on towards Reisterstown Road, about eight miles southwest of Towsontown. Bringing up the rear of the column, to keep his tired cavaliers awake, Gilmor himself soon dozed off. He later wrote that he was awakened by a loud "Halt!" In unfamiliar surroundings, he suspected that he had run afoul of a Federal picket line. Protesting that he was a Federal scout looking for Harry Gilmor, he was able to slip away. Crossing the Northern Central Railroad near today's Riderwood Station, he eventually located Joppa Road, leading west from Towsontown. Upon reaching the vicinity of Reisterstown Road, he found his command fast asleep, on the grounds of "the home of a Mr. Cradock."[24] In dire need of sleep, they had somehow dragged themselves through the Greenspring Valley, stopping at the valley's western end, just east of Reisterstown Road. Their horses were tied to bushes, to each other, or to anything available. Franklin and the other Federal prisoners had been kept in a fenced off area on the grounds. However, when Gilmor arrived, Franklin was nowhere to be found.[25] Cursing emphatically, Gilmor couldn't bring himself to punish his men, given their debilitated condition.

Franklin described his escape: "About 12 A.M., while the party having me in charge was resting & their horses feeding, I made my escape. Being much disabled, I only succeeded in getting about 22 miles [sic; 2 miles] away from them, but I hid in the woods until Tuesday night when I managed to get about one mile farther. On Wednesday morning I fell in with some Union citizens who kindly cared for me, and made my case known to the commanding officer at Baltimore. An escort of cavalry was sent for me on Wednesday night, and I arrived at Baltimore on Thursday morning."[26] Hallucinating and very hungry, Franklin found the home of a Unionist farmer on Wednesday morning, and was taken in and cared for. He later described the Greenspring Valley there as being "a mile wide." Since the Greenspring Valley is about a mile wide northeast of the Cradock home, Franklin must have been walking northeast, perhaps crossing the track of the Western Maryland railroad. Gilmor's men didn't look in that direction; thus they didn't find him. Franklin left a valise with his personal effects behind in the carriage. Gilmor arranged to have it returned to him.[27]

Gilmor and his troops spent most of Tuesday, 12 July, in the vicinity of Pikesville. Legend has it that Benjamin O. Howard, a well-known politician, and Gilmor's cousin, persuaded him not to burn the Federal armory and barracks in Pikesville. Howard reportedly told Gilmor that many local residents were Confederate sympathizers, and if Gilmor burned the armory, Federal authorities would retaliate against them.[28] Heeding the advice, he left the armory and barracks alone. Leaving Pikesville around 3 P.M. they camped that night a few miles away, at Randallstown. At dawn on the 13th, they departed Randallstown for Rockville. Traveling on back roads to avoid Federal troops, they rode all night, rejoining Johnson's brigade at Poolesville, at dawn on 14 July. Gilmor's men assisted Johnson's force in keeping the pursuing Federal 6th Corps at bay until the Army of the Valley was safely back in Virginia. They crossed the Potomac at sundown. Gilmor reported to Early, at headquarters at Big Spring, near Leesburg. General Breckinridge greeted him cordially. Staying at headquarters the entire evening, he dined with Early and Breckinridge, telling of his success in eluding Federal pursuers on the outskirts of Baltimore, and opining that with a few more men he could have captured that city.[29]

Johnson Rides South—Almost

While Gilmor was visiting his family at Glen Ellen, Johnson was also enjoying Sunday afternoon, at Hayfields, the home of his friend John Merryman. An outspoken southern sympathizer before the war, Merryman was involved in the destruction of a Northern Central railroad bridge in April 1861. He was arrested and interned at Fort McHenry, and President Lincoln ignored a writ of habeas corpus from Chief Justice Roger B. Taney pleading for his release. Johnson described his brief visit at Hayfields: "The charming society, the lovely girls, the balmy July air and the luxuriant verdure of Hayfields, all combined to make the scene enchanting to soldiers who have been for months campaigning...."[30] However, he dispatched a friend, Colonel James Clarke, to visit Baltimore to determine the number and condition of the Federal troops in the city, and to find out if reinforcements were coming up from the Army of the Potomac at Petersburg. He then left Hayfields, leaving behind two messengers to secure Clarke's report, and moved on with the brigade through the Green Spring Valley.

Before entering the valley, Johnson's brigade passed close to the home of Maryland governor Augustus Williamson Bradford. Johnson decided to burn Bradford's home, in retaliation for General Hunter's burning of Virginia governor John Letcher's home, at Lexington. He dispatched a squad, led by Lt. Henry Blackistone, to do the deed. Bradford was then in Baltimore, conferring with Mayor John Chapman and Federal commanders on how best to counter the Confederate invasion. Blackistone's squad arrived at the home, a few miles north of Baltimore, around 7 A.M. Monday, 11 July. He most likely gave Mrs. Bradford and her children some time to remove their valuables from the house, and one writer asserted that Blackistone directed his men and a few local residents to help them.[31] However, in his complaint, Bradford later wrote that Blackistone set the house on fire before informing Mrs. Bradford of his purpose. However Blackistone did it, the burning of Governor Bradford's home, while in some measure satisfying to southerners, created more anti–Southern feeling among Maryland residents. It also resulted in Johnson's indictment for treason, on Federal and State levels, after the war.[32]

Johnson and the brigade bivouacked that evening at The Caves, the home of his friend John N. Carroll, in a forested area close to the Greenspring Valley in Owings Mills. Around midnight, he received a message from Colonel Clarke, delivered by the two couriers he had left at Hayfields. Clarke's message told Johnson that the 19th Corps and part of the 6th Corps of the Army of the Potomac were on transport ships off Locust Point (near Fort McHenry), waiting to disembark upon General Emory's arrival. All available cars and locomotives of the B & O railroad were concentrated there, waiting to take the troops to Washington. Johnson informed Early by courier.

Early the next morning, just beyond the Painter farm in Owings Mills, Johnson's brigade came upon three wagons, loaded with Painter's ice cream, bound for the Baltimore market. As breakfast rations hadn't been issued, Johnson permitted them to feast on the "frozen mush." Lacking forks and spoons, the hungry troopers used anything available, scooping the vanilla, lemon, and raspberry ice cream into their canteens and hats. One rebel from southwestern Virginia stuffed his mouth with ice cream, "then clapped his hands to both sides of his head and jumped up and down" as the frozen delicacy made contact with rotten teeth. Most of Johnson's men saved the ice cream in their canteens,

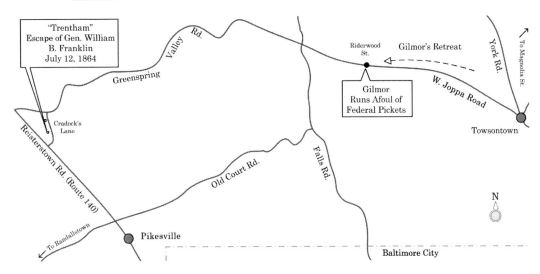

"Trentham"
Escape of Gen. William
B. Franklin
July 12, 1864

Valley Rd.

Riderwood St.

Gilmor's Retreat

York Rd.

To Magnolia St.

Greenspring

Gilmor
Runs Afoul of
Federal Pickets

W. Joppa Road

Cradock's
Lane

Towsontown

Reisterstown Rd. (Route 140)

Old Court Rd.

Falls Rd.

N

To Randallstown

Pikesville

Baltimore City

Gilmor rides around Baltimore, July 12–13, 1864

eating it when it melted. They enjoyed the "Painter's ice cream caper"; most would remember it long after the war.

As Blackistone's squad caught up with the main body of troops, Johnson headed southwest, away from possible Federal pursuit, and crossed the shallow Patapsco River. They then destroyed the tracks of the B & O railroad, west of Woodstock in Howard County. Johnson then took another lunch break with another friend, John Lee Carroll, at his Doughoregan Manor estate, a Georgian style brick mansion that still stands west of Ellicott City. Carroll would be elected governor of Maryland in 1875. They camped that evening further south at Tridelphia. After receiving an unexpected warning of a Federal cavalry force in nearby Brookeville, Johnson prepared to attack them, only to have scouts confirm that the Federals had hastily departed.

However, Johnson's brigade was supposed to be in the vicinity of Point Lookout on the morning of 12 July, making preparations to attack the compound; in fact, they were well over a hundred miles away. When he received the information about the Federal reinforcements waiting to disembark at Locust Point, Johnson realized that Early wouldn't be able to penetrate Washington's defenses. Nevertheless, he took an inordinate amount of time—five hours, traversing the eight miles between New Windsor and Westminster, suggesting that he might have still been annoyed at not being allowed to capture Frederick and then being assigned a near impossible task. Whatever the reasons, Johnson's efforts during the Point Lookout raid were without enthusiasm. However, as events unfolded, an enthusiastic effort would have been wasted.

Shortly after daybreak on 12 July, Johnson's force "passed through Mechanicsville [Olney], [then] went towards Colesville. Near Rockland Gate, they took Uncle Benjamin off his horse and took his favorite mare [Andy] and several other horses," related Sandy Spring resident R.B. Farquhar.[33] They then headed towards Laurel, where they were to have crossed the B & O's Washington branch line. When scouts reported a strong Federal force in Laurel, the brigade detoured six miles farther south, crossing the B & O's tracks at Beltsville. They immediately burned about twenty construction cars and cut down eight telegraph poles, thereby cutting Washington's telegraph service to the north, and to Grant's headquarters at City Point, Virginia. Federal troops inside Fort Lincoln, near the District boundary, looked through their field glasses and saw smoke curling above the northern horizon. Three to four hundred cavalry left the fort to investigate, mounted on green and unruly horses.

J.B. Fry, provost marshal at Fort Lincoln, told of their encounter with Johnson's brigade, as well as the unprepared condition of Washington's defenses in that sector, as occurring around 2:00 P.M.: "A force of rebel cavalry has within the last few hours been engaged with about 300 of our cavalry, at the Baltimore pike where it crosses Paint Creek, about three miles beyond Bladensburg. The rebel force was accompanied by light artillery, which up to the time my informant left had fired about fifteen shots. My informant is one of our cavalry, just in, who was wounded in the skirmish. Our 300 cavalry were yielding their ground slowly.... The line of rifle pits from this fort westward is entirely unmanned. There is not a soldier on the line as far as I can see it, and but two companies of 100-days' men and a few convalescents in this fort. The pike is really open to a cavalry dash."[34] The gray-clad cavalry were ready for the Union horsemen, as Johnson had deployed his troops and artillery. Southern cannon fire scattered the Federal horsemen, and they "skedaddled in fine style" back to Fort Lincoln. After the skirmish, Johnson's force arrived on the campus of the Maryland Agricultural College, where he briefly used the Rossborough Inn as headquarters. Local lore has it that Johnson's men held a ball at the inn that evening, inviting eligible local belles.[35]

Federal authorities expected Johnson's brigade to attack Washington's defenses between Forts Lincoln and Saratoga, where the Baltimore Turnpike and the B & O railroad entered the city. Johnson, however, didn't have time for an assault on the nation's capitol as his men were scouring the neighborhood for fresh horses and mules in preparation for the ride to Point Lookout. He "hoped to make a rapid march and get to Point Lookout early on the morning of the 13th."[36]

He sent men southward, along the road to Upper Marlboro, to inform residents of their approach so fresh mounts would be available. The brigade left the Maryland Agricultural College, but just as they turned onto the Upper Marlboro road, a courier from Early arrived, informing Johnson that the Point Lookout raid had been cancelled and that the brigade should rejoin the Army of the Valley at Silver Spring "on the Seventh Street road." The courier couldn't explain the reasons for the cancellation. However, this was a fortunate turn for Johnson. Had the raid not been cancelled, the brigade probably would have arrived at the compound the next morning, far too late to coordinate with Wood's seaborne assault.

Wood's force consisted of 800 sailors and marines; the garrison at Point Lookout totaled 1654 troops, with varying degrees of battle experience, and there were a fair number of cannon on the grounds. In addition, Federal authorities found out about the raid on 7 July, the day after a Confederate deserter wandered into General Benjamin Butler's camp, at Bermuda Hundred, Virginia, and told him that Early's expedition was to include a raid on Point Lookout Prison.[37] Butler promptly telegraphed the War Department in Washington with the news. Federal authorities had already appointed a new commander for the prison on 2 July, Brigadier General James Barnes, a competent soldier who had fought in a number of engagements and had been cited for gallant conduct at Gettysburg.

The raid was common knowledge in southern Maryland by 12 July, and Sergeant Malone commented in his diary, on 13 July, "And it was repoted that General Ewel was a fiting [fighting] at Washington. And that our Cavalry was in 4 miles of this plaice ... the Yanks was hurried up ... and run their Artilry [Artillery] out in frunt of the Block house and plaised it in position."[38] Word of the raid had preceded it; however, it didn't matter, as Jefferson Davis had cancelled the raid on 10 July. He had discovered, upon reading the *New York Herald*, that the newspaper's Washington correspondent had learned of the plan three days earlier, subsequently publicizing the transfer of "most of the prisoners at Point Lookout" to the facility at Elmira. In fact, most of the prisoners had remained at Point Lookout, and a coordinated land-sea assault probably would have succeeded in freeing a fair number of them.

Subsequently, Johnson's brigade retraced their steps. Riding all night, they moved past the northeast sector of the capital's defenses, well within range of the heavy guns in Forts Totten, Slemmer, Slocum, and Bunker Hill. Surprisingly, the Federals let them pass without firing a shot. They rejoined the Army of the Valley late that evening, near Rockville, with Johnson reporting to Early around midnight.

Thus the Johnson-Gilmor raid ended, without freeing any prisoners at Point Lookout or significantly damaging the Northern war effort. The raid did accomplish the destruction of the Northern Central and P.W. & B. railroads north of Baltimore and cut off telegraphic communication between Baltimore and the north and between Washington and City Point, Virginia. However, travelers going north from Baltimore simply took steamships to Havre de Grace, going around the wrecked Gunpowder River bridge. Once in Havre de Grace, they boarded trains for points farther north. Work crews repaired the bridge within three weeks, and telegraph communication between Washington and City Point was restored in days. The Northern Central and P.W. & B. railroads were likewise repaired quickly; thus none of the destruction had significant effect. Had the intended Point Lookout raid succeeded in freeing the prisoners, with the freed prisoners rejoining Confederate forces, a lot would have been accomplished. Southern destruction of northern railroads, with their subsequent quick repair, was an exercise in futility. Short of capturing and destroying the Mount Clare roundhouse and machine shops, or similar facilities in Cumberland, there was no way to permanently destroy the B & O railroad (or any other railroad) as the Confederates discovered, too late.

CHAPTER 7

Back to Virginia

Around 7 P.M. on 12 July, the Army of the Valley began their retreat from Fort Stevens. While the forward elements of Early's force engaged Bidwell's brigade, the reserve troops began their retreat from the vicinity of Silver Spring. Bidwell's assault underscored the wisdom of Early's withdrawal, and by midnight the Army of the Valley was in full retreat with the rear guard, led by Henry Kyd Douglas, following the main body.

A mile or so beyond Silver Spring, as they trudged up the Seventh Street Road, Douglas' attention was directed towards "a bright light behind us." The bright light proved to be Montgomery Blair's home, Falkland, going up in flames. Silver Spring was spared from the torch and serious vandalism by the vigilance of General Breckinridge. Early denied ordering the destruction of Falkland, and Union troops insisted that the fort's artillery set the mansion ablaze. The identity of those responsible has never been proved, however, Falkland was most likely destroyed by Confederate stragglers in retaliation for General Hunter's burning of Governor Letcher's home on the VMI campus at Lexington, Virginia. Nevertheless, the destruction of Falkland and Montevideo (Governor Bradford's home) provoked outrage in the North. The war had taken a hard turn, and retaliation was the order of the day. The Federal high command responded in kind, with Major General Ben Butler sending a gunboat up the Rappahannock to burn the home of Confederate secretary of war James A. Seddon, terrorizing his family. Blair would rebuild Falkland.

Around midnight, Bradley Johnson and his 1st Maryland Cavalry rejoined the Army of the Valley. Early assigned Johnson rear-guard duty, and the 1st Maryland would be heavily engaged with the pursuing 2nd Massachusetts Cavalry on 13 July and all through 14 July. The last of the rear guard left the vicinity of Fort Stevens around 5 A.M. Wednesday.[1] Crossing over to the Rockville Pike, through present-day Kensington, Early's 11,500 grimy battle-hardened veterans tramped through Rockville most of Wednesday morning and into the afternoon, more than twelve hours ahead of pursuing Federal infantry. Early and a few officers again had breakfast at the Montgomery House hotel. As the troops streamed through the town, on West Montgomery Avenue and Commerce Lane, Early watched them from a balcony, while poring over his maps, cigar in hand, trying to determine the best place to cross the Potomac. As the main body passed beyond Courthouse Square, towards the western edge of town, Early rolled up his maps, mounted his horse and followed them, never to set foot in Rockville again.

Federal Pursuit

All through Wednesday morning and well into the afternoon, as the Army of the Valley retreated towards the Potomac, Federal units occupying Washington's forts and rifle pits remained in their camps, cooking and eating breakfast, clearing brush and digging trenches. At dawn, General McCook had sent two companies of infantry after Early's retreating column to determine their route of retreat. Losing their focus, they did nothing but capture stragglers between Fort Stevens and Leesborough (Wheaton). While some Federals claimed that they lacked cavalry in sufficient numbers to pursue Early's column, in fact the only serious pursuit during the first part of Wednesday was mounted by the 800 troops of Colonel Lowell's 2nd Massachusetts Cavalry. Cavalry was available; however, infantry pursuit failed to materialize, which disgusted President Lincoln and underscored the need for a unified command structure with clear lines of authority.

While neither Halleck, Augur, McCook or Wright offered a coordinated plan of pursuit, Lowell's California Brigade left Tennallytown, riding out from Fort Reno on Rockville Pike. They discovered the tail end of the Confederate column, about 4½ miles below Rockville, around 9:15 A.M. Lowell got to within a half mile of Rockville that morning, determining that Early's Confederates were retreating in two columns: one from Sligo, passing "by the old city road from Leesborough," and the other disappearing up Rockville Pike from the vicinity of Bethesda Church. At 10:15 A.M., Lowell sent a message to the Federal high command in Washington, stating, "Any serious attempt against them with infantry must, I think, be made soon." However, the tail end of Early's retreating column left Rockville around 1 P.M., and still no Federal infantry appeared. Lowell waited with the 2nd Massachusetts on a hill, a mile and a half south of town, until the last of Early's troops left Rockville.[2]

A few hundred Californians had come east in 1862 to fill the ranks of the 2nd Massachusetts as part of an agreement between Massachusetts governor John Andrew and J. Sewall Reed, a Bay State native living in California. They had seen frustrating duty chasing Mosby's Rangers without success and had endured the mind numbing routine of picket duty. The Californians were eager for a fight, but Lowell had no desire to engage Early's main army with his small force. Nevertheless, he continued to track the Army of the Valley, and about a half hour after the last Confederate left, the 2nd Massachusetts entered Rockville.

The Army of the Valley headed towards Poolesville, 15 miles due west, marching first along West Montgomery Avenue, then making a sharp left turn around a curve, onto the Darnestown Road. Meanwhile, Lowell had placed Major Fry's brigade on high ground, east of town near St. Mary's church, and the road to Baltimore. He then ordered Lt. Colonel Caspar Crowninshield to take four companies and keep an eye on the Rebels as they retreated up the Darnestown Road. However, unknown to Lowell, Early had been informed of the Federal presence in Rockville, probably by Confederate sympathizers. Lowell accompanied the remaining eight companies into town, halting them in formation along Montgomery Avenue, a short distance west of Courthouse Square.

Meanwhile, the Confederate rear guard, composed of infantry under Colonel William Lowther Jackson, and Johnson's 1st Maryland Cavalry, took up defensive positions along Watts Branch, a shallow stream running parallel to West Montgomery Avenue. Jackson's infantry halted on both sides of the stream, on Montgomery Avenue and Darnestown Road, with Johnson's brigade nearby, out of sight around the bend in the road. Jackson was a cousin of Major General Thomas J. "Stonewall" Jackson. He had been a lawyer and judge in West Virginia before the war. However, thus far he held an undistinguished combat record, and in December 1863 Jackson had nearly failed to intercept a Federal cavalry force, retreating from a raid on the Virginia & Tennessee railroad, at Salem, Virginia (Jackson attacked the tail end of the Federal column). For that near failure and a few more conspicuous failures, he became known by the derisive nickname "Mudwall."

Lowell and a few officers had dismounted and walking back into Courthouse Square climbed the steps of the Montgomery House hotel a few minutes after 2 P.M. While his officers had dinner, Lowell sat down to write a report, with the troops still mounted on Montgomery Avenue. However, angered at his rear guard for allowing Lowell's Federals to get so close, Early ordered Johnson to re-capture Rockville and drive the 2nd Massachusetts back down the road towards Washington.

Johnson had just formed the 1st Maryland into attack formation, around the bend on Darnestown Road, when Crowninshield's portion of the 2nd Massachusetts appeared over the hill from Rockville, trotting westward on unpaved Montgomery Avenue. Crowninshield spied Jackson's infantry along Watts Branch, mistakenly assuming that they comprised the entire Federal rear guard. He formed his four companies into attack formation, and as the blue-coated troopers were drawing their sabers to charge Jackson's infantry, Johnson's Maryland line cavalry came charging around the bend in a fierce onslaught. Pistols cracked and sabers drew blood, and the Watts Branch Valley echoed with the sounds of battle. The Federals fired a volley at Jackson's troops, then fled back towards Rockville with Johnson's cavalry close on their heels. Several Union troops fell, badly wounded. Only a few minutes after Johnson's counterattack, Lowell heard the sounds of the fighting coming closer. In the midst of writing his report, he put down his pen, and hurried out of the hotel. As he mounted his horse, riderless horses and panic-stricken troops from Crowninshield's column came racing back into town and into the mounted troops in formation near Courthouse Square.

With no time to form a battle line, Lowell shouted above the din, "Halt! Dismount! And let your horse go!" About 50 or 60 Federal troops obeyed the order, taking up defensive positions along two sides of the Courthouse Square triangle. A volley from Lowell's troops, using rapid-fire, seven-shot Spencer carbines, broke the momentum of the Confederate cavalry charge, with two or three gray-clad troopers falling from their saddles. In the heat and humidity, choking dust clouds obscured both man and beast as Johnson's rebels regrouped with Lowell's Federals shooting at them from behind trees, woodpiles, and houses. Panicked residents waited out the fighting in their cellars. The 1st Maryland charged a second time, only to be met with a second volley from the Federals' Spencer carbines. Johnson responded by bringing up infantry from Watts Branch.

Time seemed to stand still as blue and gray clad troopers exchanged fire in and around Courthouse Square and along the dusty streets of Rockville. Captain Wilson C. Nicholas, of the 1st Maryland, was captured by the Federals. At one point, Johnson himself was nearly captured. Hit by a Confederate bullet, Private James Hill managed to make it inside the gate of the three story Beall house. Margaret Beall opened the door, and dragged Hill inside, under a hail of Confederate bullets. She nursed him and treated his wound, and several days later Hill was taken to a hospital in Washington. He would return to Rockville twenty years later to thank Margaret Beall.[3]

Johnson's Confederates were armed with single-shot, muzzle-loading rifles and cap-and-ball pistols, not nearly as effective as the Federals' Spencer carbines. Nevertheless, the more numerous Confederates began to push Lowell's Federals out of Rockville. The 2nd Massachusetts fell back slowly, firing as they went. Johnson attempted a flanking maneuver, to strike them from behind, but that failed. Lowell's force retreated to a hill, about a mile and a half south of town. Finally satisfied that the Federals were gone, Johnson left 30 men to guard the town, then rode west with the rest of his force to join the main army.

While Johnson was engaging the 2nd Massachusetts, the Army of the Valley had marched westward, along the Darnestown Road, stopping that evening in the vicinity of Poolesville. Arriving in the vicinity a few hours later, Johnson established a defensive line a few hundred yards west of the Seneca Creek crossing on the road to Poolesville, awaiting pursuing Federals. The next morning, he greeted Harry Gilmor's cavalry, returning from their raid on Magnolia Station. Johnson greeted Gilmor cordially, exclaiming that he thought Gilmor had been captured, and expressing great satisfaction at his arrival.

Wright's infantry, 14,000 strong, finally began their pursuit of Early, leaving Fort Stevens around 3 P.M. on 13 July. They marched in a southwesterly direction to Tennal-lytown where they took the River Road westward. By 8 P.M., they had advanced as far as Offutt's Crossroads (Potomac), but the troops were played out by their 15-mile march, scanty rations, and the ever-present heat and humidity. Wright had his troops on the march again at 4:30 the next morning. Marching west towards Poolesville, most of the Federal force arrived there around 6 P.M. However, the tail end of Wright's column was still close to Washington, and the 19th Corps, led by Major General William H. Emory, camped ten miles short of Poolesville. Wright, however, didn't appear to be confident that his force was sufficient to the task of catching Early. In a telegram to Halleck, he described his force as "wholly insufficient to justify the following up of the enemy on the other side of the Potomac." Wright then commented about awaiting further instructions, and rested his force the next day, curious behavior for a commander engaged in a vigorous pursuit. Meanwhile, Early pushed his troops hard on 13 July; as Johnson's cavalry engaged the 2nd Massachusetts in Rockville, the main body of the Army of the Valley rested near Seneca Creek. That evening, Early's infantry was on the move again, tramping through Poolesville and camping near White's Ford around midnight.[4]

White's Ford, where the Potomac was shallow, was a crossing point of choice for Confederates throughout the war. It was (is) located about two and a half miles below the mouth of the Monocacy River, just upstream from the northern end of Mason's Island.[5] The river banks on the Virginia side had to be dug down to permit access by Early's wagon trains and artillery; on the Maryland side, the C & O canal posed an obstacle for the Confederates. Bridges over the canal locks and culverts under the canal had been constructed when the canal was built. Culverts allowed people and vehicles to reach the river; however, Early's wagons proved too large to pass through them. Another bridge, for the wagons, had to be built over a lock on the canal.

Early's infantry and artillery crossed unopposed all day on 14 July, as Johnson's rear guard cavalry kept the pursuing 2nd Massachusetts at bay. Along with the troops, thousands of cattle and horses were herded across into Virginia, and in his saddlebags Early carried $220,000 in new Northern greenbacks, ransomed from Hagerstown, Frederick, and Middletown. The money was used to reimburse some residents south of the Potomac whose homes had been burned by Federal troops. By the evening of 14 July, the Army of the Valley had completed crossing the Potomac, bivouacking at Big Spring, two miles north of Leesburg. Johnson's 1st Maryland Cavalry crossed the Potomac, at White's Ford, on the evening of 14 July. However, Early realized that Wright's pursuit was not aggressive, and he gave the Army of the Valley a well-earned rest day at Big Spring. The only note-worthy event occurring on 15 July was an execution, on Poolesville's town common.

"As we entered the village of Poolesville this morning, a staff officer told me to turn right upon reaching the Common and march across it. We did so and much to our surprise and horror we saw a man dangling by the neck at the end of a rope attached to a scaffold. He proved to be a soldier named Heimes who belonged of the 65th New York Volunteers who had been acting as a spy for the rebels. Being detected, he was tried by a court martial, promptly found guilty, sentenced to die and hung. He had on part of a uniform and was a miserable looking fellow. I understand that he had made several visits to the enemy."[6] Wright also gave his troops a rest, not crossing the Potomac until 16 July. By then, the Army of the Valley was on its way through the Blue Ridge, at Snickers Gap, on the other side of Loudoun County. Privately seething at the fact that the Army of the Valley had "accomplished all they wished to or rather expected to — carried off all they needed from Maryland, while we were squat around Washington, trembling in our boots,"[7] President Lincoln expressed his disgust at the slow pace of Wright's pursuit: "He [Wright] thinks the enemy are all across the Potomac but that he has halted and sent out an infantry reconnaissance, for fear he might come across the rebels and catch some of them."[8]

Part of the problem with the Federal pursuit of Early was the conflict between Grant's vague orders and his publicly stated suggestions as to how best to destroy the Army of the Valley. Wright's force was to continue to pursue Early as long as there was a chance of "punishing" him; then they were to return to the Army of the Potomac at Petersburg. With well over 100,000 troops in the lines at Petersburg, opposing approximately 50,000 Confederates, it is difficult to appreciate why Grant needed Wright's force of 14,000 returned, especially since his public comments rang with phrases such as "getting south of the enemy," "following him to the death," and that Early could be destroyed "if they will push boldly from all quarters."[9] Grant was at City Point, Virginia, concentrating on defeating the Army of Northern Virginia, too far removed from Washington and the Shenandoah Valley for his authority to be completely effective. In addition, the lack of an adequate response from the commanders on the scene — generals Wright and Hunter — made for an unsuccessful pursuit of the Army of the Valley.

Hunter's army arrived at Cumberland, Maryland, on 8 July, by the B & O railroad. Advance elements of his force arrived in Martinsburg, West Virginia, a few days later. There he received a message from Wright, at Poolesville, on 14 July, requesting that his Army of the Kanawha join forces with his at Leesburg. The next day, 15 July, he received a telegram from Halleck, directing him to put his troops under Crook's command, or send them to Wright and serve under Wright. Considering himself insulted, Hunter asked to be relieved of command. He dispatched 7,000 infantry, led by Brigadier General Jeremiah C. Sullivan, and 2,000 cavalry, led by Brigadier General Alfred Duffie. However, instead of marching to Leesburg, they followed Hunter's orders, turning right at Hills-borough, marching through Purcellville towards Aldie, at the foot of the Blue Ridge. Sullivan and Duffie would have cut off Early's line of retreat had they kept on marching towards Leesburg. Had that happened, the Federal force might well have kept the Army of the Valley occupied until Wright's force crossed the Potomac and came up behind Early's force. However, Sullivan's and Duffie's forces camped at Hillsborough on the evening of 15 July, out of harm's way. As the Army of the Valley slowly advanced towards Snickers Gap the next day, General Crook arrived at Hillsborough, taking over command of the combined 9,000 Federals bivouacked there from Sullivan. Crook ordered Duffie to find the Army of the Valley, and he did, with a unit of Federal cavalry attacking Early's columns near Purcellville, just after noon.[10] Led by Colonel William Tibbits, 300 Federal horsemen charged the Confederate wagon train, capturing 37 wagons and burning 40.

His pride preventing him from serving under Wright, Hunter didn't participate in tracking down the Army of the Valley. Possibly in response to the 15 July telegram from Halleck, but entirely in character, he ordered the burning of the homes of a few influential secessionist residents of Jefferson County, West Virginia. On 17 July, Hunter ordered Captain F.G. Martindale, of the 1st New York Cavalry, to take a few men to Charlestown and "burn the dwelling house and out-buildings of Andrew Hunter," his [Hunter's] first cousin. Andrew Hunter was a well-known attorney who had served as prosecutor for the Commonwealth of Virginia during the trial of John Brown. Martindale's squad arrived, gave Mrs. Hunter and her family a few minutes to evacuate then burned their home. Following General Hunter's orders closely, Martindale didn't allow Andrew Hunter's family to remove any clothing, family portraits, or furniture from the house before burning it (Andrew Hunter was not at home). In addition, Andrew Hunter often wore a gold ring, given to him out of affection by "Cousin David," as it was inscribed.

Martindale also burned Fountain Rock, home of Andrew R. Boteler, a member of the Confederate Congress, and Bedford, the home of Edmund J. Lee, first cousin of Robert E. Lee, where Hunter's niece, Helen, was often welcomed. Neither Colonel Boteler nor his wife were at home when Martindale's squad arrived. Fountain Rock was then occupied by their two daughters, Helen, and Mrs. David Shepherd, a widow with three children, ranging in age from eighteen months to five years. Some of Martindale's troops plundered the house, as Boteler's daughters pleaded to be allowed to save some personal property. They were able to save a few things, however, Martindale's men piled furniture in the rooms, then set it ablaze with kerosene. Helen Boteler, a musician, begged the blue-coated troopers to save her piano, in vain. Enveloped in smoke, with fire consuming an adjacent room, she sat at the piano, playing and singing "Thy Will be Done." As the flames crept closer, she closed and locked the piano, and left the house. Less than half an hour after Martindale's squad arrived, Fountain Rock was engulfed in flames.[11]

Boydville, the home of Charles J. Faulkner, at Martinsburg, was spared when President Lincoln intervened, probably because Faulkner had been a congressman and a member of the U.S. Diplomatic Service. However, Hunter threatened to burn down all of Charlestown, as he had earlier burned the entire town of Buchanan, Virginia, on the way to Lynchburg. In addition, Hunter threatened to burn every house in Clarke County, because that locale had recorded only two votes against the Virginia ordinance of secession in 1861. At that point, burning the homes of civilians had become part of the Federal policy of total war, to which Lincoln assented.[12]

Henrietta Lee's reaction provides some insight into the suffering of Americans south of the Potomac, at the hands of Federal troops. Heart-broken, she wrote the general,

> Yesterday your underling, Captain Martindale ... executed your infamous order and burned my house. You have had the satisfaction ... of receiving from him the information that your orders were fulfilled to the letter, the dwelling and every out building, seven in number ... being burned. I, therefore, a helpless woman whom you have cruelly wronged, address you, a Major General of the United States Army, and demand why this was done? My husband was absent — an exile. He has never been a politician or in any way engaged in the struggle now going on.... The house was built by my father, a Revolutionary soldier, who served the whole seven years for your independence. There I was born; there the sacred dead repose. It was my house and my home, and there had your niece, Miss Griffith, who lived among us all this horrid war, up to the present moment, met with all kindness and hospitality at my hands. Was it for this, you have turned me, my young daughter, and little son out upon the world without shelter? ... Hyena-like, you have torn my heart to pieces ... and demon-like, you have done it without even the pretext of revenge, for I never saw or harmed you ... your very name is execrated by your own men for the cruel work you give them to do.... Your name will stand on History's pages as the Hunter of weak women and innocent children.... Can I say "God forgive you"? No prayer can be offered for you! Were it possible for human lips to raise your name heavenward, angels would thrust the foul thing back down again, and demons claim their own....[13]

Hunter then instituted a program of retribution against Confederate-sympathizing residents of Maryland in response to the damage and ill-will caused by the depredations of Early's

Major General David Hunter (Library of Congress)

troops on their march through the Free State. In response to an 18 July complaint from Major John I. Yellott, Federal provost marshal in Frederick, concerning the actions of Confederate sympathizers during Early's raid, which included pointing out the dwellings of Unionists, Hunter ordered the immediate arrest of all persons known to have engaged in such acts. He ordered male heads of household to be placed in the Federal military prison in Wheeling, while their families were to be sent south, beyond Federal lines. Yellott mitigated the severity of Hunter's order in Frederick by merely having all male residents of Frederick take the oath of allegiance; however, on 1 August, Hunter ordered the arrest and expulsion of known Confederate sympathizers in Frederick. Lincoln, however, suspended the order. In addition, John W. Baughman's secessionist newspaper, the *Frederick Citizen*, was silenced, as were a few others.[14]

Nevertheless, despite Hunter's enthusiasm for targeting civilians and destroying their homes, action taken against Maryland's Confederate sympathizers was largely limited to forced monetary reimbursement of Unionists who had suffered damages during Early's raid. As for Hunter, he was formally relieved of command by Grant on 7 August. He would later serve on the military tribunal trying the conspirators charged in Lincoln's assassination. After 42 years in the army, he lived out the remainder of his life on his military pension in Washington, D.C., dying in February 1886, at age 83. However, try as he might, he never re-established relations with his Virginia relatives, and never set foot in the Shenandoah Valley again.[15]

The Battle of Cool Spring — Island Ford

Perhaps no event during Early's raid illustrated Federal incompetence at catching and punishing the Army of the Valley better than the fight at Cool Spring, also known as Island Ford. After leaving their camp at Big Spring on 15 July, Early's force had marched west from Leesburg, along the Winchester Pike, through the pleasant hill country of western Loudoun County, then through Snickers Gap in the Blue Ridge. As the troops passed through the gap, along a rough country road, they were treated to awesome scenery ahead and behind. Around noon, Early's veterans halted on a small plateau on the western slope of the Blue Ridge, taking in the scenery. To the west was the Shenandoah Valley, with glimpses of the Shenandoah River, the "shining door" to the valley, winding northwards to greet them. To the east was the Loudoun Valley, a checkerboard of farm fields, orchards and well appointed manor houses. After crossing the Shenandoah, a short distance west of and below the Gap, the Army of the Valley bivouacked about two miles west of the river, posting strong pickets at the ford at Castleman's Ferry. By mid-afternoon, however, the east bank of the Shenandoah swarmed with blue-coated troops, many cooking dinner, with "all the liberated hogs, chickens, honey and potatoes" they had taken from the farms of Loudoun County, demonstrating that there was, in fact, sufficient food in that locale to have supported the Army of the Valley in their advance on Washington.[16]

Part of the Federal 6th Corps, a unit of the 22nd Pennsylvania Cavalry, the 23rd Illinois Infantry, and the 10th West Virginia Infantry, rested on the western slope of the Blue Ridge. They made three attempts to cross the Shenandoah over two days but were driven back each time. Wright ordered Crook, popular among his West Virginia infantry, to follow the

Army of the Valley to determine their line of retreat. Duffie's cavalry and Mulligan's Illinois infantry pushed remaining Confederates across the river on 17 July. Several subsequent Federal attempts to cross were driven back. However, Crook, standing on a bluff observing the action, continued to believe that Confederate resistance was only cavalry.

A short time thereafter, Wright and advance units of the 6th and 19th Corps began to arrive at Snickers Gap. Wright learned that an enemy force had crossed the treacherous, 300 yard wide Shenandoah, and was holding the ford at Castleman's Ferry. Since Crook believed the enemy force to be cavalry, Wright didn't have more accurate knowledge and stayed with his original plan "to cross the river if practicable and attack."[17] Wright ordered Crook to send troops across the Shenandoah to determine Early's strength. Sometime before 2 P.M., Crook, brevetted a major general that day, ordered Colonel Joseph Thoburn to take three brigades, march farther north on the east side, cross the river, then march back south, and dislodge the presumed Confederate cavalry force holding Castleman's Ferry. Crook hoped that Thoburn's foray would clear the ferry of Confederates, allowing the rest of the Federal forces to cross, and determine the whereabouts of the main Confederate force.[18]

As Thoburn's troops marched northwards, Crook and Wright climbed to a bluff about 200 feet above the river, and surveyed the scene below. They were soon joined by a battery of the 5th U.S. Artillery. They could see distant Confederate pickets on the hills on the west side of the Shenandoah. The rebel pickets could also see them. On the evening of 17 July, Early had ordered Breckinridge to "make a most determined resistance if any attempt at a crossing was made!" Responsible for the areas above and below the crossing, Breckinridge posted a strong picket from Gordon's division near Castleman's Ferry. Gordon's pickets had rebuffed earlier Federal efforts to cross.

As Thoburn's infantry continued their northward trek, the 5th U.S. Artillery opened on a conspicuous circle of enemy wagons about a mile to the west, towards the main Confederate encampment near the Winchester Pike at Webbtown. Thoburn was guided by a Confederate deserter who knew the forest trails and river fords. His troops turned right, into a forest on the property of Judge Richard Parker, who had presided at the trial of John Brown. Marching through the fields of the Retreat farm, they eventually came to a place two miles north of Castleman's Ferry, called Parker's or Island Ford, after two small islands in the middle of the Shenandoah, with the Westwood and Cool Spring farms on the opposite side. The islands were separated from the west bank by a narrow channel made shallow by dry summer weather. On the east bank, the terrain dropped abruptly to the narrow riverbank, while west of the river the terrain was undulating, with several ridges about a third of a mile distant from the riverbank. The height of the ridges above the riverbank gave the defending Confederates an advantage over their Federal attackers.

The head of Thoburn's column, the 34th Massachusetts Infantry, led by Colonel George D. Wells, crossed the Shenandoah and captured a number of Confederate pickets. They told Thoburn that two infantry regiments guarded Castleman's Ferry, and that Rodes' and Gordon's divisions were in the rear. Thoburn forwarded this news to Crook; the courier came back with orders from Crook not to advance any farther and to await the arrival of a division from the 6th Corps. Thoburn arranged his units in two lines, with Wells commanding on the left, Colonel Daniel Frost in the center, and Colonel

William Ely on the right. The first line formed behind a ridge about 75 yards west of the river, and the second behind a low stone fence near the riverbank. In front of the Federals, the ground gradually rose to a low ridge several hundred yards away, shortly to be occupied by Confederate infantry.

Soon thereafter, the Federals saw a large dust cloud to the west, indicating the approach of a large body of troops. Rodes' infantry struck Ely's Federals on the right flank, enfilading them. The rebel infantry retreated, facing the combined fire of Frost's and Wells' troops. The Confederates regrouped and charged a second time, causing Ely's Federals to flee towards the low stone fence. The panic among Ely's troops affected Frost's men; they too turned and fled towards the stone wall, and in turn, Wells' men did likewise. However, the Federals behind the stone wall arose and fired a punishing volley into Rodes' pursuing Confederates, sending them back over the ridge.

Meanwhile, Crook had asked Wright for permission to withdraw, since no other Federal unit had crossed the river in support. Wright refused, instead ordering General Ricketts, who had fought at Monocacy, to cross over and support Thoburn. After witnessing Rodes' attacks, Ricketts refused Wright's order. In response, Wright did nothing. Neither Crook nor any of Thoburn's troops could understand why they were sacrificed; Crook never forgave Wright. As Crook stated, "Gen. Ricketts' division was lying just in the rear of my men. He and I rode down together to where the crossing was to be made. By the time we had reached this place, the enemy had shown such strength that Gen. Ricketts declined to go to their support, and allowed many of my men to be sacrificed. I lost some valuable men here, murdered by incompetency or worse. I reported the facts to Gen. Wright, but that was the end of it, while I suffered in the estimation of my men as having made a useless sacrifice."[19] Ricketts, who had brought charges against Colonel John Staunton for failing to arrive on the Monocacy battlefield in support of Wallace, now himself had failed to support Thoburn. Staunton was cashiered; no action was taken against either Ricketts or Wright.

Rodes' troops charged yet again, but were repelled a third time. Some Federals, however, panicked and fled into the Shenandoah, a few drowning in the treacherous waters. However, with darkness fast approaching, Crook ordered Thoburn to withdraw across the river. Thoburn, who had coolly made a stand against the hard-charging Confederates, withdrew across the Shenandoah, sustaining losses of 65 killed, 301 wounded, and 56 missing. Confederate losses were somewhat less than 400. Troops of the 170th Ohio National Guard were the last Federals to cross the river around 9 P.M. Some of the wounded were carried across where a few died on the east bank; the troops arrived back in camp soaking wet, hungry, covered with mud, and bewildered and angry at the lack of support. Colonel Ely, who had led the Federal right during the battle, and whose regiment had been winnowed down to 60 troops, remarked, "I am willing to lead you against an equal, or even double your number of rebels, but this being shut up in a slaughter pen I cannot stand." Undoubtedly Wright's dilatory pursuit of Early, and approaching darkness, influenced Rickett's refusal to obey his order.[20]

Casualties on the Confederate side were also heavy, partly because of the lack of medical care. Many badly wounded rebels, suffering terribly, lay on the ground unattended, with nothing but a blanket between them and the ground. The surgeons and their attendants appeared unconcerned, and made little or no effort to find wounded troops in the darkness. Billy Beavans, a popular soldier, of the 43rd North Carolina Infantry, had been shot in the calf. He lay on the ground, at an improvised hospital in a rear area. The surgeons removed his leg, without anesthesia. Beavans died of shock and infection some days later.[21]

But perhaps the saddest epitaph to the Island Ford battle was the death of Colonel Daniel Frost. He had led Thoburn's third brigade, in the center of the Federal defensive line. Before the fighting began, Frost encountered his brother-in-law, a member of the 170th Ohio National Guard. Frost showed him some pictures of his family, commenting on how much he would give to see them again. During the fighting, Frost was mortally wounded, shot in the abdomen. He was carried to a log house near the Winchester Pike. Living nearby was Eben Frost, a well-known local resident, and Colonel Frost's cousin. Preparing his last will and testament, Frost requested his cousin visit him on his deathbed. Eben Frost refused; a staunch secessionist, he stated to the effect that if Colonel Frost had stayed home, he wouldn't have been shot.

The Island Ford battle ended with an artillery duel, with red-hot shells tracing fiery arcs through the darkened sky, lighting up the night. In the words of Crook's West Virginians, the three hour engagement had been "a right smart little fight." Many had been sacrificed, but Wright's Federals were no closer to catching and punishing the Army of the Valley.[22]

Stephenson's Depot — Ramseur Defeated

With the slow pace of his pursuit, and his failure to support Crook's troops at Island Ford, it became clear that Wright was avoiding a full-scale confrontation with Early. All through 19 July, scattered Federals and Confederates shot at each other while their comrades rested. Early received a report that a large Federal cavalry force, led by William Averell, was advancing on Winchester, menacing his rear. He responded by ordering Ramseur to march his division, along with Brigadier General John C. Vaughn's cavalry, to Winchester, 17 miles to the west. Ramseur was to drive Averell's cavalry northwards, and remove the sick and wounded, and stores from Winchester. Dawn on 20 July found Ramseur and his brigade two miles north of Winchester. He sent Vaughn northward to scout the approaching Federals. Several hours later, in response to a request from Vaughn, Ramseur sent a battery of cannon, and instructed him to push the Federals back to Bunker Hill, twelve miles north of Winchester. Two hours later, an officer from Vaughn's command arrived to request of Ramseur that he prepare an ambush into which Vaughn would entice the Federals. The North Carolinian declined. Two hours later, Ramseur heard gunfire to the north. Ordering his division to march towards the firing, he soon encountered Vaughn, retreating southwards. Inquiring as to why Vaughn was retreating, Ramseur learned that Averell's force wasn't large — he led one regiment of infantry and one regiment of cavalry, and a battery of four cannon. Relying on Vaughn's information, without getting verification, he thought the Federals less numerous than his own force; he sensed a chance for victory. With the troops of Brigadier General Robert Johnston on the right, those of Brigadier General W. Gaston Lewis on the left, and those under Brigadier General Robert D. Lilley in reserve, Ramseur's force marched forward to engage Averell's Federals.

Woods obscured a good part of the field as Ramseur's troops came within range of the Federal guns. What happened next was described by a Confederate artillerist, Private Henry Robinson Berkeley: "Just as we reached the farther edge of a piece of woods, while our men were still in line of march; the Yanks opened on us from behind a stone fence at close quarters before our line of battle could be formed, or our men load their guns which were empty. Our men gave way and, [with] the Yanks charging when they saw our confusion, the whole thing soon became a panic. We lost our entire battery, bringing out only one limber and a caisson. We had twenty-five horses killed and four men killed in our battery."[23]

Ramseur was unpleasantly surprised to observe at least three large regiments to the right of Lewis' troops, approaching rapidly and overlapping Lewis' left by at least 200 yards. He ordered Lilley to move his reserve troops to cover Lewis's left. However, Lilley's men moved very slowly, and before they could carry out their orders, two of Lewis' regiments unaccountably broke and ran. The panic was contagious; soon most of the Confederates were fleeing towards the rear. He desperately attempted to rally the panic-stricken men without success. Averell's Federals drove the rebel infantry through the woods and fields towards Winchester. Confederate losses were 73 killed and 130 wounded, with 17 officers and 250 men captured. The Federals lost 53 killed, 155 wounded and 6 missing, a total of 214. However, fortunately for the Army of the Valley, Averell thought himself greatly outnumbered and retreated fifteen minutes later without seriously pursuing Ramseur.

In response to an article printed in a Richmond newspaper a short time later, claiming that John Pegram's Virginia infantry saved Ramseur's brigade from annihilation, North Carolina infantry Colonel C.C. Blacknall gave his experience of the fight at Stephenson's Depot:

> The truth of the matter ... was as follows: General Ramseur marched the division down the Winchester road and from the reports of the officer commanding our cavalry in front, was led to believe that the enemy in small force were at a point more distant than we found them to be after reaching the body of woods where our cavalry were in line of battle. General Ramseur formed Hoke's brigade on the left and Johnston's on the right of the road. Pegram being in the rear when we suddenly found the enemy in a field, immediately in our front, we advanced and engaged him without hesitation, our men advancing under a heavy and destructive fire in splendid style. The enemy's line in the meantime overlapping Hoke's left and pouring into his flank a heavy enfilade fire which caused his left regiment to give way, the panic being communicated to the other regiments of the brigade, each one in turn falling back hastily and in some confusion. While this was going on, Johnston's brigade was steadily advancing.... The left of our brigade, the Twelfth and Twenty-Third Regiments, had advanced to within sixty yards of the enemy's line of battle, and every man was standing up manfully when our left was suddenly uncovered by the falling back of Hoke's brigade, the enemy pouring in a large force immediately on our flank. Our little brigade being alone and unsupported, were ... compelled to retreat or be captured.[24]

Upon learning of his defeat, Early stated that Ramseur had advanced "without taking the proper precautions," that is, without obtaining corroborating information concerning the number of troops in Averell's brigade, and their proximity, and without giving his men sufficient time to load their guns. However, even though two Richmond newspapers published scathing accounts of the defeat at Stephenson's Depot, Early, Rodes, and Gordon all came to Ramseur's defense; Lee whitewashed the battle, observing that Ramseur attacked, fought a much superior force, and "was compelled to fall back on fortifications at Winchester." Robert Rodes, a close friend, defended Ramseur in a report, dated 12 September, by pointing out that he relied on Vaughn's (an unreliable cavalryman) information concerning the size of the Federal opposition; he thus held Pegram's brigade in reserve. Rodes concluded that Ramseur wasn't responsible for the defeat; rather it was the fault of the "panic-stricken men."[25]

Second Kernstown — Early Defeats Crook

Meanwhile, Wright's pursuing Federals had at last crossed the Shenandoah on 20 July. Wright had assumed, without the slightest evidence, for at least three days that Early was in retreat to join the Army of Northern Virginia at Petersburg to reinforce Lee. In a dispatch to Halleck on 17 July, sent from Clark's Gap, Wright stated, in part: "I have no doubt that the enemy is in full retreat for Richmond, but the cavalry reports ... will settle the matter. He [Early] is represented as much demoralized, though this is doubtful as regards his old infantry force." The battle at Island Ford failed to convince him that Early wasn't on the way to re-join the Army of Northern Virginia. At Berryville, Wright ordered his column to about-face and march back to Washington. In a dispatch to Halleck on 21 July, he explained his abrupt retreat: "Conceiving the object of the expedition to be accomplished, I at once started back.... Two days easy march will bring the command to Washington." Wright further stated, "Our losses at Snicker's Ferry will not exceed 200." He either wasn't aware that Federal casualties at Island Ford were 422 killed, wounded and missing, or refused to admit it.[26]

Early took full advantage of Wright's abrupt retreat. On the morning of 23 July, President Lincoln wired Hunter, inquiring, "Are you able to take care of the enemy when he turns back upon you, as he probably will on finding that Wright has left?" An hour later, Hunter replied in the negative, claiming that his "latest advices from the front ... do not lead me to apprehend such a movement. General Crook has information, upon which he relies, that Early left his position at Berryville suddenly upon the arrival of a courier from Richmond with orders to fall back upon that place."[27] Wright, Hunter, and Grant were expecting Early's force to rejoin Lee's army at Petersburg. Blundering again, Grant ordered Wright's pursuit force to return to City Point, hoping to use them to launch an attack on Lee's army before the Army of the Valley could return. However, Early refused to cooperate with Grant's perceptions.

Upon Wright's withdrawal, Crook's 12,000 troops advanced up the Valley to Kernstown, four miles south of Winchester. Crook had three infantry divisions plus Averell's cavalry, numbering about 2,500. Crook had Duffie's cavalry reconnoiter southward, but as Crook stated, "He [Duffie] came in one day and reported the enemy advancing in force, infantry, artillery, and cavalry. Having but little confidence in him, I took an escort and went in person some distance beyond the point where Gen. Duffie reported the enemy, and, finding nothing, returned. The next day he made a similar report. I had so little confidence in anything he said or did, that I placed but little confidence in his report."[28]

However, early on the morning of 24 July, Crook's pickets discovered Early's entire force moving towards them, northwards down the Valley Turnpike. The Army of the Valley applied intense pressure all along Crook's front. At Bartonsville, Ramseur's division was ordered west along back roads to the Middle Road. Gordon's, Rodes', and Gabriel Wharton's troops continued northwards, down the Valley Turnpike. Early then sent one column of cavalry to the west, and another to the east, to converge just north of Winchester, with the goal of cutting off Crook's retreat. A cavalry screen led the army's advance down the pike, engaging Crook's main force at Kernstown around 10 A.M. Early's infantry reached Kernstown around noon, with Gordon's troops deploying to the left of the turnpike, and Wharton's to the right. Ramseur's force fanned out across the Middle Road, while Rodes' deployed east of the turnpike, into and through some ravines.

Meanwhile, Crook's force deployed on Pritchard's Hill; upon receiving word that Early's troops were approaching, he formed a battle line with two of his three divisions just north of Hogg's Run. Crook's center was led by the outgoing Colonel James Mulligan, who posted his troops behind a stone fence at the Pritchard House. Mulligan was supported by Captain Henry DuPont's artillery, on Pritchard's Hill, to the rear of the Pritchard House. Brigadier General Issac Duval's two brigades were posted, one on each of Mulligan's flanks, with the brigade of future President Rutherford B. Hayes deployed east of the Valley Turnpike. Colonel Thoburn's division was held in reserve on Pritchard's Hill, while a skirmish line was thrown out near Opequon Church, with cavalry screening both Union flanks.

Around noon, Gordon's troops engaged Mulligan's Illinois infantry, west of the turnpike, near Opequon Church. Mulligan counterattacked, supported by Hayes, taking possession of the churchyard. The stone fences and cemetery headstones provided cover for Mulligan's men, under intense Confederate fire. Regrouping, Gordon's troops advanced again, forcing Mulligan to retreat a few hundred yards to the stone fence along Pritchard's Lane. Gordon's troops were stopped at Opequon Church. Crook regrouped and repositioned his troops as one of Wharton's brigades occupied Gordon's right flank. One of Duval's brigades was moved west, athwart Middle Road, while Thoburn's division was employed filling the gap between Mulligan's and Duval's troops. Some of Duffie's cavalry was brought up in support of the right flank on the Middle Road; they were also posted on Cedar Creek Grade, to the west.

Ramseur's division came forward to occupy Gordon's left flank and advanced with Gordon's men, west of Opequon Church, against Thoburn's Federals. Taking the initiative, Gordon's troops dislodged some of Thoburn's blue-coats from behind two stone fences. In response, Thoburn retreated to the base of Pritchard's Hill, with his line facing north, exposing Mulligan's right flank. Ramseur's troops turned right, engaging Thoburn's, while enfilading Mulligan's line. Meanwhile, east of the turnpike, Wharton's division threatened Hayes' brigade. In concert with Ramseur's advance, Wharton attacked around 3 P.M., turning Hayes' left flank, forcing him to retreat to the stone wall bordering the valley turnpike. Hayes, however, rallied his brigade and now faced east, at right angles to Mulligan's troops, in the center of Crook's line.

Mulligan's troops were now under fire from three directions. Mulligan himself, hit by no less than five bullets, fell mortally wounded. Resisting efforts of assistance, he ordered, "Lay me down and save the colors!" He died a short time later. Federal resistance in the center of Crook's line soon collapsed; blue-coated troops began a hasty retreat through the streets of Winchester. Hayes' brigade made a stand atop Pritchard's Hill, allowing DuPont's artillery to escape; Duffie's cavalry counterattacked along the Middle Road, allowing Thoburn's infantry to leave the battlefield intact.

Meanwhile, Rodes' division marched northwards, to cut off the Federal retreat, following the Union troops as far as Stephenson's Depot, four miles north of Winchester, capturing hundreds of prisoners. However, Early's cavalry failed to advance, allowing the greater part of Crook's troops to escape. Major General Robert Ransom, commander of the rebel cavalry, sat out the action at Kernstown because of illness. Early made no effort to replace him; however, he did blame his cavalry for the army not being able to catch and destroy Crook's force. Leaderless, the rebel cavalry wasn't a factor in the battle. Crook's routed Federals retreated all the way to Bunker Hill; they reached and crossed the Potomac, arriving at Williamsport, Maryland, on 27 July. From there, they retreated behind the fortifications atop Maryland Heights, across the Potomac from Harpers Ferry. Having expelled the Federals, Early was once again master of the Shenandoah Valley. He was succeeding in his mission of diverting attention from Lee's besieged Army of Northern Virginia at Petersburg, and of posing a continuing threat to Washington and the North. In the succeeding weeks, Grant would finally be forced to address that threat, once and for all.[29]

CHAPTER 8

Chambersburg — Twice Sacrificed

In the wake of Crook's defeat at Second Kernstown, the route of the Federal retreat, from Winchester to the Potomac, was strewn with debris, mute testimony to the speed of the Union withdrawal. Twelve caissons and seventy-two wagons, most of them burned, greeted the Army of the Valley as they pursued Crook's Federals.[1] In a heavy rain on 25 July, Early's troops chased Crook's demoralized force into Martinsburg, where some fought the hard-charging Confederates in the streets. That evening, Crook withdrew his force to the Potomac opposite Williamsport; the next day, 26 July, the exhausted Federals withdrew across the river, camping that evening near Boonsboro. Averell's cavalry retreated to the vicinity of Hagerstown, while troops from Averell's and Duffie's commands guarded fords on the Potomac, from Williamsport to well south of Hagerstown.

At Martinsburg, in accordance with Lee's orders, Early's men destroyed the B & O railroad warehouses, machine shops, rolling stock, and track. Lee's purpose in destroying the B & O was to halt, or severely reduce, coal shipments to Northern cities, especially Washington, D.C., such that Northern civilians would be deprived of it, during the upcoming fall and winter seasons. Coal was essential to survival and comfort, particularly in the large Northern cities on the East Coast. Lincoln realized the importance of continuing coal shipments and said as much in a letter to B & O president John W. Garrett in January 1865. Had a few more residents of Northern cities been deprived of it during the previous fall, Lincoln might have lost the election.[2]

Meanwhile, very concerned that Early would make another thrust at Washington, Hunter had retreated east of the Blue Ridge, keeping his force in the vicinity of Frederick, between the Army of the Valley and the Federal capital. However, his continuing pyrotechnic campaigns, this time against the homes of prominent residents of Jefferson County, West Virginia — Alexander Boteler, Edmund Lee, Andrew Hunter, and a few others — and his threat to burn the entirety of Charlestown, forced Early to make a difficult decision, and seek some form of revenge. Most of the Federal forces were located east of the Blue Ridge, with very few troops available to defend the Mason-Dixon border area. Thus the Cumberland Valley, extending well into Pennsylvania, lay open to invasion. Early therefore decided to awaken the Northern civilian population to the full horror of Federal depredations in the Shenandoah Valley. An example would be set, by way of retaliation. Chambersburg, Pennsylvania, seventeen miles north of the border, was selected as the target. As Early explained after the war, "I came to the conclusion it was time to open the eyes of the people of the North to this enormity [Federal burning of Southern homes], by an example in the way of retaliation."[3]

A force of Confederate cavalry would advance into Pennsylvania, up the Cumberland Valley's hundred mile long, level green plain, enter Chambersburg, and demand, in writing, of municipal authorities $100,000 in gold or $500,000 in greenbacks, in lieu of burning the town. The money was to be to be given directly to those whose homes Hunter had burned, in West Virginia. If the money wasn't forthcoming, Chambersburg was to be "laid in ashes." General McCausland, known as "Tiger John" to his men, received Early's order to advance on Chambersburg late in the evening of 28 July. He was to be accompanied by Bradley Johnson's brigade, consisting of over 1,500 troops from the 8th, 21st, 22nd, 27th, 34th, and 36th Virginia Cavalry, and the 1st and 2nd Maryland Cavalry; two cannon from Carter Braxton's battery, and two cannon from Johnson's Baltimore Light Artillery, the total numbering about 2,900 troops. McCausland was to be in charge; Johnson was second in command. On the evening of 29 July, the two brigades assembled near Hammond's Mill, in Berkeley County, West Virginia, preparatory to crossing the Potomac. In a few short hours, they would begin their advance northwards.[4]

Crossroads of War

Strategically located, Chambersburg played a key role in the conflict between North and South from the beginning. Abolitionist John Brown and a few of his men had stayed there in the summer and early fall of 1859. At the boarding house of Mrs. Mary Ritner, Brown and his followers devised a plan to attack the Federal arsenal at Harpers Ferry and emancipate the slaves. Brown chose Chambersburg as his base because it was the headquarters of the profitable Cumberland Valley Railroad that provided easy access to Harrisburg and Hagerstown, a short distance from Harpers Ferry. Chambersburg's role as a stopping point on the Underground Railroad may have also influenced Brown's choice.

In August of that year, Brown met with African American leader Frederick Douglass at Chambersburg, talking about capturing the arsenal at Harpers Ferry and asking him to join the expedition. Douglass declined, stating that Brown's planned attack on the U.S. arsenal "would be an attack upon the federal government," therefore treason. Brown replied, "Douglass, I must have you with me." He responded, "But it's sheer madness. You'll die. I know it." Douglass believed that Brown's planned raid was inimical to law and order and that slavery had to be ended in other ways. After Brown's October raid, some of his men escaped from jail, and seven went back to Chambersburg. Two of them were captured and returned to Charlestown where they died on the gallows.[5]

In April 1861, as the war began, Chambersburg became a Federal supply center and a staging area for the first Federal invasion of Virginia. On 15 April, the same day President Lincoln called for 75,000 troops to invade the South, Colonel A.K. McClure, a prominent Republican attorney and local resident, reached an agreement with Lincoln and General Winfield Scott whereby Pennsylvania would quickly furnish 14,000 volunteers. Two days later, at a meeting at the Franklin County Courthouse, several committees were formed to facilitate support for the war effort. Large sums were raised for the support of families of the departing soldiers.

As May began, an isolated group of wood-cutters was fired upon by local secessionists at Shade Gap, about 20 miles northwest of town.[6] In the uproar that followed, one Chambersburg newspaper editor shouted that the "secessionist traitors should be shot down like dogs." Meanwhile, large numbers of Federal troops began to gather at the town. Most were camped on and around Fairground Hill, west of town, while some were billeted in private homes. Many of those on Fairground Hill had no tents; sleeping in the open, they became sick; Franklin Hall became a hospital, soon filling with patients.

Meanwhile, Confederate troops led by Major General Joseph E. Johnston concentrated at Harpers Ferry as another Confederate force, led by Major General Pierre Beauregard, gathered at Manassas Junction, Virginia, about 25 miles southwest of Washington. To stop these two forces from combining, a Federal force, nearly 20,000 strong, gathered at Chambersburg. Led by Major General Robert Patterson, a 69 year old Mexican War veteran, who had arrived to great fanfare some days earlier, they marched south on 7 June. As Patterson's troops advanced into Maryland, Johnston's army evacuated Harpers Ferry, retreating to Winchester. On 2 July, a short distance into Virginia, Patterson's men engaged Confederates under Colonel Thomas J. (later "Stonewall") Jackson, at Falling Waters. Defeated, they lost 4 killed, 16 wounded, and 49 missing, with 20 Confederates wounded.

However, once in the Shenandoah Valley, Patterson inexplicably stopped his pursuit of Johnston, moving his force instead to Charlestown. This allowed Johnston to combine with Beauregard, and the Confederates went on to win the first Battle of Manassas on 21 July. Two days later, Patterson read of his removal from command in a newspaper, and he passed through Chambersburg, nearly unnoticed, on his way home.

In October 1862 in the aftermath of the Battle of Antietam, Chambersburg was the target of a Confederate raid led by Major General J.E.B. Stuart. Five miles north of town, the Cumberland Valley Railroad crossed Conococheague Creek. If the bridge there was destroyed, reasoned Robert E. Lee, the Army of the Potomac would lose the use of the railroad and the supply depot at Hagerstown. In addition to destroying the bridge, Stuart was to denude the countryside of horses, needed for the Army of Northern Virginia. In addition, Lee told Stuart that he should capture "citizens of Pennsylvania holding state or government offices ... that they may be used as hostages, or for our own citizens that have been carried off by the enemy."[7] The town surrendered to Major General Wade Hampton, leading the Confederate advance. Stuart's 1,800 troops entered Chambersburg a few minutes after 8 P.M., 10 October. A force led by Colonel William E. "Grumble" Jones was immediately dispatched to destroy the railroad bridge over Conococheague Creek. Returning shortly thereafter, they were frustrated; the bridge was made of iron and indestructible.

Stuart's raiders spent the remainder of their time in Chambersburg looting railroad warehouses; by 7 A.M. the next day, Stuart and his officers were mounted, awaiting the return of those that had gone foraging for horses. A.K. McClure noted that a number of Confederate troops had begun to loot stores; Stuart had them arrested and the goods returned. Stuart's force left town around 8 A.M., just 12 hours after they arrived. Although they were unable to destroy the Conococheague Creek bridge, they carried off 1,200 horses; Federal property and Cumberland Valley railroad property valued at $250,000 was destroyed with 30 hostages taken. Stuart's raid embarrassed the Federal government and the Army of the Potomac, particularly since the raiders avoided Federal pursuit, escaping into Virginia with none killed and only two wounded.[8]

During the Gettysburg campaign, Chambersburg was again a crossroads of war and a supply base for the Army of Northern Virginia. Late in the evening of 15 June 1863, lead elements of Brigadier General Albert Jenkins brigade of Virginia cavalry, numbering about 1,500 troops, entered the town, cantering into the Diamond, illuminated by the newly installed gaslights that ringed the square. The next day, Jenkins established headquarters at the Montgomery House hotel. He sent a few squads to occupy Gelsinger's Hill, four miles to the north. He then sent a detachment, armed with black powder torpedoes, to destroy the Scotland railroad bridge, 16 miles northeast. A number of Jenkins' troops spent the day searching for runaway slaves; one Confederate detachment arrived at Thaddeus Stevens' Caledonia Iron Works, about ten miles east of town. The rebels demanded, and got, all of Stevens' horses and mules, but in return, refrained from burning the place. Congressman Stevens, who was present as the rebel horsemen approached, was persuaded to leave to avoid capture. Belligerent and hostile, he was unwilling to go. In response to unsubstantiated rumors of a large Federal advance, Jenkins retreated to Greencastle.

However, on 26 June, Jubal Early led his brigade into Caledonia and burned Stevens' iron works to the ground. Stevens estimated his losses at about $90,000. Most of the buildings, including cottages housing workers, were destroyed; all of his livestock and horses were taken or driven off, and the iron-making equipment was destroyed. Stevens was stoic about the destruction, however, and since he had strongly favored the burning of "all rebel mansions," many thought that he had received his just deserts.[9]

Meanwhile, on 10 June, the War Department in Washington had established the Department of the Susquehanna, a separate military district, to defend Pennsylvania. Forty-one-year-old Major General Darius Nash Couch, recently of the Army of the Potomac, was put in command. Disillusioned with his superior, General Joseph Hooker, because of his poor performance during the Battle of Chancellorsville, Couch had asked to be relieved of command. His request was granted, and Couch soon found himself recruiting in the Mason-Dixon border area for full-time, temporary duty troops.

He didn't have much time; Jenkins' cavalry appeared in Chambersburg on 15 June; on 22 June, Rodes' division of Ewell's corps, about 8,000 troops, crossed into Pennsylvania and encamped at Greencastle. Not far behind was the rest of the Army of Northern Virginia, nearly 70,000 troops in all. Opposing them, Couch had about 1,000 men, largely consisting of the 1st New York "Lincoln" Cavalry, two regiments of New York state militia, some Pennsylvania cavalry, and a few naval guns from the Philadelphia Navy Yard. After an ambush near Greencastle of 35 troops of the Lincoln cavalry by some of Jenkins' brigade, Couch ordered the Federals, led by Brigadier General Joseph Knipe, to retreat to Carlisle. Knipe's men panicked, rushing to the train station in Chambersburg. They left behind their spare clothing, rations, equipment, and artillery, and the 71st New York Infantry, who were obliged to march to Carlisle, 35 miles away. After they had gone, Chambersburg residents looted their encampment. Jenkins' cavalry returned, and residents soon found their town a thoroughfare for the Army of Northern Virginia. Rebel infantry marched through the Diamond on the morning of 24 June, preceded by the Confederate band, playing "The Bonnie Blue Flag." Their supply and ordnance wagon trains followed, and the men, animals and vehicles passed through the surrounding countryside, looting and destroying crops. Later that day, General Ewell arrived, setting up headquarters at the Franklin Hotel. Several hotels were requisitioned for mattresses and bedclothes; Ewell then demanded supplies from town residents.

Two days later, Lee arrived, conferred briefly with General A.P. Hill in the Diamond, then established his headquarters a short distance east of town (Near present-day Chambersburg Hospital). There he learned from one of General Longstreet's spies that the Army of the Potomac was encamped near Frederick, Maryland, and that Major General George Meade had recently replaced General Hooker as commander. Realizing that the Federals would threaten his route of retreat, Lee cancelled plans for an advance on Harrisburg and on 28 June decided to fight Meade's force east of the mountains. The Battle of Gettysburg occurred three days later. Chambersburg also witnessed large numbers of wounded Confederates passing through, retreating from Gettysburg. Thus by the time of McCausland's raid, town residents had come to know the Confederates.

To defend Chambersburg and the Maryland-Pennsylvania border area in July 1864, Couch had a force of fewer than 400 troops. The responsibility for this alarming situation lay squarely with the confusing Union command structure, President Lincoln, and Secretary of War Edwin Stanton. In the first part of July, Couch had been authorized by Pennsylvania governor Andrew Gregg Curtin to raise up to 24,000 militia volunteers for defense of the border area. However, Pennsylvania's response was slow because most of the state's able-bodied men had been sent to replace those killed in Grant's bloody campaign at Petersburg or to defend Washington. Couch's small force included the Patapsco Guards–Maryland Volunteer Infantry, two companies of mounted local militia, and two guns from Battery A, 1st New York Light Artillery. In addition, on 26 July, Couch's command was augmented by 45 troops of the 6th U.S. Cavalry, led by Lt. Hancock McLean.[10]

Anticipating this situation, Governor Curtin had attempted to retain some control over the state's militia. In a letter dated 21 July 1864, addressed to "His Excellency Abraham Lincoln," Curtin and Maryland governor Augustus Bradford proposed to raise a militia force from Maryland and Pennsylvania for the specific purpose of defending the Mason-Dixon border area from Confederate incursions. The letter stressed that there was a "pressing necessity" for raising a force "for home or local defense," as "the complete protection of this part of our frontier (is) as of admitted national importance." Curtin and Bradford urged Lincoln to comply with their request, and grant the authority necessary to raise local defense forces. The reply, dated 1 August, sent on behalf of Secretary of War Stanton, was negative, stating, "I am directed by the Secretary of War to inform you that the proposition has been fully considered and that the authority asked for cannot be granted."[11]

This denial was made despite the fact that Lincoln himself based his April 1861 call for 75,000 volunteers on a 1795 law relating to Pennsylvania's Whiskey Rebellion, allowing the president to call on state militias in times of crisis. In addition, the fact that the Pennsylvania militia had successfully defended Carlisle during the Gettysburg campaign was ignored.[12]

On 22 July, Couch wrote to Secretary Stanton, informing him that several hundred citizens of York had armed themselves and were prepared to defend their city. He also told Stanton that residents of Pennsylvania favored immediate action to counter the threat of Confederate invasion, and he recommended that "the war department encourage the movement by authorizing the loan or issue of uniforms." The reply, written on 1 August, on behalf of Stanton, stated: "The subject has been carefully considered by the Secretary of War, who cannot sanction the issue of the clothing in question." Again, Stanton had refused to allow local defense efforts. These refusals, and the refusal of the War Department to allow Curtin to fill the depleted ranks of the well-regarded Pennsylvania Reserves, resulted in Chambersburg being undefended at the time of McCausland's raid.

In addition, Couch's authority didn't extend beyond the narrow confines of the Department of the Susquehanna. On the evening of 29 July, with refugees streaming northwards through the town in advance of the approaching Confederates, consternation among town residents became bewilderment as they witnessed a long Federal supply train, destination Harrisburg, pass through. The train had been ordered to safety by General Hunter and was guarded by 1,700 troops. However Couch had no authority to order any of them to leave the train and defend the town. Hunter, in charge of the Middle Department, apparently thought the safety of his supply train more important than the safety of Chambersburg and failed to detach any of the troops to defend the town.[13]

Equally important, a signal corps detachment that could have tracked the Confederate raiders as they approached Chambersburg had been sent to Maryland Heights (Harpers Ferry) at the beginning of July. On 22 July, Couch sent an urgent appeal to the Signal Bureau in Washington requesting the return of this unit, led by Lt. Amos Thayer. The appeal stated, in part: "During the recent raid I suffered much for the want of Lt. Thayer and the signal detachment." Couch's appeal was denied, and the signal corps detachment remained at Harpers Ferry until 10 August.[14]

The Raiders Approach

At 1 A.M. on 29 July, McCausland ordered Harry Gilmor to secure McCoy's Ferry Ford, near Clear Spring, Maryland, for crossing the Potomac. Gilmor had determined the strength of the Union pickets along the river the previous evening. Inexplicably, Gilmor's Maryland cavalry didn't reach the Potomac until sunrise; they then quickly dispersed Federal pickets and secured the crossing for McCausland's main column. Before McCausland crossed, he ordered Gilmor to send out scouting units along the National Road, towards Hagerstown and Cumberland, to create the impression that the main strike would be against Hagerstown. Gilmor's force was ambushed at Spikler's Hill, near Clear Spring, suffering 17 casualties. The dismounted Federal cavalry — the 14th Pennsylvania — were armed with breach-loading carbines, shooting at the Confederates from behind stone walls, trees and fences. Gilmor eventually joined McCausland at Mercersburg. While Gilmor was fighting the 14th Pennsylvania, Early was feinting at Hagerstown and Harpers Ferry to distract the Federals.

Hagerstown had become a gathering place for stragglers from various Federal commands. By mid-morning, there were at least 3,000 Federal troops there, many of whom had been with Crook's force at Kernstown. Many were deserters and more than a few were drunk. Nevertheless, four companies of Cole's Maryland cavalry fought J.C. Vaughn's Tennessee horsemen in the streets of Hagerstown for a few hours that day, slowly surrendering possession of the town to the Confederates. The Federals withdrew to the northern perimeter of town where they were met by Averell's division — about 2,500 troops, formed in line of battle, covering their retreat.

Averell's role in the burning of Chambersburg caused a firestorm of controversy in the aftermath of the raid and has caused discussion to the present day. Could he have prevented the destruction of the town?

Cole's Maryland cavalry joined Averell's brigade as they withdrew northwards into Pennsylvania, arriving at Greencastle at sundown. Ignoring a company of militia in Greencastle's town square, Averell withdrew a mile further north, camping that evening on the farm of Archibald Fleming, about 10 miles south of Chambersburg. Averell and Couch had been in contact, by telegraph, throughout the day on 29 July and into the early morning of 30 July. In a communi-

Major General Darius N. Couch, commander — Department of the Susquehanna (Library of Congress)

cation on 29 July, Couch was clearly apprehensive, asking Averell, "Should the enemy turn your right flank and move into this state, will you pursue them, provided they threaten your front; or, if they move on your right flank in overpowering numbers, will you fall back into this Valley or move to the left?" While he wasn't certain of the Confederate destination, Averell knew that Couch was anticipating their arrival in Chambersburg, Union army headquarters for the Department of the Susquehanna. Averell's reply, sent at 9 A.M. on 29 July, is revealing: "I shall not uncover you if I can help it." That evening, from Greencastle, Averell again wired Couch: "I think that these operations of the enemy, which I have reported, are made to cover a movement in the direction of Bedford or a retreat. If they come this way I shall remain here to see what they do it with, and avail myself of any opportunity to attack them."[15] A movement towards Bedford by whom? Strangely enough, Governor Curtin was a guest at the Bedford Springs Hotel, a few miles south of Bedford, during McCausland's raid, though it's unlikely that Averell knew that.[16]

While Averell was in a difficult position, with Vaughn's Confederates in his front, his message to Couch on the evening of 29 July indicates that he was deceived by Confederate feints. While a few of Vaughn's troops had advanced beyond the Mason-Dixon line to a point about four miles south of Greencastle, the bulk of his force had remained in Hagerstown. However, instead of attempting to learn more about Confederate activity, Averell was content to remain near Greencastle, passively awaiting events to unfold. As the general and a few of his officers sat down to dinner with the Fleming family, McCaus-land's column was about eight miles away, beginning their advance on Chambersburg by way of Mercersburg. Nevertheless, one writer has said that by 10:30 P.M., Averell had probably been made aware of the Confederate occupation of Mercersburg.[17]

What happened next shed some light on Averell's intentions. After dinner, the general lay down "at a late hour" in the front yard of the Fleming house to rest without telling anyone where he was. He had left three aides at the telegraph office in Greencastle the previous evening and notified the telegraph operator, Dr. H.R. Fetterhoff, where he had established headquarters. Late in the evening of 29 July, and into the early morning of 30 July, Couch sent at least four messages to Averell. At 10:15 P.M., he telegraphed Averell that a unit of the 6th Federal Cavalry, led by Lt. McLean, had been driven from Mer-cersburg. Around 12:30 A.M., he telegraphed that McLean's pickets had been driven from Bridgeport, closer to Chambersburg. At 2 A.M., Couch sent another message to Averell, informing him that McLean had been forced to withdraw from St. Thomas, and was falling back on Chambersburg.

When each message was received, Dr. Fetterhoff sent it with an orderly to deliver to Averell. However, upon arriving at Fleming farm, none of the orderlies could locate him. At 3:30 A.M., Couch telegraphed Averell yet again — twice, telling him that the Confed-erates were on the outskirts of Chambersburg, and asking him what he was going to do, and telling him he [Couch] would "endeavor to hold the town until daylight." There were no orderlies left to deliver the messages. Providentially, however, Thomas Bard, assis-tant to the superintendent of the Cumberland Valley Railroad, having fled Hagerstown on a hand car up the Franklin railroad the previous day, was in the telegraph office when Couch's 3:30 A.M. messages arrived. Volunteering to deliver them, he set off on horseback into the early morning darkness. On the way, he met the orderlies returning to Greencastle after having failed to locate the general. Persuading the aides of the importance of the telegrams, they turned them over to him, and he bade them to follow him. The party arrived on the Fleming farm around 4 A.M., disturbing the early morning quiet of the camp site. Searching frantically for Averell, Bard found him asleep by a fence in the front yard.[18] In California, twenty years later, he recalled the incident:

"On being awakened, he raised upon his elbow and heard the information I had brought. I had handed him the telegram, but as there was no light I told him what they contained, and informed him that they had been delivered to his orderlies hours before. He made no reply and, as I thought, was about to turn over and go asleep. Minutes seemed hours to me, and growing impatient I said to him, General Averell if you wish me to convey any answer to General Couch, I beg you to let me have it quickly, for it is barely possible I can get back before telegrapher communications will be cut off. Without rising to put his troops in motion, or without the slightest manifestation of intent in the condition of General Couch, or in the peril to which the loyal people of Chambersburg were exposed, he merely said, 'Tell Couch I will be there in the morning.'"[19] At that point, even if Averell had immediately awakened, gathered his troops together, and advanced towards Chambersburg, it would have been nearly impossible to prevent the Confederates from entering the town. In addition, the Federal command apparatus, with various military districts having arbitrary boundaries, designated Averell as reporting to Hunter, not Couch.

Writing after the war, Chambersburg merchant Jacob Hoke, whose home and business were destroyed by McCausland's raiders, implied that Averell's failure to stop the Confederate advance was because he was drunk, without explaining how or when he might have become intoxicated. Drunkenness was a popular 19th century public accusation, frequently leveled at those whose behavior failed to live up to expectations. However, a much more likely cause for Averell's lack of enterprise was the physical exhaustion of his troops, his horses, and himself. Nevertheless, by 4 A.M. on 30 July, Averell and his troops had had about five hours sleep, while McCausland's Confederates rode all night long, the main column reaching the vicinity of Chambersburg around sunrise.

In addition, McCausland's 2,900 man column had been harassed throughout the night by the intrepid McLean and his 45 man command. McLean's Federals periodically shot at the advancing Confederates, slowing them down. Around 3:00 A.M. the head of McCausland's column ran into an ambush, set up by McLean, about a mile west of town. One rebel trooper was killed, and several wounded, by canister fire. As the sleepy Confederate horsemen began to deploy, McLean's command withdrew. The raiders were held up for about two hours as the Federal cannon fired a few more rounds. Couch and his few troops were thereby provided enough time to evacuate Chambersburg, around 5 A.M., on the last Cumberland Valley Railroad train out of town. McLean's small force withdrew towards Shippensburg. Before sunrise, McCausland met with his officers at the home of Henry Greenawalt, also about a mile west of town, where they were informed of the plan to ransom or burn the town. McCausland favored an immediate advance, to burn the town before sunrise, but Johnson and Gilmor voiced strong objections, and he backed down. Leaving the vicinity of the Greenawalt house, the raiders lined up on Fairground Hill, and at 5:30 A.M., to announce their presence, they fired two or three artillery rounds into town.

The 8th and 36th Virginia Cavalry were sent into town on foot to determine conditions. Immediately thereafter, Gilmor's cavalry blocked all the town's exits. Around 6 A.M., McCausland, Johnson, Gilmor and their staffs were sitting down to breakfast at the Franklin Hotel, on the town square. Upon finishing breakfast, McCausland ordered more than 50 of Chambersburg's leading citizens detained, while the 21st Virginia cavalry, led by Colonel William Peters, occupied the town. However, most of McCausland's force remained outside of Chambersburg.[20]

The Burning

Attorney J.W. Douglas hurried up Market Street, in Chambersburg, some minutes before 7 A.M., on a bright warm Saturday morning, 30 July. About an hour earlier, he had stood on the veranda of a nearby house, with a number of other residents, watching McCausland's cavalry file into the square, and begin feeding their horses at the curb. Sometime later, a gray-clad officer in the square called to Douglas, asking him to come down to the street. In the square, the officer introduced himself, "I am Captain Fitzhugh, formerly of General Jenkin's staff. We met last year and then your Burgess directed me to you to inform your people of some things we wished done. I now ask you to be our bearer on this occasion."[21] Douglas told Fitzhugh that he remembered him then asked him what he wanted.

Fitzhugh explained the ransom demand; Douglas asked him "by what authority he asked such a sum of money and threatened to lay in ashes the homes of our defenseless families if the demand was not complied with?" Fitzhugh then showed him a copy of Early's order, demanding a ransom payment of $100,000 in gold, or $500,000 in greenbacks, in lieu of burning the town. He then told Douglas to "go immediately and see your people and tell them of this demand and see that the money is forth coming, for I assure you that this order will be rigidly enforced." Stunned, Douglas read the order, then ran, then walked through the square. Encountering a number of residents, he later wrote, "I then went up Market street and told everyone I met of the rebel demand. They generally laughed at first, and when I spoke earnestly about the terrible alternative, they said they were trying to scare us, and went into their houses." Turning up Main Street, Douglas again told everyone he met of the Confederate demand, with similar results. One member of the town council, when informed of the ransom demand, quickly answered that "the citizens would not pay five cents."[22]

Despite the fact that a number of residents had heard Confederate artillery fire about 5:30 that morning, and had noticed the gray-clad troopers entering their town, denizens of Chambersburg didn't believe McCausland's threat. Lt. Fielder C. Slingluff, of Johnson's 1st Maryland Cavalry, later wrote: "They treated it [the demand] as a joke, or thought it was a mere threat to get the money, and showed their sense of security and incredulity in every act." Harry Gilmor, whose unit had been ordered into Chambersburg to seal off escape routes, wrote: "General Early's order was now published.... Just then some scouts returned with a prisoner from Averill's [sic] command, reporting him to be not more than two or three miles off, with a heavy force of cavalry. The citizens knew it too, and positively refused to raise the money, laughing at us when we threatened to burn the town." Several members of the town council said they "were not frightened by the threat — a Federal force was close at hand."[23] The strict rein that Generals J.E.B. Stuart and Robert E. Lee had imposed on the Southern troops, and their subsequent gentlemanly behavior in 1862 and 1863 had sedated Chambersburg's residents into a false sense of security concerning the danger they were in. In addition, many residents didn't realize that only about one-fourth of the raiders had entered their town; that many more awaited events, on the outskirts of Chambersburg.

Finding Fitzhugh in the town bookstore, Douglas told him that "all the bank funds" had been removed from town, and that wealthy residents had fled. As they were conversing, McCausland approached; Douglas anxiously repeated what he had told Fitzhugh. Taking Douglas by the arm, McCausland led him out into the square, asking "Are you sure you have seen your public men? I should be very sorry to carry out the retributive part of the command of my superior officer. Can't you ring the Courthouse bell and call the citizens together and see if this sum of money cannot be raised?" Douglas again stressed that since the town had been warned of the Confederate approach, local bank officials had fled, taking their funds with them, and that the Courthouse was locked up. McCausland responded by ordering a few of his men to break open the Courthouse door, and ring the bell.[24] In response, a number of the town's leading citizens, having been gathered together by Gilmor, appeared in the Diamond, and McCausland was again informed that the town had no money to give.

After again hearing that town residents lacked sufficient funds to pay the ransom, how long did McCausland wait before ordering Chambersburg torched? After the war, he claimed that he gave the town six hours to comply with the ransom demand. This is too long, as the raiders left the area sometime between 11 A.M. and noon. Jacob Hoke claimed that buildings were fired as early as 7:30 A.M., which would have meant that McCausland's order to burn the town was given almost immediately after the ransom demand was read. Reliable accounts, including those of Bradley Johnson and Sgt. William Kochersperger, one of Couch's troops, who was unable to evacuate, indicate that he gave the order to fire the town "some three hours" after the raiders arrived, perhaps a few minutes before 9 A.M.[25] Some residents claimed that individual Confederates, acting on their own, had fired a few houses before McCausland's order was given.

Fires were set in about a dozen places, and in less than an hour, the town center — most of Chambersburg — was in flames. The most common method of firing houses involved a few of the raiders using crowbars to break down a front door, entering the house, then smashing furniture into kindling. The broken furniture was then doused with kerosene, after being piled in the middle of the floor. A lighted match was then set to the pile, and within a few minutes, the house was a roaring inferno. In most cases, the occupants were given a few minutes to leave, many with nothing but the clothes on their backs. The burning of the town also occasioned a general breakdown in the morale and behavior of the Confederate troops, with many becoming intoxicated, and robbing the residents of their valuables.

The Reverend Joseph Clark, in an August article in *Presbyterian*, commented,

> The burning was executed in the most ruthless and unrelenting manner. A squad of men would approach a house, break open the door, proceed to the most convenient part of the house and kindle a fire, with no other notice to the inmates, except to get out of it as soon as they could. In many cases, five, ten, fifteen minutes, were asked to secure some clothing, which were refused. Many families escaped with only the clothing they had on, and such as they could gather up in their haste. In many cases they were not allowed to take these, but were threatened with instant death if they did not cast them away and flee. Sick and aged people had to be carried to the fields. The corpses of one or two persons, who had recently died, were hastily interred in the gardens, and children, separated from their parents, ran wildly screaming through the streets. Those whose stupor, or eagerness to save something, detained them, emerged with difficulty from the streets filled with the sheeted flames of their burning homes ... no provocation had been given; not a shot was fired on them in entering the town, and not until the full crisis was reached, did desperation, in a few instances, lead to desperate acts, and a few of the incendiaries left their bones to smoulder in the ruins.

> As to the result ... the entire heart or body of the town is burned. Not a house or building of any kind is left on a space of ... ten squares of streets, extending each way from the center, with some four or five exceptions, where the buildings were isolated. Only the outskirts are left. The court-house, bank, town hall, German Reformed printing establishment, every store and hotel in the town, and every mill and factory ... and two churches, were consumed. Between 300 and 400 dwellings were burned, leaving at least 2500 persons without a home or hearth. In value, three-fourths of the town were destroyed. The scene of desolation must be seen to be appreciated. Crumbling walls, stacks of chimneys and smoking embers, are all that remain of once elegant and happy homes. As to the scene itself, it beggars description.... The day was sultry and calm, not a breath stirring, and each column of smoke rose black, straight and single, first one,

and then another, and another, and another, until the columns blended and commingled; and then one vast and lurid column of smoke and flame rose perpendicular to the sky, and spread out into a vast crown, like a cloud of sackcloth hanging over the doomed city; whilst the roar and the surging, the crackling and the crash of falling timbers and walls broke upon the still air with a fearful dissonance, and the screams and sounds of agony of burning animals, hogs and cows and horses, made the welkin horrid with the sounds of woe. It was a scene to be witnessed and heard once in a life-time.[26]

On the Confederate side, surgeon Malcolm Fleming described the scene in a letter to his mother, "Nothing exaggerated can be said about the burning of Chambersburg.... I entered the Town with a stiff neck & stubborn heart, but as much as I hate the Yankees, I could not stand it long ... the citizens refused to pay the tribute; whereupon McCausland at once ordered the city to be laid in ashes — The scene which followed baffles all description — Shrieking children & panic stricken men & women running in every direction begging assistance. I saw several women faint upon the side walks ... the town was sacked — soldiers turned loose upon private houses & then the order issued to burn."

That the raiders disintegrated into an armed mob once the order to burn the town was given is not surprising. In the preceding months, Early made little or no attempt to better the lot of his cavalry — neither their armaments, clothing, rations or discipline had improved. McCausland made no attempt to discipline or restrain them; he himself was seen exiting a bookstore, with an armload of books, as the town burned. While McCausland was exhorting Douglas to locate the town's leading citizens, his troops began to indulge in looting and strong-arm robbery. Bradley Johnson later described the scene, "Every crime in the catalog of infamy has been committed, except murder and rape." The raiders, many now drunk, preyed upon Chambersburg's residents without mercy, unceremoniously robbing them at gunpoint, of hats, coats, boots, watches, and anything else of value. Shops and stores were broken into, with the troops stealing food and clothing, including jars of candy and handfuls of cinnamon.[27]

In some instances, the drunken raiders, many burdened with loot, forced residents to ransom their homes, with the promise of sparing them from the torch. Johnson, in his report on the raid, noted: "While the town was in flames a quartermaster, aided and directed by a field officer, exacted ransom of individuals for their houses, holding the torch in terror over the house until it was paid. These ransoms varied from $750 to $150, according to the size of the habitation. Thus, the grand spectacle of a national retaliation was reduced to a miserable huckstering for greenbacks."[28]

Nevertheless, some Confederate officers restrained themselves, with a few refusing to carry out McCausland's order. One was said to have wept publicly at the order, while another, a Mason, posted a guard around the town's Masonic temple, sparing the building from the torch. A few of the raiders assisted residents in saving their valuables from the flames. McCausland ordered Colonel William Peters, leading the 21st Virginia Cavalry, to fire the town, then rode away before Peters could answer. Peters found Johnson, who affirmed the order. Unwilling to make war against the women and children of Chambersburg, Peters said he would break his sword and throw it away before obeying the order. Johnson then ordered Peters to round up his command and leave town, which he did. About a mile from Chambersburg, he received a note from McCausland, asking if he had understood the order, and why he hadn't obeyed. Peters replied that he understood, and that he told Johnson, his immediate superior, that he refused to obey it. McCausland had Peters arrested, but rescinded the arrest the same day. Peters and the 21st Virginia performed capably as the column's rear guard when they left town later that morning. After the war, John Mosby said of him: "Col. Peters was ordered with his men to set fire to Chambersburg; he refused, and was never called to account for it. He was right." Johnson also found the order repulsive, but told Harry Gilmor to fire the town, and he willingly obeyed.[29]

Not surprisingly, many in Chambersburg on that fearful morning must have wondered, "Where is Averell?"

Indeed, where was Averell? After spending the evening on the Fleming farm, about ten miles south of the town, he probably heard the Confederate artillery fire at 5:30 A.M., gathered his men together, and ordered them to saddle up and advance northward. However, at Marion, about three miles north of Greencastle, Averell curiously ordered his brigade to turn northeast, towards New Franklin and Greenwood, instead of advancing straight towards Chambersburg. There is some evidence to show that the Union general thought McCausland's raiders would leave Chambersburg by way of the Gettysburg Turnpike, heading east, since that was the direction that J.E.B. Stuart's force had taken in 1862. Logical as that thought may have been, it contradicts Averell's telegram of the previous evening to Couch, which stated, in part: "These operations of the enemy ... are made to cover a movement in the direction of Bedford [west of Chambersburg]."[30]

Averell thus avoided the direct route northwards. Had he marched directly towards the town, he might have trapped McCausland's raiders inside Chambersburg. At least, he might have surprised and defeated them as they left, as "two-thirds of their party were in a state of intoxication," burdened with loot, and barely able to ride. However, J. Milton Snyder, a local resident, observed the Federal cavalry pass through New Franklin around 10 A.M. The smoke and flames from the burning town, only a few miles to the north, could easily be seen. Yet Averell's force continued their march eastward, another five miles to Greenwood. Snyder also noted that many of the troops were angry with their commander for not advancing directly to Chambersburg.[31] When scouts reported that the Confederates had departed, heading west on the Loudoun Turnpike, Averell's force was nearly ten miles away. Turning westward at Greenwood, they approached Chambersburg along the Gettysburg Turnpike, arriving in the burning town around 2 P.M. Although some of Averell's troopers had seen smoke rising above the town that morning on their way to Greenwood, most were unprepared for the appalling scene of devastation that greeted them upon their arrival.

With houses on both sides of the streets on fire, thick clouds of fetid black smoke hanging above the town in the humid July air, gutted shells of buildings, and piles of charred bricks where fine homes once stood, Chambersburg was a roaring inferno. Leaning forward on their frightened mounts, Averell's troopers galloped through the town as fast as they could. Nevertheless, a few had their clothing singed by the flames. Groups of helpless residents stood on street corners, proud men "with bowed heads," dumbstruck by the horror around them, a few women fainting on the sidewalks, and children, clinging to their parents, reduced to tears. A few residents that were able to waved and cheered the passage of the Federal cavalry through the blackened ruins, while a number of soldiers vowed to "Remember Chambersburg!" as they exited the town, riding after the gray-clad horsemen.[32]

McCausland's raiders had more than a two hour head start on the pursuing Federal cavalry, having departed Chambersburg shortly after 11 A.M. They left behind a scene of staggering devastation. The core of the town — 20 square blocks — was nearly completely destroyed, with 537 structures — residences, businesses, and warehouses — burned to the ground. The town's paper mill, flour mills, axe factory, chair factory, distillery and brewery were destroyed, and "all the places of business that gave employment to the poor were swept away." All of the town's stores and hotels, and most of the residences, were destroyed, with at least 2,000 inhabitants rendered homeless. Many of the homeless were made destitute, living out the remainder of their lives in poverty. The value of real and personal property destroyed was estimated at about $1.2 million.[33]

Surprisingly, however, only one death among the town's residents was known to have occurred, that of Daniel Parker, an aging former slave whose home was destroyed. He had arrived in Chambersburg as a youth, by way of the Underground Railroad. Upset at the destruction of his home, and overcome by smoke and heat, he died that evening. Three Confederates were known to have been killed by town residents. Two of the raiders, bent on looting, inadvertently locked themselves inside Miller's drug store. Proprietor Andrew Miller allegedly shot them dead. Captain Caulder A. Bailey, adjutant of the 8th Virginia Cavalry, had become inebriated and was captured by civilians. He escaped, but was shot and wounded, and took refuge in the basement of a burning home. When the heat became too intense, he exited the cellar, but was cornered by a crowd of angry residents. After begging for his life, he was shot a second time by someone in the crowd and buried in a local cemetery.[34]

The Last Rebel Bivouac in the North

McCausland's raiders left Chambersburg, heading west on the Loudon Turnpike, towards McConnellsburg, 23 miles away (www.mapquest.com). The undisciplined and inebriated rebel horsemen littered the road with "merchandise of every description" — various articles of clothing and utensils stolen from houses in Chambersburg, now serving to make Federal pursuit certain. Nevertheless, the vandalism and thievery didn't stop when they left Chambersburg. A trail of burning barns marked the rebel line of retreat, and upon entering McConnellsburg, population 556, between 3 P.M. and 5 P.M., the gray-clad cavalry promptly cut the telegraph wires and destroyed the equipment in the telegraph office.

McCausland demanded 2,600 rations from McConnellsburg's residents in lieu of burning the town. As the residents struggled to meet the ransom demand, the Confederates began to loot stores and private houses. As in Chambersburg, citizens were robbed at gunpoint, of money, clothing and jewelry, while squads of gray-clad troops rode through the surrounding countryside, robbing homes and farms. The strong-arm robberies and looting intimidated the Pennsylvanians, however, the harassment caused the raiders to lose valuable time. Time was important to McCausland, because in addition to burning Chambersburg, Early had instructed him to destroy coal mines and colliery equipment in and around Cumberland, Maryland, and if possible capture that city. However, McCausland made no attempt to discipline or restrain his men, and his continuing ransom demands, sometimes on civilians sympathetic to the Confederacy, indicated that he no longer acknowledged any restraining rules nor felt any sense of obligation to civilians.

Many of the raiders had degenerated into little more than criminals, and it showed at Chambersburg and at Hancock, Maryland, the next day.

The raiders camped in the vicinity of McConnellsburg that evening, on the lookout for Federal pursuit, guarding the road from Chambersburg. Johnson's brigade camped south of town, on and around the John B. Patterson farm, a mile or so south of McConnellsburg. Many of the raiders camped between McConnellsburg and the Patterson farm, making the area one enormous camp site.

Johnson pitched his tent under a big tree, behind the barn, and told Mrs. Patterson to cook dinner for them. The former Maryland attorney and newspaper editor and 25 of his officers sat down to a dinner of fried chicken, hot biscuits, and rye coffee in the Patterson dining room that evening. During the meal, Mrs. Patterson overheard Johnson complain about the behavior of the troops in Chambersburg. Accordingly, he posted guards around her farm house and yard to keep the troops out. Johnson also breakfasted at the Patterson house the next morning, and Mrs. Patterson was paid $600 for the two meals. Their camp at the Patterson farm has been called "the last Confederate bivouac in Pennsylvania."[35]

The burning of Chambersburg had little military value. However, many Confederates agreed with ordnance chief Josiah Gorgas when he stated, "It gives intense satisfaction."[36] While the destruction of Chambersburg satisfied rebel desires for revenge, trouble and failure lay ahead for McCausland and his raiders. Chambersburg had been sacrificed twice, once to satisfy Confederate thirst for revenge, and a second time, abandoned to Stanton's desire to keep state militia out of the conflict.

Residents of Chambersburg were reimbursed $500,000 by an appropriation of the state legislature in February 1866, and under a second appropriation in May 1871, by which the certificates of some 650 claimants were reimbursed, but only when the claims were first paid by the Federal government.[37]

However, the destruction of the town was not entirely in vain. The burning of Chambersburg shocked Northern civilians into demanding a successful conclusion to the war and awakened Lincoln and Grant to the necessity of a unified Federal command structure, with new leadership, that would finally put a stop to Early's incursions and eventually destroy the Army of the Valley.

Discord at Hancock

Sunday morning, 31 July, saw Averell's cavalry crossing 2,300 feet high Sideling Hill, west of McConnellsburg, in pursuit of McCausland's raiders but still a few hours behind. Around 8 A.M., Federal advance units drove rebel pickets off the mountain, killing and capturing several. Nevertheless, local residents who had followed the blue-coated cavalry westward, expecting to see a battle that would avenge Chambersburg, were greatly disappointed. However, Averell's appearance in the Confederate rear forced the raiders to cancel a westward thrust towards Bedford, supposed to have been carried out by Gilmor's 2nd Maryland Cavalry with units of the 37th Virginia. Instead, the raiders turned south, heading for Hancock, Maryland, and the Potomac River.

At that point, Yankee technology and ingenuity intervened. A 15-year-old telegraph operator in McConnellsburg, Thomas F. Sloan, correctly anticipating the raiders destroying the telegraph, hid an extra set of telegraph instruments. As the Federals arrived in McConnellsburg, Sloan assembled the spare equipment, and Averell telegraphed Brigadier General Benjamin Franklin Kelley, commander of Federal forces in Cumberland, requesting aid in stopping the raiders from crossing the Potomac at Hancock. Ten miles south of McConnellsburg, the Confederates entered Hancock, population 700, around 1 P.M. After resting and eating, many of the raiders began robbing and looting again. The town's stores, situated along the C & O canal, were all robbed and partially destroyed, and several canal boats were burned. A Maryland cavalryman was "nearly brained" for preventing the robbery of a woman by another raider, one resident was robbed of $1000 in greenbacks, and the local Catholic priest was robbed of his gold watch.[38]

Even more than the raiders' behavior, McCausland's actions at Hancock fragmented his command, according to state loyalties, and intensified a dangerous rift between himself and Johnson that had begun when McCausland was seen pilfering from a book store in Chambersburg.[39] While many Confederate troops were stealing from the town's residents, McCausland levied another ransom demand. Hancock's residents were to pay $50,000 and give the raiders 5,000 cooked rations, or the town would meet the same fate as Chambersburg, despite the fact that many of Hancock's residents were loyal to the Confederacy. The ransom demand was intolerable to Johnson, Gilmor, and the other Marylanders. As Johnson's adjutant, Captain George W. Booth stated: "General Johnson and myself were being entertained at the house of a southern sympathizer when this action of McCausland was reported to him, with urgent request to intervene, as it was simply a matter of impossibility to raise the money in that little burg. Johnson was indignant, and directing me to accompany him as a witness, sought out McCausland and told him Hancock was a Maryland town, with many southern residents, whose relatives were in the Confederate army, and intimating in most direct and positive language that the Maryland men of his brigade would submit to no such violent treatment." Johnson further reminded McCausland of his less than acceptable behavior at Chambersburg, and that "the attention of the proper authorities would be brought to his conduct on our return."[40]

Johnson also advised the town's prominent citizens to raise as much money as possible and pay the ransom. To prevent further looting, he had Gilmor post two guards at every house and store. Nevertheless, the Maryland contingent came very close to a mutiny and might have fought McCausland's troops in the streets of Hancock but for the arrival of Averell's cavalry around 5 P.M. While Averell's Federals fought Gilmor's troops in the hills east of Hancock and in the streets of the town, Johnson and McCausland broke off their argument, and the main rebel column mounted their horses and left. A Federal armored train, sent by Kelley to support Averell, was hit by Confederate artillery fire, tipping the smokestack, and it steamed back towards Cumberland. However, the spat between McCausland and Johnson would continue, with very serious consequences for the entire Confederate war effort.

Westward to Cumberland

Strategic objectives halted the raiders' harassment of civilians as McCausland's column departed Hancock, heading westward towards Cumberland on the National Road. The capture of that city would have in large measure advanced the Confederate cause and would have threatened western Pennsylvania. In Pittsburgh, town authorities strengthened city defenses, and at a large public gathering residents determined how to meet the threat. Cumberland was a very important B & O railroad center, containing repair shops and a large number of locomotives and hundreds of passenger and freight cars. The city was also a very important coal mining center, and if McCausland could destroy the railroad and colliery equipment, General Lee's goal of disrupting coal shipments to East Coast cities would be realized. The capture of Cumberland, with the resulting disruption of coal shipments, would be a very serious blow to the Northern war effort and might result in Lincoln's defeat in the fall election.

McCausland's column, weighed down with wagonloads of plunder from Chambersburg and other towns along their route, advanced towards Cumberland, 35 miles west of Hancock. Late that evening, they made their way up the eastern slope of 1,300 foot high Polish Mountain, pausing to rest at Bevansville atop the mountain around 3 A.M. on 1 August. At sunrise, they were on the move towards Cumberland again, going down the long western slope. As they advanced westward, they felled trees and destroyed bridges behind them, successfully retarding pursuit by Averell. However, Averell was in no condition to follow, having wired Kelley that his horses were "used up," and his men "have had no rations for two days." He asked Kelley for 60,000 rations and 40,000 pounds of forage and warned that McCausland would escape across the Potomac at Oldtown. Kelley dutifully replied, "Your wants shall be supplied promptly."[41] However, Averell was unable to pressure the Confederates from behind.

Meanwhile, Kelley had anticipated a Confederate strike on Cumberland a week earlier, when Crook's troops were driven northwards across the Potomac in the aftermath of Kernstown. A B & O freight agent before the war, he had drawn a difficult assignment—guard the entire length of the railroad, from Hancock west to the Ohio River, with less than 3,000 troops. Making matters worse, a large part of Kelley's force consisted of 100-day men, stragglers from the battle at Kernstown, and town residents; the enlistments of one regiment, the 153rd Ohio National Guard—700 troops—would end in a few days. He wired Washington, asking for reinforcements, on 25 July, but Halleck had none to spare. Kelley also had at his disposal several units of the 6th and 11th West Virginia Infantry, the 152nd and 156th Ohio National Guard, some Ohio cavalry, one unit of the 1st Maryland (Union) Light artillery, and two units of the 1st Illinois Light Artillery.

Excitement turned to panic in Cumberland on 31 July when word arrived of the approach of "a strong force of Confederates." Rumor also had it that a smaller force was coming by way of Bedford, Pa. Cumberland's merchants loaded their wares into wagons, sending them to safety, while B & O administrators sent their rolling stock westward, away from the advancing Confederates. At a town meeting that evening, the mayor, Dr. Charles Ohr, addressed the assembled citizens, stressing the need for their assistance in defending the city, urging the formation of militia companies. Three companies were organized, consisting of about 200 men. Kelley sent his son, Lt. Tappan Kelley, with a squad of Federal cavalry, to monitor the advance of McCausland's columns. By noon on 1 August, the raiders were reported at Flintstone, only 12 miles east of town, and approaching rapidly. Kelley sent the 153rd Ohio southeast to block the ford across the Potomac at Oldtown, anticipating Confederate retreat in that direction. He also sent the 156th Ohio and the 11th West Virginia, with 9 cannon, to the Evitts Creek Valley, a strong defensive position about 3 miles east of town. There the Federals dug trenches and posted their artillery on high ground overlooking the National Road near a mill owned by John Folcks, known as Folcks Mill. Kelley stationed the remainder of his troops closer to town.

The action opened around 3 P.M., as several companies of McCausland's cavalry crossed Evitts Creek bridge, drawing within range of Federal small arms fire. Kelley's troops fired upon the advancing raiders, with their rifles and artillery. The Confederates found cover behind the mill, and various other outbuildings in the vicinity. From there, they opened a heavy fire against the Federal artillery. McCausland's troops formed a skirmish line, and he posted his four cannon on a hill, about 700 yards behind the skirmishers. The fighting continued throughout the afternoon, but as the sun was setting, McCausland realized that his attack had stalled and that further attempts to capture Cumberland would be futile. They had suffered 8 killed and over 30 wounded, while Federal casualties were only 1 killed and 4 wounded.[42] In consultation with Johnson, McCausland concluded that, at that point, his best option was to retreat across the Potomac and return to Virginia. Accordingly, he sent for Harry Gilmor, who in his memoirs noted, "We had Kelly, with twice our force, in front in trenches; Averill [sic] coming up in our rear; the Potomac, seven or eight miles off, to the left; the mountains of Pennsylvania on our right, with our commanders not on the best of terms with each other."

McCausland was atop the hill, behind the Confederate skirmish line, observing his artillery fire at Kelley's Federals. To Gilmor he said, "Major Gilmor, do you know this country well?" Gilmor replied, "No, sir, I was never here before." "Have you no guides?" asked the Confederate chieftain; "Unless we get out of this predicament soon, I fear it will be too late to save our guns and wagons, and we shall, besides, lose a good many men."[43] Gilmor agreed to make a reconnaissance in the direction of Oldtown and left to find a route of retreat.

He found a local resident, persuading the man at gunpoint to guide them to the river. They found a road to the Potomac, leading up the side of a mountain. Darkness overtook Gilmor after he had made a little over 3 miles. About 1 A.M., his reconnaissance squads were about 1½ miles from the river. After trading shots with Federal pickets stationed near the Potomac, Gilmor decided not to press his luck and prudently led his troops into a forest to bivouac until daylight. In the wee hours of the morning, he sent scouts to determine Federal strength at the Potomac crossing at Oldtown.

Action at Oldtown

At dawn, the scouts reported that the ford was held by a strong Federal force; these were the 700 troops of the 153rd Ohio National Guard, led by Colonel Israel Stough. Just after daybreak, a courier arrived from Johnson informing Gilmor that his brigade was on the way to the ford. Responding to the message, Gilmor led another reconnaissance to the ford, discovering that the Federals had burned the small bridge that crossed the canal at Oldtown. A Federal ambush caused Gilmor to halt, dismount his men, and await the arrival of Johnson's brigade.

After observing Federal troops dismantling the bridge across the C & O canal, Johnson at 5 A.M. led a frontal assault against the Federals, with the 27th and 8th Virginia Cavalry. Meanwhile, the 21st Virginia Cavalry, commanded by Colonel Peters, rapidly constructed a bridge across the canal and struck both flanks of the Federal line. After responding with an ineffective volley at 300 yards, the Federals fled the scene, retreating to Green Spring Station on the Virginia shore. About 90 troops of the 153rd Ohio found refuge in a strong two-story blockhouse about a hundred yards from the river. The remainder posted themselves in a strong defensive position behind a railroad embankment on high ground, near the river bank.

Presently a strange-looking train appeared, causing some consternation among the Confederates. This was the train that had fired on them at Hancock; now six cars long, with the locomotive in the center, with three cannon and infantry in each end car, on the south bank of the Potomac, directly in their front. The entrained Federal infantry consisted of Company K, 2nd Potomac Home Brigade, firing on Johnson's Confederates through numerous openings. The iron-clad opened fire, and an exploding shell killed Johnson's horse under him.

A Confederate frontal assault, led by Gilmor, stalled under heavy Federal fire, with the raiders forced to stand in knee-high water. Confederate artillery fire was rendered ineffective by thick groves of trees that protected the blockhouse. Realizing his precarious position, Gilmor re-crossed the river, and found Johnson and McCausland together, planning the raiders' next move. He impressed them with the need for stronger artillery support; they acknowledged the heavy Federal fire, but doubted the ability of the horses to withstand it and the effectiveness of stronger artillery support. Taking matters into his own hands, Gilmor rode into Oldtown to find Lt. John McNulty, leading the Baltimore Light Artillery, and persuaded him to bring up his big guns. Gilmor found McNulty "ready for anything." As he described it, "We took two pieces down to the bridge; crossed it at a gallop; had two horses killed, which we dragged along dead in their harness; got a position on the ridge; unlimbered the pieces, already shotted and primed. The gunner was a Baltimorean named McElwee, and, though a brisk fire was opened on him, he coolly sighted his piece, and put a six-pound shell through the boiler, which exploded with a loud report."[44] Further shots disabled the iron-clad train, and the crew and soldiers abandoned it. However, the blockhouse remained in their front, keeping up a heavy fire.

Gilmor described the blockhouse as "really the greater obstacle, from the fact that it could not be seen from the Maryland side of the river. Lieutenant McNulty wasted about fifty shells feeling for it, only one of which pierced it through the roof." A direct frontal assault by one of Johnson's regiments failed, incurring heavy casualties. The stalemate continued for an hour and a half, with the Confederates pinned down; as Gilmor stated, "We were all collected in a body under the Virginia shore, and if anyone showed his head above the bank a bullet was sure to whistle very near it."[45]

Finally, McCausland decided to make "a sudden and fierce assault" against the blockhouse; however, just before the 8th and 21st Virginia regiments positioned themselves to attack, someone suggested that he first demand the immediate surrender of Stough's Federals, under the threat of no quarter when the blockhouse was taken. Johnson wrote the surrender demand, and two troopers of the 2nd Maryland were sent towards the blockhouse with it, waving a white flag. To the Confederates' great relief, Colonel Stough agreed to surrender, on condition that his men be immediately paroled; that their personal property be left alone; that his men be allowed to retain "canteens, blankets, haversacks, and rations," and that his wounded be allowed to return to Cumberland on a hand car. McCausland quickly agreed to the terms, as a direct assault would have cost him heavily in casualties and time. Stough and 82 Federals exited the blockhouse and took their parole; their surrender had saved many lives.[46]

As they exited the blockhouse, McCausland arrived, demanding the Federals surrender their canteens, rations, blankets and haversacks. Stough refused. A lively conversation ensued: McCausland inquired whether Stough had ever been in the 44th Ohio Infantry; Stough replied in the affirmative. McCausland asked, "Were you a captain?" Stough admitted he was. McCausland rejoined, "Were you not the leader of the scouting parties who used to capture my pickets on the Greenbrier River every two weeks?" "I am that man," Stough replied. McCausland responded, "We are old acquaintances. You are all right. You can have your haversacks, canteens, blankets, and rations."[47] Stough's determination earned Confederate respect, and they treated the Federal troops accordingly.

Nevertheless, his surrender underscored the fact that unexpectedly stiff Federal resistance at Hancock, Cumberland, and Oldtown, along with the undisciplined raiders' tendency to prey on civilians, had until then robbed McCausland of victory. Stough's surrender notwithstanding, McCausland's only option at that point was to return to Virginia. After destroying the blockhouse, the iron-clad train, and a section of track, the raiders rode nine miles further, resting that evening and the next day at Springfield, West Virginia, along the South Branch of the Potomac. With the rebels south of the Potomac again, the Chambersburg raid ended.[48]

CHAPTER 9

Debacle at Moorefield

Railroads often played a crucial role in the effective movement of troops and supplies in the Civil War; whoever had the most efficient railroad system enjoyed a distinct advantage. A good example was the action at New Creek, West Virginia, 4 August, where the timely transport of Federal troops on the B & O railroad again robbed McCausland's raiders of victory.

During their day's rest at Springfield, McCausland decided that an attack on the B & O might result in badly needed success for his demoralized troops. Federal forts at New Creek, West Virginia, 22 miles southwest of Cumberland, that guarded the railroad and contained huge military storage buildings, provided tempting targets. Again, however, strong Federal defenses, with blockhouses, abatis and interlocking fields of fire; the steep terrain; and the timely arrival of reinforcements by train from Cumberland proved too much for McCausland's ill-equipped tatterdemalions to overcome.

The New Creek Valley was described by an officer of the U.S. Army engineers: "The New Creek Valley is bounded on the east by a range of abrupt wooded hills or mountains [New Creek Mountain] some 800 or 900 feet high, immediately at the base of which New Creek runs ... on the west of the Creek ... the ground is low, level, and cleared for a width of some 300 or 400 yards, then rises gradually for about the same distance to a range of steep wooded hills or mountains [Thunder Hill], forming the western boundary of the valley." On the north, "the New Creek Valley crosses the Potomac Valley ... the Potomac is from 40 to 60 yards in width, rapid and fordable at three or four points in the Valley, the bottom stony." The New Creek Valley ends at a ridge on the north, atop which the Federal forts lay.[1]

Federal fortifications at New Creek, forts Fuller and Piano, were protected on the north by the North Branch of the Potomac. Fort Fuller lay southeast of the town of New Creek, atop a very steep hill, a short distance south of the river. Adjacent Fort Piano lay east of town, also atop a high hill. Both commanded strategic views of local roads leading to the Shenandoah and South Branch valleys. The B & O railroad ran immediately north of the forts. Constructed by General John C. Frémont earlier in the war, Fort Piano had been abandoned because it was atop a high, steep hill that made it largely inaccessible. However, not only did the rugged countryside militate against the Confederates achieving victory at New Creek, the feud between McCausland and Johnson intensified, resulting in failure of coordination between their brigades. Out of necessity, they had cooperated with one another at Oldtown, and the raiders had fought their way out of a precarious situation. Now, however, the danger posed by Kelley's possible pursuit, with Stough's Federals leading, had ended. They were south of the Potomac again, and Johnson and McCausland drew further apart.

Nevertheless, determined to achieve victory, the Confederates arose at first light on 4 August and headed for New Creek, McCausland's brigade in the lead. Arriving at New Creek (today's Keyser, W. Va.), the Rebel chieftain briefly delayed his attack, awaiting the arrival of Johnson's brigade. Johnson arrived late, and his explanation reflects the ill-will that had developed between the two commanders: "When his [McCausland's] advance reached New Creek I was two miles and one-half in his rear. The reason of this was that I marched from beyond Romney, he from the mouth of Mill Creek, making my march fully seven miles longer than his. When I reached the foot of the mountain I found his column ... halted, and he having taken a road twenty-five miles from Romney to New Creek, instead of one eighteen miles ... having changed the route without informing me, other than the bare order to follow him."[2] Johnson, however, admitted, "He had halted long enough for me to close an interval of seven miles. I, therefore, also stopped."[3] Failing to ascertain why McCausland had changed their route, Johnson came upon McCausland's ambulances at the foot of Mill Mountain. He mistakenly assumed they were the tail end of McCausland's column, and stopped for an hour, to rest and let his horses graze.

Meanwhile, McCausland's brigade had arrived at the New Creek forts around 1 P.M. Soldiers of the 154th Ohio Infantry camped two miles south of the forts on the Romney Turnpike (today's Route 220) heard shooting to the north, strapped on their equipment, and followed their commander, Colonel Robert Stevenson, "on the double-quick" for Fort Fuller. Upon reaching the fort, two or three companies, including a mounted patrol from the 2nd Maryland Potomac Home Brigade, were sent to determine McCausland's strength.

McCausland's men drove the Federals back to the fort, and about a half hour later, Stevenson telegraphed Kelley that New Creek was under attack, stating "the force is more than McNeill. They have infantry, cavalry, and artillery with them."[4] Kelley wired Stevenson to hold the forts at all costs, and that he was sending reinforcements.[5] A mile south of Fort Fuller, McCausland formed his troops in an east-west line of battle across the width of the valley. Part of the brigade advanced on Fort Fuller, while the remainder marched towards Fort Piano, on the crest of New Creek Mountain.

Upon arriving, Johnson was ordered to advance up Thunder Hill, on the west side of the valley, to position his big guns, and open fire on Fort Fuller. Johnson told McCausland that his two guns had 11 rounds of shot between them; nevertheless Johnson was ordered to proceed. At 3 P.M., he ordered his men to dismount and advance up the hill. The Marylanders and Virginians found the hill too steep to climb, let alone position artillery. They struggled up the hill, and found "a blockhouse, a palisaded work, and abatis" awaiting them. The 6th West Virginia Infantry, occupying the works, opened a heavy fire on Johnson's men, halting their advance. Meanwhile, McCausland's brigade had overrun Fort Piano. He then sent a few hundred troops down the fort's steep western slope towards Fort Fuller. On the way down, they engaged units of the 154th Ohio, and fighting spread across the narrow valley. By 3:30 P.M., the raiders were pushing Stevenson's Federals backwards, and the Confederate capture of Fort Fuller seemed imminent.

Enter Federal reinforcements, arriving at 4 P.M., by train from Cumberland. They charged up the mountain, forcing McCausland to evacuate Fort Piano, and the Rebels retreated down the southern slope. Nevertheless, McCausland wasn't finished. He led his men on another charge up the mountain and pushed the Federals back down the western slope. However, artillery fire from Fort Fuller caused the rebels to withdraw back up the mountain.

Meanwhile, Johnson, already low on ammunition and unable to move his artillery up Thunder Hill, decided that unacceptably high casualties would result from storming the hill and ordered a withdrawal. McCausland might have achieved victory at New Creek, but for the arrival of Federal reinforcements, the lateness of the hour, and Johnson's difficulties in capturing Thunder Hill. McCausland withdrew, with Johnson following. The rebels covered 17 miles before camping late that evening at Burlington, and Colonel Stevenson didn't discover their retreat until early the next morning. Continuing to retreat southeast, McCausland and Johnson arrived at Moorefield, a Confederate sympathizing town in the South Branch Valley, the next day.

The Valley of the South Branch was known in the 18th century as Wappatomaka, (Great South Branch Valley) to the Shawnee and Delaware tribes. During the French and Indian War, it was on the path leading from Fort Duquesne to the Shenandoah Valley, where Native warriors often attacked settlers' cabins. Fielder Slingluff described the South Branch Valley: "There is no lovelier spot in all Virginia than this little mountain-locked valley; and as it had escaped the desolation of war, it was the very spot for rest." The South Branch of the Potomac was about narrow and shallow in the Old Fields–Moorefield area, and the bottom covered with large round cobblestones.[6]

Ignoring advice from a well-known local partisan, Captain John Hanson McNeill, who warned him against camping in exposed positions near the river, McCausland ordered his brigade to encamp on the south bank. Johnson bivouacked a mile away, in the flatland on the north bank, near the Romney Turnpike, at Old Fields. Angered and humiliated at being ignored, McNeill withdrew his force eight miles upriver, to Dashers, camping there that evening. Johnson established headquarters at Willow Wall, home of Daniel McNeill, cousin of Captain McNeill. Willow Wall, a 22 room brick mansion, built in 1802, is on the east side of the Romney Turnpike. The 1st Maryland camped in a field across the road, while Gilmor slept at the home of his friends, the Van Meters, a half mile to the north. However, McCausland succumbed to a tempting offer from his wealthy friend, merchant Samuel A. McMechen, to sleep in his comfortable home, a large 3 story structure on Moorefield's Main Street. Ominously though, the McMechen home was three miles away from his command; making headquarters there rendered McCausland absent in the event of a surprise attack.[7]

Disaster Strikes

A gray-clad private, William H. Maloney, galloped down Moorefield's darkened Main Street around midnight 6–7 August 1864. He was at the end of a long and tedious 25-mile ride from Romney where, that morning, he had observed the arrival of General Averell's brigade, about 2000 strong. Maloney pulled his panting mount to a stop in front of the McMechen home, then dismounted. After tying his horse to the railing, he climbed the front steps and pounded on the door. "Message for the general!" he shouted.

After being admitted, the courier met with McCausland. Private Maloney excitedly explained that a large force of Federal cavalry commanded by Averell had left Romney the previous evening and was on the way to Moorefield. Expressing disbelief upon hearing the news, McCausland nevertheless scribbled out orders to Col. James Cochran, whom he had left in charge, and Johnson. One writer has stated that McCausland's orders to Johnson included instructions to "stand ready, strengthen the pickets, and to occupy the ford of the South Branch"; however, another account states that his order merely instructed him to "saddle up [his troops] and send out a scout on the Romney Road."[8] Whatever McCausland's order contained, it said nothing about an attack or in any way stated that the Confederates were in danger. After listening to Maloney for a few minutes, McCausland went back to sleep. Rising around dawn, he mounted his horse and left Moorefield. Heading back to camp, he encountered fleeing troops from his command and soon realized that his brigades had disintegrated under Averell's attack.

Meanwhile, Johnson received McCausland's order at 2 A.M., "a verbal order by courier from him [McCausland], informing me that Averell had passed through Romney the preceding evening with three brigades of cavalry, and directing me to saddle up my command, and send out a scout on the Romney Road." Johnson obeyed immediately, sending a courier to each regimental commander, and sending out a squad of 20 men and one officer on the Romney Road with instructions to look for the enemy. Lt. Fielder C. Slingluff, of the 1st Maryland, described the situation "when, in the middle of the night, the order came to 'saddle up.' We were soon ready for a reported advance of the enemy, but after waiting an hour or two ... the men gradually got under their blankets and went to sleep."[9]

Johnson further stated, "this was the first, last, and only intimation I ever received from General McCausland of the proximity of the enemy, and the only order I ever received from him on the subject. The order itself was calculated to assure me that there was no danger of immediate attack." Despite Maloney's warning, McCausland failed to inform Johnson that a Federal assault was likely. However, unknown to McCausland, Averell's brigades had spent the evening of 6 August resting only about 10 miles from Moorefield.[10]

Averell was unable to follow the raiders to Cumberland, mainly because 300 of his horses were exhausted and shoeless, rendering only 1,300 troops fit for riding. Since May, Averell's troopers had marched from West Virginia to participate in Hunter's attempt to capture Lynchburg, back into West Virginia on their retreat, then into Pennsylvania and Maryland, a distance of over 1,400 miles, without a remount. However, on 3 August, still at Hancock, he received an urgent telegram from Hunter, concerning the importance that Lincoln and Grant placed on destroying McCausland's raiders, and "directing me to pursue, by the most expeditious route, that portion of the enemy's forces and attack it wherever found." Also at Hunter's order, 500 troops from the 1st New York Lincoln Cavalry, the 22nd Pennsylvania Cavalry, and other units augmented his command. McCausland may have realized that Averell's horses were exhausted. Nevertheless, Averell crossed the Potomac, arriving at Springfield, West Virginia, on the afternoon of 5 August, where he discovered that McCausland's column was heading for Moorefield. They arrived in Romney about 11 A.M. the next day.[11]

From Romney, Averell sent a unit of the 22nd Pennsylvania Cavalry, about 100 troops led by Major George T. Work, to guard the Wardensville Turnpike, a winding, twisting mountain road east of Moorefield, to cut off possible Confederate retreat in that direction. South of Romney, Averell's scouts captured one of McCausland's dispatches, verifying that Moorefield was in fact the raiders' objective. Considering a dawn attack, Averell ordered a halt around 6 P.M. to let the troops rest and eat. By 1 A.M., they were mounted and moving toward Moorefield again. About three hours later, they encountered Johnson's troops.

Averell and his troops used surprise and stealth to great effect, while a steady rain that morning turned the roads soft and tended to deaden the noise of horses' hooves and gunshots. In addition, warm temperatures produced a heavy, thick fog that kept both sides from seeing all but the shortest distances. Their first night in the Moorefield area, 5 August, Lt. Samuel G. Bonn and "about 10 men" of the 2nd Maryland, went on picket duty on the Romney Road. As Slingluff described Bonn's men, "So wearied were the men that after the first night's duty, Lieutenant Bonn sent word to camp and begged to be relieved, stating that his men were absolutely unfit for duty.... His appeal was unheeded."[12] Through an oversight on Johnson's part, Bonn and his squad had had neither relief nor rations since their arrival in the Moorefield area two days earlier. Nevertheless, just before dawn on 7 August, about two dozen gray-clad horsemen rode into Bonn's camp. Confederate satisfaction at being relieved quickly turned to shock and dismay, when the gray-clad relief force quickly surrounded them and drew their guns, capturing them. Too late, Bonn and his men realized that the relief force were Jessie scouts — Federal cavalry wearing Confederate uniforms.

Meanwhile, Averell himself, leading a small squad south on the Romney Road, captured two scouts moving in front of the main rebel force. After interrogating the prisoners, and learning the location of the main rebel patrol, Averell sent 15 men, led by Captain T.R. Kerr of the 14th Pennsylvania Cavalry, to capture them. Kerr's troops left the main road and came up behind the Confederate patrol. When the pickets of the 8th Virginia inquired their identity, the Federals replied that they had come to relieve them. The hapless Confederates soon found themselves prisoners, with nothing but two miles of empty road between the advancing Federals and Johnson's brigade.

Averell learned from Bonn's men that the Confederates had been warned of his approach, and assumed that he had lost the element of surprise, and that McCausland anticipated an attack. However, Averell kept his force moving, and around 5 A.M. trotted through Reynolds Gap, a narrow defile on the Romney Road, heading straight towards Johnson's camp. He stated that Johnson's brigade was "posted in line of battle on both sides of the road, one mile north of the South Branch of the Potomac River." He further stated that his advance unit, the 14th Pennsylvania Cavalry, led by 22-year-old Major Thomas Gibson, charged the rebels, and "with an eager shout," broke the Confederate position. This is unlikely, because, according to Slingluff, by the time Averell's troops appeared, the gray-clad horsemen had decided that the anticipated Federal attack was a false alarm, with many retiring and falling asleep.[13]

Johnson stated that "about daylight a squadron in Confederate uniform moved by the camp of the First Maryland straight to my headquarters. Those who were up and saw them supposed them to be a returning scout or picket, and took no notice of them."[14]

They didn't fire until they had nearly reached Willow Wall, and they were closely followed by a large force of Federal cavalry which rode through the camps of the First and Second Maryland, forcing them back to the McNeill house (Willow Wall). Johnson was lying on the floor of the upstairs front bedroom, head resting on his saddle, when Averell's Federals came calling. After his adjutant's shouted warning, Johnson was ready seconds later. He ran out the front door, and nearly into the arms of the fast approaching blue-coats. The Federals dismounted, firing their carbines, chasing the gray-clad general back into the house.

Johnson probably climbed out a second story rear window of Willow Wall and onto the roof of the back porch. Jumping from the roof, he ran from the house, and was given an empty mount, and briefly rallied the 8th Virginia. However, little was accomplished as his brigade was swept over the steep banks and across the river, and into McCausland's brigade, by the tidal-wave momentum of the Federal assault. Leading part of the 8th Virginia, Johnson was surrounded by blue-coated cavalry and captured. However, he mingled among the other prisoners and shortly thereafter made good his escape to Moorefield.[15]

Johnson's description of his escape from Willow Wall refers to the Federal rifles, rapid-fire seven-shot Spencer carbines, a gun that provided Averell's troops with far greater firepower than the single-shot, muzzle-loading rifles and cap-and-ball type revolvers the Confederate horsemen possessed. Johnson's brigade also suffered from a lack of sabers. As he commented: "This great disaster would have at once been retrieved but for the insufficient armament of the command. Besides the First and Second Maryland and a squadron of the Eighth Virginia there was not a saber in the command. In that open country, perfectly level, the only mode to fight charging cavalry was by charging, and this the men were unable to do. The long Enfield musket once discharged lay helpless before the charging saber." The Federal advantage in firepower accounts for some of the Confederate inability to stop Averell's assault, and the blue-coated horsemen rode through the rebel encampments at will.[16]

Meanwhile, at the Van Meter home, a half mile north of Willow Wall, Gilmor was having a lively time of it. As he described events, "About 3 A.M. I received orders to saddle up ... not a word about the Federals coming, and I thought we were merely making an early start for the Valley; accordingly I saddled my mare and rode over to camp ... I tied my mare ... rested my head on a fence log, and was soon asleep. It was not long before I was roused by a shot in the direction of the 1st Maryland, and so near that I took it to be someone cleaning his pistol. Even a second shot hardly caused me to open my eyes, for our men had a bad way of firing whenever the fancy struck them." Shortly thereafter, Gilmor heard the command, "Get up, damn you!" The northern accent was unmistakable, and the speaker simultaneously fired at Gilmor, the bullet hitting the rail on which his head rested. He saw two mounted men nearby, and the head of a gray-clad column on the road. Confused, Gilmor stood up, as one of the horsemen fired at him again. He drew his pistol and shot the man, but his comrade yelled, "What in the hell are you doing? You are killing your own men!" Gilmor, now further confused, nevertheless asked him what unit he belonged to. The gray-clad horseman replied, "To Captain Harry Gilmor's command." When he failed to give the proper rank, Gilmor shot and killed him, realizing the gray-clad horsemen were Federals.[17]

As daylight began to poke through the early morning fog, Gilmor and about 50 of his troops charged, driving some Federals backwards, but he observed large numbers of blue-coats on both flanks, riding through the 1st Maryland's camp. While he had been engaged with the two gray-clad Jessie Scouts, Averell's advance, the 14th Pennsylvania and 8th Ohio Cavalry, along with elements of the 1st and 3rd West Virginia, led by Major Gibson, deployed about 500 yards from the Confederate encampment. The 14th Pennsylvania was on the right of the road, and the 8th Ohio to the left. The 1st and 3rd West Virginia, of Colonel William Powell's brigade, formed on the left, not far from the South Branch. With cries of "Remember Chambersburg!" they rode through the 1st Maryland's camp, shouting "Surrender, you house-burning scoundrels!" and "Kill every damned one of them!" and began sabering the hapless Confederates, many just awakening. They didn't fire a shot until reaching the immediate vicinity of Willow Wall, where they began their pursuit of Johnson. Observing Johnson fleeing Gibson's Federals, one of Gilmor's men, Lt. William Richardson, Company F, 2nd Maryland, dismounted, giving Johnson his horse. Shortly thereafter, Richardson was captured.[18]

Slingluff described the blue-coated advance through Johnson's camp: "Just at the break of day I felt a rude shock, which I supposed came from the careless tread of a comrade, and I made an angry remonstrance. This was followed by a kick which I thought came from a horse. I, furious, threw the blanket from over my head and found a couple of Averill's men, with cocked pistols at my head, one of whom said: "Get up, you----- Chambersburg burning-------!" Slingluff arose, and claimed that he "had nothing to do with the burning of Chambersburg" and considered it "wicked and unjustifiable." Slingluff "saw the blue-black column of Averill winding down the road and breaking off into the fields where our men slept ... dashing in among the men and waking them up from their sleep ... our rout was complete and irretrievable and the rallies, as I afterward heard, were without vigor on our part."[19]

Shortly thereafter, on the south bank, Averell's assault was temporarily halted as Colonel Peters, leading about 300 troops of the 21st Virginia, formed in line of battle. Confederate artillery fire repulsed two Federal attempts to cross the river, and the South Branch was soon crowded with Union corpses. Among the dead was Major Seymour B. Conger, of the 3rd West Virginia. Thereupon, Averell ordered a brigade commanded by Colonel Powell to cross the river and make another assault on the Confederate position. Under heavy fire, Powell's Federals crossed the Potomac, routing the raiders, sending them fleeing towards Moorefield.

About 1,200 troops of McCausland's brigade made a stand in a cornfield where the road to Moorefield divided about a mile from the river. About 200 Federals of the 1st New York Lincoln Cavalry and 3rd West Virginia had crossed the South Branch, coming upon the mounted rebels in the tall corn behind a strong skirmish line. Realizing that the Confederates would run them down if they retreated, the Union commander urged his small force forward, exhorting them to yell. The blue-coats charged straight towards the middle of the butternut battle line, yelling and waving their sabers. Their charge proved too much for McCausland's demoralized raiders. Though outnumbering the attacking Federals more than six to one, they broke and ran, scattering in every direction. Another Federal attack, on the rebels' right flank, chased many of those remaining into the hills east of Moorefield while others fled towards the town. McCausland himself left Moorefield sometime between daybreak and sunrise, not arriving on the scene until after his brigade had scattered.[20]

Many of McCausland's men fled into and through Moorefield, two miles away, where they were yelled at and humiliated by disgusted residents, most of whom were Confederate sympathizers. A few hundred, however, fled into the hills along the Wardensville Turnpike; 45 were captured, by squads of Work's 22nd Pennsylvania. Work met Averell in Moorefield around 3 P.M., turning over about 35 prisoners and 100 horses.[21]

Private Maloney, who had spent the night at the McMechen house, went to the barn just after daybreak to saddle his horse. Back at the house, he had his breakfast interrupted when a servant girl rushed in and warned, "Run Mr. Maloney! De town am full ob Yankees!" Forgetting breakfast, Maloney ran out the back door towards the stable, hearing horses' hooves, sabers clanking, and the noise of men talking coming from the front of McMechen's home. Peering through a crack in the wall, he observed a mob of fleeing Confederates on Main Street, many yelling, "Go on! Go on!" as they retreated in mass confusion. Mounting his horse, Maloney waited for the frightened mob to pass before entering the street. He refused the request of an officer to assist in halting the frightened men; the officer and his horse were thrown to the ground by the mob.[22]

Meanwhile, the noise of the mob had awakened many of Moorefield's residents. As Maloney drifted along at the tail end of the crowd, he heard one woman, standing on her front porch, yelling: "Shame! Shame! Oh, Shame! Go back and fight! Don't run! Go back and fight! If we had our South Branch men here they would not run!" One of the raiders replied, "Madam if your South Branch men had been over in Pennsylvania stealing as much as we have, they would run too."[23] Only after the raiders had fled through the town did Maloney realize that no Federals had appeared. Johnson managed to rally the undisciplined mob into some semblance of order. When Averell's Federals halted their pursuit after penetrating a short distance into the town, the rebels retreated about thirty-five miles southeast, to Early's headquarters, atop Rude's Hill in the Shenandoah Valley, near Mt. Jackson, Virginia.

The Confederates suffered a total of 150 killed and wounded, 678 horses captured, and all artillery and equipment destroyed. About 420 troops from McCausland's brigade were captured. Averell reported 9 killed and 32 wounded. Most of Johnson's brigade was sent to Camp Chase, Ohio, where they finished the war. McCausland blamed Johnson for the defeat; Johnson requested an investigation, but none was ever conducted. Who was responsible?

Captain George W. Booth, Johnson's adjutant, though not an impartial witness, nevertheless described McCausland's leadership accurately: "McCausland's management and conduct, from the time we reached Chambersburg until the fateful day at Moorefield, was destructive of discipline, without ordinary precaution and care, and found a fitting sequel in the disaster which overtook his command ... and the cause sustained a serious loss in morale and material from which this particular body of troops never fully recovered. The hope of converting them into more efficient soldiers disappeared, and we were fearfully handicapped for the remainder of the campaign."[24]

As the overall commander of the raiders, McCausland bore the greater portion of responsibility. He knew that Averell's Federals were tracking his command, yet he ignored Captain McNeill's advice about not camping in exposed positions in the flatland near the South Branch. He failed to inform Johnson that Averell's force was approaching, and failed to return to his command upon hearing Maloney's message. However, Johnson wasn't blameless. He too was aware that Averell's force was tracking them. He obeyed McCausland's order, sending word to his scattered units to be mounted and ready. However, he failed to respond in a thorough, systematic way; failed to warn his men of Federal troops dressed as Confederates; failed to issue rations; and failed to personally lead his men until Averell's Federals were in his camp.

One writer has stated that Early was satisfied that the blame for the defeat at Moorefield "did not lie entirely with Johnson," that Johnson's removal from command "had nothing to do with" the events at Moorefield, and that "Early refused to order an official investigation, despite several requests" since "the good of the service did not require, and rather mitigated against, such procedure." This was true — Early's cavalry was then in such poor condition that an official inquiry would have done more harm than good.

Johnson stayed with the Valley Army through the battles of Winchester, Fisher's Hill, and Tom's Brook, and fought well. However, because of his poor performance during the Washington raid and at Moorefield, and because Johnson had fewer men left to command, Early recommended his removal. Lee removed him from command in early November, but appointed him commandant at Salisbury Prison, in Salisbury, N.C., where he finished the war.

However, Early reorganized his cavalry after Moorefield, ignoring McCausland and giving command to Major General Lunsford Lomax. Curiously, McCausland, a Virginian and former instructor at Virginia Military Institute, wasn't censured. His attempt to ransom Hancock resulted in part from the contempt that many Marylanders harbored for the Confederate cause in July 1864, and reflected Confederate ill-will towards Maryland over that state's failure to secede. The sentiments of many Marylanders, perhaps a majority, towards the Confederacy in mid–1864 was expressed in a *New York Herald* article that referred to the Chambersburg raiders as "a contemptible squad of less than five hundred rebel ragamuffins."

Though Hancock's residents were Confederate sympathizers (unusual in Western Maryland), McCausland evidently didn't care. McCausland's feud with Johnson escalated because of the incident at Hancock, leading to defeat at Moorefield. Thus Johnson's removal from command to an administrative appointment, when the Confederate Army sorely needed field officers, had political overtones.

The defeat at Moorefield was caused by low morale, poor discipline, lack of adequate weapons among Confederate troops, crucial mistakes by McCausland, and "a wretched carelessness" on the part of McCausland and Johnson. As he stated, "Had there been less plunder, there would have been more fighting at Moorefield."[25] The disaster came at a critical time for the Confederacy, when the Army of Northern Virginia was struggling against Grant's forces at Petersburg, and when General Sherman's Federals were closing in on Atlanta. The destruction of Johnson's brigade and the scattering of McCausland's troops weakened the Army of the Valley at a time when Grant had come north to Maryland, finally turning to the task of straightening out the Federal command structure. Grant would choose a commander for the Army of the Shenandoah, Major General Phillip Henry Sheridan, who would prove more than a match for Jubal Early and the Army of the Valley.

CHAPTER 10

Northern Victory in Sight

Peace Charades

Abraham Lincoln paced up and down the Oval Room in the White House on a sweltering humid afternoon, 23 August 1864, awaiting the arrival of the cabinet members for their weekly meeting. That morning, he had written a memorandum, expressing strong doubt about his re-election, "This morning, as for some days past, it seems exceedingly probable that this administration will not be re-elected. Then it will be my duty to so cooperate with the President elect as to save the Union between the election and the inauguration; as he will have secured his election on such ground that he cannot possibly save it afterward."[1] Lincoln put the memorandum inside a sealed envelope. As the cabinet members entered the Oval Room, he had each of them sign the envelope, leaving them wondering what they had signed.

Lincoln's dismal appraisal of the prospects for his re-election was a result of his political support rising and falling with the battlefield fortunes of the Union armies. Public approval of his administration hit bottom in August, mostly because of the frustrating stalemate that had resulted when Grant's spring offensive in Virginia was blunted by Lee and the Army of Northern Virginia. With the implementation of Grant's plan to simultaneously attack various Confederate targets, Northern civilians had hoped for an end to the war by August. Instead, Grant's bulldog tenacity had thus far resulted in bloody stalemates at the battles of the Wilderness, Spotsylvania Courthouse, and Cold Harbor, and in the Army of Northern Virginia entrenching at Petersburg, stifling the Army of the Potomac, since mid–June.

Two other prongs of Grant's grand strategy were previously blunted while the Army of the Potomac was fighting at the Wilderness and Spotsylvania Courthouse. On 5 May, Major General Benjamin Butler attempted to capture Richmond from the south by landing at Bermuda Hundred, on the banks of the James River, with 30,000 troops, about midway between Richmond and Petersburg. Those cities were defended by only about 5,000 Confederates, and their commander, Major General P.G.T. Beauregard, recently re-assigned from Charleston, was still in transit. Had Butler moved fast, his force could have captured Richmond while Lee and the Army of Northern Virginia were fighting at the Wilderness, sixty miles to the north. Had Richmond been captured, along with the Confederate government, the war might have ended.

However, Butler's force didn't move on the Confederate capital until a week later. In the meantime, Beauregard had brought up reinforcements from South Carolina, and attacked Butler at Drewry's Bluff, eight miles south of Richmond. In a hard-fought contest, the blue-coats were driven back to a narrow peninsula between the Appomattox and James rivers, with Beauregard's rebels cutting them off "as if it had been in a bottle strongly corked," as Grant later described Butler's defeat.[2]

In addition, Major General Franz Sigel's force of 6,500 Federals, marching up the Shenandoah Valley to capture Staunton, destroy the Virginia Central Railroad, and threaten Richmond from the west, was met and defeated at New Market on 15 May by a scratch force of 5,000 Confederates, led by General Breckinridge. The rebel contingent included a detachment of 247 teen-age cadets from the Virginia Military Institute. The Confederates began the day defending the Bushong house, a large white frame farmhouse with several outbuildings.

Breckinridge's troops climbed Manor Hill, pushing through Sigel's first line of defense. After establishing a new line farther north, on Bushong's Hill, Union artillery blew open a gap in the rebel line. Breckinridge reluctantly ordered the cadets into the gap to charge the Union line. They advanced into the teeth of Union artillery fire, incurring heavy casualties, but caused the momentum to swing to favor the Confederates. Among the charging cadets was Moses Ezekiel, later to achieve fame as a sculptor. Among the dead was 18-year-old Thomas Garland Jefferson, a descendant of President Thomas Jefferson.

At the beginning of the fight, Sigel had ridden out in front of his troops, braving enemy fire. Sigel was a native of Baden, Germany, immigrating to the United States in 1852. Largely to satisfy German-Americans, the majority of whom voted Republican, he had been awarded command of the Army of the Shenandoah. However, he failed to inspire his men, and as the VMI cadets reached the crest of Bushong's Hill, the Federal lines gave way, and the blue-coated soldiers were pushed into a northerly retreat. Hunter replaced Sigel four days later.[3]

In Georgia, Sherman's 100,000-man Army of Tennessee had, since May, pushed approximately 54,000 Confederates, now under General John Bell Hood, back towards their base at Atlanta. Sherman's Yankees were now maneuvering around that city, to the southwest towards Jonesboro, to cut the last remaining railroad line into Atlanta. However, they hadn't yet isolated Atlanta, an important manufacturing and transportation center and gateway to the Lower South — southern Georgia, Florida, Alabama, Mississippi, and Louisiana. After more than three years of brutal warfare, Federal armies continued to appear helpless, and the lack of any definite indication of ultimate Northern victory had nearly destroyed Lincoln's chances of re-election. Though slowly staggering towards final defeat, the Confederacy still had a lot of fight left.

The incumbent president's lack of confidence in his ability to win re-election was reflected in the strong groundswell of anti–Lincoln sentiment across the political spectrum as expressed not only in the negative opinions of opposing Democrats, but also in those of Lincoln's fellow Republicans. As summer's end approached, Lincoln could do nothing right; he was soundly criticized by Radical Republicans for not prosecuting the war strongly enough, for "dictatorial usurpation" of powers and responsibilities that in their view lay with Congress, and for his vetoing of the Wade-Davis reconstruction bill, which contained draconian measures for reconstructing the South. Among these was the repudiation of the entire Southern war debt and the restriction of suffrage to whites. Henry Winter Davis, a Radical Republican from Maryland, also favored congressional oversight of Reconstruction to the exclusion of the president. From the other side of the political spectrum, Lincoln was roundly condemned by Peace Democrats and Copperheads merely for continuing the war, while War Democrats were uncomfortable with his increasing commitment to end slavery.[4]

Meanwhile, at local Democratic gatherings throughout the North, a spate of peace resolutions appeared. Newspaper editorials thundered against the war, and Union battle losses caused the peace movement to grow in strength to the extent that New York Republican "Boss" Thurlow Weed, on 6 August, stated, "Lincoln is gone, I suppose you know as well as I. And unless a hundred thousand men are raised sooner than the draft, the country's gone too."[5] Lincoln's re-election seemed so uncertain that some Republicans, including Horace Greeley, started a campaign to run General Benjamin Butler for president, and a few were even thinking about Grant. In addition, at a separate convention that spring in Cleveland, Radical Republicans had nominated John C. Frémont for president.

Contributing to Lincoln's depression that July and August was the appalling state of the nation's finances. Under the administration of Secretary Salmon P. Chase, the Treasury had incurred a debt of nearly two billion dollars, an unheard-of sum. The Legal Tender Act, signed by Lincoln in February 1862, in response to dwindling gold reserves in New York banks, created irredeemable paper money — the greenback — backed only by the "full faith and credit" of the Federal government as legal tender for debts.

Chase did nothing to stop the implementation of the greenback, and Attorney General Edward Bates upheld the constitutionality of the new paper currency. However, by 1864, the greenback had so depreciated in value that loans to the government became very risky. In addition, in June the income tax on those making $600 or more increased, from 3 percent to 5 percent. The income tax had, for the first time, been imposed on Americans on 1 September 1862, to help pay for the war. In addition to the above quoted rate, the rates were 5 percent on incomes greater than $10000, 1.5 percent on interest, and 5 percent on all property of any kind.[6]

Chase had tendered his resignation, for the fourth time, at the end of June, over a disagreement with Lincoln and New York senator Edwin Morgan, concerning his choice for the new assistant secretary of the Treasury in New York, Radical Republican Maunsell Field. This time Lincoln accepted his resignation. Chase considered the president his intellectual inferior; nevertheless, he had brought the credit of the government to its lowest point and so reduced confidence in the U.S. Treasury that his departure proved a blessing.[7] Chase had resigned on at least three previous occasions, using resignation as a way of protecting his rights and privileges as treasury secretary, with Lincoln refusing to accept. The president had once taken advantage of Chase's absence to fire a West Coast customs collector. Upon returning, Chase promptly resigned upon learning of the firing. Lincoln refused it.

Jefferson Davis attempted to take advantage of Lincoln's dilemma, and the steadily increasing desire of Northern civilians for peace, by sending representatives — peace commissioners — to Canada. The idea behind the mission was for the commissioners to locate and encourage influential Northerners who favored a quick end to the war through negotiation and who approved Southern independence. After first discussing the matter in secret session with the Confederate Congress, Davis worked closely with Secretary of State Judah P. Benjamin and Georgia senator Herschel V. Johnson, searching for suitable candidates. He finally appointed Jacob Thompson of Mississippi, Clement C. Clay of Alabama, and James Holcombe of Virginia as peace emissaries in April 1864. Thompson was a former U.S. congressman and had served as secretary of the interior in the Buchanan administration while Clay had been a Democratic senator in the 1850s. Holcombe was a legal scholar who had favored settlement of sectional differences without war and had played a role in the Washington Peace Conference in 1861. He had been a professor of law at the University of Virginia and had served in the Confederate Congress from 1862 until 1864. Clay, Thompson and Holcombe were on friendly terms with a large number of Northern Democrats.[8]

The commissioners received informal instructions from Davis, who sent them on their way "with a view to negotiation with such persons in the North as might be relied upon to aid the attainment of peace. The commission was designed to facilitate such preliminary conditions as might lead to formal negotiations between the two Governments."[9] Clay and Thompson were to support and encourage peace groups and disaffected individuals in the North, meddle in Northern politics, and weaken the Northern monetary system in any way they could. Leaving for Canada, they slipped through the Federal blockade at Wilmington, North Carolina, and arrived in St. Catherines, Ontario, close to Niagara Falls, some weeks later. They spent the next two months making contacts among Northern peace advocates, slowly realizing the complex thinking of many of them. They observed that Northern Peace Democrats were willing to make broad concessions to the South to achieve reunion but were uncomfortable with the idea of Southern independence.

Nevertheless, the commissioners thought they could work with the Peace Democrats, if they avoided making strident statements demanding Southern independence. Instead, they put forth the idea that a cease-fire would result in a restoration of the Union. They also favored a prolonged armistice to avoid unpleasant intervention by foreign powers.[10]

Complementing increasing Northern peace hopes was an intense longing for peace on the part of many Southerners. Indeed, rumors of an impending armistice swept through the South. A number of soldiers in the Army of the Valley thought that an armistice would result from their nearly successful attempt to capture Washington. One southern editor commented "that our independence is already conquered and won; that even though we may yet suffer some reverses, yet the neck of this war is broken." Another southerner stated, "It is manifest that peace principles are constantly gaining ground," while Confederate ordnance chief Josiah Gorgas observed, "Peace begins to be very openly talked about."[11] However, given Lincoln's pre-conditions for negotiation — abandonment of slavery and taking the oath of loyalty to the Union, and Davis' pre-conditions — Southern independence with slavery intact — rumors of an armistice were more reflective of emotional longings for peace rather than realistic expectations.

Not unreasonably, Northern political developments were a major factor in maintaining strong Southern military resistance and a correspondingly high level of civilian morale. Throughout the south, civilians believed that successful Confederate resistance would result in Lincoln's defeat in the fall election. Union troops escaping from southern imprisonment, traveling through the countryside towards Union lines, noticed that "the

South is now waiting for the election, in hopes of a peace candidate being elected. Vallandigham or McClellan they wish for, so long as they can defeat Lincoln." However, expectations of peace were common in the Confederate armies. Brigadier General James Conner, a South Carolina infantry officer, commented in an August 1864 letter, "I think there is every prospect of peace by the end of the year. Grant has played out badly. He is now moving his army to Maryland or thereabouts ... I look to see the whole campaign shifted to the Potomac, and perhaps, the annual Manassas fought over again, but the peace feeling is growing stronger and stronger at the North. The idea is becoming settled that fighting will not stop the war, that negotiations must come in, and that once commenced, I don't think they will ever get up any more battles ... Old Abe has lost ground amazingly of late, and may be he too will come out the strongest peace man of all."[12]

Nevertheless, Southern civilian sentiment was often at odds with Jefferson Davis' thinking and strategy, and he did little to cultivate it. However intense the longing for peace by most southerners, it wasn't enough to persuade Davis to change Confederate military strategy. Although he realized that battlefield events affected civilian opinion and hoped that Early's raid would result in the capture of Washington, he remained adamantly opposed to military operations conducted solely for political gain.

Davis remained true to his basic cordon-defense strategy; believing, even after more than three years of war, that the best way to get the Lincoln administration to negotiate was to continue to demonstrate Confederate military strength, to the near exclusion of other options. In addition, Davis entertained contrary thoughts. Partly because of widespread starvation in the South, and the increasing rate of desertion in Confederate armies, he was apprehensive that the election of a Northern peace candidate might make his goal of Southern independence unattainable. Unlike Lincoln, a Northern peace candidate would make concessions to the South, making reunion a very attractive option.

The Uprising That Wasn't

Chicago provided the setting for further Southern attempts to disrupt the Northern war effort. Founded in 1837, as a railroad and industrial center, Chicago had grown dramatically during the war. With a population of 109,000 in 1861, the city counted 178,000 residents four years later.

On the evening of 28 August, the day before the Democratic National Convention, a large band of Confederates, including a number of soldiers in civilian dress, brazenly entered the Sherman House hotel, where Clement Vallandigham, former congressman and Copperhead leader, was staying. The soldiers were escapees from Northern prison camps, led by Captain Thomas H. Hines and Lt. Jacob B. Castleman. Hines and Castleman had participated in Major General John Hunt Morgan's raid into Indiana and Ohio the previous summer, and both had been captured, spending time in the Ohio penitentiary. Both good soldiers, they eventually escaped from confinement, making their way south. Hines persuaded Davis to send him to Canada in March, along with Castleman.

Even before leaving for Canada, they came up with plans to foment chaos in the North and make Northern civilians experience the harshness of war. Among these was a plan to raid Chicago's Camp Douglas and free Confederate prisoners there during the

Democratic National Convention. Another plan was to seize the U.S.S. *Michigan,* an iron-hulled warship on Lake Erie, and use it to free Confederate prisoners incarcerated at Johnson's Island.

Traveling with Jacob Thompson, Hines and Castleman arrived in Halifax on 19 May. Realizing the need for immediate action to help the Confederacy, Thompson parted company with them. After a brief stop in Montreal, where he deposited his working capital — one million dollars — with the Bank of Ontario, he traveled to Windsor, Ontario, where he met with Vallandigham. As an advocate of free trade, Vallandigham had spoken out strongly against the Morrill tariff in Congress in July 1861. Furious at Lincoln and the Republicans for supporting tariff legislation that protected the monopolies of wealthy New England and Pennsylvania industrialists while Midwestern farmers went bankrupt, Vallandigham founded the Sons of Liberty, a radical organization, of which he was supreme commander. Another source of Vallandigham's ire was the loss of southern markets, occasioned by Federal blockade of the Mississippi River, resulting in widespread economic depression that reportedly caused 95 bank failures in Illinois by the spring of 1863. In addition, a large number of illegal and arbitrary arrests of those who disagreed with Federal war policy and fear of emancipated slaves competing for scarce jobs added to growing Midwestern discontent.[13]

Lincoln termed the Sons of Liberty, with their affiliated Copperheads, "the fire in the rear." In the spring of 1863, he responded to Vallandigham by having him arrested and jailed without charge. Under the supervision of Major General Ambrose Burnside, he was then escorted into Kentucky, where he was briefly a guest of the Confederates at the headquarters of Major General Braxton Bragg. From Kentucky, Vallandigham journeyed to Wilmington, North Carolina, where he boarded a blockade running steamship and sailed for Canada.

At their meeting in Windsor, he told Thompson that the Sons of Liberty numbered about 170,000 in Ohio, Indiana, and Illinois — a gross exaggeration — with growing membership lists in Missouri and Kentucky. Vallandigham stressed that the Sons of Liberty were strongly against the war and strong supporters of state's rights and state sovereignty but didn't necessarily favor Confederate independence. Nevertheless, for the preservation of state sovereignty and free trade, Vallandigham opined that his organization might be willing to set up a Northwest Confederacy, consisting of Illinois, Indiana, Ohio, Kentucky and Missouri, satisfying Thompson.[14] He offered Vallandigham money to finance the establishment of a Northwest Confederacy. Vallandigham himself refused it; however, the money was subsequently accepted by the Sons of Liberty for distribution to local chapters.

Thompson believed that with Confederate encouragement, which he hoped would include an invasion of Kentucky and Missouri, the Sons of Liberty would revolt and establish a Northwest Confederacy. Such an entity would be hostile to Northern interests and would intensify Northern civilian desires for an end to the war. However, Thompson and his fellow commissioners misjudged the intentions and character of the Peace Democrats.

Vallandigham's return to the United States from exile in Canada and subsequent arrest by Federal authorities was supposed to trigger the uprising. However, upon his reappearance in Ohio, Federal authorities ignored him, and no uprising occurred. Following a request for military action from Thompson, Jefferson Davis and Secretary of War

James A. Seddon decided to give the Copperheads a push. They picked General Morgan's cavalry, defending the important salt-mining region of southwestern Virginia, to work in tandem with the Copperheads to start the revolt. After successfully defending Saltville, Virginia, from a Federal cavalry raid, Morgan was ordered to lead 2,500 threadbare, weary and hungry troopers into Kentucky during the first week of June despite the objections of his commander, General Bragg. Nevertheless, Davis and Seddon overlooked the fact that Morgan cared little for the Butternuts (as he called the Copperheads) and that Morgan's raid the previous summer had hurt the Copperhead cause.

About a week later, Morgan's men captured and burned Cynthiana, Kentucky, supposed to be the signal to begin the uprising. Morgan waited for instructions from Copperhead leaders in Louisville, but none arrived. Nearly out of ammunition, the rebel raiders desperately fought off Federal pursuit, leaving their dead floating in the Licking River as they retreated eastward. Kentucky Copperhead leaders later claimed that Morgan's expedition occurred too soon — they weren't ready to rebel. The planned uprising had to be postponed.[15]

Morgan's defeat further dampened Copperhead desire for a rebellion in the Midwest, as Hines discovered when he met with their leaders in Chicago in July. The uprising was now put off until 4 July, the day the Democratic National Convention was to begin. However, the convention was postponed, and the Copperheads in turn asked for another postponement. Hines agreed to 20 July. On that day, they again said they weren't prepared to revolt, causing Hines to realize that many Copperheads liked to talk about rebellion, but only a few were willing to "sacrifice life for a cause," as he later wrote.[16]

Thus when Hines, Thompson, and Clay next met with Vallandigham, they insisted that the uprising begin on 29 August, the day the Democratic Convention was again scheduled to begin in Chicago. Many of the delegates would be Peace Democrats. With an estimated one hundred thousand conventioneers and tourists in town, lodging was scarce, with men sleeping three and four to a bed. The wooden sidewalks and dusty streets were crowded with sightseers and assorted troublemakers, many inebriated, a perfect setting for an insurrection. A critical part of the plan was the assault on Camp Douglas, led by Hines himself, to free the approximately 5,000 Confederate prisoners incarcerated there. Hines chose Camp Douglas because of the large number of Morgan's raiders imprisoned there. Simultaneously, local chapters of the Sons of Liberty and other assorted Copperheads were to revolt in Ohio and Indiana, attacking Federal troops, cutting telegraph wires, taking over courthouses and jails, and establishing a Northwest Confederacy.

Hines was hoping to act swiftly and decisively to shock Copperhead leaders into starting a widespread uprising throughout Ohio, Indiana, and Illinois. Such an opportunity arose when 3,000 Federal troops arrived in the city, on the eve of the convention. They came in response to the pleas of Colonel Jeffrey Sweet, commandant at Camp Douglas, who suspected that trouble was afoot. However, opportunity requires ready and willing participants.

Hines was staying at the Richmond House, and on the evening of 28 August he met with a group of confused and frightened Copperhead leaders in his suite. Charles Walsh, leader of the Chicago chapter of the Sons of Liberty, told Hines and Castleman that "something has gone wrong"; they had failed to send instructions to revolt to local Copperheads in Indiana and Ohio. Furious, the two former cavalrymen had no choice but to await action by the reluctant radicals. Their anger simmered as they watched the conventioneers march through the city that evening, in a torchlight parade.

The following morning, as the convention opened, Hines and Castleman again met with the Copperheads. They emphasized that the Union troops were in Chicago to disrupt the convention, to "interfere with the rights of the people." Hines and Castleman stressed that an arrest would provide a pretext to riot; they urged Walsh's men to attack the blue-coated troopers. Throughout the day on 29 August, and well into the evening, Federal troops patrolled Chicago; although Walsh had promised Hines and Castleman that the Sons of Liberty would revolt, not one Federal soldier was assaulted.

At a second meeting that day, the two former cavalrymen outlined an ambitious plan for capturing Chicago's Federal arsenal, then marching on the state capitol in Springfield, with another plan to destroy the Federal installation at Rock Island. They briefly inspired the Copperheads; but although they pleaded for 500 men, only 25 volunteered. Hines and Castleman knew there would be no revolt, and told the Confederate troops with them they were free to go home.[17] When push came to shove, the specter of "the Northwest in flames" terrified most of the Copperheads. In the end, Vallandigham and his followers, despite their anger at the Lincoln administration, had no desire to further fragment the Union. In accordance with their willingness to allow the South to secede peacefully, they were opposed to the war. However, the great majority of Copperheads weren't willing to actively help the South achieve independence.

Political Suicide

While Hines and Castleman were plotting, the Democratic National Convention got under way in an enormous wooden fire-trap of a building called the Wigwam, close to Lake Michigan. Built to accommodate over 15,000 people, the building had a "grand entranceway"—a "spacious passageway 15 feet wide"—on Michigan Avenue. The entranceway led directly to a central platform that could accommodate 600 delegates and reporters. Around the platform ran a narrow pathway by which those on the platform could come and go without walking through the galleries. Two huge galleries overlooked and surrounded the central platform, one for women, and women with male escorts, the other exclusively for men. The entire inside was decorated with "the national flag" and other patriotic bunting. A number of railroads disembarked at the Wigwam, while "the State Street cars" ran a short distance away. Sunrise on 29 August witnessed a crowd beginning to gather, and as the morning wore on, the lines extended down to the lakeshore.

With the band playing patriotic and popular songs, the proceedings began at noon; inside, the delegates were seated on the raised platform, surrounded by vast crowds. August Belmont, chairman of the Democratic National Committee, called the assembled delegates to order. In his opening statement, Belmont remarked, "The American people have at last awakened to the conviction that a change of policy and administration can alone stay our downward course.... Four years of misrule, by a sectional, fanatical, and corrupt party, have brought our country to the very brink of ruin." He confidently predicted "the utter disintegration of our whole political and social system amidst bloodshed and anarchy" should Lincoln be re-elected.[18]

William Bigler of Pennsylvania was chosen president of the convention. Governor of Pennsylvania from 1851 through 1854, Bigler's political philosophy reflected pre-war Democratic and Unionist support for the Fugitive Slave Law, and war-time Democratic desire for reunion with slavery intact. Though personally opposed to slavery, as governor he allowed Federal enforcement of the Fugitive Slave Law, and supported the Kansas-Nebraska Act of 1854.[19]

After roll call, a letter from an imprisoned Kentucky delegate was read, urging the convention to "save a bleeding country" and reassert the rights of habeas corpus and trial by jury. Washington Hunt, former Whig congressman and one time governor of New York, then proposed an armistice "with a view to terminate the pending conflict and restore the blessings of peace."[20] Nominations for president were closed on the second day.

McClellan Nominated

On 31 August, the third day, the convention voted overwhelmingly for General George B. McClellan as their nominee for president. McClellan received 202½ electoral votes, versus 23½ tallied for Thomas Seymour, a Peace Democrat and former congressman from Connecticut.

As the delegates from each state declared for McClellan, the vast crowds surrounding them became wildly enthusiastic, their shouts mingling with the discharge of cannon and the reverberating strains of music emanating from the building. Gentleman in long frock coats waved their stovepipe hats, while ladies waved handkerchiefs. Wave after wave of applause shook the building, while the crowds outside, unable to get in, echoed the shouts and enthusiasm of those inside.

As the assembled delegates and spectators quieted down, several members of the McClellan executive committee entered the hall carrying a huge portrait of the general, inscribed in large letters, "McClellan, Our Country's hope and pride," and "If I cannot have the command of even my own men, all I ask is to be permitted to share their fate on the field of battle." The portrait was hoisted onto a canopy above Bigler's chair, accompanied by wild cheering and music from the band, playing "Hail to the Chief!"[21] It underscored McClellan's position as a War Democrat, favoring reunion as the sole condition of a peace settlement, with slavery intact.

Nevertheless, one or two outspoken delegates opposed the former Army of the Potomac commander; their criticism pointed out intractable problems with McClellan's background and the Democratic platform. Benjamin Harris of Maryland told the convention that "General McClellan was the very first man who inaugurated the system of usurping state rights ... Maryland has been cruelly trampled by this man, and I cannot consent ... to allow his nomination to go unopposed." Harris then read a September 1861 directive from McClellan, ordering General Nathaniel Banks to arrest the Maryland legislature in Frederick, "and be sure that none escape." Harris then told the assembly that McClellan had imprisoned the Maryland legislature; McClellan was therefore a tool of Lincoln, "and all the charges you can make against ... Lincoln ... I can make and sustain against this man, George B. McClellan."[22] Amid a cacophony of boos and shouts for order, George W. Morgan of Ohio rose to refute Harris, claiming — falsely — that there was a conspiracy between the Maryland legislature and General Joseph Johnston, by which Johnston was to lead a Confederate army into Maryland when the legislature passed an Ordinance of Secession. In 1861, however, McClellan believed that the evidence for this conspiracy was credible, even though the Ordinance of Secession was tabled, and the so-called conspirators were arrested, languishing in prison without trial. Harris questioned McClellan's judgment, making many in the vast crowd uncomfortable. Alexander Long of Ohio, a Peace Democrat, also strongly opposed McClellan's nomination.

However, McClellan had two big problems at Chicago that proved fatal to the Democratic cause. His interests weren't strongly represented at the convention, and the Peace Democrats, led by Vallandigham, proved stronger and more vociferous than expected. In addition, New York governor Horatio Seymour offered himself as a compromise candidate between the two Democratic factions, posing a credible threat to McClellan's nomination. The general's campaign manager, Samuel L.M. Barlow, fearful of the influence of other Democratic leaders, refused to attend the convention, telling the "Young Napoleon" that his presence would hurt his chances. McClellan, however, didn't insist that Barlow attend.

Meanwhile, mild-mannered Samuel J. Tilden, a member of the Committee on Resolutions, was one of the New York delegates representing "Little Mac" at Chicago. He was entrusted with the task of designing the party platform to reflect McClellan's thinking. However, Vallandigham's presence in the committee was very strong, and as a concession to the Peace Democrats he was named to the seven delegate subcommittee entrusted with the actual writing of the party platform. Achieving a four to three majority, Vallandigham inserted his well-known war failure resolution as the second part of the platform; after four years of failure to restore the Union "by the experiment of war ... justice, humanity, liberty and the public welfare demand that immediate efforts be made for a cessation of hostilities, with a view to an ultimate convention of the States, or other peaceable means, to the end that at the earliest practicable moment peace may be restored on the basis of the Federal Union of the States."[23]

"Immediate efforts ... for a cessation of hostilities, with a view to an ultimate convention of the states" was fancy talk for an armistice, with no pre-conditions for negotiation; it was not the type of plank that McClellan, a soldier needing the soldier vote, should have accepted. McClellan's supporters on the platform committee then tried to adopt a plank that made reunion a precondition for peace, but failed, gathering only three votes. The war failure resolution was accepted by a voice vote of the delegates after Vallandigham exaggerated the numbers of Midwestern Copperheads, threatening to withhold their support, in the upcoming campaign. The war failure plank was a disaster for the Democrats, not only because it gave credence to an ideological split in the party, confusing the voting public, but also because it had the effect of robbing the still popular McClellan of the badly needed soldier vote.

However, Vallandigham's threat was an illusion. The number of Midwestern Copperheads wasn't close to "two hundred thousand," and the Sons of Liberty wasn't a strong or even a well-organized group. Nevertheless, the convention delegates believed it was, with the result that the war failure plank became an integral part of their platform. The Democrats then compounded their mistake, nominating George H. Pendleton, an outspoken Ohio Copperhead, for vice president. The war failure plank and Pendleton's presence on the ticket confused voters, contributing to McClellan's defeat in the fall election.

However, battlefield events would make his defeat certain. "Little Mac" accepted the nomination in an 8 September letter, stating in part, "The existence of more than one government over the region which once owned our flag, is incompatible with the peace, the power, and the happiness of the people."

McClellan revealed a Unionist stance that affirmed slavery and ignored Southern hopes for independence and further stated, "I could not look in the face of my gallant comrades of the army and navy who have survived so many bloody battles, and tell them that their labors and the sacrifices of so many of our slain and wounded brethren had been in vain; that we had abandoned that Union for which we have so often periled our lives." However, by accepting the war failure plank, "Young Napoleon" signaled that he would, in fact, accept the dissolution of the Union, and ignore the "sacrifices of so many of our slain and wounded brethren."[24]

Southern Death Knell — Atlanta Falls

By August, the war in the east had long since settled into a bloody and tedious stalemate. Early re-crossed the Potomac a few times, raiding the countryside, frightening Maryland residents into thinking a full-scale invasion was in progress. Federal forces in Maryland, led by General Hunter, proved unequal to the task of handling the Army of the Valley. At Petersburg, Virginia, by 30 July, with the approval of Generals Burnside, Meade, and Grant, the 48th Pennsylvania Infantry, which included many coal miners, dug a tunnel more than 500 feet long under a strong Confederate salient. They placed more than 4 tons of gunpowder in the tunnel. The resulting explosion blew a hole 170 feet long, 60 feet wide and 30 feet deep in the Confederate line, burying an entire gray-clad regiment and battery of artillery. However, failure to commit specially trained African American troops, poor leadership of the Federal infantry attack that followed the explosion, and vigorous Confederate counter-attacks resulted in 4000 Federal casualties without penetrating the Confederate line. The war to restore the Union had stalled in the East, greatly depressing Northern civilian morale. Therefore many in the North looked westward for progress against the Confederacy.[25] In addition, Robert E. Lee advised Davis to the effect that if Georgia couldn't be held, then Virginia would also be forced to surrender. Therefore if Atlanta fell to Federal forces, the days of the Confederacy were numbered.

While the Democrats were debating in Chicago, seven hundred miles away, Federal armies led by General William Tecumseh Sherman were closing in on Atlanta, a vitally important manufacturing and transportation center. Little more than a frontier town in 1860, Atlanta had become known as "the Arsenal of the Confederacy." Attracted by Georgia's efficient railroad system and abundant water supply, the Confederate government had, since 1862, strongly supported that state's munitions production; munitions factories included the Confederate States Powder Works in Augusta, a naval yard in Columbus, and various machine shops and a very large rolling mill in Atlanta. Sherman had often seen rebel ammunition boxes marked "Made in Atlanta." The capture of that city was thus one objective of Grant's plan to subdue the South.[26]

Atlanta was also the gateway to the Lower South. One hundred fifteen miles southeast of Chattanooga, with a population of about 20,000 by 1864, Atlanta was located at the confluence of the Western & Atlantic, Macon & Western, Atlantic & West Point, and Georgia railroads. With New Orleans already in Federal hands, the fall of Mobile in August guaranteed that whoever controlled "The Gate City" would control access to the Lower South — Georgia, Florida, Alabama, Mississippi, Louisiana, and Texas. More important, the capture of Atlanta would isolate the Confederate government in Richmond from these states, weaken southern will to continue the war, and likewise revive flagging northern civilian morale.

Sherman's three armies, nearly 100,000 troops, with 254 pieces of artillery, began their advance on Atlanta on 7 May with an attack on outlying elements of the Confederate Army of Tennessee at Tunnel Hill. The Federals consisted of the Army of the Cumberland, led by Major General George H. Thomas; the Army of the Tennessee, led by Major General James B. McPherson; and the smaller Army of the Ohio, led by Major General John M. Schofield.[27] Sherman chose the particular route of the Federal advance because that was the route taken by the Western & Atlantic. No other practical approach through the rugged frontier country of northwestern Georgia existed. Thus the railroad was indispensable to Sherman's advance, supplying his huge army — a city on the move — with food, munitions, clothing and medicine. Sherman protected the road by building blockhouses at strategic points, garrisoned by troops and by mobile repair crews who could rebuild the track as fast as Confederate cavalry could destroy it. In addition, a few of the bridges had locked wooden gates protecting the track.

Angling southeast from Chattanooga, the Western & Atlantic snaked into Ringgold, then climbed into the mountains, going through an impressive 1500-foot-long tunnel, in the aforementioned Tunnel Hill, which the Confederates curiously made no attempt to destroy. Had they destroyed the narrow tunnel, the Federal advance on Atlanta would have been delayed for a month, or perhaps two — long enough to affect the fall presidential election.

Leaving the mountains, the tracks entered the flatlands around Dalton, 30 miles southeast of Chattanooga, without benefit of a road bed. The line then went straight south through Resaca and crossed the Oostanaula River, a tributary of the Etowah River, at Adairsville. The tracks again turned southeast at Kingston, crossing the Etowah at Cartersville, then immediately climbed to thousand foot high Allatoona Pass, then ran down through the town of Big Shanty. South of Big Shanty, the tracks skirted the base of 1800 foot high Kennesaw Mountain, then ran down into Marietta, and eventually crossed the quarter-mile-wide Chattahoochee River. About six miles farther south, the Western & Atlantic entered Atlanta. Despite the railroad, in 1864, Cherokee Georgia was still a sparsely settled wilderness. But for Sherman's railroad supply line, and his successful defense of it, the advance on Atlanta wouldn't have occurred.

Facing Sherman, and led by General Joseph Eggleston Johnston, throughout May, June, and part of July, the Confederate Army of Tennessee numbered 63,408 troops and 189 pieces of artillery.[28] Sherman's blue-coated minions repeatedly engaged Johnston's troops, usually avoiding head-on attacks, in the rugged Appalachian highlands of Cherokee Georgia, once home to the Cherokee tribe. With methodical precision, Sherman repeatedly opted to outflank Johnston's army, at times veering away from the railroad, then coming back to the line of the Western & Atlantic. Nine May found the Army of Tennessee at

Dalton, expecting Sherman's Federals to strike from the north, down the length of the East Tennessee & Georgia railroad.[29]

Johnston may have been lulled into expecting an attack from the north, as Rocky Face Ridge, a seemingly impenetrable mountain barrier, protected Cherokee Georgia from attack from the west and northwest. Rocky Face Ridge is actually a series of rugged, high ridges; however, it was rather easily penetrated—12 miles southwest of Dalton at Dug's Gap and also at Snake Creek Gap. Troops marching through Snake Creek Gap, 15 miles due south of Dalton, would quickly find themselves between the Army of Tennessee and Atlanta. While a brigade of Kentucky cavalry guarded Dug's Gap, inexplicably, Johnston failed to guard Snake Creek Gap, 10 miles farther south.[30]

Sherman took advantage of Johnston's failure by sending McPherson's Federals to advance on Resaca through Snake Creek Gap; thus Johnston was forced to abandon Dalton and retreat towards Atlanta. After combat at Resaca on 13-14 May, Johnston was again outflanked and forced to retreat when Sherman's Federals, at Lay's Ferry, using pontoon bridges, gained the south bank of the Oostanaula River ahead of the Confederates.[31]

Despite being badly outnumbered, Johnston had no overall plan for attacking Sherman's army, opting instead to use the advantage of the defensive to counterattack. One place where this strategy might have worked was at Cassville on 19 May. However, more than any other engagement during Sherman's advance, the Cassville Affair bewildered and demoralized the Army of Tennessee, already discouraged by 12 days of retreating.

Johnston had drawn up a plan that took advantage of the terrain—the road to Atlanta split at Adairsville, and Johnston correctly anticipated that Sherman's Federals would advance down both roads. Kingston was at the base of the western leg of the triangle, while Cassville was at the base of the eastern leg, about 5 miles apart. Johnston's plan was to strike with his entire force—74,000 troops—the wing of Sherman's army coming down the Cassville Road, less than 35,000 troops, led by Schofield and Major General Joseph Hooker. Meanwhile, the western column of Sherman's army was several miles away, over rough terrain; one division was in Rome, over 20 miles west of Cassville.

Johnston, confident of success, declared to his troops: "I lead you to battle," eliciting thunderous cheers. Hood's corps, marching north, parallel to the Cassville Road, was to strike first. The Louisiana troops of Lieutenant General Leonidas Polk, the "Fighting Bishop," were about a mile west of Hood's troops, northwest of Cassville. The two corps were supposed to trap Hooker's Federals between them; however, Johnston and Hood had failed to sufficiently reconnoiter the surrounding area, and it soon showed. While Polk's division awaited the Federals, in ominous silence, for two hours, Hood quickly discovered a sizeable force—"a heavy line" of Federals, on his right. Had he turned westward to face them, as instructed, they would have been in his rear. Halting his deployment, Hood ordered out a line of skirmishers. But by that time, Sherman's main column was arriving, after an unexpectedly quick march eastward from Kingston, robbing the rebels of the element of surprise. A Confederate officer sent a report back to Johnston. Stunned and disbelieving upon reading it, Johnston called off the attack without attempting to verify it.

Although Johnston re-assembled his army that afternoon on a high ridge east of Cassville, Sherman quickly brought up his artillery, subjecting the Confederate position to a heavy crossfire. At a conference that evening, Johnston was advised that their position was untenable. Johnston later claimed that Hood and Polk urged him to retreat. However,

Hood's biographer points out that he was "in favor of fighting if allowed to attack," and that both he and Polk urged Johnston to attack. Another general might have attacked; but Johnston chose to ignore their suggestion, and again ordered a retreat, across the Etowah.[32] Although the Army of Tennessee occupied strong defensive positions the next day, they were coming uncomfortably close to Atlanta.

Later in May, at New Hope Church, Pickett's Mill, and Dallas, referred to collectively as the Hell Hole, the Army of Tennessee temporarily stopped Sherman's Federals, winning back some of their flagging self-respect. At Kennesaw Mountain, on 27 June, Sherman's advance again ground to a halt after an entire day of fruitless frontal assaults against entrenched Confederate positions. However, while Sherman was sacrificing his troops in futile headlong charges, Schofield found a way around the Southern fortifications. Accordingly, on 2-3 July, Sherman moved his Federals around the southern side of Kennesaw Mountain, seizing Marietta the next day.[33] Establishing a supply depot at Vining's Station, just north of the Chattahoochee River, Sherman's Federals made preparations to cross while panic stricken residents of Atlanta began leaving town, crowding the roads and railroad depots. Schofield's troops were the first Federals across the river, using pontoon bridges, on the morning of 8 July. They flanked Johnston yet again, forcing him to withdraw further towards Atlanta.

Meanwhile, in Richmond, Jefferson Davis had become very concerned about Johnston's inability to stop Sherman's Federals and about his failure to communicate. Davis had urged Johnston to take the offensive ever since he took command of the Army of Tennessee in December 1863. Johnston responded by repeatedly asking for reinforcements and additional supplies.[34] Johnston was so intractable in this regard that Davis and his chief military advisor, Bragg, acquiesced to his demands, and tried to find the reinforcements he requested. However, as the Federals advanced on Atlanta, Johnston's passivity and failure to stop Sherman took on a new importance and forced Davis to act. The Confederate president responded by sending Bragg to Atlanta, on 9 July, to determine Johnston's plans and suitability for further command. Arriving at Johnston's headquarters, Bragg soon wired Davis, "I cannot learn that he has any more plan for the future than he has had in the past."[35]

Already anticipating relieving Johnston, Davis wired the general the next day, asking to be informed of the current state of the conflict with Sherman's blue-coats, and "your plan of operation so specifically as will enable me to anticipate events." Bragg reported to Davis on 15 July that both Johnston and Lieutenant General William Hardee had repeatedly favored retreat during the entirety of Sherman's advance, and that Hood, Polk, and Major General Alexander P. Stewart favored taking the offensive. Bragg qualifiedly endorsed Hood for command. Because of Hood's battle record and prior meetings with Davis, the Confederate president respected him. However, Hardee outranked Hood and had more experience managing an army.[36]

In a sparsely worded telegram on the 17 July, Davis relieved Johnston of command, appointing Hood to lead the Army of Tennessee. Hood's reaction was curious. He telegraphed Adjutant General Samuel Cooper, asking that Johnston not be removed, with Davis replying that he could not revoke the order without making the situation worse. That afternoon, Johnston left for Atlanta and apparently never returned to the army. While it did some good to replace Johnston with a more aggressive commander, the

Atlanta railroad yard and train depot (Library of Congress)

change couldn't have come at a worse time — in the middle of a campaign, on the successful outcome of which the very existence of the Confederacy depended. Morale in the Army of Tennessee, not high to begin with, plummeted. General Hood, while a good fighter, was not known for his diplomatic abilities. In any event, facing a huge Federal army, he didn't have time to improve his troops' morale.

Although Hood immediately took the offensive against Sherman's Federals, attacking the blue-coats at the Battles of Peachtree Creek on 20 July, Atlanta two days later, at Ezra Church on 28 July, and during August at Jonesboro, he proved no more effective than Johnston at stopping Sherman. He missed an opportunity to destroy part of ;Sherman's army at Peachtree Creek, leaving 4,800 dead and wounded on the field. Though Hood's aggressiveness caused Sherman to respect him, it resulted in 3 disastrous defeats

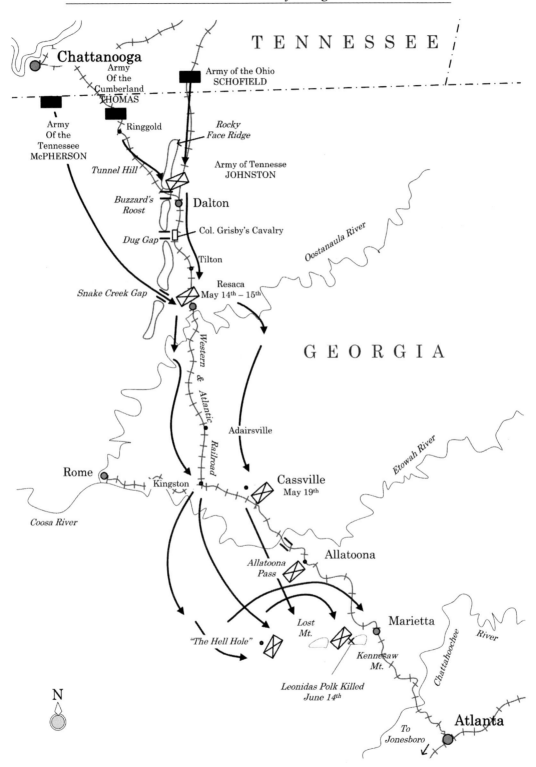

Sherman's advance on Atlanta, May–August 1864

and 13,000 casualties in only 9 days.[37] Failures of coordination, timing, and lack of support from subordinate officers dogged Hood. However, the inexperienced Hood compounded these defeats with a grave error that gave Sherman the chance to capture Atlanta.

After the repeated failure of Hood's attacks to stop Sherman, effective disruption of Federal supply lines was perhaps the Confederate commander's best option. Indeed, ever since Hood had replaced Johnston, the Davis administration had urged him to attack Sherman's supply lines, as they had so urged Johnston.[38] Johnston, however, failed to act on their suggestions, correctly fearing the consequences of sending away his cavalry. Instead, Johnston had asked the Davis administration to order Mississippi cavalry, led by Brigadier General Nathan Bedford Forrest, to attack Sherman's supply lines. Such an action by Forrest could have delayed the Federal advance, since Forrest's troops destroyed railroads more thoroughly than most Confederate cavalry units; however, though urged by Polk, Hardee, and Robert E. Lee, the asked for raid was never ordered. The result was that Sherman's supply line remained intact through May, June and July. However, the pressure on Hood to force a Federal retreat was now greatly increased.[39]

Hood responded in August by ordering the greater part of his cavalry, 5,000 troops, led by Lt. General Joseph Wheeler, northwards to Sherman's rear to destroy the Western & Atlantic. Hood's biographer states, "He envisioned merely a quick strike against the railroad and expected that Wheeler would be absent for only a few days. Details of the raid were left to Wheeler's discretion, a necessity ... since the Confederates did not have exact knowledge of conditions in Sherman's rear, but unfortunate because, as it turned out, Wheeler was not capable of handling the responsibility."[40]

Wheeler's biographer implies that Hood ordered Wheeler to cross the Tennessee River above Chattanooga and ride westward through Tennessee, towards Nashville, destroying the railroad on the way. He was to leave 1,200 troops in Tennessee to ensure that the railroad was not repaired and return to Georgia with the rest of his command, destroying the Western & Atlantic again on his way south. Riding northward on 10 August, Wheeler destroyed a few miles of the Western & Atlantic, but was chased into Tennessee by Federal troops, led by General James B. Steedman, whom Sherman had placed in charge of railroad security. In Tennessee, Wheeler was thwarted by high water at crucial river crossings, which forced him to make time consuming detours. He destroyed a few miles of railroad, but lost the confidence of his troops, and didn't rejoin Hood's army until 10 September.

Wheeler accomplished his mission, but lost over half his command in the process, bringing back only 2,000 troops. His biographer states, "So far as permanently endangering Sherman's line of communication, he had accomplished nothing." As far as endangering Sherman's supply lines, Wheeler had likewise accomplished nothing. His raid into Tennessee proved largely a waste of time and manpower, and worse. Whether or not Hood intended "a quick strike" in ordering the raid, it left his army without eyes for a month, at a very critical time.[41]

Sherman took advantage of Wheeler's absence, realizing that he could now destroy Hood's remaining railroad supply line with relative impunity. On 18 August, he sent his own cavalry to destroy the Macon & Western railroad at Jonesboro, about 12 miles south of Atlanta. Hood's remaining mounted troops managed to fend off the Federal horsemen, and trains continued to run into "The Gate City" from the south.

However, Hood gave too much credence to reports praising Wheeler's raid, believing that Sherman was retreating across the Chattahoochee, when scouts brought word that Federal trenches north and east of the city were empty on the morning of 26 August. Although Hood anticipated a Federal raid on the Macon & Western, because of Wheeler's absence, he had no idea that Sherman had shifted 6 of his 7 infantry divisions to the southwest of Atlanta, to destroy the railroad and isolate the Army of Tennessee. Nor did Hood make any special effort to defend the Macon & Western — he had no one in charge of railroad security, no blockhouses at strategic points, and no designated repair crews as Sherman had with the Western & Atlantic. Unable to determine Sherman's whereabouts, Hood indulged in a fantasy — that as a result of Wheeler's raid, Federal troops were on short rations and that Sherman had retreated northwest, back across the Chattahoochee. Late on 30 August, he still wasn't aware that nearly all of Sherman's troops were south of Atlanta, on their way to wreck the Macon & Western.

Nevertheless, he summoned Hardee and General Stephen D. Lee to headquarters early that evening and ordered them to march their corps to Jonesboro, attack whatever Federal units they found, and drive them across the Flint River, away from the railroad. Two telegrams to Hardee early on the morning of 31 August underscored these orders. Though Hardee's and Lee's troops marched through the night, their assault on the Federals didn't begin until afternoon. They failed to dislodge Sherman's Federals from the Macon & Western.

Still thinking that Federal troop presence in Jonesboro was a diversion, Hood ordered Lee back to Atlanta at 6 P.M. to help defend against the main attack on the city that he was sure would follow. Hood didn't realize that Sherman had concentrated most of his army around Jonesboro. Attacking the greatly outnumbered Hardee there on 1 September, Sherman consolidated his hold on the railroad. With the Macon & Western no longer available, Hood finally realized that evacuation of the city was his only option. The first units left around 5 P.M. The last rear guard cavalry evacuated after midnight, firing the reserve ordnance train: 81 cars loaded with ammunition and 5 locomotives blew up, shaking the ground miles from the city, and creating a hell on earth that burned for five hours. Twenty-six miles away, at Lovejoy's Station, Sherman heard the explosions, concluding that they probably signaled Confederate evacuation.

Several hours later, around 11 A.M. on 2 September, Mayor James M. Calhoun and a few companions, searching for Sherman, encountered lead elements of Major General Henry Slocum's XX Corps. After a brief discussion, Calhoun surrendered the city to Colonel John Coburn, of the 33rd Indiana Infantry, asking in the surrender note for protection for "non-combatants and private property." Slocum sent a note to Sherman, still south of the city at Lovejoy's Station, informing him of Atlanta's surrender. At 6 A.M. the next day, Saturday, 3 September, Sherman sent a telegram to Washington, received the next day, stating in part: "So Atlanta is ours, and fairly won."[42]

Northern Reaction

Upon publication of the news of Atlanta's surrender, Northern civilian morale, so long depressed, soared high with wild enthusiasm, as those north of the Mason-Dixon

Line began to realize that their cause would prevail. As the news of the city's fall spread throughout the north, a traveler taking a night train from New York to Chicago related that "the shouts of rejoicing multitudes" were a constant refrain, and the "glare of bonfires" often illuminated the track. In an editorial of 5 September, titled "The Fall of Atlanta," the *New York Times* said that Sherman's capture of that city "thrilled the nation with a joy not less heartfelt, if somewhat less demonstrative, than that of France, when through the streets of Paris ran the cry: *Sebastopol est pris.* Indeed, the Sebastopol of Georgia has fallen, and with this splendid achievement, one-half of the great campaign of the Summer is finished, and the seal of success already set upon the military operations of the year 1864. With nothing more done, the sum of that which has been done is victory."[43]

The editorial explained how Sherman's campaign had decimated the Army of Tennessee, and further stated, "Atlanta is ours — the point of which that far-seeing speculator, John C. Calhoun, prophesied, in the year 1850, that it would be the greatest inland city of the entire South, and at no distant day ... the capital of a Southern Confederacy. This is the place which, while rapidly approaching the fulfillment of Calhoun's prediction, has been seized by the Union arms. At once, the workshop, the granary, the storehouse, and the arsenal of the Confederacy, Atlanta and its environs were of incalculable value. The foundries, furnaces, rolling mills, machine shops, laboratories, and railroad repair shops; the factories of cannon and small arms; of powder, cartridges and percussion caps, of gun carriages, wagons, ambulances, harnesses, shoes and clothing ... are ours now."[44] Upon receipt of Sherman's 3 September telegram, Abraham Lincoln proclaimed a national day of Thanksgiving, and ordered the firing of 100-gun salutes in more than a dozen northern cities.

Sherman, who had been vilified in the press for years, was now lauded as the greatest general since Napoleon, and described as "brilliant" and as a "genius." He was mentioned by both Republicans and Democrats as a prospective candidate for president or vice president. Lincoln, Seward, Stanton, Grant, Sumner and others hailed him publicly. Predictably, but also inaccurately, New York's leading newspaper, strongly supportive of Lincoln, the day before had glorified Sherman, as having "resisted all pressure tending to extravagant expenditure of life."[45] In fact, more than a few of the Federal casualties during the campaign — perhaps as many as one-fifth — were sustained by reckless frontal assaults against fortified positions, such as at Kennesaw Mountain and Ezra Church.

However, Sherman spoiled the luster of his victory the day after he arrived in the city. Thoroughly in keeping with his theory of the collective responsibility of Southern civilians for the war, Sherman on 8 September issued Special Field Order No. 67, ordering all civilians, except "such civilian employees as may be retained by the proper departments of government" to leave Atlanta. The directive came after they had endured a brutal, unrelenting daily artillery bombardment for seven weeks, and despite the fact that most had nowhere to go, and no provision for food or shelter in the war-ravaged Georgia countryside. Sherman provided rail transportation for those Atlanta residents who went northwards. Those who went south were transported in wagons for about 20 miles, to Rough N' Ready, where they became the responsibility of the Confederate army. However, poor harvests in 1863 and 1864 in northwest Georgia made matters worse, and in the immediate aftermath of Atlanta's surrender, Federal foraging parties had so thoroughly stripped the surrounding area of food that many local residents were close to starvation. Hood was unable to satisfy the 1,000 applications for rations received daily from refugees and locals alike, and many wound up camping in the woods that fall, starving and freezing.

Sherman's depopulation order drew a sharp letter of protest from Hood, and was likewise strongly condemned in the Southern press. However, not only was most of the northern press silent about the forced expulsion of Atlanta's civilian population, the Lincoln administration tacitly approved, with Secretary of War Henry Halleck telling Sherman, "Not only are you justified by the laws and usages of war in removing these people, but I think it was your duty to your own army to do so.... We certainly are not required to treat the so-called non-combatants and rebels better than they treat each other. Even here in Virginia ... they strip their own families of provisions, leaving them as our army advances to be fed by us or to starve without our lines." Federal reluctance to feed Southern civilians made destitute by the war, easily accomplished, played a role in Sherman's decision to depopulate Atlanta. Sherman's order resulted in 1,644 civilians leaving Atlanta, a figure that included 79 slaves.[46]

While Northern reaction to Atlanta's capture was joyous, Southern reaction was predictably very solemn. An example was the subdued front page of a border state newspaper, *The* (Baltimore) *Sun*. Various news items confirmed the fall of Atlanta, Wheeler's raid into Tennessee, and gave a graphic description of civilian suffering in Atlanta as a result of the heavy Federal bombardment, and subsequent destruction, of their city:

> On Wednesday night a large 42 pound shell entered the Presbyterian church on Marietta street, and after passing through the pulpit exploded in the basement, in [the] Sunday School room. Several families living in the vicinity having taken refuge there, were more or less stunned and injured by the explosion, and one man had his right arm taken off. The scene in the room was frightful — it was after midnight, and all the inmates were sleeping peacefully, perfectly confident of security. Mothers caught up their children hurriedly, and rushed frantically into the streets screaming, though without any definite purpose in view, save that of escaping ... from the scene which had struck such terror into their souls — and there, out upon the open streets, they stood crouching.... Shell after shell in rapid succession came screaming through the air, and as the light of each terrific explosion ... quivered over them, striking terror into their souls — and there, out upon the open streets, they stood; the figure of one pale-faced mother could be described ... vainly hoping to shield her little ones from the falling fragments.[47]

The Federal bombardment of Atlanta had no military purpose. Major O.M. Poe, Sherman's chief engineer, experienced the unease of a guilty conscience regarding the killing of women and children during the bombardment. Soon after the city fell, Poe wrote to his wife, saying that he was opposed to the bombardment, "for it did no good at all, and only brought harm to innocent people." He further opined that the shelling didn't cause the city's fall "a single second sooner" than it would have fallen without it, and went on to explain that it was Sherman's movement around the south of the city that caused the rebels to evacuate. Like many in the Federal ranks, Poe couldn't understand the need for Sherman's war of terror against Southern civilians, which had begun in 1862 when Sherman ordered the destruction of the entire town of Randolph, Tennessee, because from that location someone had fired on Federal steamboats in the Mississippi River.[48]

However, the assertion of some modern historians that Atlanta's munitions factories were located in residential neighborhoods, implying that Federal artillerists couldn't help the destruction of civilian residences, is inaccurate and misleading. Federal artillery crews used 30-pound Parrott rifles and 4 1/2-inch cannon, guns that Sherman knew could hit precisely targeted buildings from great distances. Sherman himself requested these guns, and they destroyed many a civilian residence, evidence that he was deliberately targeting non-combatants. That he derived gratification from doing so is apparent, as he described corpses of women and children in Atlanta's streets as "a beautiful sight."[49] The scale of Sherman's war of terror against Southern civilians was without precedent.

The fall of Atlanta caused John C. Frémont to abandon his presidential aspirations. More important, the city's surrender negated the war failure plank adopted by the Democratic National Convention — the war was now seen as successful — and made Lincoln's re-election almost certain. The city's surrender quickly brought most Southerners to the brink of despair. Mary Boykin Chesnut, a volunteer nurse in Columbia, S.C., expressed the thinking of most Southerners: "Atlanta is gone. That agony is over. There is no hope, but we will try to have no fear."[50]

The fall of "the Southern Sebastopol" also affected the Army of the Valley. When Sherman's advance stalled during August, many of Early's troops thought peace close at hand. Robert Rodes thought there would be an armistice before year's end. Stephen Ramseur knew that the fate of Atlanta would greatly affect Lincoln's chances of re-election, and hoped that Hood's Army of Tennessee would force Sherman to retreat. However, even with the city's surrender, the confusing and disappointing platform adopted by the Democrats at Chicago, and McClellan's warlike acceptance letter, Ramseur was confident that Early's army would sustain Confederate hopes and defeat the Federals in the Shenandoah Valley. He wrote, "Everything depends upon the issue of this fall [military] campaign." With the fall of Atlanta, Confederate hopes for holding Virginia certainly did.[51]

CHAPTER 11

Failure in the Shenandoah Country

Early on the morning of 16 September 1864, in Winchester, Rebecca Wright opened the front door of her boarding house ever so slightly and peered through the crack at the tall, elderly African American standing on the porch of her North Loudon Street residence. She inquired of his purpose. Thomas Laws explained that he had come at the behest of Major General Philip H. Sheridan and that he had a message for her. A Quaker and schoolteacher, Wright was well known in Winchester for her Unionist sympathies.

Living just beyond Union lines near Millwood, several miles southeast of Winchester, Laws had been given a permit by the Confederate commander to travel into town three times a week to sell vegetables. Recruited by Major H.K. Young, director of Sheridan's intelligence department, Laws gathered information on Confederate activities in and around Winchester, and passed it to the Federals. Meanwhile, General Crook, a frequent visitor at the boarding house, had told Sheridan that Wright was a trustworthy source and a reliable contact. Wright's boarding house was also frequented by Confederate soldiers.

Two of Young's scouts brought Laws to Sheridan's headquarters, where he was questioned by "Little Phil." Satisfied that he was trustworthy, the Irish general then discussed a dangerous mission: make contact with Wright and deliver a message from Sheridan. Laws agreed to the rendezvous with Wright. The fiery Sheridan wrote out the message on tissue paper, asking if she could tell him the location of Early's army, the "number of divisions" it contained, their numerical strength, and "his probable or reported intentions." Sheridan then asked if the Army of the Valley had received any reinforcements, or if any were "coming or reported coming." He wrapped the message in tinfoil, and instructed Laws to carry it in his mouth. If he was captured by Confederates, he was to swallow the tinfoil.

Ironically, Wright had heard from a wounded Confederate officer at her boarding house the previous evening that Kershaw's division, led by Major General Richard H. Anderson, had departed to rejoin the Army of Northern Virginia at Petersburg. After first consulting her mother, Wright replied to the diminutive general. She said that though she had "no communication whatever with the rebels," General Kershaw's division, along with the twelve guns of Cutshaw's artillery battalion, "have been sent away." Refuting the convincing and often repeated rumor that Early's force numbered 20,000 to 30,000 troops, she stated "no more are expected" as they "cannot be spared" and that the Army of the Valley "is much smaller than represented." Wright further stated, "I will take pleasure ... in learning all I can of their strength and position, and the bearer may call again." Laws delivered her reply to Sheridan.[1] Wright commented, "Many times during the next day ... I wondered what had become of the messenger, and what would result from my note. " The noise from the third battle of Winchester ended her uncertainty two days later.[2]

Wright's information proved very useful to Sheridan; he now had verification of crucial information concerning the size and disposition of the Army of the Valley. Sure of himself and the capabilities of his troops, "Little Phil" could now take the offensive against the much smaller Confederate force facing him and end the frustrating, month-long game of maneuver the two armies had been engaged in.

Ever grateful, Sheridan later gave Wright a made-to-order gold watch, chain and breast pin. However, she was cordially hated in Winchester after the war, as she had given Sheridan information that helped him to eventually destroy the Army of the Valley and defeat the Confederacy. Badly wanting to leave her hometown, Wright paid Sheridan a visit, and he helped her obtain a job at the U.S. Treasury Department in Washington in 1868.

Grant Comes North

The burning of Chambersburg and the debacle at the Battle of the Crater, both occurring on 30 July, underscored glaring deficiencies in the unwieldy Federal command structure and strengthened the presidential campaign of George B. McClellan. As July turned into August, these disasters, combined with Early's unabated threat to Washington, D.C., and Maryland, began to interfere with Grant's ability to successfully prosecute the war. Grant wanted to consolidate the four military departments impacting Washington, D.C., and the Mason-Dixon border area into one and end the threat posed by the Army of the Valley for good.* Grant realized the necessity of a Federal army "getting south of the enemy" but also understood that he would get little or no support for a change in strategy from the War Department, where the top priority was keeping a Federal army between Early's force and Washington. The Federal commander-in-chief appealed directly to Lincoln.

After a 31 July conference with the president at Fort Monroe, Grant informed Chief of Staff Henry Halleck that the four military departments should be consolidated into one, and that he was sending Sheridan to Washington for orders. Anticipating Stanton's disapproval, because of Sheridan's youth and relative inexperience, Grant nevertheless wired Halleck on 3 August, "I want Sheridan put in command of all the troops in the field, with instructions to put himself south of the enemy and follow him to the death." The Union's top commander desired that General Hunter, senior to Sheridan, act as the new department's administrative director. Lincoln, however, understood that to imple-

*The departments were Susquehanna, West Virginia, Washington, and the Middle Department.

ment a sea change in the Federal command structure, accompanied by a change in strategy, more than a telegram to Halleck was needed. He advised Grant accordingly, "Do not count on the War Department to help prosecute a vigorous campaign in the Shenandoah. I repeat to you it will neither be done nor attempted, unless you watch it every day and hour and force it." Even with Lincoln's support, Grant realized that he would have to implement the change himself.[3]

Accordingly, he left City Point, Virginia, taking a troop steamship up the Chesapeake Bay to Washington, where he caught a train for Hunter's headquarters at Monocacy Junction, 42 miles northwest. Some hours later, Grant stepped onto the platform at the junction and was greeted by an escort of Federal officers. Early on the evening of 5 August, the commander of all the Union armies strode into the parlor of Araby, the battle scarred house that had survived the engagement at Monocacy; where he was introduced to the C. Keefer Thomas family, owners of the mansion. After greeting the Federal officers present, he quickly got down to business. He inquired, "General Hunter, where is the enemy?" Shame-faced, Hunter replied, "I do not know, General Grant." Hunter then explained that he had been besieged with conflicting orders from the War Department "moving him first to the right then to the left" so that he had lost all trace of the enemy." Occupying himself with the details of organizing a 30,000 man army, the 62-year-old Hunter had failed to locate the Army of the Valley.[4]

Grant's goal was the destruction of Early's Confederates; the first step was to find them. He immediately ordered Federal forces in the region to concentrate at Halltown, Virginia, four miles south of Harpers Ferry; the infantry was to use the railroad. Early's reaction would indicate the Army of the Valley's location. If Early was in Maryland or Pennsylvania, he would have to return to the valley rapidly to avoid being cut off; if he was in the Upper Valley, he would have to move northwards to meet the threat. Grant then wrote out detailed instructions for Hunter, stating in part:

> In pushing up the Shenandoah Valley, as it is expected you will have to go first or last, it is desirable that nothing should be left to invite the enemy to return. Take all provisions, forage, and stock wanted for the use of your command. Such as cannot be consumed, destroy. It is not desirable that the buildings should be destroyed — they should, rather, be protected; but the people should be informed that so long as an army can subsist among them recurrences of these raids must be expected, and we are determined to stop them at all hazards.
>
> Bear in mind the object is to drive the enemy south; and to do this you want to keep him always in sight. Be guided in your course by the course he takes. Make your own arrangements for supplies of all kinds, giving regular vouchers for such as may be taken from loyal citizens in the country through which you march.[5]

Grant then suggested that Hunter, an old friend, "establish the headquarters of the department at any point that would suit him best, Cumberland, Baltimore, or elsewhere"; Sheridan was to lead the troops in the field. Hunter realized that he was being sidelined; he immediately asked to be "relieved entirely" of command, as Halleck "seemed so much to distrust his fitness for the position he was in" that "he did not want to embarrass the cause." Impressed by the apparent selflessness and patriotism of the "brave old soldier," Grant quickly acceded to Hunter's request. He then telegraphed Sheridan, requesting that he come to Monocacy Junction.[6]

Sheridan reported to Grant the next day. Their meeting lasted less than two hours, with Grant giving him the same orders he had given Hunter. With the Army of the Shenandoah already on the way to Halltown, the two generals parted. The preliminaries to the deadly earnest cat-and-mouse game between the Valley Army and the much larger Army of the Shenandoah had begun. Where was Early? Sheridan would soon find out.

Up the Valley and Down Again

Grant had chosen 33-year-old Philip Henry Sheridan to lead the Army of the Shenandoah because of his noteworthy war record, his singular ability to motivate troops in the field, and because of personal affinity.

A casual observer looking at the diminutive Sheridan — he stood five feet three inches tall, and weighed about 130 pounds — wouldn't think that "Little Phil" was suited to a military career. However, the effect that he had on his troops was described by Captain Henry A. Dubois, a Yale Medical School graduate who served as an assistant medical director in the cavalry corps:

> He [Sheridan] talked freely, said little about himself, but seemed interested in the Army of the Potomac and in the character of its officers and in their current reputation. He drew both of us out and in return gave us his ideas of cavalry and how it could be used. I can now recall him ... his short legs and long body; his peculiar shaped head with a large bump on its back just where his cap fitted; his quiet and rather dull look when not speaking, and the sudden change which came over his face when speaking and the animation of his whole body ... when interested in what he was saying. He inspired me with confidence — but more than this I felt a personal liking for him — why I could not at the time understand nor can I after all these years explain.
>
> He wore the uniform of a Major General but there was no constraint in his manner in talking to us ... nor on the other hand did we feel any reserve towards him on account of his rank. At first I thought that this was due to politeness alone, but soon found it was his natural manner, that was absolutely destitute of any feeling of superiority on account of his rank, but even when I found this out it did not account for the feeling ... of personal attraction ... which soon was so firmly fixed that before his orders had been made out ... I felt as if I had known him long and should have defended him ... as I only could have done for an old and personal friend.... I found that others felt much as I did, that we had a personal ownership in him, that he would at all times acknowledge, and this without any feeling of superiority....
>
> Later on I found that this same feeling was not confined to officers but that the soldiers in the ranks felt much the same way ... much as they would towards a brother in whom they had unlimited confidence and whose interests were also theirs.... This magnetic influence seemed to spread ... to a whole army at times.... His appearance in front of the line of battle, without his saying a word, changed the character of every man in a moment, so far at least as his military utility in the pending battle was concerned.[7]

However, Sheridan had a dark side: he could be a domineering, tyrannical man who never admitted mistakes and often displayed a foul temper; he treated subordinates poorly and was sometimes insubordinate to superior officers as well. In November 1864, a Confederate cavalry force led by Brig. General Thomas L. Rosser captured Federal forts at New Creek, West Virginia, on the B & O railroad, and threatened Cumberland, Maryland. The Federal commander at Cumberland, Brevet Maj. Gen Benjamin F. Kelley, telegraphed Crook, stating: "I will fight Rosser to the last if he attacks me." Sheridan read the telegram, and angrily fired back, "I give you no credit for this remark, as I expect you to do so." Kelley, however, stood his ground, telling Sheridan, "I certainly do not expect or claim any credit for the remark. My only object in making it was to advise my superior officer that, notwithstanding the small force at my command, I would defend the town and public property to the best of my ability. This I deemed proper and respectful, and I exceedingly regret you do not so regard it." Sheridan backed down a bit; three days later he telegraphed Halleck, "I respectfully present the name of Brevet Major General Kelley for being exceedingly cautious when there is no danger and not remarkably so when there is."[8]

The dialog between Sheridan and Kelley is interesting, not least because Sheridan often claimed credit for events that he had little or nothing to do with, regardless of the facts. Conversely, he sometimes couldn't (or wouldn't) tolerate others claiming or receiving due credit for events in which they played a significant role. For example, Sheridan claimed credit for the capture of Missionary Ridge at Chattanooga in November 1863. In fact, the troops of Maj. General William B. Hazen captured Missionary Ridge, along with 18 cannon on the summit and a large number of prisoners. His troops carried the crest long before any troops from Sheridan's units arrived. Hazen denied Sheridan's claim in writing; nevertheless "Little Phil" stood by his pretentions, repeating them many years later.

In his formal report on the Valley campaign, written at New Orleans in February 1866, Sheridan took credit for the plans that resulted in his army defeating Early's Confederates at 3rd Winchester and driving them from Fisher's Hill three days later: "This night I resolved to use a turning column again, and that I would move Crook unperceived, if possible, over onto the face of Little North Mountain and let him strike the left and rear of the enemy's line, and then, if successful, make a left half-wheel of the whole line of battle to his support." His use of the word "again" refers to the flank attack made by Crook's men against Gordon's division that finally resulted in the Federal victory at Winchester. The credit for these maneuvers rightfully belonged to Crook, who proposed and executed them. Sheridan promised to give Crook due credit but never did, even though the idea of turning Early's left flank never occurred to him. After the war, an adoring public heaped praise on Sheridan; he rose to command the entire U.S. Army; the relatively unknown Crook reverted to the rank of lieutenant colonel and saw others, perhaps less deserving, promoted over him. Understandably, he became embittered, turning against Sheridan after the war.[9]

Of Irish descent, Sheridan spent his youth in Somerset, Perry County, Ohio, in the middle of the state, a short distance southwest of Zanesville.[10] Entering the military academy at West Point in 1849, he spent summer breaks at home in Ohio, working as a clerk in a dry goods store where he acquired a strong aptitude for accounting. He would later use these numerical skills as a quartermaster officer in St. Louis. However, Sheridan's combative streak almost cost him his military career. He was nearly expelled from West Point in 1852 for using a bayonet to attack a cadet sergeant whom he decided had addressed him in a disrespectful tone. Sheridan halted before he lunged with the weapon. Nevertheless, he was suspended for a year. He spent his suspension working at the dry goods store. He returned to graduate in 1853, 34th out of a class of 52. While at West Point, he became well acquainted with a number of cadets who would become important later on. These included Henry Slocum, George Crook, James B. McPherson, John M. Schofield, and John B. Hood. Crook in particular would prove his worth to Sheridan many times over.

In July 1853 Brevet 2nd Lieutenant Sheridan was assigned to the infantry at Fort Duncan, Texas, where he served for a year. He spent most of the next seven years serving in the Pacific Northwest, near the Columbia River, fighting Indians, making geographic surveys, and learning to speak Chinook, the coastal tribal language.

Sheridan had a pronounced ability to make a good first impression, particularly where his services were in great demand. Ordered east in the fall of 1861, he found himself a captain in the 13th U.S. infantry at Jefferson Barracks, Missouri, under the command of Colonel William T. Sherman. But before he could settle in, he was chosen by Major General Henry Halleck to conduct an audit into the financial and administrative mess left by the previous commander in Missouri, John C. Frémont. Sheridan straightened matters out quickly, and Halleck rewarded him by appointing him chief quartermaster and chief commissary of the Army of Southwest Missouri. Transportation and supply work occupied him until early summer 1862, when Austin Blair, Republican governor of Michigan, offered him the command of the 2nd Michigan Cavalry with the rank of colonel. Shortly thereafter, he won his first victory over a much larger Confederate force at the Battle of Booneville (Mississippi).

As a result, his superiors were so impressed that on 30 July they telegraphed Halleck, urging Sheridan's promotion to brigadier general, stating, "Brigadiers scarce; good ones scarcer. The undersigned respectfully beg that you will obtain the promotion of Sheridan. He is worth his weight in gold."[11] Halleck complied, and Sheridan thereby rose from captain to brigadier general in 35 days. His commission was made retroactive to July 1, the date of the Battle at Booneville. Nevertheless, a short time later, he was given command of the 11th Infantry Division, which he successfully led at the Battles of Perryville and Stones River. Ironically, however, Sheridan became better known for his leadership of the Union cavalry.

Grant appointed Sheridan to command the Cavalry Corps of the Army of the Potomac on 4 April 1864. At that time, he had had about 90 days' experience commanding cavalry. About five weeks later, on 11-12 May, Sheridan's troopers met a Confederate cavalry force led by Major General J.E.B. Stuart at Yellow Tavern, Virginia. Stuart took a bullet in the stomach and died a short time later, but the Federal force was kept away from Richmond.

A month later, attempting to cut the Virginia Central Railroad near Gordonsville, and join Hunter's army at Charlottesville, Sheridan's horse soldiers were met by a Confederate force led by Major General Wade Hampton and defeated in a terrific two-day battle at Trevilian's Station. Sheridan failed to destroy the Virginia Central and was kept from joining Hunter. However, during the months of May, June and July, his cavalry was engaged daily, and averaged 150 remounts per day. Nevertheless, on 1 August, "Little Phil" was relieved of command of the Cavalry Corps. He was needed to conduct a campaign against Jubal Early and the Army of the Valley.[12]

Taking command of the Army of the Shenandoah on 6 August, Sheridan knew by the evening of the 7th that Early's Confederates were encamped at Bunker Hill, across Opequon Creek about 12 miles west of Halltown. On 9 August, he ordered an advance, to begin between 4 A.M. and 5 A.M. the following day. Attempting to "get south of the enemy," Sheridan's Federals arrived at Berryville about 5 P.M.; but as "Little Phil" expected, Early abandoned his position at Bunker Hill, withdrawing his army south to Winchester, where they camped that evening. The Federal advance and Confederate retreat continued 11–12 August, two exceedingly hot days in which many troops suffered from thirst and sunstroke. The evening of the 12th found the blue-coats camped along Cedar Creek, near Middletown; the Army of the Valley rested a scant four miles south, on Fisher's Hill, a rounded prominence overlooking Strasburg. In only three days, marked by constant skirmishing, the Federals had maneuvered Early's Confederates out of the Lower Valley.[13]

However, illusion and politics intervened. Sheridan refrained from attacking the Army of the Valley as he believed the Confederate force was much larger than it actually was, and in August 1864, the Lincoln administration could ill-afford another defeat, particularly so close to Washington. Ever since the advance on Washington, Early had enthusiastically cultivated the impression that his force numbered between 20,000 and 30,000 troops. This was accomplished by spreading rumors to that effect, by frequently marching his infantry back and forth, and by attacking bridge guards. These efforts had their intended effect, to the point where Grant believed that the Army of the Valley contained as many as 40,000 troops, as he telegraphed Halleck on 12 August: "Inform Sheridan that it is now certain two divisions of infantry have gone to Early, and some cavalry and twenty pieces of artillery ... Early's force, with this increase, cannot exceed 40000 men, but this is too much for Sheridan to attack." The following day Sheridan ordered a reconnaissance towards Fisher's Hill, but the Federals stopped at the top of Hupp's Hill, a large hill about half a mile north of Strasburg.[14]

The effect of Early's rapid back and forth marching to deceive the Federals is reflected in Sheridan's telegram to Halleck, dated 5 September: "My estimate of Early's force is about 27000 infantry." Sheridan wasn't the only one fooled by Early's maneuvers. About two weeks later Sheridan said, "The people of Winchester say that Early had yesterday [19 September] on the field 28000 infantry." In fact, at the battle of Winchester, the Army of the Valley numbered less than 13,000 troops, infantry, cavalry and artillery. In stark contrast, the Army of the Shenandoah mustered about 39,700 on the field, and 45,509 altogether. Most of the difference was the Harpers Ferry garrison, numbering about 4,800 troops. Sheridan's Federals also enjoyed a pronounced advantage in firepower; many were armed with 7-shot Spencer carbines — a gun that one could "load on Sunday and fire all week"— or the lever-action Henry repeating rifle. Early's Confederates were armed with single-shot muzzle loading Enfield rifles and a few shot-guns and pistols; many of the gray-clad cavalry lacked sabers. The blue-coats were also better clothed and fed.[15]

It was just as well that the Federal reconnaissance stopped on Hupp's Hill, because on 6 August Davis and Lee had decided to send Major General Joseph B. Kershaw's division, 3,500 strong, accompanied by the 12 guns of Major Wilfred Cutshaw's artillery battalion, and the cavalry division of Major General Fitzhugh Lee, northward to Culpeper to threaten Sheridan's flank. Traveling on three different railroads, Kershaw's Confederates, led by Major General Richard H. Anderson, arrived at the northern end of the Luray

Valley — Front Royal — on 14 August. Their presence denied Sheridan the use of the Luray Valley as a means of getting behind Early's rebels and forced the Irish General to conduct a two day retreat from Cedar Creek. At dawn on the 17th, Early, watching from atop Fisher's Hill, discovered the empty Federal encampments. He ordered pursuit at once and ordered Anderson's force to meet the Army of the Valley at Winchester. Early's advance units engaged and defeated Sheridan's rear guard south of Winchester that afternoon; however, the Federals continued to retreat, filing into their old encampments at Halltown five days later.

Meanwhile, Major General Wesley Merritt's cavalry had already begun to turn the Valley into a barren waste — per Grant's orders — burning barns, haystacks, and outbuildings on "the Front Royal and Winchester roads" and driving large herds of cattle, sheep and horses through towering columns of smoke that marked their grisly work. Going beyond the army chief's orders, Merritt's troops burned a number of homes on the Valley's eastern side. Sheridan agreed with the Federal policy of making war on Southern civilians, later expressing his opinion:

> I endorsed Grant's programme, for I do not hold war to mean simply that lines of men shall engage each other in battle, and material interests be ignored. This is but a duel, in which one combatant seeks the other's life; war means much more, and is far worse than this. Those who rest at home in peace and plenty see little of the horrors attending such a duel, and even grow indifferent to them as the struggle goes on, contenting themselves with urging those who are able-bodied to enlist in the cause, to fill up the shattered ranks as death thins them. It is another matter, however, when deprivation and suffering are brought to their own doors. Then the case appears much graver, for the loss of property weighs heavily with the most of mankind; heavier, often, than the sacrifices made on the field of battle. Death is popularly considered the maximum of punishment in war, but it is not; reduction to poverty brings prayers for peace more surely and more quickly than does the destruction of human life, as the selfishness of man had demonstrated in more than one great conflict.[16]

Sheridan, however, was a bit disingenuous. While it is true that the "reduction to poverty" brought the war directly to the doorsteps of Southern civilians, the policy of burning homes didn't begin with Grant, nor in 1864. In the fall of 1861, Federal troops under Brigadier General Louis Blenker burned a number of homes in the Valley; destruction of Southern civilian property continued throughout the war. While there is some truth to the contention that the destruction of the Valley's crops and forage shortened the war, there is no evidence to show that burning civilian homes had the same effect. These were destroyed to wage war on Southern civilians and to establish and enforce the authority of the Federal government. More than a few Federal troops found burning civilian homes distasteful and when ordered to do so refused. However, this policy resulted in the burning of thousands of homes, and entire towns, throughout the South. It was designed, and frequently enforced, with a vindictive spirit that changed the relationship of American civilians to their government and contributed to a bitter legacy in the South.[17]

The Army of the Shenandoah was puzzled by Sheridan's withdrawal, but most of the troops were aware that 1864 was an election year with summer and fall the peak campaign season. Thus many of the troops realized the army's retreat resulted from Sheridan's desire to avoid defeat and soothe the worries of politicians and administrators in Washington. As the Irish General later stated, "I deemed it necessary to be very cautious; and the fact that the Presidential election was impending made me doubly so, the authorities at Washington having impressed upon me that the defeat of my army might be followed by the overthrow of the party in power, which event, it was believed, would at least retard the progress of the war, if, indeed, it did not lead to the complete abandonment of all coercive measures."[18]

Nevertheless, Sheridan's retreat to the safety of his lines at Halltown was all too familiar to many Northerners; the withdrawal reminded them only too well of the long string of demoralizing defeats in the Valley at the hands of "Stonewall" Jackson, and after the 7-Days Battles, Fredericksburg, and Chancellorsville. A firestorm of public criticism descended on Sheridan; Northern newspapers demanded his relief, while another invasion of Maryland and Pennsylvania was predicted.[19]

However irrelevant Sheridan's intentions were to the Northern public, the Federal retreat to Halltown worked in the Irish General's favor. The Army of the Valley wasn't terribly impressed with Sheridan; his retreat resulted in Early harboring a growing contempt for him. Early became satisfied that "the commander opposed to me was without enterprise, and possessed an excessive caution which amounted to timidity." Early thus became overconfident, which soon proved fatal to the Confederate cause in the Shenandoah Valley and played a significant role in the defeat of the entire Confederacy. Early was partially correct in his assessment of Sheridan—"Little Phil" sometimes lacked initiative on the battlefield. Very partial to headlong frontal assaults, Sheridan also came up short as a tactician. However, Early went overboard in his low opinion of his opponent. How an army commander with Early's combat experience in an adverse situation—badly outnumbered and outgunned—could so thoroughly underestimate his opponent is little short of incredible.[20]

Early's subsequent actions underscored his low opinion of the Federal commander. On 25–26 August, in a rash attempt to lure the Federals into pursuit, he divided his force, marching his army up the Potomac, feinting at crossing into Maryland. However daring a maneuver this may have been, it left Anderson's 3,500 troops isolated at Charlestown, completely at Sheridan's mercy. "Little Phil," however, believing intelligence reports that further rebel reinforcements were on the way, remained stationary at Halltown. The Federals followed the Army of the Valley in their retreat towards Bunker Hill the next day, but by 3 September, the Army of the Shenandoah was encamped behind impregnable fieldworks stretching eight miles from Berryville to Summit Point. The pattern of advance and rapid retreat, feinting and following, ended; the two armies, divided by the line formed by Opequon Creek, remained at rest until 18 September.

Into the Storm

The fall of Atlanta increased the importance of events in Virginia, bringing into sharp relief the relationship between events in the Valley and the increasing pressure Grant was exerting on the Army of Northern Virginia at Petersburg. Equally important, Sherman's capture of the "Gate City" had a dampening effect on the Army of the Valley. Stephen Ramseur learned of Atlanta's fate the first week in September and wrote to his wife, "My darling this is certainly the time to try our souls. We see in Yankee papers that Sherman has defeated Hood and captured Atlanta! We do not wish to believe this — but are compelled to be apprehensive and anxious." While still respecting the offensive power of Early's army, Sheridan patiently watched and waited for a chance to strike.[21]

The fall of Atlanta subtly influenced participants on both sides; however, Early committed two blunders during September that directly resulted in Sheridan's attack on his army at Winchester. In the latter part of August, Grant forced Lee to extend his already thin lines to cover Richmond. The Army of the Potomac had also denied the Confederates the use of the Weldon railroad, a very important supply line that ran from Petersburg into North Carolina. The result, as Early's biographer explains, was Lee asking for the return of Anderson, along with Kershaw's division and Cutshaw's artillery battalion. However, the issue of Kershaw's return was a bit more complicated.[22]

Anderson wasn't under Early's direct command, and his orders from Lee were characteristically vague, allowing room for Anderson's judgment. For his part, Early failed to devise a plan for coordinating his force with Anderson's, and as was his habit failed to consult him concerning the best course of action. Anderson grew frustrated with the murky situation and the lack of precise instructions and most likely tired of Early's cantankerous behavior. He decided to return to Petersburg, with or without his men.

Brigadier General James Conner, one of Kershaw's subordinates, in a letter home dated 9 October, described the suffering of Valley residents, then criticized Early, "And to think that their sufferings were brought about by the bad passions and bad feelings of one man. Had Early been less selfish and more harmonizing, our Division need never have left Winchester. If he had told Anderson that he needed it Anderson would have left it, but they did not harmonize. We were carried off and the result was his defeat. The officers all deeply deplore our having left."[23] In a similar letter about eighteen days earlier, Conner had described their situation, "We certainly are not needed at Petersburg, and it is comforting to think that 'Robert' does not need us, for he wrote General Anderson to leave our Division up there, and to return himself to Petersburg."[24] Kershaw's brigade, with Anderson leading, left the Valley on 14 September. Had Kershaw's division remained with the Army of the Valley, the outcome of the 3rd battle of Winchester might have been different. Sheridan received Rebecca Wright's message that Kershaw's brigade had departed on the evening of 16 September.[25]

Meanwhile on the 14th, Grant had received a message from Halleck, complaining that "the long and continued interruption of the Ohio and Chesapeake Canal and the Baltimore and Ohio Railroad is very seriously affecting the supply of provisions and fuel for public and private use in Baltimore, Washington, Georgetown and Alexandria. Unless the canal can be opened very soon a sufficient supply of winter's coal cannot be procured before the close of navigation. The gas companies are already thinking to stop their works for want of coal.... They, therefore, urge the great importance of driving Early far enough south to secure these lines of communication from rebel raids, and that if Sheridan is not strong enough to do this he should be reinforced."[26]

Probably in response, Grant decided that the time had come to drive Early's Confederates up the Valley. Not trusting written orders to go through the War Department, the lieutenant general departed City Point for a face to face meeting with "Little Phil." Upon hearing that Kershaw's South Carolinians had departed, Sheridan had begun preparations to attack the Valley Army at Newtown. But shortly thereafter, a message from Grant summoned him to a meeting at Charlestown. Leaving his headquarters at Clifton immediately, Sheridan rode to Charlestown, where he met with Grant, under a large oak tree. As the two officers conversed, the Irish General spread out a map of the area around Opequon Creek. The Army of the Valley was encamped on the west bank, and Sheridan had telegraphed Grant on 11 September describing the Opequon as "a very formidable barrier" with "formidable" banks. However, frequent reconnaissance patrols had since taught him a lot about the terrain on the east bank; thus he had little trouble convincing Grant that his plan of attack would work. Grant then asked, "Could you be ready to move by next Tuesday?" "Oh, yes" answered Sheridan, "I can be off before daylight on Monday." Grant replied simply, "Go in."[27]

The Plains of Winchester

The third battle of Winchester, also known in the North as the battle of the Opequon, was the most important engagement of Sheridan's Valley campaign. Arguably, it was also the most important battle of Grant's spring campaign in Virginia. It was the opening act of the destruction of the Army of the Valley; it foretold the Confederacy's failure to hold and preserve the Shenandoah Valley and the eventual surrender of the Army of Northern Virginia at Appomattox. The Federal victory at 3rd Winchester shattered the confidence of the Valley Army in Jubal Early's leadership. Along with the rout at Fisher's Hill three days later, it destroyed their morale. After these twin defeats, the chance of any Confederate victory in Virginia was greatly diminished, likewise the chance of the Confederacy achieving some measure of independence. However, the first full-scale battle between Early and Sheridan need never have happened at Winchester, where the terrain favored the Army of the Shenandoah.

On 17 September, Early learned that repair crews were at work on the B & O railroad near Martinsburg, 22 miles north of Winchester. Despite the fact that his troops had kept the B & O in a more or less continual state of disrepair, and knowing that Sheridan "had at least 35,000 infantry against me," Early left for Martinsburg without corroborating the information. Leading the divisions of Rodes and Gordon, "Old Jube" soon had the Army of the Valley dangerously scattered. Braxton's artillery and Lomax's cavalry accompanied the infantry, while the brigades of Breckinridge and Wharton remained at Stephenson's Depot, six miles north of Winchester. Ramseur's division, guarding the crossing of the Opequon on the Berryville Pike, was nearly 25 miles away from Early. Major Henry Kyd Douglas described Early's march to Martinsburg: "It was simply bravado ... I remember well the anxiety felt at our Headquarters when we knew of this movement, and it would have been greater had we known that General Grant was then at Harpers Ferry in consultation with General Sheridan and giving him his orders. The air seemed to have a sulphurous smell."[28]

However, the Martinsburg junket proved a waste of time; the repair crews were nowhere to be found. Lomax's cavalry destroyed a railroad bridge, while Early's quartermaster officers purchased coal for the army's blacksmiths with Northern currency—greenbacks. More important, Early accompanied a squad that broke into the telegraph office;

they found copies of telegrams divulging Grant's visit to Sheridan two days earlier. Word of the discovery of Grant's visit quickly spread, alarming the troops and probably Early as well. With Rodes in the lead, the Army of the Valley immediately turned about, hastening to get back to Winchester as sundown approached that quiet Sunday, 18 September. Rodes camped at Stephenson's Depot that evening, but Gordon's division advanced only as far as Bunker Hill, 14 long miles from Ramseur's division on the Berryville Pike. Rodes was closest to Ramseur, about six miles away.

Well before daylight on 19 September, the Army of the Shenandoah began their advance across Opequon Creek against Ramseur's depleted division, which counted no more than 2,000 troops. Sheridan found out from Averell, whose brigade had been driven out of Martinsburg, that Early and two divisions had gone there the previous day. He determined to attack Ramseur's isolated units.[29] The Irish General's plan was fairly simple: Major General Alfred Torbert, Sheridan's cavalry chief, along with Merritt's 1st Division Cavalry, would advance from Summit Point, capture two of the Opequon crossings, and link up with Averell, coming south from Darkesville on the Valley Turnpike, near Stephenson's Depot. Simultaneously, Brigadier General James H. Wilson's 3rd Division Cavalry would capture the Opequon crossing on the Berryville Pike, then advance westward, uphill through the narrow Berryville Canyon. They would then hold the flat open country at the canyon's western entrance as General Wright's 6th and 19th Corps Infantry, 20,000 strong, came up behind them. Wilson was then to move south to Abraham's Creek to cover Sheridan's left flank as Wright's infantry occupied the ground west of the canyon.

After Wilson's cavalry had dispersed Ramseur's pickets, Wright's infantry was to attack Ramseur's 2,000 foot soldiers, while the 10,000 troops of the 8th Corps, led by General Crook, was held in reserve on the east bank of Opequon Creek. They were eventually supposed to block the Valley Turnpike south of Winchester, turning back any retreating Confederates, while Merritt's cavalry did likewise.[30]

Wilson's troopers arrived at the Berryville crossing of the Opequon sometime between 4 and 4:30 A.M. On the west bank, at the eastern entrance to the Berryville Canyon, Brigadier General John B. McIntosh, one of Wilson's brigade commanders, positioned his vanguard, the 2nd and 5th New York Cavalry, backed up by the 18th Pennsylvania Cavalry and two batteries of artillery. McIntosh's troops advanced into the two-mile long canyon, thickly forested on each side, with the 2nd New York in the lead. Some minutes later, they came out the western end, surprising rebel pickets of the 23rd North Carolina Infantry, led by Brigadier General Robert D. Johnston. Fumbling in the pre-dawn darkness, the North Carolinians at first fell back before the New Yorkers' rapid-firing Spencer carbines. Regrouping, they fell back slowly and stubbornly, firing as they went, as the Federals began exiting the canyon's western end, deploying across the pike. They encountered stubborn resistance from Johnston's brigade, who fired volley after volley at the charging New Yorkers, stopping them in their tracks at close range.

Meanwhile, at dawn that Monday, Ramseur received a messenger from Johnston, who had taken position straddling the pike about five hundred yards west of the entrance to the canyon. The messenger announced that Sheridan's Federals had swarmed across Opequon Creek, pushing aside Johnston's thin line of pickets, and were advancing on Winchester. Ramseur came to Johnston's aid immediately, supported by William Nelson's artillery, deploying his entire brigade across the pike, on an elevated plain between two tributaries of the Opequon, Red Bud Run on the north and Abraham's Creek on the south.[31]

Badly outnumbered and outgunned, Ramseur's division stubbornly resisted Sheridan's advance, buying time for Gordon's and Rodes' divisions to arrive on the battlefield. However, one writer has stated that Ramseur, "by deploying Johnston several hundred yards from the canyon, the establishment of a lone regiment at the western mouth and his neglect to post an advance vidette" on the west bank of the Opequon, "permitted Wilson's troopers to surprise the pickets and acquire a foothold on the open terrain. If Johnston's brigade had barricaded the gorge's embouchure, no enemy force, charging along a front the width of the road, could have penetrated the brigade's line. Sheridan's dangerous enterprise could have died aborning, instead Ramseur's isolated division faced annihilation and Early's army a piecemeal destruction." Ramseur also failed to investigate the possibility of ambushing any force that came through the canyon. However, as matters stood, Wright's twenty thousand troops became bottled up in the narrow canyon, which one writer has described as "a narrow gorge between picturesque hills so steep and so densely covered with forests and underbrush as to be impassable to any force but unencumbered infantry."[32]

A soldier who marched through the defile described the scene: "The army at this moment was engaged in the perilous movement of filing through a narrow gorge and deploying in face of a strongly-posted and veteran enemy. The road was crowded with artillery, ammunition wagons, and ambulances, all hurrying forward. On each side of it a line of infantry in column of march stumbled over the rocky, guttered ground, and struggled through the underbrush. The multitudes of men who belong to an army, yet who do not fight — the cooks, the musicians, the hospital attendants, the quarter-masters' and commissaries' people, the sick, and the skulkers — sat on every rock and under every bush, watching us pass. Here, too, were jammed the troopers of the cavalry advance, who, for the present, had finished their fighting, having cleared the passage of the Opequon Creek, and opened the way thus far for the infantry and artillery. Presently we met litters loaded with pale sufferers, and passed a hospital tent, inside of which I saw surgeons surrounding a table, and amputated limbs and pools of blood underneath it. The stern and sad business of the day had evidently begun in front, although the sound of it was not yet audible to us, excepting an occasional boom of cannon, deadened to a dull *pum pum* by the woods and the distance." The same soldier later stated, "We lost something like six hours in getting over a distance of about three miles; and the chance of attacking Early by surprise, before he could concentrate, was utterly lost." The 6th and the 19th Corps took five to six hours to exit the 2-mile-long canyon and deploy; the 6th Corps was immediately followed by their baggage train, and thereby blocked the 19th Corps from getting to the battlefield.

As Sheridan stated, "A good deal of time was lost in this movement through the cañon, and it was not until perhaps 9 A.M. that the order for the advance in line was given." Wright's infantry wasn't fully deployed until well after 9 A.M. Sheridan forced twenty thousand troops through a very narrow defile when half that number would have sufficed. However, he had three roads of approach but used only one. Part of his force could have crossed the Opequon at Tanqueray's Ford, a mile north of the Berryville Pike, and advanced along the Burnt Factory Road that ran parallel to the canyon then angled towards the Berryville Pike, intersecting it a few hundreds yards west of the defile. "Little Phil" also could have sent his force westward along another road running parallel to the Berryville Turnpike, about a mile to the south. Although Ramseur had posted part of A.C. Godwin's brigade to guard this road, he concentrated most of his force to defend the Berryville Turnpike; had Sheridan used all three roads, the Federals could have rapidly advanced through the canyon and approached the 27-year-old major general's division from three directions at once and quickly defeated them. However, Sheridan might have also sent part of his force towards Winchester, farther south along the Senseney Road, and approached Ramseur from behind.

As it was, Sheridan's poor judgment gave Early time to concentrate his army; by the time Wright's infantry fully deployed, Rodes' and Gordon's divisions had arrived on the field. Because of this error, "Little Phil" lost his chance to destroy Ramseur's division, and Early's army, piecemeal.[33] Many years later, Sheridan admitted that Wright's infantry was delayed in the canyon, but never took responsibility as to the cause: "The battle was not fought ... on the plan ... with which marching orders were issued ... I adhered to this purpose during the early part of the contest, but was obliged to abandon the idea because of unavoidable delays by which I was prevented from getting the Sixth and Nineteenth Corps through the ... defile ... early enough to destroy Ramseur while still isolated. So much delay had not been anticipated.... My idea was to attack Ramseur and Wharton at a very early hour ... but I was not in condition to do it until nearly noon." The arrival of Gordon's and Rodes' divisions forced "Little Phil" to make a major change in his battle plan; however, years later he wrote, "yet I have always thought that by adhering to the original plan we might have captured the bulk of Early's army."[34]

Meanwhile, Early had camped the evening of 18 September with Rodes' division at Stephenson's Depot, five miles north of Winchester. He received Ramseur's message concerning Wilson's attack at daybreak. After telling Rodes of the Federal attack, he left camp, galloping towards Ramseur's location. Upon arriving, he quickly appraised Sheridan's advance and ordered the Army of the Valley to reconcentrate, close to Ramseur's division, on the plains west of Berryville Canyon.

Rodes was ready to march when Early's order came; he arrived between 9 and 10 A.M. and posted his four brigades — led by brigadier generals Bryan Grimes, William R. Cox, Philip Cook, and Cullen Battle — on Ramseur's left. Gordon's division, marching from Bunker Hill, to save time abandoned the Valley Turnpike, cutting diagonally across fields and arriving on the plain west of Berryville Canyon some minutes before 10 A.M. However, Rodes and Gordon completed their deployment over an hour before the Federal assault began. The Army of the Valley now manned a line running from south of Senseney Road, where the cavalry of William Lowther "Mudwall" Jackson and Lunsford Lomax were posted; northwards to Abraham's Creek, where Bradley Johnson's cavalry had protected Ramseur's flank since daybreak; and further north, past the divisions of Ramseur, Rodes, and Gordon, to the north bank of Red Bud Run. North of the stream, Fitzhugh Lee's horse soldiers completed Early's line, more than two miles long. Rodes' and Gordon's arrival added over 5,000 muskets to the Valley Army's defense line.[35]

The Federal line ran from Abraham's Creek, where Wilson's cavalry and a few infantry from Colonel Daniel Bidwell's brigade were posted, northwards to the remainder of George W. Getty's division. Across the Berryville Pike was Frank Wheaton's brigade, with that of Colonel James Warner's Vermont infantry on Wheaton's right. Still further north, completing the Federal line, were the two brigades of Brigadier General James Ricketts, led by Colonels J. Warren Kiefer and William Emerson, and the brigades of David A. Russell.[36]

The 2nd Division of the 19th Corps, led by Brigadier General Cuvier Grover, had advanced northwest, away from the 6th Corps, into a large patch of forest known as the First Woods. Grover aligned his brigades into two lines, led by Colonel Jacob Sharpe on the left and Brigadier General Henry W. Birge. Grover's brigades were followed by those of Brigadier General William Dwight. The red-headed corps commander, Major General William H. Emory, known to the troops as "Old Brick Top," completed their deployment, placing other units around Dwight's men.

The main Federal attack began at 11:40 A.M., on a beautiful early autumn day that belied the imminent carnage. The 19th Corps advanced uphill across approximately 1,100 yards of rolling terrain, farm fields with patches of woods with steep ravines and deadfalls interspersed. From the Federal position, on the plain west and northwest of the Berryville Canyon, only the skirmishers and snipers of Ramseur's force were visible, while the troops of Rodes and Gordon were concealed by the patches of forest. Elements of the 19th Corps initially drove some of Gordon's troops from the woods, towards Colonel Thomas Carter's artillery. Carter couldn't fire at the attacking Federals without hitting gray-clad troops. Finally, when the Federals had closed to within 60 yards, Carter's artillery, loaded with canister, opened fire, sending the blue-coated infantry running rapidly in the opposite direction.[37]

Grover's lead brigades charged across an open field, 600 yards wide, towards a second patch of forest, as the gun signaling the attack fired. As they marched towards the far patch of forest, the Second Woods, they were subject to a terrific enfilading fire from a six-gun battery of horse artillery north of Red Bud Run. Clusters of men fell as exploding canister fire opened gaps in the Federal advance, but Birge's troops, ahead of the others, drove the gray-clad skirmish line well back into the woods. The Federal charge was answered by the counter-charge of the 31st Georgia Infantry in a ravine in their front. The two lines struggled in hand-to-hand combat; the air was thick with minie balls and rent by the groans of the wounded and dying. The 31st Georgia wavered, then for the first time broke and ran. Birge's troops pursued them beyond the woods for some minutes, but Braxton's artillery stopped the Federal attack.

As Birge's and Sharpe's Federals retreated, Gordon's two brigades, accompanied by the 31st Georgia, came screaming out of the deep woods in a counter-attack and fell upon them with a vengeance. The Federals retreated back into and through the Second Woods, disrupting the remaining two brigades of blue-coated infantry, led by Colonels David Shunk and Edward Molineux. Coming back through the Second Woods, Grover's blue-coats were subjected to a murderous fire from Gordon's men, who had outflanked them on two sides and had approached to within 60 yards. Fully one-half of Shunk's officers were killed, and the Confederates captured most of the 159th New York and 13th Connecticut Infantry. Taking intense fire from three sides, the blue-coated infantry soon disintegrated; they turned and ran for the First Woods.[38]

Sheridan, however, had made another mistake. As Gordon observed the Union retreat, he also noticed the blue-clad infantry of the 6th Corps advancing to the right, away from him, following the Berryville Turnpike as it slanted southwest, as instructed

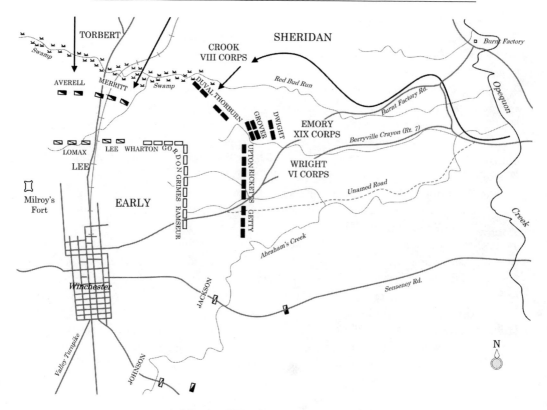

3rd Battle of Winchester, September 19, 1864

by Sheridan. This movement created a gap between the 6th and 19th Corps. Realizing that "Little Phil" had given the Army of the Valley another opportunity, Gordon decided to take advantage of it. In a brief conference, Rodes and Gordon decided to send their divisions through the widening gap. Gordon returned to his troops as Rodes prepared to send Cullen Battle's Alabama brigade through the several hundred yard wide disconnect between the two Union corps. However, in the blink of an eye, fate intervened. As Rodes urged his men forward, a Federal artillery shell exploded above him; a fragment struck Rodes behind the ear, crushing his skull. He briefly leaned forward then fell backwards off his horse. The stalwart general, long a pillar of the Confederate war effort and widely respected in the South, was dead when he hit the ground. Learning of Rodes' death soon afterwards, Gordon controlled his shock and horror, taking temporary command of the dead general's division.

Rodes' four Alabama brigades came storming out of the woods, with Cullen Battle's brigade in the lead, furiously assaulting Kiefer's regiments. They pushed Kiefer's troops and Emerson's brigade off the plateau, firing volley after volley at the retreating Federals. To escape the murderous Confederate fire, fleeing Union troops took any available cover. With the disintegration of Keifer's and Emerson's brigades, Ricketts' vaunted 6th Corps collapsed, and Sheridan's army was very close to defeat. Watching the rout of his troops, the Irish General responded quickly, ordering Brigadier General David A. Russell's fresh division to move forward and restore the Union line.

While Federal artillery kept the Alabamians at bay, Russell's men deployed across the Berryville Turnpike. While supervising their deployment, Russell was hit in the chest by a minie ball, but he remained at his post. His troops were soon facing Rodes' entire division — Battle's Alabamians, Grimes and Cox's North Carolinians, and Cook's Georgians. Many of Russell's Federals had an advantage in firepower — they were using seven-shot Spencer carbines. Nevertheless, Confederate units fought their blue-coated attackers to a standstill for over half an hour, amid dry grass and undergrowth set aflame by sparks and overheated gun barrels. Superior rebel marksmanship, rifle handling, and tracking skill sometimes cancelled the Spencer carbine's greater firepower; Federal units using them still had difficulty defeating the Rebels.

Now, however, it was the Army of the Shenandoah's turn to lose a general. Fragments from an exploding shell killed Russell; his loss deeply affected his men and commanding officers, particularly Wright and Sheridan. Grimes' North Carolina infantry charged but was met by a devastating volley from Russell's 3rd Brigade, led by 25-year-old Brigadier General Emory Upton. The enfilading fire from Upton's brigade slowed, then stopped Grimes' and Gordon's counter-attack, and gave Union reinforcements, coming through the Berryville Canyon, time to arrive and take position. The rebel regiments retreated in the face of the 3rd Brigade's flanking fire, and the fighting in and around the Second Woods gradually came to a halt, with both sides exhausted. However, had it not been for Upton's counterfire, Russell's 1st Division and Getty's 2nd Division would have been outflanked and routed. One writer stated, "The situation was extremely critical and the Union army was on the verge of a serious defeat, if not an absolute disaster, it being patent ... that considerable time must necessarily elapse before the reserve [Crook's Corps] could possibly reach the field." After a march of nearly an hour, struggling through traffic in the canyon, Crook's reserve units arrived about 1:30 P.M. Their placement east of the Opequon had nearly cost Sheridan the battle.[39]

The fighting had now raged for over eight hours; a little less than thirteen thousand Confederates had destroyed most of two Union corps, fighting about thirty thousand Federals to a standstill. Had the battle ended there, Early could have justifiably claimed victory. Sheridan was temporarily in dire straits; his original plan for capturing Early's army had failed, and he needed assistance. He would get it — from his cavalry, and from his friend, George Crook.

Defeat Brings Despair

The aroma of boiling coffee wafted through the camp of Brigadier General Wesley Merritt's 1st Division Cavalry a few minutes after midnight on 19 September. Merritt's troopers were among the first in Sheridan's army to awaken on a day that one Union soldier would describe as "the hardest days fight I ever saw."[40] They cooked and ate breakfast, then broke camp and were ready to march by 1:30 A.M. Merritt's three brigades, numbering something over 3,000 troops, were led by Colonel Charles R. Lowell, Brigadier General George A. Custer, and Colonel Thomas Devin. Riding approximately southwest, the troops turned due west towards the Opequon at Summit Point. Custer crossed the north-flowing Opequon at Locke's Ford, about 4½ miles north of the Berryville Turnpike crossing. About a mile south of Custer, Lowell crossed at Seiver's, or Ridgway's Ford, while Devin's brigade temporarily remained east of the 50-foot-wide stream.

Arrayed against them, west of the Opequon, were the five attenuated regiments of John McCausland's brigade; about 800 mounted troopers guarded all of the stream's crossings north of the Berryville Turnpike, then westward some distance towards Colonel George Smith's brigade of Virginia cavalry, straddling the Valley Pike. No longer fighting with Bradley Johnson's brigade, McCausland's troopers had never fully recovered from their defeat at Moorefield, six weeks earlier. The weakest link in Early's defense of Winchester, McCausland could only expect to harass and delay the Union horse soldiers.

Before daybreak Merritt ordered Lowell to cross the Opequon at Seiver's Ford. The regulars of the 2nd U.S. Cavalry crossed the stream, facing heavy fire from the 14th Virginia Cavalry, led by Colonel James Cochran, an attorney in Staunton before the war. After securing the western bank, the Federals overwhelmed McCausland's overmatched troopers, taking some prisoners and forcing them to retreat.[41] Meanwhile about a mile to the north, at Locke's Ford, Custer's Michigan and New York regiments were checked by rifle fire from the 22nd Virginia Cavalry, posted in the woods on the west bank. Custer responded with the 6th Michigan, charging across the creek; they were repulsed with a deadly volley. The 1st Michigan then pushed across the stream and supported by the 5th and 6th Michigan drove the gray-clad troopers — cavalry and infantry — out of the woods, establishing themselves on the west bank.

Merritt's troopers also encountered Confederate infantry, led by Brigadier General Gabriel C. Wharton. Faced with this obstacle, Merritt's and Custer's regiments halted, resting for about four hours. They began their advance again around 10 A.M., when the rebels were seen retreating. About an hour later, Custer joined forces with Lowell some distance west of the Opequon. Confederate forces had meanwhile retreated westward, rejoining the rest of Wharton's brigade. They were under the overall command of John C. Breckinridge, responsible for protecting Early's left flank, north and east of town. Around 11 A.M. Custer attacked rebel infantry and cavalry led by colonels Augustus Forsberg and George Smith, part of Wharton's brigade that had earlier opposed him at Locke's Ford. Lt. Colonel Floyd King's artillery stopped the Wolverines' assault.

In the meantime, William Averell's two brigades of West Virginia and Pennsylvania cavalry, about 2,000 strong, had begun their day at 5 A.M. Advancing up the Valley Pike from Darkesville, more than 20 miles northeast of Winchester, they soon encountered the 23rd Virginia Cavalry who for three hours offered stubborn resistance, mounted on underfed and leg-weary horses. At Bunker Hill, the rebels were joined by the 62nd Virginia Mounted Infantry and the 18th Virginia Cavalry. The two sides deployed; with artillery support, Averell's troops charged the gray-clad cavalry. Outnumbered and outflanked, the Virginians quickly withdrew. Averell's blue-coats pushed the overmatched rebel horsemen southwards up the pike but failed to pursue them.

However, at 11:40 A.M., the time of the main Federal assault, Early ordered Breckinridge to send Wharton's brigade and King's artillery to a position on the Valley Pike north of Winchester. Less than an hour later, he summoned Breckinridge, Wharton and King to a position east of town. Early transferred some cavalry from the northern perimeter to a position south of Abraham's Creek and also gave Fitzhugh Lee command of the cavalry north of Red Bud Run. However, his repeated shifting of troops indicated that the Valley Army was badly outnumbered, unable to adequately defend important sectors of the field, an ominous portent of the battle's outcome.

Around 1:30 P.M., Merritt had his entire division advance towards the Valley Pike. Devin with his five regiments crossed the Opequon, while those of Custer and Lowell were close by on his right flank. About a mile east of the pike, Devin's Federals met McCausland's five depleted regiments drawn up in line of battle. Under a Federal artillery barrage and mounted charge, McCausland's troopers quickly scattered. Devin was momentarily stopped by the counterattack of Colonel Smith's 23rd Virginia. The action went back and forth until Devin simultaneously attacked Smith's flank and front, forcing the gray-clad cavalry to withdraw up the valley after McCausland's retreating troopers.

Meanwhile, Averell had advanced to Stephenson's Depot where his two brigades joined forces with Merritt's three. The combined force advanced slowly southward, up the Valley Pike, Averell on the west side, Merritt on the east, sabers glittering in the bright sunshine and cool, dry air, daring the Confederate horsemen to attack.

In the woods about a mile to the south, the fleeing Confederate horsemen met Fitzhugh Lee, leading the brigade of William Payne. In the two hours he had commanded the cavalry north of Red Bud Run, Lee hadn't taken part in the fighting. But as the Federals approached, their bands playing popular martial tunes, Lee's recombined forces burst from the woods, firing their pistols, charging the "compact mass" of Federals. Just as quickly, the rebel charge was broken, with Lee taking a bullet in the thigh, and his favorite horse, Nellie Gray, killed under him. Merritt's Federals were slowed by King's artillery; King expended his ammunition as Averell came into the fray. Further volleys from Colonel George S. Patton's Virginia infantry, concealed in the woods, finally stopped the Union horsemen.[42]

As the clock approached 3 P.M., the fighting died down to an exhausted stand-off, with most of Early's troops in the same positions they had occupied two hours before. Early's Confederates and Sheridan's Federals had seen hard fighting since 5 A.M. Many a Federal soldier had been marching and fighting since 1:30 A.M. without food or rest; many a Confederate had been marching and fighting since well before dawn, also without food or rest. Neither Sheridan nor Early wanted to immediately renew the casualty producing charges and counter-attacks. However, outnumbering Early three to one, "Little Phil" retained the initiative, and he wasn't about to quit. Nevertheless, the 6th Corps and the 19th Corps had seen more than their share of fighting thus far; both were fairly well spent. To continue the struggle, Sheridan would need a good deal of support.

Anticipating such a need, the Irish General had summoned his reserve troops — ten thousand battle-hardened veterans of the 8th Corps — the Army of West Virginia, led by his long-time friend George Crook. Sheridan ordered the future captor of Geronimo to bring his corps forward from east of the Opequon, through the Berryville Canyon. His aides delivered the orders to Colonels Issac Duval and Joseph Thoburn, whose six thousand troops were resting on the stream's east bank, opposite Spout Spring. Duval's men crossed the Opequon first, entering the narrow canyon. They found the defile still crowded with ambulances, wagons, and stragglers and wounded, walking in the opposite direction. As a result, like the 19th Corps that morning, the Army of West Virginia was reduced to marching single file on each side of the road.

When the 8th Corps exited the canyon, Sheridan ordered them to position themselves in the rear and to the right of the 19th Corps. Around 4 P.M., Merritt's and Averell's cavalry were again advancing along the Valley Turnpike against Breckinridge's woefully thin line of infantry north of town. Half an hour later, Crook's two divisions, led by Duval and Thoburn, began a flanking attack on Early's left, across a morass named Red Bud Run. About thirty yards wide with a thick green top coating of algae, with forbidding growths of impenetrable grass and upstart scrub trees along the banks, stagnant Red Bud Run was more of a swamp than a stream. Worse, it wasn't visible until the attacking Federals came very close. Nevertheless, Duval's troops, led by Colonel Rutherford B. Hayes' 23rd Ohio Infantry, plunged into the chest high water, struggling through, while under fire from Gordon's Confederates.

As Hayes described the crossing, "My horse plunged in and mired down hopelessly, just as by frantic struggling he reached the middle of the stream. I jumped off, and down on all fours, succeeded in reaching the Rebel side — but alone. Perhaps some distance above or below others were across. I was about the middle of the brigade and saw nobody else, but hundreds were struggling in the stream." Thoroughly soaked, Hayes was one of the first across. Somehow, nearly all the troops made the hazardous crossing, including Crook.[43]

Refusing his line to the left, Gordon and his troops offered stiff resistance to the unexpected flank attack. Crook's attack bent the Confederate line into an inverted L-shape, extended some distance westward. The 8th Vermont and 12th Connecticut Infantry, led by Brigadier General James McMillan, hit Gordon's position hard. A stone wall offered the Confederates some protection, but the swamp had been breached, and by five o'clock Gordon's troops were beginning to fall back towards Winchester.

Meanwhile, on the Confederate right, along the Senseny Road, Wilson's cavalry pressured Lomax's gray-clad horsemen back towards town, attempting to cut off Early's anticipated retreat. Ramseur's and Rodes' divisions were still battling hard against the westward thrust of the 6th and 19th Corps. However, the rising din of battle to their left and rear indicated that Gordon's men were slowly being pushed backwards. Responding to a false report that his right was being flanked, Early ordered a general withdrawal. Discovering his mistake, he immediately cancelled the order, but the damage was done. The troops paid no attention, continuing to withdraw. Then, north of town, Merritt's entire division charged, three brigades under Devin, Lowell, and Custer. Sabers glittering, several thousand Federal cavalry swept down on the half-demoralized and overextended rebel infantry. Overrun by the irresistible mass of blue horsemen, they broke and ran pell-mell for the rear. They ran towards Winchester, every man for himself, joined by Ramseur's and Rodes' troops.[44]

Early's hungry and exhausted men streamed through Winchester on their way south as the sun began to fall below the horizon and evening shadows lengthened. They had fought hard and executed well all day, but had only their soldier's pride to show for it. Defeated, demoralized, and disorganized, they stumbled through the streets and up the Valley Pike, somehow keeping ahead of the pursuing Federals. As General Gordon retreated with his men, riding through the war-torn town, he was alarmed to find his wife, Frances "Fanny" Rebecca Harrelson Gordon, and Mrs. Breckinridge on foot on the street as Federal bullets and artillery shells landed nearby. She had stopped at the home of her friend, Mary Greenhow Lee, who ran a boarding house in town. She had stayed there several times since July, long after she had become known among her husband's troops as "The Bride of the Battlefield." She quickly became a close friend of Mrs. Lee, and a welcome guest. Henry Kyd Douglas described the retreat through Winchester, "Mrs. Gordon ... was compelled to wait for her ambulance. It was a critical moment. The last of our skirmishers, driven by the enemy, were coming in, much demoralized, on the Berryville road. Mrs. Gordon, on the pavement, grappled several of these and ordered them to stop and make a stand; but neither her example, her rank, nor her beauty stayed them, and they trotted on. Riding back for her, I saw ... the enemy coming ... not far off, and several shots advised me that I need not wait for them."

Gordon described the scene a bit differently. He claimed that as the retreating Confederates passed Lee's home, Mrs. Gordon stood on the veranda, imploring them to return to the fight. Gordon found her in the street, distraught, after she had observed his troops passing the house. He ordered her into the house, but she didn't stay inside long. With shells falling around the stable, a few of Gordon's troops retrieved her carriage. Fanny Gordon, with her six-year-old son, Frank, Mrs. Breckinridge, and a wounded officer, boarded the conveyance, and they left town, southward along the Valley Pike. Federal pursuit was maintained into the evening; as Gordon stated, it only ended "when night came and dropped her protecting curtains around us."[45]

The defeat at Winchester shattered the morale of the Army of the Valley and also destroyed much of their confidence in Early. The condition of the army on their retreat and the despair of many a rebel soldier were described by Gordon: "Lucky was the Confederate private who knew his own captain, and most lucky was the commander who knew where to find the main body of his own troops.... Little was said by any officer.... What was the morrow to bring, or the next month, or the next year? There was no limit to lofty courage, to loyal devotion, and the spirit of self-sacrifice; but where were the men to come from to take the places of the maimed and the dead? Where were the arsenals from which to replace the diminishing materials of war?"

Early's sarcastic humor intruded on the melancholy silence of the retreat. In his shrill falsetto voice, he needled Breckinridge, "What do you think of the 'rights of the South in the Territories' now?," a reference to their political differences before the war when Early was strongly Unionist, and when the Kentuckian had become vice president, and had been, in 1860, the Democratic candidate for president. The normally resilient Breckinridge made no reply. For the first time, Stonewall Jackson's foot cavalry had been defeated. Another officer characterized Winchester as "this most fatal defeat." Early and what remained of the Army of the Valley, "now converted into a mob," fled south to Fisher's Hill.[46]

Disintegration at Fisher's Hill

Two days after the retreat from Winchester, another blow fell on the Army of the Valley. Breckinridge and his troops were ordered to return to southwestern Virginia, where he was stationed prior to coming to the Valley in May. Breckinridge had fought capably in defeating Sigel at New Market, through the raid on Washington, and afterwards. His departure underscored the fact that the Confederacy didn't have enough troops to adequately defend their steadily shrinking domain against the advance of Federal armies and moderate the ever-worsening problem of desertion.[47]

John O. Casler, a private in the 33rd Virginia Infantry, commented to the effect that after Winchester, the troops had lost all confidence in Early, and that he couldn't accomplish anything with them. Their lack of confidence in Early's leadership became obvious in the debacle at Fisher's Hill.[48]

The Army of the Valley now occupied a very strong defensive position atop the hill, at its highest, several hundred feet above the valley floor. The Fisher's Hill battlefield consists of two roughly parallel undulating ridges, with the Army of the Valley on the higher southern ridge, facing north towards the Federals. The hill stretches three and a half miles, coming to an abrupt halt on the east, at the North Fork of the Shenandoah, and on the west, leveling out into a small valley, about a half mile from the slopes of Little North Mountain. It was bisected by the Back Road, the Middle Road (which occupied roughly the position of today's I-81) and the tracks of the Manassas Gap railroad, coming from Strasburg. Running roughly northwest to southeast, a 2-foot-deep, 15-foot-wide stream, Tumbling Run, also bisected the hill, emptying into the Shenandoah. Not far from the hill's east end, 1,365-foot-high Three Top Mountain towered over the entire scene, giving the Confederates a birds-eye view of Federal troop movements. Not for nothing did the Confederates describe Fisher's Hill as their "Gibraltar," and one Union trooper called it "the bugbear of the valley."[49] Had Early's army occupied Fisher's Hill on the 18th and 19th, American history might have been different.

Early's army had two days' rest before Sheridan resumed the Federal offensive on the 22nd, but given the weakened state of the Valley army, and the lack of confidence in Early, it did no good. On his far right flank, "Old Jube" placed the small division of Gabriel Wharton. Gordon's command was placed immediately to Wharton's left, straddling the Manassas Gap railroad. Continuing to the left, Ramseur's old division — three brigades, now led by Brigadier General John Pegram, took position straddling the Middle Road. Ramseur's command was placed to the left of Pegram's, and on the far left, closest to Little North Mountain — his most vulnerable point — Early put his most vulnerable command, Lomax's cavalry. Lomax's troopers occupied a wooded ridge parallel to Fisher's Hill, just to the south. Their units were undermanned, hungry, poorly armed — many lacked sabers — and were demoralized; Early was blaming them for the defeat at Winchester.

Another blow was the loss of Fitzhugh Lee, rendered *hors de combat* the previous day. The popular Lee would have supported them, but he was en route to a hospital in Staunton. These egregious mistakes on the part of an army commander with Early's combat experience indicated a self-destructive streak that proved fatal to the Confederate cause. Their situation was made worse by poor visibility from the wooded ridge they were defending, with the entire army thinly spread over a 3 mile front, with less than 9,500 troops available.[50]

Facing the rebels on the hill, the Army of the Shenandoah mustered about 34,000 troops. On his far left, close to where the hill abruptly ends in a steep cliff, close to the North Fork of the Shenandoah, Sheridan positioned Grover's brigade. Those of Dwight and Wheaton were to Grover's right, straddling the railroad, while the troops of Getty and Ricketts were to their right. Initially, the two lines were about a half mile apart, with the Federals occupying a lower ridge, looking up at Early's fortifications.

That evening of the 20th, Emory, Wright and Crook met with Sheridan at his head-quarters tent, close to the Valley Pike and the North Fork of the Shenandoah. All four rejected the idea of a frontal assault against the high, rock studded hill front facing them. Sheridan then proposed the turning of Early's right flank, a nearly unassailable position. This plan would have involved crossing the North Fork and attacking the high bluff that comprised part of the eastern end of the hill while under the gaze of Confederate signal-men atop Three Top Mountain. Sheridan quickly realized that the idea wouldn't work. Crook then suggested a flanking movement around the Confederate left, at Little North Mountain. Sheridan approved; Wright and Emory didn't. The idea was adopted when brigade commanders Rutherford B. Hayes and Joseph Thoburn came to the meeting and approved it.

The plan had two parts. Crook's turning maneuver would depend heavily on surprise, and that in turn depended on his ability to move his troops up the slope of Little North Mountain undetected. Thus the 8th Corps would move into position at night and stay hidden in the woods on the mountain the next day. The second part involved the cavalry. After combining with Wilson at Front Royal, Torbert was to take the cavalry, rid the Luray Valley of any gray-clad troops, cross Massanutten Mountain through New Market Gap, and cut off Early's retreating army as they fled south from Fisher's Hill. Crook would attack at first light on 22 September. At the same time, the 6th and the 19th Corps would demonstrate against the hill front. If the Confederates fled southward, Sheridan would have the Army of the Valley "bagged" by the next day.[51]

However, the plan wasn't altogether successful. The next day Early sent Fitz Lee's cavalry, now led by Brigadier General Williams C. Wickham, to the Luray Valley, a smaller valley east of the Shenandoah Valley, to protect his rear. According to plan, Sheridan sent Wilson's and Merritt's divisions, led by Torbert, to clear Wickham out. They were then to cross Massanutten Mountain at New Market Gap, and form a barrier across the valley. On the evening of 20 September, Wickham's force took position on the south bank of the Shenandoah River, near Front Royal. At daybreak, Wickham's men held their ground against a Federal attack but were eventually driven southward by 1st Vermont and 1st New Hampshire infantry, which followed them as they retreated to Front Royal. The rebel cavalry retreated southward that evening and occupied a strong position the next morning at Milford, where the valley narrows to a gorge. The Confederate horsemen were between the Shenandoah and a spur of the Blue Ridge with a stream in their front. After some skirmishing, Torbert gave up on driving them out of Luray Valley, retreating seven miles northward. Not until two days later did Torbert advance, after the battle on Fisher's Hill, clearing the Luray Valley of a few remaining Confederates. Wickham's stand had preserved the valley army's line of retreat.

Thus Sheridan lost the chance to bag the Army of the Valley. As he later commented, "To this day I have been unable to account satisfactorily for Torbert's failure. No doubt, Wickham's position near Milford was a strong one, but Torbert ought to have made a fight ... it does not appear that he made any serious effort at all to dislodge the Confederate cavalry," which "not only chagrined me very much, but occasioned much unfavorable comment throughout the army."[52]

Meanwhile, back at Fisher's Hill on the 21st, Sheridan noticed a smaller hillock, occupied by Confederate sharpshooters, between the Federal lines and the main hill. The

Federal commander realized that possession of the hillock, known locally as Flint Hill, would give him a birds-eye view of Early's defenses. "Little Phil" ordered the storming of Flint Hill, but the first two forays failed. Then four regiments of Vermont infantry quickly captured the hillock at a cost of 38 casualties, giving Sheridan his advanced observation post. The capture of Flint Hill was the first crack in the Confederate defenses. Early later claimed that after the Union capture of Flint Hill, he "began to think that he [Sheridan] was satisfied with the advantage he had gained and would not probably press it further."

The capture of Flint Hill re-aligned the deployment of the VI Corps, dictating a shift of troops westward by Getty and Wheaton. This was accomplished on the night of the 21st, but because of rough terrain it took several hours to complete, depriving the troops of a good night's rest. Emory's XIX Corps followed, completing their realignments by daybreak. Last, but certainly not least, Crook's 8th Corps crossed Cedar Creek at nightfall on the 21st, refreshed by their day in the woods. They camped that evening near Hupp's Hill, a large hill about three-quarters of a mile north of Strasburg, on the Valley Turnpike. They would draw the most difficult assignment against Early's Confederates the next day.

The 22nd dawned cool and dry, with Sheridan in the saddle, riding among the troops, urging his division commanders to "press the enemy." But it was on the west end of the lines that Early got an ominous foretaste of the day's action. Around 1:30 P.M., two brigades of Ricketts' division attacked Ramseur's division on Early's far left. Ramseur's troops broke and ran. Early later cryptically stated that after Ricketts' attack, he learned that "on the afternoon of the 22nd, another attack was contemplated, and orders were given for my troops to retire, after dark, as I knew my force was not strong enough to resist a determined assault." He also later claimed that as a result of Ricketts' attack, he discovered that his position "could be flanked" and sent orders down the chain of command to withdraw at sunset.[53]

Did he mean a flanking attack when he said "another attack was contemplated"? Nevertheless, given Early's extensive combat experience, and the immense size of the area his troops were defending, it's difficult to believe that the possibility of a flank attack didn't occur to him sooner. But Early's state of mind was illustrated by his placement of Lomax's cavalry, isolated —"in the air"— several hundred yards to the west of Ramseur's hill. They were poorly armed with little or no support.

However, one writer states that by mid-afternoon of the 22nd Early "possessed no intelligence that his left flank was endangered." At that point, where was Early and what did he know? The record is silent as to his whereabouts on the afternoon of the 22nd, but his arthritis made it unlikely that he was atop Three Top Mountain. However, it may be inferred that he was on some vantage point, surveying his defenses, through his ever-present field glasses. The slopes of Little North Mountain were visible from one or two points on the left. Henry Robinson Berkeley, a private in Thomas J. Kirkpatrick's Amherst Artillery, on Early's far left, indicated in his diary that he had witnessed "the Yanks ... moving heavy columns of infantry to their right all day. We can see them plainly climbing up the side of [Little North Mountain]." Berkeley assumed that Early knew about the Federal flanking movement and did nothing to send the news up the chain of command.[54]

Nevertheless, Bryan Grimes, a division commander, also witnessed Crook's troops ascending the mountain, around three o'clock, and sent a courier to Ramseur with the news. Grimes urged Ramseur to reinforce Lomax's dismounted troopers with a brigade of infantry. Without orders from Early, Ramseur declined, even though he had met with Lomax and they had agreed that the gray-clad horsemen would offer only token resistance. Assured of enough ammunition by the army quartermaster, Ramseur nevertheless failed to ask Early for orders, and the Confederate commander failed to send any. Failure to communicate indicated low morale in the Army of the Valley, and implied the existence of a rift between Ramseur and Early over the troop placements on the hill.[55]

Early's biographer states that Early, "watching what he could see of Sheridan's preparations for the assault, now concluded that he would not be able to withstand it. Jubal had not changed his mind about Sheridan, but he was nonetheless capable of acting prudently. As he recalled the decision in his memoirs, 'I knew my force was not strong enough to resist a determined assault.' He gave orders to pull back off the ridge at nightfall. Most unfortunately for him, however, it was well before dark when Crook brought his hard-bitten columns out of the woods and attacked Early's dismounted cavalry."[56]

A little after 4 o'clock, Crook's 5,500 West Virginia and Ohio infantrymen began their assault, an ocean of blue roaring down the mountain towards Early's left flank, in two battle lines, one behind the other. As Crook described their advance, "I gave instructions not to yell until I gave the word, intending to march quietly until within a short distance of the open valley where the enemy's line was before commencing the charge. But their shells and round shot were crashing the trees in our midst so fiercely that when I gave the command to face to the front and move forward, they started to yell. And unless you heard my fellows yell once, you can form no conception of it. It beggars all description."[57] As they charged down the mountain, Crook followed, with an armload of rocks, throwing them at stragglers. By the time the blue-coats reached the valley bottom, the demoralized troopers of Johnson's, Jackson's, and Smith's brigades, so few in number that Crook mistook them for a line of pickets — had fired a few shots, then broke and ran. Some climbed the western end of Fisher's Hill, while others fled southward along the Back Road.

Minutes later, Crook's Federals hit Grimes' and Cox's brigades like a tidal wave, while Federal 6th Corps troops under Ricketts hit Early's left flank from the front, and the units of Getty and Wheaton pressured the gray-clad infantry further to the right. Ramseur ordered Cullen Battle's Alabama brigade into line on the far left, while Early ordered Pegram's troops to shift to the left, to meet the blue-coated flood. From a "lookout tree" atop the hill, Ramseur's troops could see the Federals approaching. Battle's men stood and fought valiantly, with Battle himself walking up and down the line with a big cedar stick, hitting anyone that ran. Ramseur's men on the hilltop soon found themselves "wrapped in a deadly pocket of Federal fire" from Ricketts men assaulting their front, and Crook's infantry coming in on their left and around to their rear. They held firm for perhaps half an hour or more, buying time for the rest of the Army of the Valley to retreat. Then they began to retreat off the hill, slowly at first, then rapidly. As Early's left disintegrated, the rest of the army quickly followed, a confused mob of men, horses, wagons, and artillery pieces fleeing southward towards Woodstock, crowding the Valley Turnpike.

Trying to restore some semblance of order to Grimes' fleeing North Carolinians, Early ordered the troops of the 13th Virginia Infantry to shoot their routed comrades. He

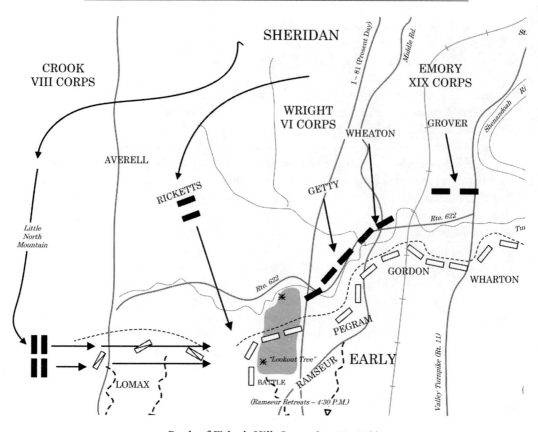

Battle of Fisher's Hill, September 22, 1864

was mortified when they not only refused his order, but quickly joined the rest of the army in their headlong flight. The Confederates lost 14 artillery pieces, and most of them bivouacked late that evening at Woodstock, 25 miles south of Fisher's Hill.

Sheridan lost about 500 killed and wounded. Early's casualties were light — 30 killed with 210 wounded; but the retreat had a heavy cost: 995 troops were missing, of whom about half were prisoners. In addition, Lt. Colonel Alexander "Sandie" Pendleton, Early's promising chief of staff, was killed, five days shy of his 25th birthday, attempting to rally the fleeing troops for a stand against pursuing Federals near Woodstock. Many of the Confederates traveled all night, finally stopping at Mt. Jackson. There they formed in line of battle, and repulsed pursuit the next day, withdrawing that evening to Port Republic and Brown's Gap. Although Sheridan claimed "only darkness has saved the whole of Early's army from total destruction," it was Wickham's stand against Torbert, in the Luray Valley, that kept him from sealing off Early's retreat from Fisher's Hill, allowing the Army of the Valley to escape.[58]

In the immediate aftermath of "The Affair at Fisher's Hill" (as Early called the fight in his memoirs) the morale of the Army of the Valley fell further. Sheridan commented, "I do not think that there ever was an army so badly routed. The Valley soldiers are hiding away and going to their homes." Most of the troops had lost all confidence in Early's leadership; many had lost hope in the Confederate cause. Bryan Grimes, who had narrowly escaped capture while Early's left was disintegrating, in a letter to his wife of 30 September, commented, "God forbid that I should again ever experience such sensations of misery as I did that evening and night of the 22nd. Then I felt for the first time that we would not establish the Confederacy." Grimes expressed the thoughts and beliefs of many in the Army of the Valley.[59] However, Early's Confederates were not yet finished. Most of the troops, though badly shaken and discouraged, were still able-bodied and willing, and Sheridan had failed to cut off their retreat. As the warmer days of September gradually gave way to October's chill, there would be another day of reckoning for Sheridan and the Army of the Shenandoah.[60]

CHAPTER 12

Ordeal by Fire

From Fisher's Hill, Early's shattered army retreated about 70 miles southward, finally stopping near Brown's Gap, a few miles east of Staunton, on the same ground where Stonewall Jackson's foot cavalry had camped in June 1862. At the end of September, the Army of the Valley mustered about 7,200 infantry and 3,000 cavalry with a scant 23 guns and 850 artillerymen. Some of Early's remaining troops had served under "Old Jack," and the memory of his successful valley campaigns added a humbling twist to their present mournful circumstances. They were hungry and dirty, with their uniforms in tatters, and many were shoeless.[1] Equally important, their fighting ability had been seriously compromised. The brigades of Ramseur, Wharton, and Gordon had lost so many field officers that maintaining discipline became impossible. In many units there were neither commissioned nor non-commissioned officers. The twin defeats in less than a week resulted in Early's proud warriors being pushed almost clear out of the valley, unimaginable under Jackson.

As a result, Early's enemies brought accusations of drunkenness and incompetence against him, resulting in loud public clamor for his removal from command. His most conspicuous antagonist was Colonel William "Extra Billy" Smith, of the 49th Virginia Infantry. An able politician and soldier, Smith had acquired the nickname "Extra Billy" by accepting extra reimbursement from the U.S. Post Office for a mail service he had run before the war. He had fought under Early at Chantilly, Antietam, and Gettysburg, and was now governor of Virginia for the second time. Smith and Early were not on good terms. Smith didn't care for West Pointers, and he most likely thought that as governor his opinions deserved more attention than Early normally gave subordinates. Smith's service under Early must have been unpleasant.

After Gettysburg, Smith resigned from the army. However, as a result of the two defeats in September, he saw an opportunity to strike at Early. In October, in a private meeting with Robert E. Lee, and in two subsequent letters, Smith discussed Early's faulty leadership and his unsatisfactory rapport with the troops. Claiming that another officer had written to him of the rank and file's opinions of their commander, Smith emphasized the troops' loss of confidence in Early's tactical decisions, and his lack of appreciation for them. The unnamed officer, whom Smith quoted, described the army's 1 October departure from Waynesboro "in the rain, and [we] marched all day through the hardest, coldest and bleakest storm of the season ... unless it [the march] was imperative it was cruel and injudicious; cruel because a great many of the command are shoeless and without blankets, and injudicious because exposure to such weather will necessarily produce a great deal of sickness ... this and other things ... have produced the impression among the men that he has no feeling for them."

Smith's informant also claimed that there were "no salutes" between Early and the troops, and "no pleasure, much less enthusiasm and cheers" when Early appeared during the day's march; "he is not greeted at all by private or officer, but is allowed to pass ... neither receiving nor taking notice." The unnamed officer further stated that the troops "once believed him a safe commander" whose caution could be trusted, but "this has been proven a delusion, and they cannot, do not, and will not give him their confidence." Smith recommended that John C. Breckinridge replace Early and urged that Lee take "prompt and immediate action."[2]

Lee recognized the gravity of Smith's charges but questioned his sources and refused to accept his information as accurate. He urged Smith to reveal the name of Early's accuser so that "justice to General Early" would be served and the matter could be officially investigated. Smith declined to offer any names, and Lee supported his lieutenant general, stating that his dispositions at Winchester were "judicious and successful until rendered abortive by a misfortune which he could not prevent and which might have befallen any other commander." Thanking Smith for his concern, Lee ended the matter: "General Early had conducted his operations with judgment, and until his late reverses rendered very valuable service considering the means at his disposal. I lament these disasters as much as yourself, but I am not prepared to say that they proceeded from such want of capacity ... as to warrant me in recommending his recall."[3]

Smith's accusations were put to rest; however, the groundswell of popular feeling against Early continued, unabated in Southern newspapers and was even taken up by the Confederate Congress. The *Richmond Enquirer* came out with an editorial on 27 September calling for Early's dismissal and suggesting James Longstreet as his replacement. However, the refusal of the *Enquirer's* editors to acknowledge the steadily deteriorating fortunes of the Confederacy was also highlighted by the comment that "neither party" had a permanent hold on the valley, and that the engagements in the valley "are mere episodes of the war." Lee reflected this thinking in a dispatch to Early of the 27th, in which he commented to the effect that Sheridan's infantry "cannot be so greatly superior to yours," and that they most likely didn't number more than 12,000 troops. Lee's estimate was greatly mistaken. Not surprisingly, Sheridan's three to one advantage in manpower over Early wasn't made public until after the war.[4]

Then drunkenness, a common 19th century public charge, reared its ugly head. A Savannah newspaper published a report that Early was seen frequently tippling from a black bottle, during the defeat at Winchester. Senator Benjamin Hill, of Georgia, even claimed to know what was in the bottle — apple brandy. As a result, Senator James Orr of South Carolina called on the Military Committee to investigate the twin defeats, allegedly caused by Early's drunkenness. Responding quickly, Early wrote a letter to the chairman of the Military Committee, demanding an investigation to prove Orr's allegations. Fortunately, John C. Breckinridge was available to testify. A widely respected witness, Breckinridge's testimony put an end to the charges of drunkenness. Early had dodged a bullet or two, but there was no escape from the bleak situation in the valley.[5]

The news of Sheridan's victory at Fisher's Hill roused Northern civilians and all but guaranteed Lincoln's re-election. Grant was duly impressed, sending a congratulatory telegram late that evening. In the lieutenant general's estimation, the Northern victory at Fisher's Hill was "most opportune in point of time and effect. It will open again ... the very important line of road from Baltimore to the Ohio, and also the Chesapeake Canal. Better still, it wipes out much of the stain upon our arms by previous disasters in that locality. May your good work continue is now the prayer of all loyal men."[6]

Meanwhile, the Army of the Shenandoah pursued Early's fleeing Confederates as far up the Valley as Harrisonburg, then halted. At that point, unsure of his immediate strategy, Sheridan gave his infantry a few days rest. Nevertheless, he sent Thomas Devin's cavalry "to press the enemy" and gave Averell verbal orders to join him. Averell, however, had encamped for the night, and didn't link up with Devin until the afternoon of the 23rd. According to Averell's report, at Mt. Jackson, both Federal units drove a "superior force of the enemy ... beyond the town ... on the heights beyond the village the army of the enemy could be plainly seen in bivouac, while a division of his infantry marched down and engaged me, opening five pieces of artillery.... The position, naturally strong, had been strengthened by artificial defenses." Averell must have been referring to a bluff immediately south of town, across Mill Creek, a strong position to be sure, but one that could have been flanked. However, he failed to attack, despite Sheridan's written warning, "I do not want you to let the enemy bluff you or your command ... I do desire resolution and actual fighting, with necessary casualties, before you retire." Later that evening, the Irish General wrote out an order relieving Averell of command, replacing him with Colonel William Powell. While there is some truth to the contention that Averell's dismissal was for political reasons, the evidence shows that both Grant and Sheridan wanted Averell relieved to maintain morale. In addition, the victor of Moorefield many times failed to help his own cause.[7]

By 26 September, Federal advance units were at Mount Crawford; by 1 October, blue-coated infantry were at Waynesboro, a scant 20 miles from Charlottesville, by way of Rockfish Gap through the Blue Ridge. The Army of the Valley had gathered near Brown's Gap; but by 1 October, the Union commander at Harpers Ferry, Brigadier General John D. Stevenson, learned that Early had left the valley through Brown's Gap, then turned around and stopped a Federal cavalry thrust farther south at Rockfish Gap. However, the Army of the Valley was now greatly reduced in numbers and efficiency; large numbers of wounded filled hospitals, churches and private homes all the way from Harrisonburg. Had Sheridan ordered his men to fill their haversacks with three days rations and march for Charlottesville, the Federals could have quickly occupied that city, destroyed the railroad and canal, and pressured the Army of Northern Virginia from the west. Had Sheridan achieved those objectives, the war might have ended that fall.

However, a strange paralysis had taken hold of Sheridan. He became very concerned about the lack of information on conditions in Brown's Gap — was the road through the Blue Ridge blocked by fallen timber? Where exactly was the Army of the Valley? In the event of a march on Charlottesville, how long would his supply line extend from Harpers Ferry? Would the Orange & Alexandria railroad be available as a supply line? What Confederate forces were east of the Blue Ridge?

Sheridan's dispatch to Grant, dated 29 September, indicated that his cavalry was busy destroying "rebel Government property" in Staunton, and an iron railroad bridge over the Shenandoah at Waynesboro. Equally important, he thought that "most of the troops which Early had left passed through the mountains to Charlottesville." "Little Phil" further promised to "go on and clean out the Valley" of Confederate troops and supplies as "I am getting twenty-five to forty prisoners daily, who come in from the mountains on each side and deliver themselves up. From the most reliable accounts, Early's army is completely broken up and is dispirited." Sheridan therefore concluded that the Army of the Valley posed no further threat to his own army there in the valley. He then said something peculiar: "It will be exceedingly difficult for me to carry the infantry column over the mountains and strike at the Central road, as I cannot accumulate sufficient stores to do so," and he proposed a retreat to Front Royal, eighty miles north of Brown's Gap. He further stated that "the destruction of the grain and forage from here [Harrisonburg] to Staunton will be a terrible blow to them."[8]

Although Kershaw's brigade was thought to be somewhere in the vicinity of Gordonsville, Sheridan could have instructed his quartermaster to butcher a few hundred of the approximately 3,000 head of cattle and sheep collected in the past few days between Staunton and Mount Crawford and turn the meat into rations. Thus supplied, a quick-striking Federal force could have marched eastward through Rockfish Gap, Swift Run Gap, or New Market Gap, and destroyed "the Central road" at Gordonsville, clearing the way for the rest of Sheridan's army to advance. He could have also sent a small force farther south to strike at Charlottesville and destroy the James River canal. However, even though he received assurances that the Orange & Alexandria railroad would be made available, Sheridan chose to concentrate his efforts and resources on thoroughly destroying the Shenandoah Valley and making war on Southern civilians. The Orange & Alexandria railroad, explained Sheridan, would have taken an entire corps to defend, against Confederate guerrillas, thus "subtracting from the chance of success."[9]

The weather had turned cold as September became October, just after Sheridan's Federals arrived at Harrisonburg. Nevertheless, for ten days thereafter, the valley's lush farms and homesteads were turned into charred heaps of ash. Homes, barns, mills and factories went up in a "holocaust of fire," and the area from Harrisonburg southward to Staunton and Waynesboro was called "The Burnt District." By day, thick roiling columns of smoke rose above the valley; by night, the entire area glowed as bright orange, yellow and red flames devoured the valley and the lifetimes of labor that many residents had given it. One Federal soldier described the scene, near Harrisonburg: "The whole country around is wrapped in flames, the heavens are aglow with the light thereof ... such mourning, such lamentations, such crying and pleading for mercy I never saw nor never want to see again, some were wild, crazy, mad, some cry for help while others would throw their arms around yankee soldiers necks and implore mercy."

Another Federal soldier commented, "The completeness of the devastation is awful. Hundreds of nearly starving people are going north. Our trains are crowded with them. They line the wayside. Hundreds more are coming ... so stripped of food that I cannot imagine how they escaped starvation."[10] Sheridan then retreated to Woodstock, and in a 6 October dispatch to Grant, he proclaimed that his troops had "destroyed over 2000 barns filled with wheat, hay and farming implements; over 70 mills filled with flour and wheat; have driven in front of the army over 4000 head of stock, and have killed ... not less than 3000 sheep."[11] The untimely death of Lt. John R. Meigs, son of Quartermaster General Montgomery Meigs, near Harrisonburg on 3 October at the hands of a Confederate patrol further fueled Sheridan's anger at valley residents.

However, the burning of the valley between Harrisonburg and Staunton was merely a foretaste of things to come. Beginning on the evening of 5 October, the Army of the Shenandoah retreated northwards. As they moved down the valley, their cavalry torched the region, destroying $20 million worth of property (in depreciated Confederate currency), rendering many homeless, and creating a bitter legacy among valley residents. A young resident of Augusta County who witnessed the burning said it best: "How my soul filled with horror as I was compelled to stand and witness one building after another consumed to ashes ... their lurid glare sent many a pang of hopelessness to houseless citizens.... Truly the great ... general, Sheridan has achieved a wonderful victory over the helpless women and children of the Valley of Virginia."[12]

Meanwhile, John S. Mosby and the 43rd Virginia Cavalry were very busy during Sheridan's burning of the valley. Derailing a number of trains, they successfully disrupted repairs to the Manassas Gap railroad after Grant had ordered it repaired in September. The task had been delegated to Major General Christopher Augur, in charge of Washington's defenses. Forcing Augur to take extreme measures to stop the guerrillas, Mosby's men denied the Federals the use of the road, a direct route from Washington to the valley. Mosby's partisans also disrupted the B & O railroad and struck Federal supply trains in the valley.

However, Early and his army, camped at Brown's Gap, could do little but seethe in frustration and watch as the valley burned. On 28 September, near Waynesboro, they stopped some of Torbert's cavalry from destroying the iron railroad bridge and tunnel through the Blue Ridge. On 1 October, they left Brown's Gap and marched to Mt. Sidney, near Staunton, staying there four days. Early's Confederates followed the Federals as they moved down the valley, with Early ordering his cavalry "to pursue the enemy, to harass him, and to ascertain his purposes."[13]

Had Early coordinated his efforts with Mosby's, both commands would have benefited immeasurably. After the war, Mosby inquired of one of Early's staff why "Old Jube" didn't tell him of the planned attack at Cedar Creek. Mosby had some idea of assaulting Sheridan's rear while Early attacked his front. Apparently someone on Early's staff did suggest the idea to him before the battle. Early replied to the effect that he was not going to do the fighting while Mosby did the plundering.[14]

Thomas Rosser Tries

On 5 October, 600 mounted troopers from the Army of Northern Virginia, led by Major General Thomas Lafayette Rosser, arrived at Early's camp. Well over six feet tall, Rosser was a native Virginian and West Pointer who had grown up in Texas. Rosser harbored very strong sentiments against partisan rangers. He had fought under Early during the Confederate pursuit of Averell's cavalry on the retreat from their raid on the Virginia & Tennessee Railroad at Salem, Virginia, in December 1863. Confederate pursuit failed to catch Averell, and Rosser soon found himself at odds with Early over having left camp to visit his wife without permission. Nevertheless, Early gradually formed a good opinion of Rosser, placing some trust in his abilities; this was very unusual given Old Jube's long standing mistrust of cavalry. Rosser's Laurel Brigade brought the strength of Early's cavalry to nearly 5,000 troops. The laurel symbolized success, and it was reflected in the Laurel Brigade's record since the flamboyant Turner Ashby organized it in 1862. Partly for that reason, Rosser came to be called "The Savior of the Valley," an appellation he came to regret.[15]

Following Early's orders, Rosser's Laurel Brigade nipped at the heels of Custer's and Merritt's brigades, harassing them and successfully attacking their rear guards. While Lunsford Lomax's troops harassed Merritt's brigade on the Valley Pike, Rosser's men attacked Custer's brigade on the Back Road, distracting the Federals and keeping them from firing homes and barns. On 7 October, Custer's and Rosser's troopers faced off at Mill Creek. Captains Dan Hatcher, Sam Myers, and Ramsey Koontz led the Confederates in a flank attack on the Union horsemen. The fighting lasted from mid-afternoon past sundown, and the Laurel Brigade inflicted a stinging defeat on the larger Federal force, capturing nine forges and fifty prisoners besides killing and wounding a respectable number of blue-coats. Custer retreated down the valley, but Captain Koontz, a 27-year-old resident of Mt. Jackson, was mortally wounded and died the next day. On 8 October, as the Federals continued their retreat, Rosser's Confederates, fighting for hearth and home, boldly continued their assaults, striking Custer's rear guard near Columbia Furnace. Pushing the Federals beyond Tom's Brook, they came dangerously near Sheridan's infantry. After Rosser's rebels repulsed a Federal flanking attempt, the day's action ended.

On the evening of 8 October, a thoroughly annoyed Sheridan, by this time indignant at Rosser's growing reputation as the valley's deliverer, summoned Torbert. Telling his cavalry chief to get an early start, "Little Phil" ordered him to "whip the rebel cavalry or get whipped himself," and to "finish this savior of the Valley."[16]

At daybreak on the 9th, Rosser's brigade, numbering less than 2,000 troops, faced the nearly 4,000 horsemen of Custer's brigade along Tom's Brook. From a ridge overlooking the stream, Custer observed Rosser's deployments, the center of which lay on Wisman's Hill, a strong position above the Wisman farm.

The rebels were worn and tired from three days of continuous fighting; the Federal horsemen were in somewhat better condition and armed with seven-shot Spencer carbines. Colonel Thomas T. Munford's troops composed Rosser's left, across the Back Road; near the road were placed two guns of Thompson's battery, supported by William Payne's 300 cavalrymen. Rosser's right was composed of the Laurel Brigade, led by Colonel R.H. Dulany. They were positioned just south of Tom's Brook, which flowed into the Shenandoah. Lomax, leading about 1,500 troops, faced Merritt's Federals along the Valley Pike.

Custer sent mounted and dismounted skirmishers against Rosser's line, accompanied by a Federal artillery barrage aimed at the hill, around 7 A.M. They encountered stubborn resistance, causing Custer to refrain from a frontal assault. The stand-off skirmish continued for two hours. Because of the strength of the Confederate defensive position and defective Federal artillery shot, Custer at first saw no way around the impasse. Reconsidering, he decided that maneuvering might result in victory. He ordered three regiments to turn the Confederate left flank. As Custer brought up troops for the attack, Colonel

Munford noticed the flanking movement. He warned Rosser, who made light of it, exclaiming to the effect that he would shortly drive the Federals back to Strasburg.

On their second attempt, the Federal horsemen succeeded in turning the rebel position; Rosser's left flank broke and ran, followed by those in the center. They made a brief stand a short time later then turned and ran again. Meanwhile, Merritt's Federals flanked Lomax's brigade; they too turned and ran. Both rebel brigades stampeded southward; Rosser's frightened men ran twenty miles, stopping at Woodstock, while Lomax's once proud troopers scampered twenty-six miles, reining up under the guns of Early's infantry at New Market. The Federal horsemen captured six guns, Rosser's wagons, desks, and papers, and the Confederate commander's overcoat. After the battle, the theatrical Custer paraded around camp wearing the gray coat, amusing his men. However, Munford never forgave Rosser for his role in the defeat and never spoke to him again.

The engagement at Tom's Brook came to be called derisively "The Woodstock Races." Ever quick with sarcastic humor, Early now insisted that the laurel was "a running vine," giving his cavalry another undeserved dose of acid. However, outflanked troopers often break and run. Had Early supported his cavalry, instead of scorning them, they might have repulsed Custer at Tom's Brook, and the Army of the Valley would have fared better against Sheridan.[17]

Cedar Creek — Early's Last Chance

Sheridan's dispatches to Grant and Halleck of 11 October reveal that "Little Phil" had relaxed after defeating Early's cavalry at Tom's Brook, assuming that the Army of the Valley, as an organized force, no longer posed a serious threat. In his dispatch to Grant, describing the results of the recent fight, the Irish General related, "I have seen no signs of the enemy since the brilliant engagement of the 9th instant.... The refugees from Early's army ... are organizing guerilla parties, and are becoming very formidable and are annoying me very much. I know of no way to exterminate them except to burn out the whole country and let the people go North or South."[18]

Later that evening, in a dispatch to Halleck, he again commented that "the enemy has not shown himself since the brilliant cavalry victory of the 9th," urged sending the 6th Corps to Alexandria, and also advised that repairs on the Manassas Gap railroad be ended. He concluded that with a division of cavalry, he could "keep the enemy running from the Valley to the railroad and from the railroad to the Valley."[19]

Considering the valley campaign to have ended, on the 12th Sheridan sent the 6th Corps marching towards Alexandria to return to Grant's army at Petersburg. At 9 P.M. that evening, he telegraphed Grant that the 6th Corps "is now at Front Royal," and that Early was thought to be, with most of his troops, at Craig's Creek, between Brown's Gap and Waynesboro. "Little Phil" further stated, "I believe that a Rebel advance down this valley will not take place."[20] He soon received a rude awakening. Early probed Sheridan's camp along Cedar Creek the very next day. Marching north from Hupp's Hill, one brigade of Kershaw's division engaged part of the Union 8th Corps in a sharp fight that lasted all morning. Kershaw's men were led by Brigadier General James Conner, who lost a leg in the fight. The 10th West Virginia Infantry was forced to retreat in disorder; Federal casualties totaled 209 killed, wounded, and missing; Confederate casualties numbered about 180. Colonel George D. Wells, leading the 34th Massachusetts Infantry, was among the slain.[21] Not surprisingly, this brief but bloody encounter failed to change Sheridan's mind about the threat posed by Early.

Then the administration intervened. Since August, Grant and the War Department had wanted Sheridan to continue his march southward and destroy two supply lines crucial to Lee's army. These were the Virginia Central Railroad, around Gordonsville, and the James River canal, near Charlottesville. From that city, the Army of the Shenandoah could advance on Petersburg from the west. However, "Little Phil" disagreed with Grant concerning the best use of his army once the threat posed by Early was ended. On 12 October, Halleck informed the Irish General that Grant wanted a base established "for future operations against Gordonsville and Charlottesville," suggesting a location near Manassas Gap. While Sheridan had some desire to destroy these important supply lines, he allowed the cost of doing so to deter him. Very wary of guerrilla attacks—"the robber bands" of Mosby—against badly extended supply lines, Sheridan was strongly opposed to Grant's strategy and to the subsequent repair of the Manassas Gap railroad, despite their potential for a quick end to the war. However, a quick cavalry raid might satisfy Grant.

On 14 October, Sheridan received an invitation from Stanton to come to Washington to discuss strategy. Despite the attack of the previous day, Early's intentions and capability were unknown, and the Union Army's Cedar Creek campsite had poor defensive potential. Thus the Irish General was uneasy about leaving the troops. Nevertheless, the conference offered a chance to impress his views on the administration. The next morning, he mounted his big black horse, Rienzi, and rode for the Rectortown train depot, accompanied by his entire cavalry force, on their way to Front Royal and Charlottesville. Then a small history altering event occurred, revealing the depth of Early's contempt for Sheridan.[22]

The Irish General had not gone far when he received an unsettling message from General Wright, whom he had left in command. Federal signalmen had intercepted a coded message addressed to Early, bivouacked at Fisher's Hill, stating, "Be ready to move as soon as my forces join you and we will crush Sheridan. LONGSTREET." Sufficiently recovered from his Wilderness wounding, Longstreet had reported for duty at Richmond the last week in September. The message proved to be a ruse, but it planted strong doubts about Early's apparent weakness. Had Early moved from Fisher's Hill? What was he planning? Was Longstreet coming to the valley?[23] Early hoped the message would cause Sheridan to retreat; however, he instead cancelled the Charlottesville raid, sending the cavalry back to the army.

Wright also feared an attack on their right flank, where Cedar Creek meanders through flat, open country, in some places less than a mile south of Belle Grove Mansion. He ended the message to his commander that he would "only fear an attack on my right, which I shall make every preparation for guarding against and resisting." While correct in his assessment, the stolid Wright didn't consider that an attack would come from the left, over difficult undulating terrain where Massanutten Mountain comes to an abrupt end, nearly on the south bank of the Shenandoah. As a result, the Federal left was lightly guarded when Early did attack, two and a half days later. Sheridan's reply sent from Front

Royal merely said, "Make your position strong.... Close in Colonel Powell, who will be at this point.... Look well to your ground and be well prepared."[24] Meeting with Stanton for a few hours on the morning of the 17th, Sheridan left Washington at noon, boarding a special train for Martinsburg. Arriving back in the valley at Winchester, late in the afternoon of Tuesday, 18 October, he spent the evening in town at headquarters, the large brick home of Lloyd Logan, a local merchant. He was fourteen miles away from the army.

Meanwhile, Early was preparing to attack. His first idea was to assault the Federal right. General Gordon, however, "was not entirely satisfied with the general plan of attack." Deciding to see the Federal encampments for himself, the Georgian took advantage of the crisp autumn weather, ascending the steep slopes of Massanutten's north end — Three Top Mountain, on the 17th. Three officers climbed to the summit with him, including Early's cartographer, Captain Jedediah Hotchkiss. Through field glasses, they observed the "inspiring panorama" from the top, including the entire Army of the Shenandoah. Three Federal infantry corps were camped along the northern (eastern) bank of Cedar Creek with Thoburn's division of the 8th Corps, supported by Dupont's artillery, about a half mile north of the creek. Several hundred yards north of Thoburn, the 23rd Ohio Infantry, led by Colonel Hayes, straddled the Valley Pike. Immediately west of Hayes' units the 19th Corps, led by General William Emory, was encamped. About a half mile northwest of the 19th Corps, the 6th Corps, led by General James Ricketts, was bivouacked. Merritt's and Custer's cavalry brigades lay still further away, directly west of Middletown. Hotchkiss made a rough map of the Federal encampments.

Sheridan's left flank was protected by only a few of Powell's cavalry from the brigade of Colonel Alpheus S. Moore; this reflected the widely held opinion that Massanutten's seemingly impassable northern end, with the river almost immediately in front, were sufficient protection against attack. Federal cavalry was nearly all deployed on the right, suggesting to Gordon that Sheridan was expecting an attack on his right or center. He was thus entirely convinced that an unexpected attack on the Union left flank would achieve complete surprise. Certain he had found a way to destroy Sheridan's army, the enthusiastic Georgian presented the plan to Early the next afternoon, offering to take personal responsibility should it fail.[25] Early approved the plan, but expressed doubts about the route to the ford. However, that day Gordon and Hotchkiss found a narrow trail leading through the woods and around the mountain to Bowman's Ford. Using the trail, Gordon's infantry could pass single file around the mountain, cross the Shenandoah, and continue their advance on the Federals.

Early now completely approved the plan, setting 5 A.M. as the time for the attack. Gordon would take three divisions across the Shenandoah, attacking the Federal left flank, while Early would direct Wharton's and Kershaw's divisions, along with the artillery, up the Valley Pike through Strasburg. Wharton would hit the Federal center — the 19th Corps — along the Valley Pike, while Kershaw would cross Cedar Creek at Robert's Ford, attacking Thoburn's division. While Rosser's cavalry was to attack and occupy Custer's horsemen to the west, Early made another grave mistake with Lomax's brigade. He sent the 1,700 troops, about half of his cavalry, on a vague maneuver through Front Royal, twelve miles southeast, by which they were to turn and attack Sheridan's rear. As a result, they weren't in the vicinity when needed. As the day wore on, Early would be in acute need of them.[26] With his small cavalry brigade, Payne was to storm Belle Grove man-

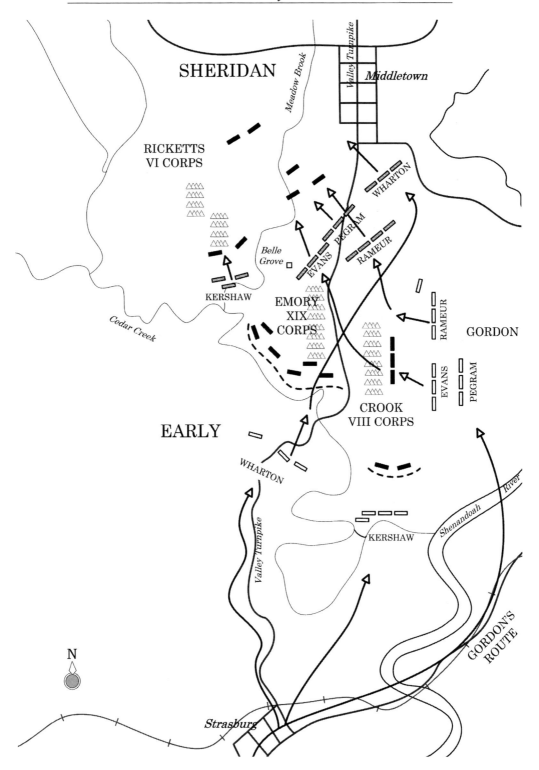

Battle of Cedar Creek, October 19, 1864

sion — thought to be Sheridan's location — and bring "Little Phil" back captive to the Confederate lines.

Gordon's infantry, including Ramseur's and Pegram's divisions, awakened at midnight, after a four hour rest. An hour later, they began their advance — without their metal canteens, talking in whispers and only when necessary — single file along the narrow precipice above the Shenandoah. A bright moon dimly lit the trail, while scouts were stationed along the route to make sure the troops took the right path. They arrived near the crossing points — Bowman's and McInturf's fords — with plenty of time to spare. Lying in the thickly matted grass near the riverbank, shivering in the October chill, they awaited the signal to cross, each man pondering his fate in the approaching battle. A few of Colonel Moore's videttes sat like statues on their horses in the river, unaware of the massed enemy infantry a stone's throw away.

As the clock neared 5 A.M., just before daybreak, Payne's cavalry plunged into the ice cold Shenandoah, overrunning the startled Union pickets. Following Payne's horsemen, Clement Evans' infantry brigade crossed the swift flowing dark water. Thoroughly soaked on reaching the north bank, they advanced "on the double quick" towards the Federal 8th Corps, about a mile away. They ran through a dense fog that had settled in overnight, obscuring the landscape and making sound judgment difficult. The entire area — from the Shenandoah north through Middletown — was blanketed; visibility was reduced to a few feet. The thick fog at first worked in Early's favor; a few hours later it worked against him.

Upon reaching the Cooley house, a white frame dwelling a half mile east of the Valley Turnpike, Gordon's infantry turned to the left, and charged through the fog. Yelling like demons, Ramseur's, Pegram's and Evans' men fell upon the unsuspecting, half-awake troops of colonels J. Howard Kitching and Rutherford B. Hayes and threw them, shocked and bleeding, across the turnpike as Kershaw's 3,000 troops, observing complete silence, had some minutes before overrun the entrenchments of Thoburn's division. Attempting to rally his men, Colonel Thoburn was shot in the back and killed. The thick fog, augmented by battle smoke, severely limited visibility and prevented the complete destruction of Thoburn's regiments as they fled across the turnpike.

Alarmed by the noise of gunfire coming from Thoburn's position, Hayes rode over to check on Kitching, whose 6,000 troop Provisional brigade had just joined Sheridan's army as reinforcements. The 25-year-old Kitching was confident, reassuring the paternal Hayes that he could "hold on" if Hayes could do likewise. Looking over his shoulder while conversing with Kitching, Hayes was startled to see wave after wave of Gordon's men come charging out of the fog. His horse killed underneath him, the future president narrowly escaped capture, taking refuge in a nearby patch of woods. Shortly thereafter, Kitching took a bullet in the foot; the wound caused his death three months later. Dazed by the surreal early morning attack, most of the 8th Corps fled westward, many unarmed and in their night clothes, disrupting the camps of the 19th Corps, west of the turnpike.

The quick rout of Thoburn's Federals failed to slow the momentum of Kershaw's Georgians, Mississippians, and South Carolinians. Like a tidal wave, they surged northward, out of the fog towards Crook's artillery, posted on two ridges several hundred yards away. However, complete success against the 8th Corps artillery eluded the butternut infantry. Led by Captain Henry A. Dupont, the 26-year-old heir to the Delaware gunpowder entrepreneurs, the 8th Corps' big guns comprised Battery B, 5th U.S. artillery, Battery D, Pennsylvania Light artillery, and Battery L, 1st Ohio Light. A widely respected, experienced officer, Dupont was very concerned about the lack of protection for the army's left flank. Investigating himself upon finding that no one knew of Powell's exact location, he found no troops on the far left. His concern mounted.

Dupont ordered his artillerymen to their guns at the first sounds of Kershaw's attack. For the next 15 minutes, Dupont's Pennsylvanians, closest to Thoburn's position, peered anxiously into the opaque haze, seeing nothing. Then a flood of blue-coated, demoralized refugees appeared out of the fog, 50 feet away, pressed closely by Colonel James P. Simms' Georgians. Afraid of hitting Thoburn's men, with almost no time to react, the Pennsylvanians bravely resisted, but were overwhelmed and their six big guns captured.

About a quarter mile away to the west, on the second ridge, with the 5th U.S. artillery, Dupont heard the sounds of the approaching conflict while deciding on how to save his big guns. When the commander of the 5th U.S. Artillery, Lt. Henry F. Brewerton, asked Dupont what to fire at, the future senator from Delaware told him to shoot in the direction of the sound. Wheeling the guns to the left, the crews fired towards the east, into the seething haze. Deciding to hide the guns in the ravine between the ridges, Dupont told Brewerton to stand fast until the Confederates became visible, then drag the guns out of sight, down into the defile, where he would be waiting with the limbers. Spurring his mount, Dupont then disappeared down the hillside.

The 5th U.S. Artillery stood fast, peppering the fog with repeated salvos, while the 1st Ohio Light fired at some Confederates south of Cedar Creek. As Kershaw's Georgians closed to within 25 yards, Brewerton's crews began dragging the big guns down the hillside. Dupont lost only one cannon, and his intrepid stand on the ridges above the 8th Corps slowed the Confederate avalanche, allowing Crook's men to escape westward across the turnpike. Dupont was promoted to brevet lieutenant colonel and later received the Congressional Medal of Honor.[27]

Meanwhile, Wharton's division, about 1,400 troops, had advanced along the Valley Turnpike, just ahead of the artillery, occupying Hupp's Hill. The wheels of the cannon had been wrapped in cloth to muffle the noise. As the big guns arrived on the hilltop, the noise of Gordon's and Kershaw's attacks dispelled the need for silence, and the cloth wrapping was removed. Wharton and the artillery then captured and held the turnpike bridge over Cedar Creek.[28]

After destroying Crook's 8th Corps, Gordon's and Kershaw's forces combined, pursuing the fleeing blue-coats across the Valley Turnpike. The dazed, half-dressed Union troops ran westward, into and through the encampment of the 19th Corps. A bit farther north, they ran through the Federal wagon park, on the front lawn of Belle Grove, a one-story 18th century Georgian style residence, now serving as General Wright's headquarters. In front of the gray limestone house sat hundreds of ammunition wagons and ambulances. As the sound of the fighting grew louder, dozens of teamsters hurried their canvas covered vehicles northward along the turnpike, through Middletown, more than a few overturning in their haste to get away.

Emory reached his forward line "in fog so dense it was impossible to see the position of the enemy or the direction of his advance"; however he placed three regiments of the 8th Vermont Infantry across the path of the oncoming Confederates. A few minutes before

Belle Grove Mansion (courtesy Belle Grove Plantation)

6 A.M. they closed with the surging divisions of Evans and Kershaw, and fierce hand-to-hand combat ruled, much of it swirling around the Union battle flags. For well over an hour, various units of the 19th Corps resisted the Confederate onslaught. Emory eventually committed all five of his brigades, but one by one they were shattered by the rebel juggernaut. Most of the 19th Corps offered strong resistance but were swept away by the irresistible momentum of the Confederate assault. Along with the shattered 8th Corps they retreated northwest, around Belle Grove, and into the camps of the 6th Corps. A routed, disorganized mob of about 9,000 Federal troops crossed two foot deep Meadow Brook, a small stream flowing southward into Cedar Creek.

Most re-formed on Red Hill, "a commanding crest which overlooked the whole open country in its front," about 1500 yards west of Belle Grove, where Emory was deploying in two lines of battle. After first covering his flanks, Emory's units joined the 6th Corps around 7:30 A.M.[29] They had left behind a scene of devastation on the plain east of Belle Grove, where some of the triumphant rebels were plundering the Union encampment. Two and a half hours after Kershaw's men began their assault on Thoburn's camp, the surging Confederates had captured 1,300 Federals and 18 cannon.

However, the battlefield remained a scene of unending confusion. The fog tenaciously clung to the landscape, mixing with black powder discharges from the muzzles of thousands of guns, creating an opaque choking haze that hampered perception and decision making. The haze helped to create doubt about the strength and deployments of the 6th Corps; Ramseur and Pegram apparently thought they were fighting the entire Corps. The murky fog also stifled reconnaissance. As the brigades of Evans and Kershaw assaulted the

19th Corps, Ramseur's and Pegram's brigades halted between Middletown and Belle Grove; 4,000 troops remained idle for over an hour. One writer states that their inaction "became a critical factor, if not decisive, in the outcome of the battle," and that "Ramseur and Pegram held the key to the battle — the Valley Pike — and did not know it. If they had been able to view the dispositions of the 6th Corps, Ramseur could have held Getty in place while Pegram could have marched down the turnpike and through Middletown." He further states that had Pegram marched through Middletown, he "would have secured the highway," thus the Federals "could not have used the road as an escape route or a point of rallying as they subsequently did."

These assertions are correct. Early's Confederates were the weaker party in the battle; time was especially critical for them. Delay postponed victory, and allowed the shattered Army of the Shenandoah an opportunity to rest and regroup. Had Ramseur occupied Getty while Pegram marched through Middletown, past the Union army's left flank, a successful flank attack against the 6th Corps would probably have resulted. Had that occurred, the 6th Corps would have been chased from the field, and the Confederate success in the morning would have had a victorious outcome. In addition, Lomax's cavalry might have executed a successful flanking attack against the 6th Corps, through Middletown, had they been present.[30] However, neither Early, nor Gordon, nor Ramseur realized that just as maneuvering was the key to their morning success, it was also crucial to driving the 6th Corps into retreat.

After hearing the sounds of Kershaw's and Evans' attacks on the 8th Corps, the 6th Corps infantry was under arms, ready to advance, by 6 A.M. Wright had requested two divisions, and the Federals advanced in two columns, east across Meadow Brook. George Getty's brigade, in the lead, crossed Meadow Brook, and formed in line of battle about "1000 yards north of Belle Grove and 500 yards from the southern limits of Middletown." Frank Wheaton's brigade held the center, behind Belle Grove, while Rickett's brigade, led by Colonel J. Warren Kiefer, was on the far right, behind Wheaton's men. Wright, however, witnessing the destruction of the 8th Corps, and seeing that "no part of the original line could be held, as the enemy was already on the left flank of the Nineteenth Corps," ordered the 6th Corps to fall back.[31] Shortly thereafter, Ricketts went down, wounded in the chest and shoulder. The 6th Corps then retreated to a crest west of Meadow Brook, where they repelled part of Kershaw's brigade pursuing the 19th Corps.

Regrouping on a ridge above and parallel to the Meadow Brook defile, Kiefer's men twice repulsed Kershaw's three brigades. Kershaw's brigade hit Kiefer's position a third time, while Evans' men assaulted the New Hampshire regiments of Colonel Joseph Hamblin. They fiercely resisted the gray onslaught, but by 8 A.M., they were retreating northward. The only Federal division still on the field was the 3rd Division, led by General Getty. As the rest of the 6th Corps was forced into confused retreat, Getty too retreated, but to a stronger position about 300 yards to the west. This was a commanding semi-circular ridge top, which proved to be the location of Middletown's cemetery. Some minutes after 8 o'clock, about 4,000 Federals, including the 2nd Vermont Volunteers and the Maine, New York, and Pennsylvania units of Colonel Daniel Bidwell, awaited another Confederate assault on the ridge top. Around 8:30 A.M. Pegram's three butternut brigades, about 1,600 men, climbed out of the shallow canyon formed by Meadow Brook, towards the ridge top, screaming the defiant rebel yell. Following orders, Getty's men waited until the Confederate tide was within thirty yards; then volley after volley mowed down the charging Rebels, silencing their unnerving battle cry. Pegram's Confederates retreated down the hill, while the troops of Bidwell and Colonel James Warner pursued, forcing them back across Meadow Brook.

Jubal Early then made another mistake. With the ubiquitous opaque haze still covering part of the field, he conferred with Ramseur and Pegram, shortly after Pegram's retreat from the cemetery crest. Responding to their request for reinforcements against the 6th Corps, he ordered Wharton's division forward, directing "Generals Ramseur and Pegram to put it where it was required."[32] This was out of character for Early; he infrequently submitted to the requests of even trusted subordinates. Ramseur and Pegram committed Wharton's brigade, Early's only reserve unit, to a futile, piecemeal attack on Getty's division, still in position on the cemetery crest. With the misuse of Wharton's brigade, the window of opportunity closed for an advance through Middletown and an assault on the Federal left flank. This was because Wright ordered Torbert, between nine and ten o'clock, to move his entire cavalry force to the left to cover Middletown and the turnpike to the north.

One writer commented that the order "was the single most important decision made by the acting army commander on this day." Union cavalry was now threatening Early's right flank. As Wharton's infantry retreated down from the cemetery crest, the fog at last began to dissipate. "Old Jube" sent them, along with one of Kershaw's brigades, north of Middletown, to oppose the encroaching Federal horsemen. Confederate cavalry, led by Thomas Rosser, outnumbered by a ratio of about eight to one, wasn't a factor in the battle.[33] Merritt's cavalry, part of Torbert's command, kept Wharton's infantry in place. Lomax's cavalry would have been a very useful addition to Wharton's brigade. Meanwhile, Getty's division of the 6th Corps withdrew northwards from the cemetery hill to "second position" of the day, directly west of Middletown. Shortly thereafter, under Rebel artillery fire from the guns of Colonel Thomas Carter, the 6th Corps retreated again to the "third position" of the day, about a mile north of Middletown, west of the turnpike. There they joined the 19th Corps, resting until the Federal counterattack late that afternoon.

Nevertheless, Early believed that all was well, despite the presence of 7,500 Federal cavalry on his right flank. Indeed, "Old Jube" felt a strong sense of vindication for the three recent defeats at the hands of Sheridan, and some measure of revenge towards "Little Phil," whom he despised. Around 10 o'clock he rode towards Middletown. As he learned of the Federal retreat, his normally taciturn countenance became joyful, and he was heard by a staff officer to exclaim, "The Sun of Middletown! The Sun of Middletown!" Paraphrasing Napoleon, he had imagined that Cedar Creek was his Austerlitz, site of the French emperor's victory over coalition forces.[34]

Another clue to his state of mind soon surfaced. Perhaps half an hour later, Early encountered John Gordon; their conversation became the grist of Civil War legend. "Well, Gordon, this is glory enough for one day!" he exclaimed. Gordon replied, "It is very well so far, General; but we have one more blow to strike, and then there will not be left an organized company of infantry in Sheridan's army." As he spoke, Gordon pointed towards the 6th Corps. Early didn't agree. "No use in that," he replied, "they will all go directly!" Gordon answered, "This is the 6th Corps, General. It will not go unless we drive it from the field." Early had the last word, "Yes, it will go, directly." Gordon was mortified.[35]

However, Early took too much for granted. A little before 6 that morning, at the Logan House in Winchester, Sheridan was awakened by the duty officer, who reported intermittent cannon fire from the direction of Cedar Creek. Sheridan replied that the noise was from the reconnaissance in force that Grover was making that morning, and that "he is merely feeling the enemy." Nevertheless, the Irish General couldn't sleep any further. A bit later, the duty officer returned, confirming the cannon fire but again claiming there was no battle. Nevertheless, Sheridan ordered the cook to hurry breakfast and ordered the horses saddled.

Between 8:30 and 9 o'clock, Sheridan and his party left the Logan House, riding through Winchester, then up the Valley Turnpike. At the edge of town, Sheridan heard the artillery fire more clearly — "in an unceasing roar." A half mile south of town, at Mill Creek, they were joined by an escort from the 17th Pennsylvania cavalry. As they trotted over the rise beyond the stream, "Little Phil" must have realized that Grover had made no reconnaissance. They were greeted with "the appalling spectacle of a panic-stricken army — hundreds of slightly wounded men, throngs of others unhurt but utterly demoralized, and baggage wagons by the score, all pressing to the rear in hopeless confusion, telling ... plainly that a disaster had occurred at the front."[36] After ordering the garrison commander at Winchester to cordon off the panic stricken retreat near Mill Creek, Sheridan increased his pace. Mounted on his huge black charger, 17 hands high, "Little Phil" rode up the valley, shouting profane encouragement, urging his discouraged troopers to go back and fight. He arrived back at the battlefield around 10:30 A.M., having traveled about 14 miles, a ride immortalized in a poem after the battle ("Sheridan's Ride," by Thomas Buchanan Read). After greeting Wright, Crook, and Emory, he set about reorganizing and reinvigorating the Army of the Shenandoah.

As the sun approached the noon zenith, Early's confidence in victory, at a high level in battle's opening stages, had slowly degenerated into hesitation and apprehension. Getty's division of the 6th Corps had repulsed three attacks, and had now retreated to the crest of a hill a mile north of Middletown. There they rested, part of the Federal defenses, awaiting further battle. The cavalry divisions of Custer and Merritt now occupied the turnpike north of Middletown, and the area east of the turnpike, threatening Early's right and canceling any chance of a flanking attack. With so many troops plundering the abandoned Federal encampments, "Old Jube" chewed a wad of tobacco, pondering the best course of action. He determined "to try and hold what had been gained," giving orders to carry off the captured and abandoned artillery, small arms and wagons.[37]

Having returned to his command, Sheridan now inspected the troops. Using his uncanny "battlefield presence" and inspiring talk, he passed by each unit, rousing the entire army. They responded with thunderous cheers, subsequently repulsing Gordon's attack around 1 P.M. Early didn't expect the attack to succeed, telling Gordon not to attack "if he found the enemy's line too strong."[38]

Early, however, had given up the fight. Even though he was aware that Sheridan's Federals remained in strength in the woods to the north, the three hour afternoon break in the action sedated him. Attempting to coordinate with Rosser's cavalry to the west, Gordon stretched his line dangerously thin on the left with a quarter mile wide gap between Evans' brigade and that of Colonel John Lowe's Georgia infantry. Signal flags atop Massanutten Mountain told the fiery Georgian that the revived Federals were massing for an attack opposite the gap. Sending aide after aide to inform Early of the danger and request reinforcements, Gordon received "no satisfactory answer." Riding to see Early himself, Gordon pleaded for reinforcements or an immediate withdrawal. Instead, "Old Jube" told Gordon to stretch his thin line even further without riding out to personally inspect his subordinate's deployment. With this nonsensical order Early abandoned his army to their fate. Sheridan had delayed his counterattack, having received erroneous reports that Longstreet was approaching from the direction of Winchester.[39]

Nevertheless, at 4 P.M. Federal bugles sounded the charge. Ramseur's, Kershaw's and Evan's brigades stood firm against the Union onslaught, their ranks islands of gray engulfed by a sea of blue. They fired on the charging blue-coats from behind stone walls, stopping their advance. The fighting settled down into a stalemate, and for an hour and a half the Army of the Valley held Sheridan's finest at bay. However, as Sheridan's Federals charged through gaps in the Rebel line, they turned and attacked "our main line on the flank" and rolled it up "like a scroll." As Gordon described it, "Regiment after regiment, brigade after brigade, in rapid succession was crushed, and, like hard clods of clay under a pelting rain, the superb commands crumbled to pieces." Gordon's Confederates at first yielded slowly, but shortly thereafter "there came from the north side of the plain a dull, heavy swelling sound like the roaring of a distant cyclone, the omen of additional disaster. It was unmistakable. Sheridan's horsemen were riding across the open fields of grass to intercept the Confederates before they crossed Cedar Creek.... As the sullen roar from horses hoofs beating the soft turf of the plain told of the near approach of the cavalry, all effort at orderly retreat was abandoned."[40]

Custer's cavalry galloped into the action around 4:30 P.M., entering the fray against some isolated units of Lowe's infantry. The Georgia troops fired one round, then fled towards Cedar Creek. Federal infantry then surprised some units of Louisiana troops who broke and ran. Shortly thereafter, they were followed by other Confederate infantry units in a panic stricken stampede towards Cedar Creek. Ramseur had two horses shot out from under him and had suffered a bullet wound himself. While mounting a third, he was hit by another bullet that penetrated his lungs. Carried to an ambulance, the 27-year-old major general was captured in transit and taken to Belle Grove. That evening, as Federal surgeons tried to save his life, the unconscious Ramseur was visited by his West Point friends Henry Dupont and George Custer. He died the following morning. On the Federal side, Colonels Charles R. Lowell and Daniel Bidwell were killed. The popular 29-year-old Lowell caught a bullet in the back, near Middletown, only moments before the Rebels fled. He died a short time later. Bidwell, the well-liked defender of Fort Stevens, had been wounded in the chest and shoulder. Sheridan signed Lowell's commission as a brigadier, posthumously, that evening.

The sun had already set as the Rebel infantry stampeded across Cedar Creek. In the growing darkness, a stone bridge over that narrow stream, on the Valley Turnpike, became a scene of bedlam as a wagon broke down and the team became entangled with passing artillery. As the sun began to set on the Army of the Valley, Jubal Early, "red-faced with rage," desperately trying to rally the fugitives, yelled "Run, run, G-d d—you, they will get you!"[41] Ignoring their commander, the battered, disorganized remnants of the once proud Valley army continued their flight throughout the evening, regrouping at New Market the following day.

Conclusion

Thus the battle of Cedar Creek, which might have resulted in a Confederate victory, ended in disastrous defeat for the Army of the Valley. John Gordon was correct in assuming that victory required driving the 6th Corps from the field. However, none of the Confederate commanders — Early, Gordon, Ramseur, Kershaw, or Pegram — seemed to realize that to defeat the 6th Corps, further maneuvering was necessary. Their lack of awareness was partly caused and abetted by the heavy fog, which kept them from realizing that they were in control of events, before Torbert's cavalry occupied the turnpike. Early must have had a good idea of the tactical importance of the Valley Turnpike, because his orders for Wharton contained the phrase "press up the Pike" through Middletown; Lomax's role was to "move by Front Royal ... and come to the Valley Pike, so as to strike the enemy wherever he might be." Yet beyond these basic requirements, there was nothing — no orders for an attack on the Federal left flank, or to occupy and hold Middletown, or the turnpike to the north.[42]

Nonetheless, there are more fundamental, but less obvious, reasons for the Confederate defeat in the Valley campaign. To be sure, a fair amount of plundering, requiring many field officers to control, contributed to the defeat at Cedar Creek. Not long after Kershaw's attack got underway, pillaging of the hastily abandoned Federal camps began. An officer of Barksdale's Mississippi brigade described it: "Then our line passed over the breastworks. Good gracious, what a feast we had! Edibles of every kind and in great abundance were there ... camp kettles on the fire were full of boiling coffee. We got some of the good things, filled our tin cups with the coffee, and moved on after the Yankees, eating, drinking and feeling big and brave." Great quantities of food and clothing were left behind, and Early's troopers were in dire need; many were shoeless, with torn uniforms, and most were hungry. Many left the ranks and supplied themselves; the pillaging continued throughout the morning. The looting "weakened our lines considerably," occupying hundreds of troops who would otherwise have been in the ranks; Early didn't have enough officers to control them. Physical exhaustion also reduced the number of troops available for an attack.[43]

Writing many years after the war, Gordon brought out Early's deficiencies in glaring relief. In his efforts to blame Early for the defeat, Gordon emphatically denied the pillaging; Early emphasized it in his report to Lee, and in his *Memoirs*, for which he was roundly criticized.[44] Despite his opinion that "this was a case of a glorious victory given up by my own troops after they had won it ... on the ground of partial demoralization caused by the plunder of the enemy's camps," Early let the truth slip out when he directed Jed Hotchkiss not to tell Lee that "we ought to have advanced in the morning beyond Middletown, for we should have done so."[45] Blaming the troops for the breakdown in discipline was not a valid explanation for the defeat.

However, referring to "Old Jube's" legendary conversation with Gordon, Early's biographer states that he was seized "by a curious numbness of mind and spirit that Gordon may have sensed at this meeting and ... at other times during the day."[46] Partly as a result of three mistakes Early made — sending away Kershaw's brigade, scattering his army in front of a much stronger enemy, and his abiding contempt for Sheridan — the Army of the Valley lost the 3rd battle of Winchester. Consequently, the troops began to lose confidence in his leadership. He in turn lost control of his troops. Thus Early may

have, in some way, given up the fight before Cedar Creek. Arguably, at Fisher's Hill, placing his most vulnerable troops — Lomax's cavalry — on the far left, the weakest point in
his defenses, is evidence for this contention. Was this negligent act — placing his weakest
troops in an isolated, exposed position — merely an inability to handle cavalry? Or was
it something more? Given the result — they were placed in what became the direct path
of Crook's attack — impartial readers may believe it was something more. With the resulting rout, Early's troops lost all confidence in their commander.

Certainly, he didn't have effective control of Confederate efforts at Cedar Creek —
John Gordon and Joseph Kershaw conducted the first three and a half hours of the battle.
Given the plundering that occurred, the misuse of his reserve troops, and his failure to conduct any reconnaissance towards the Federal left flank, Early's efforts thereafter amounted
to little. Arguably, after he took command from Gordon, he was merely going through the
motions, content to hold onto the gains of the early morning attacks. And once again, he
courted disaster by sending away his cavalry on a vague mission that wasted their efforts.

Would another attack have destroyed the 6th Corps? A coordinated, two-pronged
attack could have, but the presence of Merritt's cavalry on Early's right flank after 10 A.M.
took away that option. In addition, as time passed, Philip Sheridan's presence on the field,
after 10:30 A.M., began to make a difference as he inspirited and reorganized his army.
Gordon's tentative probing attack in the afternoon was easily repulsed. The window of
opportunity for a Confederate victory at Cedar Creek closed very rapidly. Nevertheless,
no Confederate general then on the field could have fully appreciated that. Southern
defeat at Cedar Creek began with their defeats at Winchester, Fisher's Hill, and Tom's
Brook, exacerbated by peculiar battlefield conditions on 19 October. Early wasn't entirely
responsible for the defeat at Cedar Creek. However, by 19 October, he had lost control
of the Army of the Valley and was unable to regain it.

Thus the Confederate cause in the Shenandoah Valley failed. After Cedar Creek,
part of the Army of the Valley returned to Lee's forces at Petersburg. Their final defeat,
at Waynesboro, was still a few months away, but the destitute condition of the valley and
winter's cold blast militated against further large-scale fighting. Nevertheless, badly out-
manned and outgunned, they had come very close to defeating Sheridan. Had Early not
scattered his army in front of Sheridan's superior force, making a fruitless trek to Martinsburg; had he not sent away Kershaw's division; had he not scattered his depleted army
over a 3½ mile front at Fisher's Hill; had he not placed his weakest troops at the point of
attack; had he fought Sheridan at Fisher's Hill on the 19th, instead of at Winchester; had
he coordinated his efforts with those of Mosby....

However, in a sense, Sheridan also failed. Most any competent Federal commander,
enjoying great advantages in manpower, supply, and firepower, would have defeated Early;
yet it took Sheridan nearly seven months to destroy the Army of the Valley. Had he not
forced half his army through a narrow defile, using only one road of approach, and had
he not kept his reserve force two miles in the rear, he might have bagged the Valley Army
at Winchester. Had he not assumed the Valley Army was finished after Fisher's Hill and
pursued them through Brown's Gap, and had he extended his supply lines, destroyed the
James River Canal, and pressured Lee's army from the west, the war might have ended
that fall. Instead, Sheridan chose to burn the valley, ensuring several more months of
fighting and a long residue of bitterness afterwards.

CHAPTER 13

Epilogue — Winter 1865

Twilight of the Confederacy

The fall of 1864 saw the waning of the Confederate cause. Sherman's capture of Atlanta, his March to the Sea in December, and his subsequent march through the Carolinas laid waste city and countryside and so reduced the area controlled by the Confederacy that final defeat and surrender were only a matter of time. However, Sheridan's victories over Early ensured the re-election of Abraham Lincoln.

Nevertheless, though their cause was failing, the South was still full of fight, complementing still strong anti-war sentiment in the North. As Election Day approached, in many Northern jurisdictions there was considerable fear of polling place disruption, and "all persons from the insurgent states" in New York City and the surrounding military department were required to register with local military authorities. In late October, Delaware governor William Cannon telegraphed General Wallace, in Baltimore, requesting the presence of Federal troops at polling places in the First State.[1] A few days later, Major Richard I. Dodge, Federal provost marshal at Harrisburg, received an emphatic telegram from an outlying district: "For God's sake do not withdraw any part of military force from this county until after the 8th, especially the cavalry."[2]

Secretary of War Stanton was apprehensive about the use of state militia troops to guard New York City. He doubted the motives of Governor Horatio Seymour, considered anti-administration, in calling them out. He suggested reinforcing the Federal garrison in the city with Major General Benjamin Butler commanding.[3] Stanton's worries were caused in part by exaggerated reports that several thousand Rebels were in the city, waiting to cause mischief. However, Brigadier General John A. Green, militia commander in New York City, doubted the wisdom and legality of sending Federal troops to New York. Referring to Butler's coming to the city, Green stated, in part, "The General-Commanding recognizes danger to the public peace in the proposed attempt of a Major-General holding a commission under the Federal Government to take under his care and supervision within the ... district, the election to be held as aforesaid. For this contemplated interference there is no necessity, authority or excuse. The Federal Government is charged with no duty or responsibility whatever relating to an election to be held in the State of New York."[4]

Butler wanted direct control of the state militia but was opposed by the Federal commander in New York, Major General John A. Dix. Telegraphing Stanton, Dix commented on Butler's ambitions, "I cannot think [them] right in law, and which raises a most important question of constitutional power ... unwise to raise a day or two before the election."

However, Butler didn't disappoint. Upon arriving in New York City, four days before the election, he promptly silenced Major General C.W. Sanford, the state militia commander. Without authority, Butler threatened to consider as enemies any state militia troops called upon to police the election, ordering Sanford not to call them out. Butler backed down the day before the election as a result of a telegram from Stanton: "The President thinks it expedient to avoid precipitating any military collision between the United States forces and the militia of the state of New York."[5]

On Election Day, Butler had heavily armed gunboats covering Wall Street, Five Points, and the High Bridge over the Harlem River, while a brigade of infantry guarded Federal ordnance stored at the Battery and in Lower Manhattan. Election Day in New York City was very quiet, and went off in the rest of the country without serious disturbance. However, even though Lincoln won re-election, he failed to win New York City despite the presence of Federal troops, and despite Butler's intimidation of southern residents into not voting. Lincoln won New York State by less than 7,000 votes.[6]

Nevertheless, a plot to burn the city involving Copperheads and Confederate agents was attempted, despite the arrival of Federal troops. As in Chicago, the Copperheads backed out of the plot, set for Election Day. The arrival of the troops the previous day gave them pause, leaving Confederate agents in the city to attempt it. The plot was postponed until Thanksgiving; the Copperheads again backed out. Led by Colonel Robert Martin, the Confederates set a number of the city's major hotels ablaze, using bottles of Greek fire. The fires were quickly put out; only one hotel suffered major damage. The Astor Hotel escaped major damage when one conspirator failed to open the window in the room he set ablaze. Forced to leave town that evening, the Rebel provocateurs arrived in Toronto shortly thereafter, where they reported the results of their mission to Jacob Thompson. It was later discovered that they had been betrayed by a co-conspirator, who had also disclosed to the Federals the plot to capture the U.S.S. *Michigan* and use it to free Confederate prisoners held at Johnson's Island. During their incendiary activities, the Confederates were shadowed by Federal detectives.[7] Had the Copperheads not backed out, a considerable part of the city might have burned.

The fall of Atlanta caused most Southerners to have some expectation of Lincoln's re-election; regardless, his victory further disheartened them. One resident of Richmond wrote, "There is no use disguising the fact that our subjugation is popular at the North." Robert G.H. Kean, in the Confederate War Department, wrote in his diary: "The Yankee election was evidently a damper on the spirits of many of our people, and is said to have depressed the army a good deal." With Lincoln's victory, Union armies continued to wreak havoc in the South, abetted by Confederate mistakes. Hood's strategy of suicidal frontal attacks against entrenched Federals at Franklin destroyed his army and Confederate hopes in the West. Simultaneously, the Union Navy tightened its grip on Southern ports. With no prospect that negotiation would end the fighting, desertion from Confederate armies became epidemic as weary troops forgot their loyalties rather than face further fighting for an increasingly hopeless cause.

As December became January, desertion multiplied; every morning brought new reports of troops that had disappeared. Over a ten day period in February, 1094 men deserted from the Army of Northern Virginia. Prompting the exodus was the Confederate government's leniency towards deserters. Many believed they wouldn't be shot for leaving without permission, prompting Lee to telegraph Adjutant General Samuel Cooper near the end of February, "Hundreds of men are deserting nightly, and I cannot keep the army together unless examples are made of [convicted deserters]." At the beginning of March, Confederate authorities estimated that as many as 100,000 deserters were at large. Deserting Confederates often cited Lincoln's re-election and prospects of further fighting as justification for crossing enemy lines.[8]

Last Stand of the Valley Army

Fall in the Shenandoah Valley brings with it bitter cold. In the immediate aftermath of Cedar Creek, increasingly cold weather brought snow and sleet, chilling the countryside, dampening martial ardor, and nearly halting the fighting. The remnants of the Valley Army assembled at New Market, while Early's quartermasters and inspector general, Major Samuel J.C. Moore, searched for a suitable winter camp. They found a few camp sites near Waynesboro, a small town on the South Fork of the Shenandoah, straddling the Virginia Central Railroad, near Rockfish Gap in the Blue Ridge. As fall gradually became winter, the lack of forage and destitute condition of the valley forced Early to send many troops home, on call when needed. He was forced to scatter his remaining units over a wide area to procure adequate supplies. Fitzhugh Lee's two brigades were returned to the Army of Northern Virginia; Lomax's cavalry was sent into West Virginia; Lt. Colonel J. Floyd King's artillery was sent to southwestern Virginia. However, fighting continued well into December despite Lincoln's re-election.[9]

From New Market, Early probed northwards with infantry led by Gordon, Kershaw, Pegram, and Wharton. Lomax's and Rosser's cavalry skirmished near Cedar Creek and at Mt. Jackson. In November, on a day described as "raw and cold," the fighting went back and forth, with Custer forcing Rosser backwards in the morning, and Payne scattering Custer's Federals "far and wide" in the afternoon.[10] McCausland was driven across the Shenandoah at Cedarville, but because "a blustering wind was blowing" the noise of the fighting was silenced. Early found out that evening, when the army withdrew to Fisher's Hill.

In the aftermath of Cedar Creek, Early's reputation fell further among Southern civilians; again public opinion charged him with drunkenness. He again successfully refuted the charges; however, Lee was forced to acknowledge the rising tide of public sentiment against "Old Jube." He retained Early, but partly of necessity further reduced the size of the Valley Army. On 9 December, Gordon, now in command of the 2nd Corps, along with Pegram, returned with their troops to the Army of Northern Virginia.[11]

However, Sheridan had learned to respect Early. Into late November, he believed Early very capable of taking the offensive and thought the Valley Army retained four divisions of infantry and one of cavalry.[12] Sheridan retained the 6th Corps until Gordon and Pegram left the Valley Army.

After the Valley Army returned to New Market, Kershaw's division left the valley, returning to Lee at Petersburg. Near the end of November, Rosser's cavalry crossed 2,500-foot-high Great North Mountain into Hardy County, West Virginia. On 29 November, he surprised and captured the hilltop forts at New Creek, on the B & O Railroad, along with 800 prisoners, eight cannon, a large quantity of supplies, and several hundred cattle and sheep. A Federal cavalry thrust, led by Custer, was repulsed north of Harrisonburg by Rosser and Payne a few days before Christmas. On that note, the 1864 Valley campaign ended.

The Valley Army went into winter encampment at Waynesboro, while Early established his headquarters at Staunton. The day after the new year began, Early visited Lee at Richmond. The two Generals discussed the Valley army's difficulties; Lee told Early that his mission remained to draw as many troops as possible away from Grant and instructed him to do his best. Shortly thereafter, the dutiful Early sent Rosser's cavalry on a very successful raid against a Federal force at Beverly, West Virginia. A few weeks later, with winter's end approaching, ranger Captain Jesse McNeil, with a few partisans, evaded tight security at Cumberland, Maryland, and captured generals Crook and Kelley, in their hotel rooms. The two generals were spirited away to the valley, briefly confined in Richmond and then exchanged. The raid temporarily raised the morale of soldiers and civilians in the valley but had little permanent effect.

However, on 20 February, Grant told Sheridan to advance up the valley, destroy Early's remaining forces, and then advance on Lynchburg. That very day, north of Winchester, the Irish General held a grand review of his two cavalry divisions. Realizing that their last campaign would soon begin, the troopers eagerly prepared to march. Five days later, Sheridan issued orders. His two divisions, ten thousand strong, passed four abreast through Winchester on 27 February, where the glossy coats of their horses, new saddles, red blankets and shiny accouterments made an unforgettable impression on residents. Upon leaving town, they cantered up the macadamized Valley Turnpike in a raging sleet storm, with ice-covered trees and patches of snow still on the ground. Leaving the turnpike, they advanced slowly southward, over washed out roads, some with two feet of mud, through biting winds that blew "right through us." Nevertheless, they made good time, camping the night of 28 February at Lacey Springs, about 60 miles south of Winchester.

Early responded by ordering Rosser and Lomax to delay the Federal advance. Lomax was sent to Pound Gap to flank the Federals should they advance on Lynchburg, while on 1 March Rosser's troops deployed at Mt. Crawford, south of the covered bridge over the North Fork of the Shenandoah. They set fire to stacked rails inside the bridge, but part of Custer's cavalry swam the river above the bridge, while the rest crossed the burning span before it collapsed. Custer's two-pronged attack forced Rosser to retreat to the outskirts of Staunton, however that city was successfully evacuated. Meanwhile, Early gathered about 2,000 troops from Wharton's infantry, and a few cavalry, and prepared to make a stand at Waynesboro, 15 miles away in the shadow of the Blue Ridge.

Although Sheridan's objective was Lynchburg, he couldn't allow the Valley Army to remain in his rear. He thus decided to end Early's threat once and for all, sending the bulk of his cavalry eastward, along the Richmond Turnpike, toward Waynesboro. A few blue-coated horsemen were sent to destroy the railroad depot at Swopes, eight miles west of Staunton. On 2 March, just after sunrise, Custer's troops, led by the 22nd New York

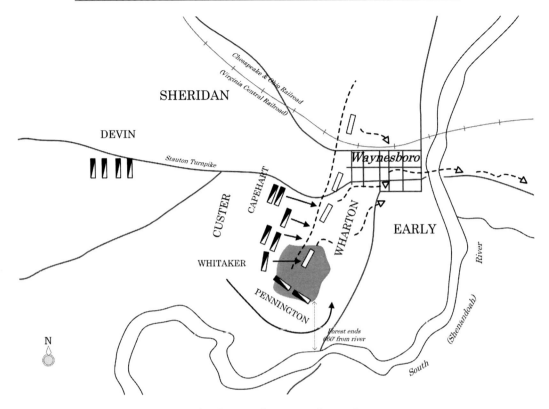

Battle of Waynesboro, March 2, 1865

Cavalry, were the first to encounter Early's skirmishers, pushing them back to the outskirts of town. Early wanted to fight a delaying action at Waynesboro to buy time to evacuate badly needed supplies stored nearby, including five cannon without teams. However, he failed to reckon with the speed of Sheridan's advance.

Waynesboro is situated on a high plateau, bounded on the west by a 300-foot-high, north-south ridge and the South Fork of the Shenandoah, called South River, on the south and east. Early had about 2,000 troops — about 1,200, Wharton's infantry and a few cavalry — form a line along the ridge top, facing the approach from Staunton. Two railroads — the Virginia Central and the Staunton-Charlottesville — crossed South River behind the ridge. Early's position was strong; a few troops dug trenches and some built crude breastworks, while Nelson's six guns faced westward, covering the highway approach from Staunton. Four of the guns were in a patch of woods on Wharton's left, 1/8 mile from the river, while the muddy fields fronting the ridge seemingly made a direct assault impossible. However, the line stretched ¾ of a mile — too long for 1,200 troops — and once again the day was lost in the details.

As had become his habit, Custer found a weakness in Early's line. Neither flank was protected or anchored by any natural feature or fortification. The right flank ended on the far side of town near a cluster of cabins across the Virginia Central railroad tracks; the left entered a grove of trees on high ground about 1,500 feet from South River, penetrating the grove only a short distance. The grove ended abruptly, about 660 feet from the river. Worse, the trees made visibility difficult, allowing an attacking force to approach with little risk of detection. After a thorough reconnaissance, Custer learned of the unprotected gap; Early's response to the gap came too late.

The 22nd New York, in the vanguard, arrived around noon, covered with mud. They immediately began to skirmish with Wharton's infantry, but Early's artillery kept the Federals at bay. However, two hours later, Custer's entire division arrived and deployed. The "Boy General" sent three regiments of Colonel Alexander Pennington's brigade, armed with Spencer carbines, towards the exposed gap while at the same time advancing against Wharton's front. Henry Capehart's brigade prepared to charge against Early's center, while Union artillery unlimbered and opened fire. Around 3 P.M., Thomas Devin's division arrived and was held in reserve. On high ground near the railroad, Early observed Custer's deployment, noticing the unprotected gap on his left. He sent a warning via courier to Wharton, but the infantry commander never received the message. A minute or so later, Federal bugles sounded the charge.

Capehart's troopers charged through the mud against Early's center while Pennington's dismounted cavalry — the 1st Connecticut, 2nd Ohio, and 3rd New Jersey — moved towards the exposed left flank. Led by Lt. Colonel Edward Whitaker, they ran undetected through a ravine near the riverbank, through the ubiquitous mud. Stopping to rest before charging up the boulder-strewn ridge, they realized they were in the Valley Army's rear. Surprised by the sudden appearance of Whitaker's Federals on the ridge, Wharton's left broke and ran. The rest of the Valley Army soon followed, scattering in every direction in wild flight. Hundreds surrendered on the streets of Waynesboro. The 1st New York and 8th New Hampshire Cavalry pursued. They raced across South River and deployed, cordoning off escape routes. By 4 P.M., a scant hour after the Federal attack, the fighting ended. About 1,600 of the 2,000 Confederates engaged were captured, along with all of Early's artillery. Watching his troops routed and captured, Early crossed South River ahead of the Federals, trying in vain to rally the few that had escaped. On the east bank, seeing that escape was cut off, Early "rode aside into the woods, and in that way escaped capture. I went to the top of a hill ... and had the mortification of seeing the greater part of my command being carried off as prisoners."[13]

Early and Wharton, with a small contingent, rode over the mountain north of Rockfish Gap, vainly trying to reach Greenwood Depot before Custer. Riding farther north, they spent a miserable night in the Blue Ridge. The prisoners were escorted to Winchester, arriving there six days later. Most of Sheridan's force went on to Charlottesville, where the mayor and the University of Virginia surrendered to Custer. Finally having achieved the destruction of Confederate military power in the valley, Sheridan headed east to join Grant.

Once again, Early unfairly blamed his men: "The only solution of this affair which I can give is that my men did not fight as I had expected them to do."[14] However, the issue was then moot. Many Southerners couldn't understand why he didn't bypass Waynesboro, making a stand at Rockfish Gap instead, and the clamor for his removal was louder than ever. In a brief conference with Lee on 16 March, Early was sent to southwestern Virginia to await further orders. Lee wanted to keep Early in command in the valley; however, an enraged public and a vocal press demanded his removal. Two weeks later, at his sister's home in Marion, Early received a telegram from Lee, dismissing him from command. A sympathetic letter, dated 30 March, arrived shortly thereafter. In it, Lee stated in part: "While my own confidence in your ability, zeal, and devotion to the cause is unimpaired, I have nevertheless felt that I could not oppose what seems to be the current of opinion, without injustice to your reputation and injury to the service."[15] Jubal Early's war was over. Ironically, a few companies of Lomax's cavalry at Lynchburg remained in the Valley Army until Lee's surrender.

Conclusion

Thus the Army of the Valley ceased to exist. However, with courage and determination, Jubal Early and his outnumbered and outgunned army had tied up 45,000 Federal troops; and threatened Maryland, Washington, D.C., and the B & O railroad for four months. Could Early have postponed Sheridan's victory in the Shenandoah Valley another month or two?

Hindsight has perfect vision, however, the facts show that they came very close to capturing Washington and halting the northern war effort. Had Early marched through Loudoun County, had he not wasted time trying to force Sigel off Maryland Heights, had he not given his troops a rest day on 4 July, had he not indulged in economic warfare, had he coordinated his efforts with Mosby, had he made better use of cavalry, had McCausland captured Cumberland, had word of the Point Lookout raid not been leaked ... little by little victory eluded him. Early might have initially defeated Sheridan in the valley, but for his tactical errors — scattering his army in front of a stronger enemy, failure to fight on favorable terrain, and later on, faulty troop dispositions. However, the failure to capture Washington, combined with the fall of Atlanta, foretold the demise of the Confederacy. Thus, even if Early had initially defeated Sheridan in the valley, such a victory would have only temporarily postponed Confederate surrender.

However, Jefferson Davis and the Confederate Congress bear the largest portion of responsibility for the Confederacy's demise. For example, a fundamental reason for Confederate defeat was the breakdown of their cavalry. Although Early contributed to that, the ultimate responsibility for the cavalry's decline lay with the Confederate government.

Rebel cavalrymen were generally superb horsemen and enjoyed a distinct advantage over their Federal counterparts during the first two years of the war. However, Confederate government policy made them responsible for supplying their own remounts. As long as horses were plentiful, finding a replacement horse wasn't difficult. But as the war continued, horses became scarce, and many cavalry units had to dismount and fight on foot as infantry units. Rebel cavalrymen, horse traders in 1862, more frequently became horse thieves by 1864. In addition, dismounting often caused wholesale desertion in Confederate ranks because of the contempt Confederate cavalrymen displayed towards Rebel foot soldiers.

In stark contrast, the Federal government maintained six remount depots, including a 625 acre horse farm, at Giesboro Point, near Washington, D.C., where a full-time staff cared for as many as 30,000 horses at a time. As a result, Federal cavalry units could count on a steady supply of fresh, well-trained horses. Similar facilities in the south would have taken the burden of finding remounts off already hard-pressed Rebel cavalrymen, thereby helping to maintain morale.[16] In some units, such as John Imboden's brigade, where an 1863 fight between two officers resulted in the death of one, morale was questionable from the start. The declining ability of Early's cavalry directly contributed to defeat at Winchester, while "Old Jube's" mistakes undermined their usefulness at Fisher's Hill and Cedar Creek.

The attempt to incite a Copperhead rebellion in the north was doomed from the start. The Confederate Commissioners, in Canada, misjudged the temper of Clement Vallandigham and his organization, the Sons of Liberty. While Lincoln termed Vallandigham and his disgruntled followers "the fire in the rear," they actually comprised the loyal opposition to his administration. Vallandigham was an anti-war Democrat, strongly opposed to emancipation (as were many Democrats that favored the war). However, his ire was also directed against economic policies that supported Northern industrialists at the expense of Western farmers. Although there were a few violent incidents in the midwest, neither Vallandigham nor the majority of his supporters were enthusiastic about Confederate independence. When push came to shove, they were unwilling "to sacrifice life for a cause"; only a few favored open rebellion against the Union.

Lincoln won re-election, aided and abetted by a huge mistake on the part of Jefferson Davis. However, his triumph wasn't the overwhelming victory that some portray. While he won 55 percent of the popular vote, having a plurality of 403,000 over George B. McClellan, his margin was only about 350,000 more votes than he received in 1860. Had Lincoln not won the badly needed soldier vote — gathering 116,887 votes out of about 154,000 cast, the election would have been very close. It would have been closer still had Davis offered peace negotiations in August 1864, when Northern civilian morale was very low. Nevertheless, impartial readers will conclude that Lincoln's margin of victory could have been greater given his frequent practice of arresting and jailing dissenters and silencing unfriendly newspapers. Lincoln's re-election assured Northern victory. The eradication of slavery and increased freedom for African Americans, encouraged by abolitionists and Radical Republicans, completed the American Revolution. In the late 1850s, and as president, Lincoln supported emancipation, but in an ambiguous and half-hearted way that left many wondering about his true position. However, Lincoln's legacy was runaway greed, endless corruption, and a quest for empire that spoiled Northern victory, ignored George Washington's warnings, and tarnished American freedom.[17]

Hagerstown Ransomed

On Wednesday, 6 July, in accordance with Early's orders, General McCausland ransomed Hagerstown, 25 miles northwest of Frederick. As his 1,500 cavalrymen approached the town, many of Hagerstown's 6,000 residents and a few city officials packed their belongings and fled to Pennsylvania, considered safe territory. Farmers hid their horses and livestock, and children stayed close to their parents as they evacuated. Early directed that McCausland demand $200,000 from Hagerstown, but an aide misunderstood the number on the original order, and $20,000 was written on the ransom letter; McCausland demanded that sum instead.

McCausland and his troops rode up Potomac Street, stopping in front of the Market House, where he established headquarters. From there, he sent for the town's treasurer, 47-year-old Matthew Barber. In response to the summons, Barber found John Kausler, a teller at the Hagerstown Bank, and both went to confer with the Confederate general. Guards were posted throughout the city as ransom negotiations got underway. McCausland ordered his troops to be alert and keep their weapons at hand; Federal cavalry had been reported close by in Pennsylvania. Barber and Kausler found the Rebel chieftain casually attired in shirtsleeves, as was his habit, in M.L. Byers' Drug Store, on one corner of Hagerstown's public square. Barber fully expected to be placed under arrest; instead, he was given a long, handwritten letter demanding $20,000 and a large amount of clothing. The letter read, in part:

> In accordance with the instruction of Lt. Gen. Early, a levy of $20,000 is made upon the inhabitants of this city. The space of three hours is allowed for the payment of this sum in U.S. funds. A requisition is also made for all government stores. The following articles will also be furnished from the merchandise now in the hands of the citizens or merchants, viz: 1500 shirts, 1500 suits of clothing, 1500 hats, 1500 pairs of shoes or boots, 1900 pairs of drawers, and 1500 pairs of socks. Four hours will be allowed for this collection. The Mayor and Council are held responsible for the execution of this order, and in cases of non-compliance the usual penalty will be enforced upon this city.

McCausland signed the order.[1]

After explaining to the angry Rebel chieftain that it wouldn't be possible to supply the amount of clothing requested, Barber went to confer with the president of the Hagerstown Bank, J. Dixon Roman, at his home a short distance from the courthouse. The ailing Roman informed McCausland that he would meet him at the courthouse; the Rebel chieftain reluctantly agreed. Besides McCausland, Roman, and Barber, bank board members William Hamilton and Isaac Nesbitt were present.

McCausland started the discussion, stating that he would allow them no more than four hours to meet his demands. He then told them that if the order wasn't obeyed, Hagerstown would be "laid in ashes."[2] Roman replied that the amount of clothing demanded simply wasn't available. "We will get all the clothing that is possible. If you burn the town for failure to do what cannot be done, you will be destroying the property of many of the warm friends of the Southern cause," he said. McCausland gradually relented, agreeing to take as much clothing as could be gathered.

However, he stipulated that "the people should be left under the impression that the redemption of the town depended upon the collection of the amount originally required and that McCausland had made no concession."[3] He then gave them three hours to collect the clothing. Barber then asked how long would be allowed for evacuation of the women and children. McCausland curtly answered, "One hour!" ending the discussion. He returned to the Market House as nervous citizens and town officials worked out a plan for clothing collection; the courthouse would serve as the collection center. As Hagerstown residents loaded bundles of clothing into wagons, Roman worked out a plan to collect the money.

At an emergency meeting of the Hagerstown Bank's Board of Directors, Roman proposed that the bank draw up a note for $10,000, with the First National Bank and the Williamsport Bank lending $5,000 each. The Board of Directors approved the plan. At a special emergency City Council session, McCausland's demands were considered. Mayor John Cook, having fled the town, was absent. Barber presented Roman's plan; it was approved. At least a hundred of Hagerstown's leading citizens signed the note, along with Barber. He obtained their signatures because he correctly foresaw that when those who had fled returned, they would object to the city's assumption of the debt. When the refugees returned, many did object to the ransom payment. However, many signatories later petitioned the Maryland legislature to issue bonds, relieving them of their obligation to pay. The legislature complied, and bonds were issued. Eventually, $39,000 worth of bonds were issued to pay the ransom-induced debt.

Barber carried the cash —$20,000 in northern notes— to McCausland. After extending the clothing collection time by two hours, the Rebel chieftain stationed a cavalry regiment in front of the courthouse to intimidate residents into compliance. However, the amount of clothing collected proved insufficient, and McCausland swore that if the clothing wasn't "forthcoming by the time specified he would carry out his threat, should it cost him his own life and that of his whole command." After a few Confederate officers interceded on behalf of Hagerstown's residents, McCausland was persuaded to accept the $20,000, 243 coats, 203 pairs of trousers, 737 pairs of socks, 123 pairs of shoes, 99 pairs of boots, 830 hats, 225 shirts, and miscellaneous clothing.[4] A receipt was given for the clothing and cash, and the Rebels departed Hagerstown around midnight.

However, the next morning, a party of about 70 Confederates returned, breaking into a few stores, claiming McCausland's demand hadn't been fully met. With great difficulty, Barber persuaded their commander, a Major Davis, to accept ten pairs of boots and leave town. A short time later, another squad of Rebels arrived, burning the railroad warehouse, and a large structure containing government hay. That day, Early's troops ransomed Middletown, a crossroads hamlet about halfway between Hagerstown and Frederick, demanding $5,000. A prominent citizen of Middletown, William J. Irving, persuaded them to accept $1500.

Chapter Notes

Chapter 1

1. Donald Dale Jackson, *Twenty Million Yankees: The Northern Home Front* (Alexandria, VA: Time-Life Books, 1985), 20–22.
2. Ernest A. McKay, *The Civil War and New York City* (Syracuse, NY: Syracuse University Press, 1990), 216.
3. Jackson, *Twenty Million Yankees*, 92.
4. *Ibid.*, 103.
5. *Ibid.*, 103–110; The History Channel (A&E Entertainment); McKay, *The Civil War and New York City*, Chapter 11: "Riot."
6. Thomas J. DiLorenzo, *The Real Lincoln: A New Look at Abraham Lincoln, His Agenda, and an Unnecessary War* (New York: Crown, 2003), 85–129.
7. John C. Waugh, *Re-electing Lincoln: The Battle for the 1864 Presidency* (New York: Crown, 1997), 89; *New York Herald*, 2 June 1864, 1; *New York Tribune*, 1 June 1864, 1.
8. George W. Smith and Charles Judah, *Life in the North During the Civil War: A Source History* (Albuquerque: University of New Mexico Press, 1966), 217–218; *Charleston Plaindealer*, 2 April 1864, as quoted in Smith and Judah, *Life in the North During the Civil War*, 218.
9. Kenneth M. Stampp, "The Milligan Case and the Election of 1864 in Indiana," *Mississippi Valley Historical Review*, no. 31 (June 1944), 41–58 (hereafter cited as "The Milligan Case.").
10. *Ibid.*, 47.
11. *Ibid.*, 52.
12. *Ibid.*, 55.
13. McKay, *The Civil War and New York City*, 235.
14. Carl Sandburg, *Abraham Lincoln: The Prairie Years and the War Years* (New York: Harcourt, Brace, 1954, 1982), 468.
15. *Ibid.*, 466.
16. Waugh, *Re-electing Lincoln*, 54; *Congressional Globe* 37th Congress, 3d Session, pt. 2, 1338.
17. Waugh, *Re-electing Lincoln*, 193.
18. www.civilwaralbum.com/misc/olusteel.htm; www.geocities.com/Athens/Aegean/6732.
19. Dwight Schultz, *The Dahlgren Affair: Terror and Conspiracy in the Civil War* (New York: Norton, 1998), 232–247; Steven Bernstein, "Marylander Commits Himself to Confederate Cause," *America's Civil War*, September 2005 (biography of Bradley T. Johnson). Confederate cavalry forces engaged in stopping the Dahlgren-Kilpatrick raid, which consisted of Wade Hampton's contingent, 306 troops, and a smaller force, led by Colonel Bradley T. Johnson. Hampton harassed Kilpatrick and Dahlgren on their retreat from Richmond. A company led by Lt. James Pollard shadowed Dahlgren and ambushed his men in King George County, Va., killing the 21-year-old lieutenant colonel. Johnson pursued Kilpatrick, with 60 men and two cannons, harassing him and causing his retreat from the outskirts of the city.
20. Waugh, *Re-electing Lincoln*, 126–131.
21. McKay, *The Civil War and New York City*, 243–244.
22. Charles C. Osborne, *Jubal: The Life and Times of General Jubal A. Early CSA, Defender of the Lost Cause* (Baton Rouge: Louisiana State University Press, 1992), 238–239.
23. McKay, *The Civil War and New York City*, 246–247.

Chapter 2

1. Author's conversation with historian Robert E. Lee Krick, Richmond National Battlefield, 23 January 2006. Krick specified that General Lee's headquarters tent was on a slope above Powhite Creek, west of the Cold Harbor battlefield, where it was sheltered from incoming Federal artillery fire.
2. Quoted in James M. Perry, *Touched with Fire: Five Presidents and the Civil War Battles That Made Them* (New York: Perseus Books, 2003), 189.
3. *Ibid.*
4. Charles C. Osborne, *Jubal: The Life and Times of General Jubal A. Early, CSA Defender of the Lost Cause* (Baton Rouge: Louisiana State University Press, 1992), 249 (hereafter cited as *Jubal*); Elizabeth Preston Allan, ed., *Life and Letters of Margaret Preston Junkin* (Boston; privately published, 1903), 196.
5. Frank Vandiver, *Jubal's Raid: General Early's Famous Attack on Washington in 1864* (New York: McGraw-Hill, 1960), 25–26 (hereafter cited as *Jubal's Raid*).

6. *Ibid.*, 26.

7. Robert C. Black III, *The Railroads of the Confederacy* (Chapel Hill: University of North Carolina Press, 1952), 85–86, 88–91,133.

8. Vandiver, *Jubal's Raid*, 33; *The War of the Rebellion: A Compilation of the Official Records of the Union and Confederate Armies* (Washington, DC: U.S. War Department 1880–1901), Series I, vol. 37, pt. 1, p. 763 (hereafter cited as *ORA*).

9. Black, *Railroads of the Confederacy*, 247.

10. Vandiver, *Jubal's Raid*, 36.

11. John O. Casler, *Four Years in the Stonewall Brigade* (Guthrie, OK: State Capital Print, 1893), 224–225.

12. Vandiver, *Jubal's Raid*, 39; Douglas Southall Freeman, *Lee's Lieutenants*. Vol. 3 (New York: Scribner's, 1944) 3, 527.

13. Vandiver, *Jubal's Raid*, 39.

14. B.F. Cooling, *Jubal Early's Raid on Washington 1864* (Baltimore: Nautical & Aviation, 1989), 12 (hereafter cited as *JERW*).

15. Osborne, *Jubal*, 257.

16. *Lynchburg Virginian*, quoted at www.historicsandusky.org/history.htm; Historic Sandusky Foundation, "Audio Driving Tour of the Battle of Lynchburg," undated; William C. Davis, "Jubilee: General Jubal A. Early," *Civil War Times Illustrated* 9 (December 1970): 11. Contains the description of Jubal Early.

17. Osborne, *Jubal*, 258; www.historicsandusky.org/history.htm; Historic Sandusky Foundation, "Audio Driving Tour."

18. Stephen Sears, *Chancellorsville* (New York: Mariner Books, 1998), Chapter 4, "The Highest Expectations"; Steven Bernstein, "Errors Costly to Victor at Kelly's Ford," *Washington Times*, 3 September 2005. General William Averell, who was with Hunter at "Sandusky," on the night of June 17, had fallen victim to the same ruse at the Battle of Kelly's Ford, 17 March 1863. His opponent, Confederate General Fitzhugh Lee, had the Orange & Alexandria railroad run locomotives up and down the track, not far from the battlefield, to create the impression that Confederate reinforcements were arriving (none were). Averell heard the locomotive whistles, broke off the fight, and ordered a retreat across the Rappahannock River. He was shortly thereafter transferred to West Virginia by his commander, Major General Joseph Hooker. Averell therefore had reason to know that the locomotive whistles and martial noise emanating from Lynchburg might have been a ruse. However, if he mentioned that to Hunter, the Army of the Shenandoah's commander didn't act on it. Hunter failed to investigate the martial noise coming from Lynchburg. Had he captured the city, Early's raid on Washington probably wouldn't have occurred, and the war might have ended sooner.

19. *Lynchburg Virginian*, as quoted at www.historicsandusky.org/history.htm.

20. *Ibid.*

21. Vandiver, *Jubal's Raid*, 60.

22. Cecil D. Eby Jr., ed., *A Virginia Yankee in the Civil War: The Diaries of David Hunter Strother*

(Chapel Hill: University of North Carolina Press, 1961), 250–251. According to Strother, Hunter's chief of staff, Crook, stated to the effect: "If we expected to take Lynchburg at all we must move upon it immediately and rapidly. I agreed with him that such be our proper and safe course but mentioned our lack of ammunition. Crook said he had plenty and if permitted would march on Lynchburg with his division alone, saying that celerity was more important than numbers or ammunition."

23. Vandiver, *Jubal's Raid*, 53; Jubal A. Early, *A Memoir of the Last Year of the War for Independence in the Confederate States of America, Containing an Account of the Operations of His Commands in the Years 1864 and 1865* (Lynchburg: Button, 1867), 44–45 (hereafter cited as *A Memoir*).

24. www.salemmuseum.org/history.htm.

25. William B. Stark, "The Great Skedaddle: General Hunter's Retreat from Lynchburg," *Atlantic Monthly* 162 (1938), 86–94.

26. Cooling, *JERW*, 13.

27. *Ibid.*, 13–14.

28. Vandiver, *Jubal's Raid*, 58.

29. www.oldandsold.com/articles11/virginia-homes-86.shtml.

30. Cooling, *JERW*, 14.

31. Vandiver, *Jubal's Raid*, 60.

32. *Ibid.*, 63.

33. Casler, *Four Years in the Stonewall Brigade*, 224.

34. Vandiver, *Jubal's Raid*, 64.

35. Harold Manakee, *Maryland in the Civil War* (Baltimore: Maryland Historical Society, 1959), 149.

36. Major Edwin Moore, Inspection report, 21 August 1864, *ORA*, I, vol. 43, pt. 2, 609–610; Freeman, *Lee's Lieutenants*, 558.

37. John B. Gordon, *Reminiscences of the Civil War* (1903; reprinted, Alexandria, VA: Time-Life Books, 1981), 318 (hereafter cited as *Reminiscences*).

38. Vandiver, *Jubal's Raid*, 66.

39. *ORA*, I, vol. 37, pt. 2, 600, Memo from Sandy Pendleton (Early's adjutant) to Breckinridge, concerning desertion, 23 July 1864: "General: The lieutenant-general commanding directs me to call your attention to the fact that your last 'field return' shows a falling off of 2,462 in the number of men reported present for duty. He wishes you to send in at once a statement showing how you account for this diminution, including your losses in killed, wounded, and missing, that there may be some means of estimating the number of men who are in the rear without authority. I am, general, very respectfully, your obedient servant, A.S. Pendleton, Assistant Adjutant-General."

40. Early, *A Memoir*, 381; Vandiver, *Jubal's Raid*, 68.

41. Author's conversation with historian Stevan Meserve, 11 December 2005.

42. Jubal A. Early, *Autobiographical Sketch and Narrative of the War Between the States*. Edited by R.H. Early (Philadelphia: Lippincott, 1912), 383 (hereafter *Autobiographical Sketch*); Vandiver, *Jubal's Raid*, 76.

43. State of Virginia, Virginia Agriculture Census (1860), Loudoun County, 347–407; Charles P. Poland, *From Frontier to Suburbia* (St. Louis: Walsworth, 1976), 294; James W. Head, *History and Comprehensive Description of Loudoun County, Virginia* (1908; reprinted Baltimore: Clearfield Publishing, 1989), 95. Loudoun developed a dairy industry in the 1870s when farmers began to sell milk to the various hotels in Washington DC, making use of the railroad to the capital. Loudoun's dairy industry therefore began in the vicinity of the county's railroad stations. In addition, Head offers further support for the strength of Loudoun agriculture: "The value of all farm property increased 25.7 percent in the decade 1850–1860, and the value of livestock increased by 26.1 percent in the same period (Table I, p. 94). And despite the destruction of the Civil War, the value of all farm property increased by 2.7 percent, between 1860 and 1870."

44. Poland, *From Frontier to Suburbia*, 225.

45. *ORA*, I, vol. 43, pt. 2, 673.

46. Quoted in *From Frontier to Suburbia*, 213.

47. *Ibid.*, 218.

48. *Loudoun Valley Mirror*, 14 June 1865, quoted in *From Frontier to Suburbia*, 223–224.

49. Shcila R. Phipps, *Genteel Rebel: The Life of Mary Greenhow Lee* (Baton Rouge: Louisiana State University Press, 2004), 147; Maurice F. Shaw, *Stonewall Jackson's Surgeon: Hunter Holmes McGuire, a Biography* (Virginia: Howard, 1993), 1, 84 (picture of McGuire's home).

50. Cooling, *JERW*, 24.

51. No author, "Martinsburg, West Virginia during the Civil War," *The Berkeley Journal*, no. 27 (2001): 89.

52. *Ibid.*, 89–93.

53. Cooling, *JERW*, 25.

54. *Ibid.*, 27; Vandiver, *Jubal's Raid*, 81; John P. Worsham, *One of Jackson's Foot Cavalry* (New York: Neale, 1912), 232–233.

55. Vandiver, *Jubal's Raid*, 91; *ORA*, I, vol. 37, pt. 2, 592.

56. Cooling, *JERW*, 28–29; *ORA*, I, vol. 37, pt. 2, 15.

57. Vandiver, *Jubal's Raid*, 88; Worsham, *One of Jackson's Foot Cavalry*, 233–234.

58 National Park Service Web site: www.nps.gov/hafe/maps/maryland.htm.

59. *Ibid.*

60. *Journal of Jedediah Hotchkiss*, 7 July 1864; Vandiver, *Jubal's Raid*, 94.

61. Paul Gordon and Rita Gordon, *Never the Like Again* (Frederick, MD: Heritage Partnership, 1995), Ch. 4, "A Family Affair"; Steven Bernstein, conversation with Paul Gordon, August 2004; untitled item, *The Frederick Examiner*, 11 February 1863. Since the Antietam campaign, when Johnson was provost marshal in Frederick, he had returned for only a few very brief visits. His former home, on North Court Street, had been used as Union Army Headquarters, inhabited by General Nathaniel Banks, in 1862. In October of that year, the former owner obtained a judgment against him, for defaulting on the mortgage some years earlier. In February 1863, the house was auctioned, and Johnson's next-door neighbor, James W. Pearre, bought it. The house was torn down in the 1920s, to make way for a synagogue that stands on part of the site today.

62. Vandiver, *Jubal's Raid*, 95; Cooling, *JERW*, 44–46.

63. Vandiver, *Jubal's Raid*, 95; Lew Wallace, *Lew Wallace: An Autobiography*. Vol. 2 (New York: Harper Brothers, 1906), 713; Worsham, *One of Jackson's Foot Cavalry*, 235.

64. Cooling, *JERW*, 45.

65. *Diary of Jacob Englebrecht*, 271–272; *ORA*, I, vol. 51, pt. 1, 1171–1174; *ORA*, I, vol. 37, pt. 2, 110; Wallace, 738–744; Cooling, *JERW*, 46.

66. Vandiver, *Jubal's Raid*, 86; Henry Kyd Douglas, *I Rode with Stonewall* (New York: Mockingbird Books, 1960), 292.

67. *ORA*, I, vol. 37, pt. 1, 194–195; *ORA*, I, vol. 51, pt. 1, 1174–1175; Wallace, 738–744.

68. Vandiver, *Jubal's Raid*, 100; Wallace, 731.

69. *Journal of Jedediah Hotchkiss*, July 7, 1864; Vandiver, *Jubal's Raid*, 101.

70. Cooling, *JERW*, 47, 48.

Chapter 3

1. Senate Subcommittee of the Committee on the Judiciary, on S. 1842, *To Reimburse the City of Frederick, MD, for Money Paid Saving Harmless Valuable Military and Hospital Supplies Owned by the United States Government.* 92nd Cong., 2nd sess., 1972 (hereafter cited as Senate Subcommittee, *To Reimburse*), 1.

2. Karen Gardner, "Mathias Wants Ransom Repaid to City," *Frederick News-Post*, October 1986.

3. Lucian Warren, "Mathias Finally Gets Senate OK to Repay Civil War Ransom," *Frederick News-Post*, 4 October 1986.

4. Jacob Englebrecht, *Diary*, entry for 11 July 1864. The details of the ransoming of Hagerstown are in Appendix A.

5. Edward Y. Goldsborough, *The Appeal of Frederick City, Maryland to the Congress of the United States, for the Payment of its Claim of $200,000 Paid as a Ransom to the Confederate Army July 9th, 1864* (Frederick, MD: Privately published, 1902) (hereafter cited as *The Appeal of Frederick City*).

6. Author's conversation with Mrs. Betty Smith, Frederick, MD, 15 October 2005, regarding Dr. Richard T. Hammond (1815–1896), Mary Agnes Hammond (1823–1894), and Robert Lee Hammond (1862–1945).

7. *Frederick News-Post*, "Saw Early Write $200,000 Order," July 1972.

8. *Ibid.*

9. Goldsborough, *The Appeal of Frederick City*, 17–18.

10. *Ibid.*, 18.

11. *Ibid.*, 18; Cooling, *JERW*, 52.

12. Goldsborough, *The Appeal of Frederick City*, 4.

13. Cooling, *JERW*, 50.

14. Goldsborough, *The Appeal of Frederick City*,

8–14; Senate Subcommittee, *To Reimburse*, 24–25.

15. Steven Bernstein, "Marylander Bradley T. Johnson Committed Himself to the Confederate Cause Before and After the War," *America's Civil War*, September 2005; Senate Subcommittee, *To Reimburse*, 15; author's conversation with historian Paul Gordon, 27 April 2006.

16. Senate Subcommittee, *To Reimburse*, 26, chart, "Storage Warehouses in Frederick Used by Government."

17. Senate Subcommittee, *To Reimburse*, 44.

18. *Ibid.*, 20; Cooling, *JERW*, 52.

19. *Ibid.*, 21.

20. Lucian Warren, "Frederick's Civil War Ransom Request Loses Battle in House," *The News*, 17 October 1986, A-3.

21. *New York Times*, "Settling an Old War Debt," 4 October 1986, as cited in Elizabeth Duthinh, "Reflections of a Senator: Charles McCurdy Mathias," *Catoctin History*, Spring-Summer 2006.

22. *The News*, untitled item, 9 September 1995.

Chapter 4

1. Lew Wallace, *Lew Wallace: An Autobiography*. Vol. 2 (New York: Harper Brothers, 1906), 810–811.

2. *Ibid.*, 804.

3. B. Franklin Cooling, *Monocacy: The Battle That Saved Washington* (Shippensburg, PA: White Mane, 1997), 38.

4. *Ibid.*, 39.

5. http://en.wikipedia.org/wiki/Lew_Wallace.

6. Cooling, *Monocacy*, 63.

7. *Ibid.*, 64; Wallace, 721.

8. Cooling, *Monocacy*, 96.

9. Wallace, 754–755.

10. *Battle Report: Colonel Allison Brown, ORA*, I, vol. 37, pt. 1, 216–219; Cooling, *Monocacy*, 114.

11. Wallace, 758.

12. *Confederate Order of Battle: The Battle of Monocacy, 9 July 1864* (National Park Service: Monocacy National Battlefield, no date).

13. Wallace, 774.

14. E.M. Haynes, *A History of the Tenth Regiment, VT. Vols.* (Rutland: Tuttle, 1894), 196–200.

15. Glenn H. Worthington, *Fighting for Time: The Battle That Saved Washington and Mayhap the Union* (Frederick, MD: Historical Society of Frederick County, 1932), 117.

16. Osborne, *Jubal*, 273–274.

17. Cooling, *Monocacy*, 119.

18. *Ibid.*, 114.

19. *Ibid.*, 119, 139.

20. Wallace, 771.

21. *Ibid.*, 773.

22. Alfred Seelye Roe, *9th New York Heavy Artillery* (Worcester, MA: privately published, 1899), 128.

23. *Report of Colonel John F. Staunton* (Washington, DC: National Archives August 1864); Author's conversation with Monocacy National Battlefield staff, 30 June 2006.

24. George Reeser Prowell, *History of the 87th*

Regiment, Pa. Volunteers (York, PA: Press of the York Daily Record, 1901), 235; "Thomas Farm Trail" (Frederick, MD: Monocacy National Battlefield, no date); Cooling, *Monocacy*, 142.

25. John B. Gordon, *Reminiscences of the Civil War* (Alexandria, VA: Time-Life Books, 1981, reprint 1906), 310.

26. *Ibid.*, 310–311.

27. Cooling, *Monocacy*, 147.

28. *Ibid.*, 148.

29. *Ibid.*, 149.

30. Worthington, *Fighting for Time*, 136.

31. Wallace, 785.

32. Cooling, *Monocacy*, 156.

33. *Ibid.*, 154.

34. E.Y. Goldsborough, "Early's Great Raid" (Frederick, MD: privately published, 1898), 25–28; Cooling, *Monocacy*, 157.

35. *Captain Edward Leib: Battle Report, ORA*, I, vol. 37, pt. 1, 221–223; Cooling, *Monocacy*, 158.

36. Cooling, *Monocacy*, 181; estimates from the U.S. Department of the Interior, Monocacy Battlefield; author's conversations with Monocacy Battlefield staff, 2007–2009.

Casualty figures for the battle of Monocacy vary. In his *Autobiographical Sketch & Narrative of the War Between the States* (Philadelphia, 1912) Early claimed losses of 700, but this is too low. In Gordon's attack alone, Evans' brigade lost more than 500; York's Louisianans lost 163 (killed, wounded, and missing), while McCausland lost about 100 in his two attacks. Terry probably lost between 30 and 50 in his assault on Wallace's far left; Rodes lost 54 at the Jug Bridge, and Ramseur likewise lost about 100. Confederate casualties totaled about 1,000. Federal losses numbered about 1,300.

37. Worthington, *Fighting for Time*, 176; Visitor Center, Monocacy National Battlefield; Jacob M. Holdcraft, *Names in Stone: Frederick Co. Cemetery Records* (Ann Arbor, MI: Genealogical, 1966).

Chapter 5

1. Douglas, *I Rode with Stonewall*, 282; Vandiver, *Jubal's Raid*, 121.

2. John T. DeSellum to friend, July 1864, Montgomery County Historical Society, Rockville; Historic marker, "Civil War Trails," at Summit Hall farm site.

3. Steven Bernstein, "Early's Summer March Chills Washington," *Washington Times*, 5 June 2004; *ORA*, I, vol. 37, pt. 2, 166; Michael Fitzpatrick, "Jubal Early and the Californians," *Civil War Times* (May 1998): 51–61.

4. *ORA*, I, vol. 37, pt. 2, 166.

5. Cooling, *JERW*, 103.

6. DeSellum to friend, 46–47.

7. *Ibid.*, 48–51.

8. Osborne, *Jubal*, 280.

9. Steven Bernstein, "Wagon Train Plays Role in Stuart's Failure at Gettysburg," *Washington Times*, 31 May 2003; "Encounter at Rockville: Confederate General Captures City's Most Prominent Citizen," *The Free-Lance Star*, 14 June 2003.

10. Steven Woodworth, *Davis & Lee at War* (Lawrence: University Press of Kansas, 1995), 64–67.

11. *Diary of Gideon Welles*, as quoted in Cooling, *Symbol, Sword and Shield: Defending Washington During the Civil War* (New York: Archon Books, 1975), 133.

12. Cooling, *Symbol, Sword and Shield*, 161.

13. Vandiver, *Jubal's Raid*, 137.

14. Margaret Leech Pulitzer, *Reveille in Washington, 1860–1865* (1944; repr. Alexandria, VA: Time-Life Books, 1980), 415–418.

15. Cooling, *JERW*, 90–91; Jackson, *Twenty Million Yankees*, 103.

16. Cooling, *JERW*, 92–93.

17. *Ibid.*, 84–85.

18. Cooling, *Symbol, Sword and Shield*, 178; *ORA*, I, vol. 37, pt. 2, 83–85.

19. Vandiver, *Jubal's Raid*, 159–160.

20. William B. Feis, "A Union Military Intelligence Failure: Jubal Early's Raid, June 12–July 14, 1864," *Civil War History* 36, no. 3 (1990); Edwin C. Fishel Papers, Special Collections, Georgetown University Library, Washington, DC.

21. Fishel Papers; *ORA*, I, vol. 37, pt. 2, 33.

22. Cooling, *JERW*, 99.

23. *Ibid.*, 108.

24. *Ibid.*, 115; Mildred Newbold Getty, "The Silver Spring Area," *The Montgomery County Story*, vol. 12, no. 1 (November 1968), 2.

25. Cooling, *JERW*, 113. Note: A successful attorney, Montgomery Blair was a great grandson of Christopher Gist, who had rescued George Washington from the freezing waters of the Allegheny River in 1753. He had been mayor of St. Louis in 1842 and 1843. He had purchased real estate in San Francisco, through an agent, in the 1850s. Though a respected attorney, his speech suffered from a lisp. He represented a runaway slave, Dred Scott, in the case *Dred Scott v. Sandiford*. However, the Supreme Court decided in favor of the slave owner and against Scott. The verdict reinforced the Fugitive Slave Law. Blair became Lincoln's postmaster general, holding that position from 1861 to September 1864. He served in the Maryland legislature after the war. Blair died in 1883. His son, Gist Blair, attended Princeton University, and became an attorney, practicing law in Silver Spring. He died in 1940. Montgomery Blair's home, Falkland, was destroyed on 7 September 1958 by the Silver Spring Fire Department to make way for a shopping center complex, still on the site. (*Blair Family Papers*, Library of Congress, Washington, DC.).

26. Cooling, *JERW*, 117.

27. J. Cutler Andrews, *The North Reports the Civil War* (New Brunswick, NJ: Princeton University Press, 1970), 593–594; Cooling, *JERW*, 134; Lt. General Jubal A. Early, "Early's March to Washington in 1864," in Clarence C. Buell and Robert U. Johnson, eds., *Battles and Leaders of the Civil War* (New York: T. Yoseloff, 1956), 497–498; Map of Washington, D.C., National Geographic Society, 1967.

28. Cooling, *JERW*, 113.

29. I.G. Bradwell, "Early's Demonstration against Washington in 1864," *Confederate Veteran*, no. 22 (October 1914); *ORA*, I, vol. 37, pt. 2, 195.

30. Walter Clark, ed., *Histories of the Several Regiments and Battalions from North Carolina in the Great War 1861–1865*, no. 2 (Wilmington, DE: Broadfoot, 1991), 122; Monocacy National Battlefield, Frederick, MD.

31. Cooling, *JERW*, 123.

32. General H.G. Wright to General C.C. Augur, 11 July 1864; *ORA*, I, vol. 37, pt. 2, 208.

33. Waugh, *Re-electing Lincoln*, 239–240; *Diary of Gideon Welles* (Boston & New York: Houghton Mifflin, 1911) entry for July 9, 70.

34. Gordon, *Reminiscences of the Civil War*, 314–315.

35. Early, *Autobiographical Sketch*, as quoted in Osborne, *Jubal*, 286.

36. Cooling, *JERW*, 137–138.

37. *Diary of Gideon Welles*, entry for July 12, 74–75.

38. George Thomas Stevens, *Three Years in the Sixth Corps: A Concise Narrative of Events in the Army of the Potomac from 1861 to the Close of the Rebellion, April, 1865* (New York: D. Van Nostrand, 1870), as quoted in Cramer, *Lincoln Under Enemy Fire* (Baton Rouge: Louisiana State University Press, 1948), 28–29.

39. Cramer, *Lincoln Under Enemy Fire*, 30–31; *Diary of Gideon Welles*, 75.

40. William C. Davis, "The Turning Point That Wasn't," in *The Cause Lost: Myths and Realities of the Confederacy* (Lawrence: University Press of Kansas, 1996), 129.

41. As quoted in Larry E. Nelson, *Bullets, Ballots, and Rhetoric* (Tuscaloosa: University of Alabama Press, 1980), 60.

42. Osborne, *Jubal*, 288–289; Vandiver, *Jubal's Raid*, 170–171.

43. Cooling, *Symbol, Sword and Shield*, 210; Douglas, *I Rode with Stonewall*, 284; Joseph McMurran Diary, entry for July 13–14, Special Collections, University of Virginia, Charlottesville; Caleb Linker to Daniel Linker, 17 July 1864, as quoted in Cooling, *JERW*, 189–190.

Chapter 6

1. Bradley T. Johnson, "My Ride Around Baltimore in Eighteen Hundred and Sixty Four," *Journal of the U.S. Cavalry Association*, Southern Historical Society Papers, Vol. 30 (September 1889), 217.

2. Joseph Judge, *Season of Fire: The Confederate Strike on Washington, DC* (Bridgewater: Rockbridge, 1994), 164.

3. Johnson, "My Ride Around Baltimore," 217–218; Judge, *Season of Fire*, 167.

4. Cooling, *JERW*, 157–158, 173–174. There were about twenty thousand Confederate prisoners at the Point Lookout facility at the end of June 1864. In response to this overcrowding, Federal authorities opened another prison facility at Elmira, New York. The exact number of prisoners at Point Lookout on 12 July is uncertain. However, by the end of July, the

compound held 14,747 prisoners and 4,528 had been transferred to the Elmira facility.

5. Wade Hampton, *The Raid on Point Lookout: A Study in Desperation*, seminar paper, American University, Washington, DC, August 1970, 7.

6. Copperas is a bluish green crystalline solid, used for water purification and for the manufacture of iron salts, fertilizer and ink. Fatal poisoning often results from drinking water containing it. Random House Unabridged Dictionary, 2006.

7. Sidney Lanier, 1842–1881. Lanier was a Baltimore native and resident who fought in Texas during the first part of the war. A statue of Lanier, playing his flute, is on the campus of Johns Hopkins University.

8. Cooling, *JERW*, 159; Edwin S. Beitzell, *Point Lookout Prison Camp for Confederates* (Baltimore: A.S. Abell, 1972), 56.

9. Gary Baker, "Gilmor's Ride Around Baltimore," at www.civilwarinteractive.com/ArticleGilmor.htm.

10. Vertical files, Carroll County (Maryland) Historical Society; J. Thomas Scharf, *History of Western Maryland* (Baltimore: Regional, 1898), No. 2; Cooling, *JERW*, 159.

11. Johnson, "My Ride Around Baltimore," 219.

12. *Baltimore County Advocate*, 16 July 1864, as cited in Baker, "Gilmor's Ride Around Baltimore," 3.

13. Harry Gilmor, *Four Years in the Saddle* (New York: Harper & Brothers, 1866), 192.

14. *Ibid.*

15. *Ibid.*, 193.

16. *Hartford County Correspondent*, 12 July 1864, as cited in Baker, "Gilmor's Ride Around Baltimore," 6.

17. Cooling, *JERW*, 168; *ORA*, I, vol. 37, pt. 1, 225–230.

18. Helen Marie Noye Hoyt letter (unpublished; 1925), as quoted in Ellen Oliver Smith, "The Magnolia Station Train Raid," http://madonna.edu/pages/lmmtrain.cfm.

19. *ORA*, CD, *Monocacy*, Ch. 49, 227, as quoted in Baker, "Gilmor's Ride Around Baltimore."

20. *Ibid.*, 230, as quoted in Baker, "Gilmor's Ride Around Baltimore."

21. Cooling, *JERW*, 169, citing Official Records of the Union and Confederate Navies in the War of the Rebellion, I, No. 5, 292–294, 458–471, 547.

22. The northern boundary of Baltimore during the Civil War was North Avenue, about four miles south of the present-day boundary. Ady's Hotel stood on York Road in what is today the middle of Towson's business district. The spot was later occupied by a movie theater.

23. Cooling, *JERW*, 166.

24. Gilmor, *Four Years in the Saddle*, 202.

25. Cradock's home and outbuildings were known as Trentham. Built in 1746, it was the home of the Reverend Thomas Cradock, minister of nearby Garrison Forest Church. The home and outbuildings still stand; the street in front is Cradock's Lane.

26. Unpublished letter of William B. Franklin, as quoted in Smith, "The Magnolia Station Train Raid," http://www.madonna.edu.

27. Mark A. Snell, *From First to Last: The Life of General William Buell Franklin* (New York: Fordham University Press, 2002), 326–329.

28. Cooling, *JERW*, 170.

29. Robert E. Michel, *Colonel Harry Gilmor's Raid Around Baltimore* (Baltimore: Erbe, 1976), 25.

30. Johnson, "My Ride Around Baltimore," 219.

31. Michel, *Colonel Harry Gilmor's Raid*, 13–14.

32. Johnson's indictment for treason, dated 10 May 1865, is on file in the Reverdy Johnson Papers at the Maryland Historical Society, Baltimore. There was a hearing in June 1865, but the charges were dropped. After the war, Johnson lived in Virginia until 1879, when he moved to Baltimore, where he practiced law, with his friend and partner John Poe. He never lived in Frederick again. Bradford's home, Montevideo, stood on the grounds of a present-day country club, on the hill behind the tennis courts, about 300 yards west of Charles Street.

33. Diary of R.B. Farquhar, *Montgomery County Story* 2, no. 2 (February 1959), 6.

34. J.B. Fry to Secretary of War Stanton, 12 July 1864, *ORA*, I, vol. 37, pt. 2, 224.

35. Johnson, "My Ride Around Baltimore," 221; George H. Calcott, *A History of the University of Maryland*, 162–163.

36. Johnson, "My Ride Around Baltimore," 222.

37. Hampton, *The Raid on Point Lookout*, 38–39.

38. Beitzell, *Point Lookout Prison Camp for Confederates* (Baltimore: Abell, 1972), 59.

Chapter 7

1. Douglas, *I Rode with Stonewall*, 284; Cooling, *JERW*, 187.

2. Cooling, *JERW*, 183; Fitzpatrick, "Jubal Early and the Californians," 51–55.

3. Cooling, *JERW*, 183; Fitzpatrick, "Jubal Early and the Californians," 59–61; Bernstein, "Early's Summer March Chills Washington," *Washington Times*, 5 June 2004.

4. Jeffry Wert, "The Snickers Gap War," *Civil War Times Illustrated*, August 1978, 30–42.

5. Charles T. Jacobs, "Civil War Fords and Ferries in Montgomery County," *The Montgomery County Story*, no. 1 (1997), 40.

6. Elisha Hunt Rhodes, *All for the Union: The Civil War Diary of Elisha Hunt Rhodes*, as quoted in Hoewing, *Poolesville: 250 Years — Indians to the Internet* (2003).

7. Signal Corps Lt. J. Willard Brown, as quoted in Cooling, *JERW*, 177.

8. As quoted in *JERW*, 188; Wert, "The Snickers Gap War," 35.

9. Cooling, *JERW*, 184.

10. *Ibid.*, 193–194; Wert, "The Snickers Gap War," 36.

11. Millard K. Bushong, *Old Jube: A Biography of General Jubal A. Early* (Shippensburg, PA: White Mane, 1990), 219.

12. Author's conversation with National Park Service staff, Harpers Ferry, WV, February 2007; DiLorenzo, *The Real Lincoln*, 246; Bushong, *Old Jube*, 221.

13. Matthew Page Andrews, ed., *Women of the South in War Times* (Baltimore: Norman, Remington, 1920), 201–204; Osborne, *Jubal*, 300.

14. Cooling, *JERW*, 207–208.

15. Richard R. Duncan, "Maryland's Reaction to Early's Raid in 1864: A Summer of Bitterness," *MD Historical Magazine*, no. 64 (1969), 277–278; Cooling, *JERW*, 215–216; Edward A. Miller, *Lincoln's Abolitionist General: The Biography of David Hunter* (Columbia: University of South Carolina Press, 1997), 260.

16. Cooling, *JERW*, 200.

17. Peter J. Meany, OSB, *The Civil War Engagement at Cool Spring* (Berryville: Clarke County Historical Society, 1980), chapters 4–8.

18. Wert, "The Snickers Gap War," 38–40.

19. Martin Schmitt, ed., *General George Crook: His Autobiography* (Norman: University of Oklahoma Press, 1960), 122.

20. Meany, "The Civil War Engagement at Cool Spring," 41; Wert, "The Snickers Gap War," 39.

21. Meany, "The Civil War Engagement at Cool Spring," 42.

22. *Ibid.*, Ch. 8.

23. William Runge, ed., *Four Years in the Confederate Artillery: The Diary of Henry Robinson Berkeley* (Chapel Hill: University of North Carolina Press, 1961), 89.

24. Walter Clark, ed. *Histories of the Several Regiments and Battalions from North Carolina in the Great War 1861–1865* (Wilmington, DE: Broadfoot, 1907), 248–250.

25. *ORA*, I, vol. 37, pt. 1, 353–354; Gary W. Gallagher, *Stephen Dodson Ramseur: Lee's Gallant General* (Chapel Hill: University of North Carolina Press, 1985), 133–135.

26. *ORA*, I, vol. 37, pt. 2, 411–412, 369.

27. *Ibid.*, 423.

28. Crook, *General George Crook: His Autobiography*, 123.

29. http://www.angelfire.com/va3/valleywar/battle/2kernstown.html; Bushong, *Old Jube*, 214.

Chapter 8

1. Ted Alexander, *History and Tour Guide of the Burning of Chambersburg and McCausland's Raid* (Columbus, OH: Blue & Gray, 2004), 11.

2. Charles Theodore Alexander, *McCausland's Raid and the Burning of Chambersburg*, master's thesis (University of Maryland Baltimore County, 1988), 17–18.

3. Early, "Autobiographical Sketch," as cited in *History and Tour Guide*, 12.

4. Alexander, *McCausland's Raid*, 14–15.

5. Ted Alexander, William P. Conrad, Jim Neitzel, and Virginia Stake, *Southern Revenge! Civil War History of Chambersburg* (Shippensburg, PA: White Mane, 1989), 15–17.

6. Alexander, et al., *Southern Revenge!*, 26.

7. Alexander, et al., *Southern Revenge!*, 50.

8. *Ibid.*, 62.

9. Hans Trefousse, *Thaddeus Stevens: 19th Century Egalitarian* (Harrisburg, PA: Stackpole Books,

1992), 134–135. There is no doubt that Stevens was anti-slavery, but some say he wasn't anti-southern. However, most southern landowners weren't slave owners. Thus Stevens' co-sponsorship of the 1860 Morrill tariff, his advocating the burning of "all rebel mansions," and his frequent use of the term "conquered provinces" to describe southern states underscore his anti-southern leanings.

10. Fritz Haselburger, *Confederate Retaliation: McCausland's 1864 Raid* (Shippensburg, PA: Burd Street Press, 2000), 22–23.

11. *ORA*, I, vol. 43, pt. 1, 755.

12. DiLorenzo, *The Real Lincoln*, 95; units of the Pennsylvania Militia, led by Major General William "Baldy" Smith, repulsed JEB Stuart's cavalry during the Battle of Carlisle, 30 June to 1 July 1863.

13. *ORA*, I, vol. 43, pt. 1, 756; William J. Miller, *The Training of an Army: Camp Curtin and the North's Civil War* (Shippensburg, PA: White Mane, 1990), 195; Edward Stackpole, *Sheridan in the Shenandoah* (Harrisburg, PA: Stackpole Books, 1992), 93.

14. As cited in Alexander, *McCausland's Raid*, Ch. 3, footnote 17.

15. *ORA*, I, vol. 37, pt. 2, 507–508.

16. Conversation with staffs at Franklin County Historical Society, Chambersburg, PA, Spring 2007; William H. Egle, ed., *Andrew Gregg Curtin: His Life and Services* (Philadelphia: Avil Printing, 1912), "Curtin's Second Term," 175–176.

17. Haselberger, *Confederate Retaliation*, 36.

18. *ORA*, I, vol. 37, pt. 2, 514–515; Haselberger, *Confederate Retaliation*, 89–90.

19. Jacob Hoke, *The Great Invasion of 1863; or General Lee in Pennsylvania* (Dayton, OH: Shuey, 1887), 584–587.

20. *Ibid.*, 37–38.

21. Jacob Hoke, "Reminiscences of the War," *Public Opinion*, 1884, 112–113, also at www.openlibrary.org/a/ol/2170057a/J-Hoke.

22. Freeman, *Lee's Lieutenants*, 3, 571.

23. Alexander, et al., *Southern Revenge!* 118–119; Gilmor, *Four Years in the Saddle*, 209; Freeman, *Lee's Lieutenants*, 3, 572.

24. Statement of J.W. Douglas, in Hoke, "Reminiscences of the War," 112–113.

25. Haselberger, *Confederate Retaliation*, 39–40.

26. Samuel P. Bates, *History of Franklin County, Pennsylvania* (Chicago: Warner, Beers, 1887), 384–386.

27. Report of Brig. General Bradley Johnson, *ORA*, I, vol. 43, pt. 1, 4; Alexander, *McCausland's Raid*, 42; Letter of Malcolm Fleming, 10 August 1864, at www.lib.virginia.edu/small/exhibits/hoos/remember.html.

28. Report of Brig. General Bradley T. Johnson, *ORA*, Series I, vol. 43, pt. 1, p. 4; Alexander, McCausland's Raid, p. 42; Letter of Malcolm Fleming, 10 August 1864, at www.lib.virginia.edu/small/exhibits/hoos/remember.html.

29. John E. Olson, *21st Virginia Cavalry* (Lynchburg, VA: Howard, 1989), 31.

30. *ORA*, I, vol. 37, pt. 2, 508.

31. Haselberger, *Confederate Retaliation*, 37; Re-

port of Sgt. Will Kochersperger, 9 August 1864, *ORA*, I, vol. 37, pt. 1, 334–335.

32. Haselberger, *Confederate Retaliation*, 105–106; Alexander, et al., *Southern Revenge!*, 128.

33. *Middletown Valley Register*, "Further Particulars of the Burning of Chambersburg," 12 August 1864; Olson, *21st Virginia Cavalry*, 31.

34. Alexander, et al., *Southern Revenge!*, 127, 132.

35. Alexander, *History and Tour Guide*, 47, 81; Haselberger, *Confederate Retaliation*, 105.

36. Osborne, *Jubal*, 309.

37. Bates, *History of Franklin County, Pa.*, 390.

38. Alexander, *McCausland's Raid*, 50; Report of Brig. General Bradley T. Johnson, *ORA*, I, vol. 43, pt. I, pg. 4; Reference Desk, Carnegie Library, Pittsburgh.

39. George W. Booth, *A Maryland Boy in Lee's Army: Personal Reminiscences of a Maryland Soldier in the War Between the States 1861–1865* (Lincoln: University of Nebraska Press, 2000), 129.

40. *Ibid.*, 131.

41. *ORA*, I, vol. 37, pt. 2, 568; Alexander, *McCausland's Raid*, 54.

42. Alexander, *McCausland's Raid*, 55–56; Will Lowdermilk, *History of Cumberland* (Baltimore: Regional, 1878), 414–417.

43. Gilmor, *Four Years in the Saddle*, 215.

44. *Ibid.*, 219–220.

45. *Ibid.*, 220.

46. Alexander, *McCausland's Raid*, 60–61; Olson, *21st Virginia Cavalry*, 32.

47. Haselburger, *Confederate Retaliation*, 128–129.

48. Alexander, *McCausland's Raid*, 61.

Chapter 9

1. Haselburger, *Confederate Retaliation*, 135–136; *ORA*, I, vol. 43, pt. 1, 654.

2. Report of Brig. General Bradley T. Johnson, *ORA*, I, vol. 43, pt. 1, 4.

3. *Ibid.*

4. *ORA*, I, vol. 37, pt. 2, 588.

5. Haselburger, *Confederate Retaliation*, 139.

6. Quoted in Stephen G. Smith, *The First Battle of Moorefield: Early's Cavalry Is Routed* (Saline, MI: McNaughton & Gunn, 1998), 19; Fielder Slingluff, "The Burning of Chambersburg," SHS Papers, Vol. 37, 1909, 160.

7. Smith, *The First Battle of Moorefield*, 22; Haselburger, *Confederate Retaliation*, 145.

8. Michael J. Pauley, *Unreconstructed Rebel: The Life of General John McCausland, CSA* (Charleston: Pictorial Histories, 1992), 64; Smith, *The First Battle of Moorefield*, 25.

9. Report of Brig. General Bradley T. Johnson, *ORA*, I, vol. 43, pt. 1, 5; Slingluff, "The Burning of Chambersburg," 161.

10. Report of Brig. General Bradley T. Johnson, *ORA*, I, vol. 43, pt. 1, 5; Smith, *The First Battle of Moorefield*, 26.

11. Alexander, *McCausland's Raid*, 67–68; Smith, *The First Battle of Moorefield*, 23.

12. Slingluff, "The Burning of Chambersburg," 162.

13. Report of Brig. General William W. Averell, 8 August 1864; *ORA*, I, vol. 43, pt. 1, 494; Slingluff, "The Burning of Chambersburg," 159–160.

14. Report of Brig. General Bradley T. Johnson, *ORA*, I, vol. 43, pt. 1, 5.

15. Editors of Time-Life Books, *Shenandoah 1864: Voices of the Civil War* (Alexandria, VA: Time-Life Books, 1998), 75; Haselburger, *Confederate Retaliation*, 160; Alexander, *History and Tour Guide*, 48.

16. Report of Brig. General Bradley T. Johnson, *ORA*, I, vol. 43, pt. 1, 6.

17. Gilmor, *Four Years in the Saddle*, 222–223.

18. Haselburger, *Confederate Retaliation*, 162.

19. Slingluff, "The Burning of Chambersburg," 160–161.

20. Haselburger, *Confederate Retaliation*, 169–170.

21. *Ibid.*, 174.

22. *Ibid.*, 170–171.

23. Alexander, *History and Tour Guide*, 58; Smith, *The First Battle of Moorefield*, 37.

24. Booth, *A Maryland Boy in Lee's Army*, 140; Mt. Jackson Museum, historic marker, Mt. Jackson Va. Rude's Hill is a 980-foot-high prominence about 1½ miles southwest of Mt. Jackson. Early's headquarters were atop the hill, allowing him to observe the surrounding countryside. Johnson's headquarters were on the Meem farm, just outside of town. There was a large hospital in Mt. Jackson, with facilities for over 500 wounded, torn down by Ohio infantry in the spring of 1865.

25. Haselburger, *Confederate Retaliation*, 180–181; Booth, *A Maryland Boy in Lee's Army*, 140; *Memoir of the First Maryland Regiment*, 221, cited in, Bart Rhett Talbert, "Maryland in the War Between the States: A Lesson in the Struggle for American Freedom," Ph.D. diss. (Montgomery: University of Alabama, 1976), 129–130; Richard Duncan, "A Summer of Bitterness," *Maryland Historical Magazine* 64, 1969; *New York Herald*, 3 August 1864, 1; Report of Brig. General Bradley T. Johnson, *ORA*, I, vol. 43, pt. 1, 8. Concerning Confederate ill-will towards Maryland, after the Army of Northern Virginia retreated from the Battle of Antietam, Johnson wrote: "The whole Confederacy filled with complaints that Maryland did not rise." By 1864, Maryland was considered Union territory.

Chapter 10

1. Noah Brooks, *Washington in Lincoln's Time* (New York: Rinehart, 1958), 164–165, cited in John Nicolay and John Hay, *History of Lincoln* (New York: Century, 1890), 237.

2. *ORA*, I, vol. 46, pt. 1, 20.

3. Editors of Time-Life Books, *Shenandoah 1864: Voices of the Civil War*, (Alexandria, VA: Time-Life Books, 2000), 11–12; Columbia Encyclopedia, 6th ed. (New York: Columbia University Press, 2007).

4. Waugh, *Re-electing Lincoln*, 224.

5. Benjamin Butler, *Private and Official Correspondence of General Benjamin Butler* (Boston: privately published 1917), 5, 9; Letter of J.K. Herbert to General Butler, 6 August 1864.

6. Paul N. Herbert, "Lincoln's Odd Ways with Finances," *Washington Times*, Civil War page, 22 December 2007.

7. Gideon Welles, "The Opposition to Lincoln in 1864," *Atlantic Monthly*, March 1878, 367–368; Waugh, *Re-Electing Lincoln*, 214–219.

8. Biography Resource Center, Gale Database Co., Farmington Hills, MI.

9. *Memoirs of Jefferson Davis*, as cited in Larry E. Nelson, *Bullets, Ballots, and Rhetoric* (Tuscaloosa: University of Alabama Press, 1980), 24.

10. Nelson, *Bullets, Ballots, and Rhetoric*, 62–65.

11. Quoted in Nelson, *Bullets, Ballots, and Rhetoric*, 100; Sarah Woolfolk Wiggins, ed., *Journals of Josiah Gorgas* (Tuscaloosa: University of Alabama Press, 1995), 145.

12. Quoted in Nelson, *Bullets, Ballots, and Rhetoric*, 99; Mary Conner Moffett, ed., *Letters of General James Conner C.S.A.* (Columbia: Bryan, 1950), 147.

13. Mabel McIlvaine, *Reminiscences of Chicago During the Civil War* (Citadel Press, 1967), back cover; Oscar Kinchen, *Confederate Operations in Canada and the North* (Quincy: Christopher, 1984), 15–17; DiLorenzo, *The Real Lincoln*, 241–242.

14. Waugh, *Re-electing Lincoln*, 158; DiLorenzo, *The Real Lincoln*, 240–242.

15. James D. Horan, *Confederate Agent: A Discovery in History* (New York: Fairfax Press, 1954), 101–104.

16. Quoted in *Confederate Agent*, 121.

17. *Ibid.*, 128–131; George Levy, *To Die in Chicago* (Gretna: Pelican Press, 2000), 260.

18. Waugh, *Re-electing Lincoln*, 282; Democratic National Convention. *Official Proceedings of the Democratic National Convention, Held in 1864 at Chicago* (Chicago: Chicago Steam, 1864), 3–11. The description of the Wigwam is from the *Chicago Times* as cited in *The Sun* (Baltimore), 23 August 1864, 1.

19. www.phmc.state.pa.us/bah/dam/governors/bigler.asp.

20. *Official Proceedings of the Democratic National Convention*, 10.

21. *Ibid.*, 46–47.

22. *Official Proceedings of the Democratic National Convention*, 34.

23. Stephen W. Sears, *George B. McClellan: The Young Napoleon* (New York: Ticknor & Fields, 1988), 372–373.

24. *Official Proceedings of the Democratic National Convention*, 60–64.

25. James M. McPherson, *Battle Cry of Freedom* (New York: Oxford University Press, 1988), 758–760.

26. Lee Kennett, *Marching Through Georgia* (New York: HarperCollins, 1995), 22.

27. Samuel P. Carter III, *The Siege of Atlanta 1864* (New York: Bonanza Books, 1973), 100.

28. http://roadsidegeorgia.com/city/tunnelhill.html, www.northga.net/whitfield/tunnel.html; John P. Dyer, *From Shiloh to San Juan: The Life of Fightin' Joe Wheeler* (Baton Rouge: Louisiana State University Press, 1961), 124. Construction of the tunnel through Chetoogeta Mountain, Whitfield County, Ga., began in 1848; the first train passed through on 9 May 1850. The tunnel was closed in 1928 as an adjacent tunnel had been built to accommodate the larger trains of the 20th century.

29. Kennett, *Marching Through Georgia*, 82.

30. Northwestern Georgia was called Cherokee Georgia because the Cherokee tribe had lived there during the 1830s. They were forced to emigrate to the Oklahoma Territory on the Trail of Tears, according to President Andrew Jackson's removal policy.

31. Ronald H. Bailey, *Battles for Atlanta: Sherman Moves East* (Alexandria, VA: Time-Life Books, 1985), 48.

32. Bailey, *Battles for Atlanta*, 48–49; Carter, *The Siege of Atlanta 1864*, 128–129; Richard M. McMurry, *John Bell Hood and the Southern War for Independence* (Louisville: University Press of Kentucky, 1982), 108–109.

33. Bailey, *Battles for Atlanta*, 50–78.

34. Steven Woodworth, *Jefferson Davis and his Generals: The Failure of Confederate Command in the West* (Lawrence: University of Kansas Press, 1990), 272–274.

35. Quoted in William C. Davis, *Jefferson Davis: The Man and His Hour— A Biography* (New York: HarperCollins, 1991), 561.

36. *ORA*, I, vol. 38, pt. 5, 878–882, quoted in Davis, *Jefferson Davis*, 561; McMurry, *John Bell Hood*, 118.

37. Carter, *The Siege of Atlanta 1864*, 198–203; Shelby Foote, *The Civil War: A Narrative— Red River to Appomattox* (New York: Random House, 1974), 491.

38. *ORA*, I, vol. 38, pt. 5, 885, *John Bell Hood*, 143.

39. Steven Woodworth, *Jefferson Davis and His Generals* (Lawrence: University of Kansas Press, 1998), 278.

40. McMurry, *John Bell Hood*, 144–145.

41. Dyer, *From Shiloh to San Juan*, 146–147, 153.

42. McMurry, *John Bell Hood*, 148–149; Bailey, *Battles for Atlanta*, 152–154; *ORA*, V, vol. 38, pt. 1, 777, at http://cdl.library.cornell.edu/cgi-bin/moa.

43. Quoted in Kennett, *Marching Through Georgia*, 201; *New York Times*, 5 September 1864, 4.

44. *New York Times*, 5 September 1864, 4.

45. *New York Times*, 4 September 1864, 1; Sherman to Ellen Sherman, 30 June 1864, quoted in John Marszalek, *Sherman: A Soldier's Passion for Order* (New York: Free Press, 1993), 273–285 After the frontal assaults at Kennesaw Mountain failed, in a letter to his wife Sherman remarked, "I begin to regard the death and mangling of a couple thousand men as a small affair, a kind of morning dash — and it may be well that we become so hardened."

46. Marszalek, *Sherman: A Soldier's Passion for Order*, 285–286; *ORA*, I, vol. 39, pt. 2, 417–419, 503; DiLorenzo, *The Real Lincoln*, 185–186.

47. *Columbus* (Georgia) *Times*, quoted in *The Sun* (Baltimore), 7 September 1864, 1.

48. Letter of O.M. Poe to wife, 7 September 1864, quoted in Michael Fellman, *Citizen Sherman: A Life*

of William Tecumseh Sherman (New York: Random House, 1995), 184 (Hereafter cited as *Citizen Sherman*).

49. Fellman, *Citizen Sherman*, 184; *ORA*, I, vol. 38, pt. 5, 412, 422, 436, 447.

50. Mary Boykin Chesnut, *A Diary from Dixie* (Whitefish, MT: Kessinger, 2008), quoted in Bailey, *Battles for Atlanta*, 155.

51. Gary W. Gallagher, *Stephen Dodson Ramseur: Lee's Gallant General* (Chapel Hill: University of North Carolina Press, 1985), 136.

Chapter 11

1. Edward J. Stackpole, *Sheridan in the Shenandoah* (Harrisburg, PA: Stackpole Books, 1992), 176–178; Dan Wright, "Rebecca Wright"(undated), at www.dnronline.com/civilwar/part-2/peo-civ-wright.htm; Jeffry Wert, *From Winchester to Cedar Creek* (Carlisle, PA: South Mountain Press, 1987), 42.

2. Thomas A. Lewis, "The Slave and the Schoolmistress," in *The Shenandoah in Flames: The Valley Campaign of 1864* (Alexandria, VA: Time-Life Books, 1985), 113.

3. Time-Life Books, *The Shenandoah in Flames*, 100–101.

4. Ulysses S. Grant, *Ulysses S. Grant: Personal Memoirs*, Caleb Carr, ed. (New York: Modern Library, 1999), 485; Time-Life Books, *The Shenandoah in Flames*, 101.

5. Stackpole, *Sheridan in the Shenandoah*, 141.

6. Grant, *Personal Memoirs*, 485.

7. Stackpole, *Sheridan in the Shenandoah*, 122–124.

8. *ORA*, I, vol. 43, pt. 2, 691–692, 696.

9. *ORA*, I, vol. 43, pt. 1, 48; Eric Wittenberg, *Little Phil: A Reassessment of the Civil War Leadership of Gen. Philip H. Sheridan* (Washington, DC: Brassey's, 2002), 105–109, 135–146, 206–207.

10. Map of Ohio (Heathrow, FL: American Automobile Association, 1997).

11. Lewis, "The Slave and the Schoolmistress," 103.

12. Stackpole, Sheridan in the Shenandoah, 131; Wittenberg, Little Phil, 37–41.

13. Wert, *From Winchester to Cedar Creek*, 29–31.

14. *ORA*, I, vol. 43, pt. 1, 43, as cited in Wert, *From Winchester to Cedar Creek*, 32.

15. *ORA*, I, vol. 43, pt. 1, 23, 26, 61: Douglas Southall Freeman, *Lee's Lieutenants*. Vol. 3 (New York: Scribner's, 1944), 41.

16. P.H. Sheridan, *Personal Memoirs of P.H. Sheridan* (New York: Webster, 1888), vol. 1, 487–488.

17. DiLorenzo, *The Real Lincoln*, 177, 181–199.

18. Sheridan, *Personal Memoirs*, vol. 1, 500; Wert, *From Winchester to Cedar Creek*, 36–37.

19. Osborne, *Jubal*, 325.

20. Jubal A. Early, *Autobiographical Sketch and Narrative of the War Between the States* (Baltimore: Nautical & Aviation, 1989), 415.

21. Ramseur to Ellen Ramseur, 6 September 1864, as cited in Gary W. Gallagher, *Stephen Dodson Ramseur: Lee's Gallant General* (Chapel Hill: University of North Carolina Press, 1985), 136.

22. Osborne, *Jubal*, 330.

23. Mary Conner Moffett, ed., *Letters of General James Conner, C.S.A.* (Columbia, SC: Bryan, 1950), 157–158.

24. *Ibid.*, 154.

25. Wert, *From Winchester to Cedar Creek*, 42; Sheridan, *Personal Memoirs*, vol. 2, 4, 13.

26. *ORA*, I, vol. 43, pt. 2, 83–84.

27. Stackpole, *Sheridan in the Shenandoah*, 182–183; ORA, I, vol. 43, pt. 2, 69.

28. Douglas, *I Rode with Stonewall*, 308; Osborne, *Jubal*, 331–332; Early, *Autobiographical Sketch*, 419.

29. *ORA*, I, vol. 43, pt. 2, 106, 119.

30. Sheridan, *Personal Memoirs*, vol. 2, 4, 13–14; Osborne, *Jubal*, 332–333.

31. Gallagher, *Stephen Dodson Ramseur*, 141; Wert, *From Winchester to Cedar Creek*, 147–148.

32. Wert, *From Winchester to Cedar Creek*, 148; John W. DeForest, *A Volunteer's Adventures: A Union Captain's Record of the Civil War* (New Haven, CT: Yale University Press, 1946), 173.

33. DeForest, "Sheridan's Battle of Winchester," *Harper's New Monthly Magazine* 30 (January 1865), 195; DeForest, *A Volunteer's Adventures*, 173; ORA, I, vol. 43, pt. 1, 47; Wittenberg, *Little Phil*, 205; author's visit to Winchester Battlefield, August 2008; Wert, *From Winchester to Cedar Creek*, 51.

34. Sheridan, *Personal Memoirs*, vol. 2, 4, 18.

35. Wert, *From Winchester to Cedar Creek*, 52–53; Osborne, *Jubal*, 335.

36. Wert, *From Winchester to Cedar Creek*, 54.

37. Osborne, *Jubal*, 336.

38. Wert, *From Winchester to Cedar Creek*, 59–61.

39. Henry A. Dupont, *The Campaign of 1864 in the Valley of Virginia and the Expedition to Lynchburg* (New York: New York History Society, 1890), 113; Wert, *From Winchester to Cedar Creek*, 66–70.

40. Wert, *From Winchester to Cedar Creek*, 96–99; Jeffry D. Wert, *Custer: The Controversial Life of George Armstrong Custer* (New York: Simon & Schuster, 1996), 183.

41. Wert, *From Winchester to Cedar Creek*, 72.

42. *Ibid.*, 78–80.

43. Perry, *Touched with Fire*, 201.

44. Stackpole, *Sheridan in the Shenandoah*, 225–230.

45. Gordon, *Reminiscences of the Civil War*, 322–323; Sheila R. Phipps, *Genteel Rebel: The Life of Mary Greenhow Lee* (Baton Rouge: Louisiana State University Press, 2004), 147; Douglas, *I Rode with Stonewall*, 311; Time-Life Books, *The Shenandoah in Flames*, 122.

46. Gordon, *Reminiscences*, 324–325; John N. Opie, *A Rebel Cavalryman with Lee Stuart and Jackson* (Chicago: Conkey, 1899), 250.

47. Freeman, *Lee's Lieutenants*, vol. 3, 582.

48. Wert, *From Winchester to Cedar Creek*, 178.

49. As cited in ibid., 180.

50. Osborne, *Jubal*, 341; Freeman, *Lee's Lieutenants*, vol. 3, 581. This figure is the result of subtracting Early's casualties at Winchester, 3,611, from the Valley Army's strength on 18 September — about 12,900 troops, infantry, cavalry, and artillery.

51. Wert, *From Winchester to Cedar Creek*, 112; Stackpole, *Sheridan in the Shenandoah*, 249–250; Sheridan, *Personal Memoirs*, vol. 2, pt. 4, 18–21; Osborne, *Jubal*, 342; George Crook, *General George Crook: His Autobiography*, Martin Schmitt, ed. (Norman: University of Oklahoma Press, 1960), 130–132.

52. Sheridan, *Personal Memoirs*, vol. 2, 4, at www.gutenberg.org; G.G. Benedict, *Vermont in the Civil War: A History of the Part Taken by the Vermont Soldiers and Sailors in the War for the Union, 1861–1865* (Burlington, VT: Free Press, 1898), vol. 2, 214.

53. Wert, *From Winchester to Cedar Creek*, 118; Early, *Autobiographical Sketch*, 430.

54. Wert, *From Winchester to Cedar Creek*, 119; Henry Robinson Berkeley, *Four Years in the Confederate Artillery*, entry for 22 September 1864, as cited in Osborne, *Jubal*, footnote 44, 509.

55. Gallagher, *Stephen Dodson Ramseur*, 147–150.

56. Osborne, *Jubal*, 342; Early, *Autobiographical Sketch*, 430.

57. Crook, *His Autobiography*, 130–131.

58. Bryan Grimes to wife, 30 September 1864 (Southern Historical Collection, Wilson Library, University of North Carolina); ORA, I, vol. 43, pt. 1, 26–27; Historic marker at Ramseur's Hill interpretive site. The lookout tree still stands atop this hill, at the Fisher's Hill, Va., battlefield site.

59. Bryan Grimes to wife, 30 September 1864; Sheridan, *Personal Memoirs*, 27.

60. Osborne, *Jubal*, 343–344; Freeman, *Lee's Lieutenants*, 3, 584; Douglas, *I Rode with Stonewall*, 313.

Chapter 12

1. *ORA*, I, vol. 43, pt. 2, 882–883; Wert, *FWCC*, 135.

2. Letter of Smith to Lee, 6 October 1864, *ORA*, I, vol. 43, pt. 2, 893–894.

3. Wert, *FWCC*, 135–139; Osborne, *Jubal*, 352–354; ORA Series I, 2, No. 43, 895–898.

4. *Lee's Lieutenants*, No. 3, 611–612; Wert, *FWCC*, 138–139.

5. Osborne, *Jubal*, 354.

6. Grant to Sheridan, 22 September 1864, *ORA*, I, 1, No. 43, 61–62.

7. *ORA*, I, vol. 43, pt. 1, 500; Dispatch of Grant's to Sheridan, 1 September 1864, *ORA*, I, vol. 43, pt. 2, 3; *Personal Memoirs of P.H. Sheridan*, No. 2, 4, 23, at www.gutenberg.org; Mt. Jackson (VA) Public Library. Grant's dispatch to Sheridan of 1 September 1864 states: "The frequent reports of Averell's falling back without much fighting or even skirmishing, and afterward being able to take his old position without opposition, presents a very bad appearance at this distance. You can judge better of his merits than I can, but it looks to me as if it was time to try some other officer in his place. If you think as I do in this matter, relieve him at once and name his successor."

8. *ORA*, I, vol. 43, pt. 1, 29–30.

9. Wert, *FWCC*, 144.

10. Roy Morris Jr., *Sheridan* (New York: Crown, 1992), 564; Mark Grimsley, *The Hard Hand of War* (New York: Cambridge University Press, 1995), 184; DiLorenzo, *The Real Lincoln*, 196–197.

11. *ORA*, I, vol. 43, pt. 2, 307–308.

12. *The Madison Quarterly* 9, no. 2 (March 1949), cited in John L. Heatwole, *The Burning* (Bridgewater, VA: Rockbridge Press, 2003), 52.

13. Early, *Autobiographical Sketch*, 435; Wert, *Custer*, 189.

14. Jeffry D. Wert, *Mosby's Rangers* (New York: Simon & Schuster, 1990), 224–238.

15. Osborne, *Jubal*, 223–227.

16. *ORA*, I, vol. 43, pt. 1, 31, 431; Wert, Custer, 190; Dr. John Wayland, *A History of Shenandoah County, Virginia* (Strasburg, VA: Shenandoah, 1927), 331.

17. Wayland, *History of Shenandoah County*, 332; Osborne, *Jubal*, 355–356; *ORA*, I, vol. 43, pt. 1, 520–522.

18. *ORA*, I, vol. 43, pt. 2, 339–340.

19. *Ibid.*, 340.

20. *Ibid.*, 346.

21. Report of Colonel Thomas M. Harris, 10th W. Va. Infantry, *ORA*, I, vol. 43, pt. 1, 371–372; Osborne, *Jubal*, 358; Early, *Autobiographical Sketch*, 437.

22. Time-Life Books, *The Shenandoah in Flames*, 140.

23. *Richmond Enquirer*, 27 September 1864, 1.

24. *ORA*, I, vol. 43, pt. 2, 389–390.

25. Gordon, *Reminiscences*, 333–336; *ORA*, I, vol. 43, pt. 2, 580.

26. www.mapquest.com.

27. Wert, *FWCC*, 178–182, 181–183.

28. Gordon, *Reminiscences,* 327–340; Stackpole, *Sheridan in the Shenandoah*, 298–305; Time-Life Books, *The Shenandoah in Flames*, 144–150; *Lee's Lieutenants*, 3, 598–609.

29. Wert, *FWCC*, 189–195; *ORA*, I, vol. 43, pt. 1, 284–286.

30. Wert, *FWCC*, 206–207.

31. *ORA*, I, vol. 43, pt. 1, 158–159.

32. Wert, *FWCC*, 208–210; Early, *Autobiographical Sketch*, 445.

33. *ORA*, I, vol. 43, pt. 1, 433; Wert, *FWCC*, 214–215.

34. Osborne, *Jubal,* 368; Napoleon exclaimed, "Yonder shines the sun of Austerlitz! Today shall be a day of victory!" www.napoleongames.com.

35. Gordon, *Reminiscences*, 341; Osborne, *Jubal*, 369.

36. *Memoirs of P.H. Sheridan*, No. 2, 4, 31–32, at www.gutenberg.org.

37. Early, *Autobiographical Sketch*, 447–448.

38. Wert, *FWCC*, 226.

39. Gordon, *Reminiscences*, 347–348; Wert, *FWCC*, 229.

40. Gordon, *Reminiscences*, 348–349.

41. Wert, *FWCC*, 235.

42. Early, *Autobiographical Sketch*, 441.

43. H.H. Stevens, "Battle of Cedar Creek, Va.," *Confederate Veteran* 27, 1919: 390–391; Wert, *FWCC*, 218–219.

44. Gordon, *Reminiscences*, 363–372; *ORA*, I, vol.

43, pt. 1, 562–563; Early, *Autobiographical Sketch*, 451.

45. *ORA*, I, vol. 43, pt. 1, 582; Osborne, *Jubal*, 379.

46. Osborne, *Jubal*, 370.

Chapter 13

1. *ORA*, I, vol. 43, pt. 2, 485, 486, 531.

2. *Ibid.*, 527.

3. *Ibid.*, 519.

4. *New York Times*, 1 November 1864, Roy P. Basler, ed., *Collected Works of Abraham Lincoln*, vol. 8, 92.

5. *ORA*, I, vol. 43, pt. 2, 549, 568.

6. Benjamin F. Butler, *Butler's Book* (Boston: Thayer, 1892), 753–759; www.mrlincolnand-newyork.org, 4.

7. *Encyclopaedia Americana Database*, 2008; Horan, *Confederate Agent*, 208–223 Greek fire is a volatile mixture of distilled petroleum, pitch, sulfur, quicklime, and other ingredients, with the odor of rotten eggs. It was used before gunpowder existed, and burns on contact with water.

8. *ORA*, I, vol. 46, pt. 2, 1258; Freeman, *Lee's Lieutenants* No. 3, 624; Nelson, *Bullets, Ballots, and Rhetoric*, 157–158.

9. Early, *Autobiographical Sketch*, 459.

10. *ORA*, I, vol. 43, pt. 1, 584–585.

11. Osborne, *Jubal,* 381–383; Freeman, *Lee's Lieutenants*, vol. 3, 617.

12. *Memoirs of P. H. Sheridan*, vol. 2, 98–99; *Jubal*, 384.

13. Early, *Autobiographical Sketch*, 463; Osborne, *Jubal*, 387–389; J.W.A. Whitehorne, "Jubal Early at Waynesboro: The Last Hurrah," *Civil War* 11, no. 2 (April 1994), 24.

14. Early, *Autobiographical Sketch,* 464.

15. Osborne, *Jubal*, 390–392; Freeman, *Lee's Lieutenants*, vol. 3, 636; Early, *Autobiographical Sketch*, 469.

16. Time-Life Books, *The Shenandoah in Flames*, 110–111; Smith, *The First Battle of Moorefield*, 43; Marian Gouverneur, *As I Remember: Recollections of American Society During the Nineteenth Century* (Boston: Appleton, 1911), 320–321.

17. Sears, *George B. McClellan: The Young Napoleon*, 385–386; Waugh, *Re-electing Lincoln*, 354; Allen C. Guelzo, "A Reluctant Recruit to the Abolitionist Cause," *Washington Post*, 11 February 2001; DiLorenzo, *The Real Lincoln*, Chapters 8–10.

Appendix

1. S. Roger Keller, *Events of the Civil War in Washington County, Maryland* (Shippensburg, PA: Burd Street Press, 1995), 336–338.

2. J. Thomas Scharf, *History of Western Maryland: Being a History of Frederick, Montgomery, Carroll, Washington, Allegany and Garrett Counties, from the Earliest Period to the Present Day* (Baltimore: Baltimore Regional, 1968), 286.

3. Thomas J.C. Williams, *History and Biographical Record of Washington County Maryland* (Wilmington, NC: Broadfoot, 1906), 356.

4. *History of Western Maryland*, p. 286.

Bibliography

Primary Sources

BOOKS

Andrews, Matthew Page, ed. *The Women of the South in War Times.* Baltimore: Norman, Remington, 1920.

Butler, General Benjamin F. *Private and Official Correspondence.* Boston: Privately published, 1917.

Chesnut, Mary Boykin. *A Diary from Dixie.* Whitefish, MT: Kessinger, 2008.

Democratic National Convention. *Official Proceedings of the Democratic National Convention, Held in 1864 at Chicago.* Chicago: Chicago Steam, 1864.

Douglas, Henry Kyd. *I Rode with Stonewall.* Chapel Hill: University of North Carolina Press, 1940.

Early, Jubal A. *A Memoir of the Last Year of the War for Independence in the Confederate States of America, Containing an Account of the Operations of His Commands in the Years 1864 and 1865.* Lynchburg, VA: Button, 1867.

Englebrecht, Jacob. *Diary.* Frederick, MD: Historical Society of Frederick County, 1978.

Gorgas, Josiah. *Journals.* Tuscaloosa: University of Alabama Press, 1995.

Hotchkiss, Jedediah. *Make Me a Map of the Valley: The Civil War Journal of Stonewall Jackson's Topographer.* Edited by Archie P. McDonald. Dallas: SMU Press, 1973.

Junkin, Margaret Preston. *Life and Letters.* Edited by Elizabeth Preston Allan. Boston: privately published, 1903.

Lincoln, Abraham. *Collected Works.* 8 vols. Edited by Roy Basler. New Brunswick, NJ: Rutgers University Press, 1953.

Moffett, Mary Conner, ed. *Letters of General James Conner C.S.A.* Columbia, SC: Bryan, 1950.

National Historical Society. *The War of the Rebellion: A Compilation of the Official Records of the Union and Confederate Armies.* Series I, vol. 37, pt. 1, Washington: Government Printing Office, 1891.

_____, Series I, vol. 37, pt. 2.

_____, Series V, vol. 38, pt. 1.

_____, Series I, vol. 38, pt. 5.

_____, Series I, vol. 39, pt. 2.

_____, Series I, vol. 43, pt. 1.

_____, Series I, vol. 43, pt. 2.

_____, Series I, vol. 46, pt. 1.

_____, Series I, vol. 51, pt. 1.

Strother, David Hunter. *A Virginia Yankee in the Civil War.* Edited by Cecil D. Eby Jr. Chapel Hill: University of North Carolina Press, 1961.

Welles, Gideon. *Diary.* New York: Houghton Mifflin, 1909.

Younger, Edward, ed. *Inside the Confederate Government: The Diary of Robert Garlick Hill Kean.* New York: Oxford University Press, 2007.

GOVERNMENT DOCUMENTS

Confederate Order of Battle: The Battle of Monocacy, July 9, 1864. Frederick, MD: Monocacy National Battlefield, undated.

Goldsborough, Edward Y. *The Appeal of Frederick City, Maryland to the Congress of the United States, for the Payment of its claim of $200,000 Paid as a Ransom to the Confederate Army, July 9, 1864.* Frederick, MD: Privately published, 1902.

"Thomas Farm Trail." Frederick, MD: Monocacy National Battlefield, undated.

U.S. Congress. *Congressional Globe.* 46 vols. Washington, 1834–73.

U.S. Congress. Senate. Committee on the Judiciary, Subcommittee on S. 1842. *To Reimburse the City of Frederick, MD, for Money Paid Saving Harmless Valuable Military and Hospital Supplies Owned by the United States Government.* 92nd Cong., 2d sess., 2 August 1972.

Virginia Agriculture Census. Richmond: State of Virginia, 1860.

MANUSCRIPT COLLECTIONS

Blair Family Papers. Manuscript Division, Library of Congress, Washington, DC.

DeSellum, John T. 1864. Montgomery County Historical Society, Rockville, MD.

Edwin C. Fishel Papers. Special Collections, Georgetown University Library, Washington, DC.

Hoyt, Helen Marie Noye. 1925. http://madonna.edu/pages/lmmtrain.cfm.

Joseph McMurran Diary. 13–14 July 1864. Special Collections, University of Virginia Library.

Secondary Sources

BOOKS

Alexander, Ted. *History and Tour Guide of the Burning of Chambersburg and McCausland's Raid*. Columbus, OH: Blue & Gray, 2004.

Alexander, Ted, William P. Conrad, Jim Neitzel, and Virginia Stake. *Southern Revenge! Civil War History of Chambersburg*. Shippensburg, PA: White Mane, 1989.

Andrews, J. Cutler. *The North Reports the Civil War*. New Brunswick, NJ: Princeton University Press, 1970.

Bailey, Ronald H. *Battles for Atlanta: Sherman Moves East*. Alexandria, VA: Time-Life Books, 1985.

Bates, Samuel P. *History of Franklin County, Pennsylvania*. Chicago: Warner, Beers, 1887.

Benedict, G.G. *Vermont in the Civil War: A History of the Part Taken by the Vermont Soldiers and Sailors in the War for the Union 1861–1865*. Vol. 2. Burlington, VT: Free Press Association, 1898.

Berkeley, Henry Robinson. *Four Years in the Confederate Artillery*. Edited by William Runge. Chapel Hill: University of North Carolina Press, 1961.

Black, Robert C. III. *The Railroads of the Confederacy*. Chapel Hill: University of North Carolina Press, 1952.

Booth, George W. *A Maryland Boy in Lee's Army: Personal Reminiscences of a Maryland Soldier in the War Between the States 1861–1865*. Lincoln: University of Nebraska Press, 2000.

Brooks, Noah. *Washington in Lincoln's Time*. New York: Rinehart, 1958.

Buell, Clarence C., and Robert U. Johnson. *Battles and Leaders of the Civil War*. New York: Castle Books, 1956.

Bushong, Millard K. *History of Jefferson County, West Virginia*. Charlestown, WV: Jefferson, 1941.

_____. *Old Jube*. Shippensburg, PA: White Mane, 1990.

Butler, Benjamin F. *Butler's Book*. Boston: Thayer, 1892.

Calcott, George H. *A History of the University of Maryland*. Baltimore: Maryland Historical Society, 1966.

Carter, Samuel P. III. *The Siege of Atlanta 1864*. New York: St. Martin's Press, 1973.

Casler, John O. *Four Years in the Stonewall Brigade* Guthrie, OK: State Capital Print, 1893.

Castel, Albert. *Winning and Losing in the Civil War: Essays and Stories*. Columbia: University of South Carolina Press, 1994.

Clark, Walter, ed. *Histories of the Several Regiments and Battalions from North Carolina in the Great War 1861–1865*. Vol. 2. Wilmington, NC: Broadfoot, 1991.

Cooling, B.F. *Jubal Early's Raid on Washington 1864*. Baltimore: Nautical & Aviation, 1989.

_____. *Symbol, Sword, and Shield*. New York: Archon Books, 1978.

_____. *Monocacy: The Battle That Saved Washington*. Shippensburg, PA: White Mane, 1997.

Crook, General George. *His Autobiography*. Edited by Martin Schmitt. Norman: University of Oklahoma Press, 1960.

Current, Richard Nelson. *Lincoln's Loyalists: Union Soldiers from the Confederacy*. Boston: Northeastern University Press, 1992.

Davis, William C. *The Cause Lost: Myths and Realities of the Confederacy*. Lawrence: University of Kansas Press, 1996.

_____. *Jefferson Davis: The Man and His Hour — A Biography*. New York: HarperCollins, 1981.

_____. *Look Away! A History of the Confederate States of America*. New York: Free Press, 2002.

DeForest, John W. *A Volunteer's Adventures: A Union Captain's Record of the Civil War*. New Haven, CT: Yale University Press, 1946.

DiLorenzo, Thomas J. *The Real Lincoln: A New Look at Abraham Lincoln, His Agenda, and an Unnecessary War*. New York: Crown, 2003.

Donald, David, ed. *Why the North Won the Civil War*. Baton Rouge: Louisiana State University Press, 1960.

Driver, Robert H. Jr., ed. *58th Virginia Infantry*. Lynchburg, VA: Howard, 1990.

Dupont, Henry A. *The Campaign of 1864 in the Valley of Virginia and the Expedition to Lynchburg*. New York: New York History Society, 1890.

Dyer, John P. *From Shiloh to San Juan: The Life of Fightin' Joe Wheeler*. Baton Rouge: Louisiana State University Press, 1961.

Early, Jubal A. *Autobiographical Sketch and Narrative of the War Between the States*. Edited by R.H. Early. Philadelphia: Lippincott, 1912.

Editors of Time-Life Books. *Shenandoah 1864: Voices of the Civil War*. Alexandria, VA: Time-Life Books, 1998.

Egle, William H., ed. *Andrew Gregg Curtin: His Life and Struggles*. Philadelphia: Avil Printing, 1912.

Evans, Eli. *Judah P. Benjamin: The Jewish Confederate*. New York: Free Press, 1988.

Farrar, Samuel Clarke. *The Twenty-Second Pennsylvania Cavalry and the Ringgold Battalion, 1861–1865*. Pittsburgh: Twenty Second Pa. Ringgold Cavalry Association, 1911.

Fellman, Michael. *Citizen Sherman: A Life of William Tecumseh Sherman*. New York: Random House, 1995.

Foote, Shelby. *The Civil War: A Narrative — Red River to Appomattox*. New York: Random House, 1974.

Freeman, Douglas Southall. *Lee's Lieutenants*. Vol. 3. New York: Scribner's, 1944.

Gallagher, Gary W. *Stephen Dodson Ramseur: Lee's Gallant General*. Chapel Hill: University of North Carolina Press, 1985.

Gilmor, Harry. *Four Years in the Saddle*. New York: Harper Bros., 1866.

Glenn, William Wilkins. *Between North and South: A Maryland Journalist Views the Civil War, 1861–1869*. Madison, NJ: Fairleigh Dickinson University Press, 1976.

Goldsborough, E.Y. *Early's Great Raid*. Frederick, MD: privately published, 1898.

Gordon, John B. *Reminiscences of the Civil War*. 1903. Reprint, Alexandria, VA: Time-Life Books, 1981.

Gordon, Paul, and Rita Gordon. *Never the Like Again.* Frederick, MD: Heritage Partnership, 1995.

Gouverneur, Marian. *As I Remember: Recollections of American Society during the Nineteenth Century.* Boston: Appleton, 1911.

Grant, Ulysses S. *Personal Memoirs.* Edited by Caleb Carr. New York: Modern Library, 1999.

Haselberger, Fritz. *Confederate Retaliation: McCausland's 1864 Raid.* Shippensburg, PA: Burd Street Press, 2000.

Haynes, E.M. *A History of the Tenth Regiment, VT. Vols.* Rutland: Tuttle, 1894.

Head, James W. *History and Comprehensive Description of Loudoun County, Va.* 1908. Reprint, Baltimore: Clearfield, 1989.

Heatwole, John L. *The Burning.* Berryville, VA: Rockbridge, 2003.

Hoewing, Ray. *Poolesville: 250 Years—Indians to the Internet.* Poolesville, MD: Crafts-A-Plenty, 2003.

Hoke, Jacob. *The Great Invasion of 1863; or General Lee in Pennsylvania.* Dayton: Shuey, 1887.

Holdcraft, Jacob M. *Names in Stone: Frederick Co. Cemetery Records.* Ann Arbor, MI: Genealogical, 1976.

Horan, James D. *Confederate Agent: A Discovery in History.* New York: Fairfax Press, 1954.

Jackson, Donald Dale. *Twenty Million Yankees: The Northern Home Front.* Alexandria, VA: Time-Life Books, 1985.

Jones, James Pickett, and James Lee McDonough. *War So Terrible: Sherman and Atlanta.* New York: Norton, 1987.

Judge, Joseph. *Season of Fire: The Confederate Strike on Washington, DC.* Berryville, VA: Rockbridge, 1994.

Keller, S. Roger. *Events of the Civil War in Washington County, Maryland.* Shippensburg, PA: Burd Street Press, 1995.

Kennett, Lee. *Marching through Georgia.* New York: HarperCollins, 1995.

Kinchen, Oscar. *Confederate Operations in Canada and the North.* Quincy, MA: Christopher, 1968.

Klement, Frank L. *The Limits of Dissent.* Frankfort: University of Kentucky Press, 1970.

Levy, George. *To Die in Chicago.* Gretna, LA: Pelican Press, 2000.

Lewis, Thomas A., and the Editors of Time-Life Books. *The Shenandoah in Flames: The Valley Campaign of 1864.* Alexandria, VA: Time-Life Books, 1985.

Linn, William Alexander. *Horace Greeley.* New York: Chelsea House, 1981.

Lowdermilk, Will. *History of Cumberland.* Baltimore: Regional, 1878.

Manakee, Harold. *Maryland in the Civil War.* Baltimore: Maryland Historical Society, 1959.

Marszalek, John F. *Sherman: A Soldier's Passion for Order.* New York: Free Press, 1993.

McClure, Colonel A.K. *Recollections of Half a Century.* Salem, MA: Salem Press, 1902.

McIlvaine, Mabel, ed. *Reminiscences of Chicago During the Civil War.* New York: Citadel Press, 1967.

McKay, Ernest A. *The Civil War and New York City.* Syracuse, NY: Syracuse University Press, 1990.

McMurry, Richard M. *John Bell Hood and the Southern War for Independence.* Frankfort: University Press of Kentucky, 1982.

McPherson, James M. *Battle Cry of Freedom: The Civil War Era.* New York: Oxford University Press, 1988.

Michel, Robert E. *Colonel Harry Gilmor's Raid Around Baltimore.* Baltimore: Erbe, 1976.

Miller, Edward A. *Lincoln's Abolitionist General: The Biography of David Hunter.* Columbia: University of South Carolina Press, 1997.

Miller, William J. *The Training of an Army: Camp Curtin and the North's Civil War.* Shippensburg, PA: White Mane, 1990.

Nelson, Larry E. *Bullets, Ballots, and Rhetoric.* Tuscaloosa: University of Alabama Press, 1980.

Newcomer, C. Armour. *Cole's Cavalry: or Three Years in the Saddle in the Shenandoah Valley.* Baltimore: Cushing, 1895.

Nicolay, John, and John Hay. *History of Lincoln.* Chicago: Century, 1890.

Niven, John. *The Coming of the Civil War, 1837–1861.* Wheeling, IL: Harlan Davidson, 1990.

Olson, John E. *21st Virginia Cavalry.* Lynchburg, VA: Howard, 1989.

Opie, John N. *A Rebel Cavalryman with Lee, Stuart and Jackson.* Chicago: Conkey, 1899.

Osborne, Charles. *Jubal: The Life and Times of General Jubal Early CSA, Defender of the Lost Cause.* Baton Rouge: Louisiana State University Press, 1992.

Patchan, Scott C. *Shenandoah Summer: The 1864 Valley Campaign.* Lincoln: University of Nebraska Press, 2007.

Pauley, Michael J. *Unreconstructed Rebel: The Life of General John McCausland, CSA.* Charleston, WV: Pictorial Histories, 1992.

Perry, James M. *Touched with Fire: Five Presidents and the Civil War Battles That Made Them.* New York: Perseus Book Group, 2003.

Phipps, Sheila R. *Genteel Rebel: The Life of Mary Greenhow Lee.* Baton Rouge: Louisiana State University Press, 2004.

Poland, Charles P. *From Frontier to Suburbia.* St. Louis: Walsworth, 1976.

Pond, George E. *Campaigns of the Civil War.* Vol. 11. *The Shenandoah Valley in 1864.* 1884. Reprint, New York: Brussel, 1959.

Prowell, George Reeser. *History of the 87th Regiment, Pa. Volunteers.* York, PA: Press of the York Daily Record, 1901.

Pulitzer, Margaret Leech. *Reveille in Washington 1860–1865.* 1944. Reprint, Alexandria, VA: Time-Life Books, 1980.

Ramage, James A. *Gray Ghost: The Life of Col. John Singleton Mosby.* Frankfort: University Press of Kentucky, 1999.

Roe, Alfred Seelye. *9th New York Heavy Artillery.* Worcester, MA: privately published, 1899.

Sandburg, Carl. *Abraham Lincoln: The Prairie Years and the War Years.* New York: Harcourt, Brace, 1954, 1982.

Scharf, J. Thomas. *History of Western Maryland: Being a History of Frederick, Montgomery, Carroll, Washington, Allegany and Garrett Counties, from the*

Earliest Period to the Present Day. Baltimore: Baltimore Regional, 1968.

Schultz, Dwight. *The Dahlgren Affair: Terror and Conspiracy in the Civil War*. New York: Norton, 1998.

Sears, Stephen. *Chancellorsville*. New York: Mariner Books, 1998.

_____. *George B. McClellan: The Young Napoleon*. New York: Ticknor & Fields, 1988.

Shaw, Maurice F. *Stonewall Jackson's Surgeon: Hunter Holmes McGuire, a Biography*. Lynchburg, VA: Howard, 1993.

Sheads, Scott Sumpter, and Daniel Carroll Toomey. *Baltimore During the Civil War*. Linthicum, MD: Toomey Press, 1997.

Sheridan, P.H. *Personal Memoirs*. New York: Webster, 1888.

Smith, George W., and Charles Judah. *Life in the North During the Civil War: A Source History*. Albuquerque: University of New Mexico Press, 1966.

Snell, Mark A. *From First to Last: The Life of General William B. Franklin*. New York: Fordham University Press, 2002.

Sprague, Dean. *Freedom Under Lincoln*. New York: Houghton Mifflin, 1965.

Stackpole, Edward J. *Sheridan in the Shenandoah*. Harrisburg, PA: Stackpole Books, 1992.

Stampp, Kenneth M. ed. *The Causes of the Civil War*. Englewood Cliffs, NJ: Prentice Hall, 1974.

Thomas, Dawn F. *The Greenspring Valley: Its History and Heritage*. Vol. 1. Baltimore: Maryland Historical Society, 1978.

Trefousse, Hans. *Thaddeus Stevens: 19th Century Egalitarian*. Chapel Hill: University of North Carolina Press, 2001.

Vandiver, Frank. *Jubal's Raid: General Early's Famous Attack on Washington in 1864*. New York: McGraw-Hill, 1960.

Wallace, Lew. *Lew Wallace: An Autobiography*. Vol. 2. New York: Harper Brothers, 1906.

Waugh, John C. *Re-electing Lincoln: The Battle for the 1864 Presidency*. New York: Crown, 1997.

Wayland, Dr. John. *A History of Shenandoah County*. Strasburg, VA: Shenandoah, 1927.

Weitz, Mark. *More Damning than Slaughter*. Lincoln: University of Nebraska Press, 2005.

Wert, Jeffry. *From Winchester to Cedar Creek*. Carlisle, PA: South Mountain Press, 1987.

_____. *Custer: The Controversial Life of George Armstrong Custer*. New York: Simon & Schuster, 1996.

_____. *Mosby's Rangers*. New York: Simon & Schuster, 1990.

Williams, Thomas J.C. *History and Biographical Record of Washington County, Maryland*. Wilmington, DE: Broadfoot, 1906.

Wittenberg, Eric. *Little Phil: A Reassessment of the Civil War Leadership of Gen. Philip H. Sheridan*. Washington, DC: Brasseys, 2002.

Woodworth, Steven E. *Jefferson Davis and his Generals: The Failure of Confederate Command in the West*. Lawrence: University Press of Kansas, 1990.

_____. *Davis & Lee at War*. Lawrence: University Press of Kansas, 1995.

Worsham, John P. *One of Jackson's Foot Cavalry*. New York: Neale, 1912.

Worthington, Glenn H. *Fighting for Time: The Battle that Saved Washington and Mayhap the Union*. Frederick: Historical Society of Frederick County, Md., 1932.

ARTICLES

Baker, Gary. "Gilmor's Ride around Baltimore." www.civilwarinteractive.com/ArticleGilmor.htm

Baltimore Sun, 7 September 1864, 1.

Bernstein, Steven. "Errors Costly to Victor at Kelly's Ford." *Washington Times*, 3 September 2005.

_____. "Marylander Bradley T. Johnson Committed Himself to the Confederate Cause Before and After the War." *America's Civil War*, September 2005.

_____. "Early's Summer March Chills Washington." *Washington Times*, 5 June 2004.

_____. "Wagon Train Plays Role in Stuart's Failure at Gettysburg." *Washington Times*, 31 May 2003.

_____. "Encounter at Rockville." *Fredericksburg Free-Lance Star*, 14 June 2003.

Charleston Plaindealer, 2 April 1864.

Davis, William C. "Jubilee: General Jubal A. Early." *Civil War Times Illustrated* 9 (December 1970).

Deforest, John William. "Sheridan's Battle of Winchester." *Harper's New Monthly Magazine* 30 (January 1865).

Duthinh, Elizabeth. "Reflections of a Senator: Charles McCurdy Mathias." *Catoctin History*, Spring/Summer 1986.

Fitzpatrick, Michael. "Jubal Early and the Californians." *Civil War Times*, May 1998.

Frederick Examiner. 11 February 1863, 1.

Frederick News-Post. "Saw Early Write $200,000 Order." July 1972.

Gardner, Karen. "Mathias Wants Ransom Repaid to City." *Frederick* (MD) *News-Post*, October 1986.

Herbert, Paul N. "Lincoln's Odd Ways with Finances." *Washington Times*, 22 December 2007.

Middletown Valley Register. "Further Particulars of the Burning of Chambersburg." 12 August 1864.

New York Herald, 2 June 1864.

New York Times 5 September 1864, 4.

_____. 4 September 1864, 1.

New York Tribune, 1 June 1864.

Smith, Ellen Oliver. "The Magnolia Station Train Raid." http://madonna.edu/pages/lmmtrain.cfm.

Stark, William B. "The Great Skedaddle: General Hunter's Retreat from Lynchburg." *Atlantic Monthly* 162 (1938).

Sumner, Charles. "Our Domestic Relations; or, How to Treat the Rebel States." *Atlantic Monthly* 12 (October 1863).

Tallman, Douglas. "Ransom Notes to Be Displayed." *The News* (Frederick, MD), September 1995.

Warren, Lucian. "Mathias Finally Gets Senate OK to Repay Civil War Ransom." *Frederick News-Post*, 4 October 1986.

_____. "Frederick's Civil War Ransom Request Loses Battle in House." *The News*, Frederick, MD, 17 October 1986.

Welles, Gideon. "The Opposition to Lincoln in 1864." *Atlantic Monthly*, March 1878.

Wert, Jeffry. "The Snickers Gap War." *Civil War Times Illustrated*, August 1978.

Whitehorne, J.W.A. "Jubal Early at Waynesboro: The Last Hurrah." *Civil War* 11, no. 2 (April 1994).

Young, James Harvey. "Anna Elizabeth Dickenson and the Civil War: For and Against Lincoln." *Mississippi Valley Historical Review* 31 (June 1944).

DISSERTATIONS/THESES

Alexander, Charles Theodore. "McCausland's Raid and the Burning of Chambersburg." Master's thesis, University of Maryland Baltimore County, 1988.

Hampton, Wade. "The Raid on Point Lookout." seminar paper, American University, Washington, DC, 1970.

Talbert, Bart Rhett. "Maryland in the War Between the States: A Lesson in the Struggle for American Freedom," Ph.D. diss., University of Alabama at Montgomery, 1976.

JOURNALS/PAMPHLETS

Bradwell, I.G. "Early's Demonstration against Washington in 1864." *Confederate Veteran* 22 (October 1914).

Duncan, Richard R. "Maryland's Reaction to Early's Raid in 1864: A Summer of Bitterness." *Maryland Historical Magazine* 64, 1969.

Farquhar, R.B. "The Diary of Roger Brooke Farquhar of Montgomery County, Maryland." Pt. 2. *The Montgomery County Story* 2, no. 2 (February 1959).

Feis, William B. "A Union Military Intelligence Failure: Jubal Early's Raid, June 12-July 14, 1864." *Civil War History* 36, no. 3 (1990).

Getty, Mildred Newbold. "The Silver Spring Area." *The Montgomery County Story* 12 (November 1868): 2.

Jacobs, Charles T. "Civil War Fords and Ferries in Montgomery County." *The Montgomery County Story* 40, no. 1 (February 1997).

Johnson, Bradley T. "My Ride around Baltimore in Eighteen Hundred and Sixty Four." *Journal of the U.S. Cavalry Association*, Southern Historical Society Papers, Vol. 30 (September 1889).

Meany, Peter J., OSB. *The Civil War Engagement at Cool Spring*, Berryville, VA, 1980.

Mettam, Henry. "Civil War Memoirs: First Maryland Cavalry CSA." *Maryland Historical Magazine* 58, no. 2 (June 1963).

Moore, Virginia Campbell. "Remembrances of Life Along the Rockville Pike during the Civil War." *The Montgomery County Story* 27, no. 4 (November 1984).

Slingluff, Fielder. "The Burning of Chambersburg." SHS Papers, Vol. 37, 1909.

Smith, Stephen G. *The First Battle of Moorefield: Early's Cavalry Is Routed*. Saline MI: McNaughton & Gunn, 1998.

Stampp, Kenneth M. "The Milligan Case and the Election of 1864 in Indiana." *Mississippi Valley Historical Review*, no. 31 (June 1944).

No author. "Martinsburg, West Virginia During the Civil War." *The Berkeley Journal*, no. 27, 2001.

WEB SITES

Civil War Album: www.civilwaralbum.com/misc/olu steel.htm

The Civil War in the Shenandoah Valley: http://www. angelfire.com/va3/valleywar/battle/2kernstown.html

Civil War Interactive: www.civilwarinteractive.com/ ArticlesGilmorsRide.htm

Cornell University: http://cdl.library.cornell.edu/cgi-bin/moa

DNR Online: www.dnronline.com/civilwar/part-2/ peo-civ-wright.htm

Heritage Quest Online: http://www.heritagequeston-line.com

Historic Sandusky: www.historicsandusky.org/history. htm

Madonna University: http://www.madonna.edu

Mapquest: www.mapquest.com

Mr. Lincoln and New York: www.mrlincolnandnew york.org

Napoleon Games: http://www.napoleongames.com

National Park Service: www.nps.gov/hafe/maps/mary land.htm

North Georgia: www.northga.net/whitfield/tunnel. html

Old and Sold: www.oldandsold.com/articles11/vir ginia-homes-86.shtml

Open Library: www.openlibrary.org/a/ol/2170057aJ-Hoke

Pennsylvania Historical and Museum Commission: www.phmc.state.pa.us/bah/dam/governors/bigler. asp

Project Gutenberg: http://www.gutenberg.org/files/ 5857/5857-h/5857-h.htm

Roadside Georgia: http://roadsidegeorgia.com/city/ tunnellhill.html

Salem Museum: www.salemmuseum.org/history.htm

University of Virginia: www.lib.virginia.edu/small/ exhibits/hoos/remember.html

Wikipedia: http://en.wikipedia.org/wiki/Lew_Wallace www.geocities.com/Athens/Aegean/6732

MISCELLANEOUS

Battle of the Monocacy. Official Actor Action Reports North & South, commemorating *Biography Resource Center*. Gale Database Co., Farmington Hills, MI.

Columbia Encyclopedia. 6th ed. New York: Columbia University Press, 2007.

Frederick City's 250th Anniversary Frederick, MD: U.S. Flag Service, 1998.

Historic Sandusky Foundation. *Audio Driving Tour of Lynchburg*. Cassette tape. No date.

Map of Ohio. Heathrow, FL: American Automobile Association, 1997.

Index

229